'We cannot undo the past, but we are bound to pass it in review in order to draw from it such lessons as may be applicable to the future, and surely the conclusion from this story is that we should not intervene in these matters unless we are in earnest and prepared to carry out intervention to all necessary lengths.'

Sir Winston Churchill during the Abyssinian Debate in the House of Commons, 6 April 1936

As quoted by Harold Wilson during the Rhodesian Debate in the House of Commons, 12 November 1965

For
Nancy, Steve
Karen and Kathy
who were there

Contents

Contents

Illustrations

Preface

I recall once standing on the kopje, or small hill, which commands a splendid panoramic view of Salisbury. My white escort from the Rhodesian Ministry of Information called my attention to the sensible way the city was laid out. 'We have a prevailing wind towards the west,' he explained, 'so the industrial area was put on the western side of town and all the residential areas were put upwind on the eastern side.' I asked him mischievously where Highfield was located, the largest African township housing at least 60,000 people. It was of course far removed from the white neighbourhoods – and directly downwind from the industrial area.

This maddening obliviousness is of course a symptom and a substantial part of the problem of Southern Africa. It is also true that, because the white Southern African frequently perceives the black African to be an all-encompassing and ultimately threatening presence, he contrives, often unconsciously, to put the African's existence out of mind.

Much the same may be said of white Western perceptions of the coloured world. Certainly our obliviousness to events in Southern Africa is notorious. During an extensive speaking tour of the United States in 1967 while on leave from our African post, my family and I found ourselves constantly explaining that our country of assignment, Zambia, was *not* the same as Gambia or Zanzibar, and if our audiences responded at all to the illegal seizure of independence in neighbouring Rhodesia or to the person of Mr. Ian Smith, it was generally favourably because they knew nothing of the circumstances except that Rhodesians had had a rebellion of sorts (as had we) against the British. So the concern to write this book emerged.

It is directed at many audiences, most importantly in Britain as the book more than anything else is an account of and a statement about a British foreign policy problem. But the implications of the story touch many areas, not least the United States. Though Rhodesia in no sense was or is an 'American problem', developments in that country as in other parts of Southern Africa will one day come to preoccupy us. I say this with such certainty because I believe that in this age of immediate communication and instant involvement, it is inconceivable that two great racial revolutions (in America and in Southern Africa) can climax at roughly the same point in history without finally each affecting, exciting, and probably aggravating the other. Exactly how this interaction will work itself out is I think unpredictable. But that there will be a significant interaction I would consider inevitable.

The genre of the book is not easily defined. Since I served in Zambia as American Ambassador from March 1965 through December 1968 and since both my position and location afforded a fascinating vantage point which subsequently would prove useful in reconstructing parts of the story, the book in an odd way is a memoir. (My own role in these events, however, was tangential – largely that of an observer-commentator rather than an actor – so the use of the first person singular normally associated with memoir materials would have been both misleading and in poor taste.) Even more important, the study is based on an extensive reading of public sources, the press of the major countries involved, the records of Parliamentary debates and United Nations documentation, and some 300 private interviews arranged in the course of two visits to South Africa, Zambia and Rhodesia and four to London, as well as stops in Lisbon, Lourenço Marques, Dar es Salaam and Addis Ababa. As an exercise in contemporary history, the book inevitably is journalism of a sort.

Based upon these sources, my intention was to probe a sequence of events as fascinating and instructive as they were complex and under-reported, and then to write an interpretative account which might command some interest beyond that limited circle to which political studies of this kind are normally confined. I have therefore reduced to a minimum the conceptual baggage usually associated with scholarly ventures, while at the same time introducing enough analytical material to make the narrative elucidate the most critical issues and lessons arising from the Rhodesian rebellion and the endless array of responses to it. If labels have to be used, the resulting study may be called, I suppose, a scholarly memoir or analytical journalism.

A word must also be said about procedure. Since materials deriving from anonymous sources (unattributable interviews supplemented here and there by diplomatic insights) do not lend themselves to footnotes, and because in any event I have indicated in the text itself the sources from which much of the public material was derived,

I have decided not to festoon the story with the usual display of citational footnotes. Rather I have included at the end of the book bibliographical notes arranged by chapter and section and citing not only the principal materials used, but in some cases supplemental material as well which the student of these matters might wish to consult. In so proceeding, I am necessarily straining at the fastidious reader's scholarly sensibilities and cannot do otherwise at various undocumented points in the story than to ask that he 'take my word for it'.

My way of work in short was this: facts and interpretations garnered from public and private sources were amassed, ordered, then repeatedly checked and cross-checked. Various sections of the resulting manuscript were subsequently read by some forty knowledgeable observers of and participants in the affairs described, whose anonymous assistance and unusual patience I acknowledge with deep gratitude.

I am also in debt to a number of individuals whose assistance (and forbearance) can be acknowledged more explicitly. The research and much of the writing was financed by a grant from the Ford Foundation awarded upon my departure from Zambia. My particular thanks go to J. Wayne Fredericks who has been obliged to wait much too long for the results. The grant was managed by the School of Advanced International Studies of the Johns Hopkins University which also provided me with an academic home, for which I am most grateful to Dean Francis Wilcox and to Professors Robert Osgood and Charles Burton Marshall of the Washington Centre of Foreign Policy Research. I must express gratitude too to colleagues at the Graduate School of International Studies of the University of Denver who were obliged from time to time to put up with a rather distant Dean while this task was being completed. For research assistance I am particularly indebted to Mr. Gerald Williams. For secretarial assistance, often way beyond the call of duty, I am indebted to Mrs. Marilyn Perkins of Washington and to my secretary, Mrs. Lavonne Delahunty. Responsibility for the final result of this prolonged imposition on the patience of so many individuals is solely (in the customary disclaimer) my own.

Denver, Colorado   ROBERT C. GOOD
October 1972

I

11 November 1965

It was an insignificant beginning, considering the furore that would follow. Ian Douglas Smith, Prime Minister of the British self-governing colony of Rhodesia,* spoke into the microphone: 'Your Government has issued the following proclamation which I will read to you.'

Outside, a scattered crowd stood under the African sun in Salisbury's Cecil Square listening to loud speakers. The clock on the bell tower of the Anglican Cathedral read 1.15 p.m. It was Armistice Day, 1965. 'Whereas in the course of human affairs,' the flat voice continued in that vowel-pinched accent characteristic of many European settlers in Southern Africa, 'history has shown that it may become necessary for a people to resolve the political affiliations which have connected them with another people and to assume amongst other nations the separate and equal status to which they are entitled. And whereas in such event,' the purloined phrases droned on, 'a respect for the opinions of mankind requires them to declare to other nations the causes which impel them to assume full responsibility for their own affairs. . . .'

A bill of particulars followed. It noted that Rhodesia had enjoyed self-government since 1923. It asserted that Rhodesians had demonstrated their loyalty through two World Wars both to the Crown and to 'their kith and kin' (Mr. Smith was referring to Rhodesia's 210,000 whites who controlled the country), and that they 'now see all they have cherished about to be shattered on the rocks of

---

* The country is still technically 'Southern Rhodesia' according to the British Government, though Rhodesian authorities dropped the adjective after the dissolution of the Federation of Rhodesia and Nyasaland when the northern territories, Northern Rhodesia and Nyasaland, assumed independence as Zambia and Malawi. For convenience (having nothing to do with political preference) the simple term, Rhodesia, is used throughout this book.

expediency' (Mr. Smith had in mind the danger of rule by Rhodesia's 4.2 million blacks who presently controlled nothing). Moreover Britain had consistently refused to accede to Rhodesia's entreaties for full independence (under a constitution which would have perpetuated for an undetermined number of years rule by the white minority). Now this day by proclamation Rhodesia assumed her independence unilaterally. In so doing, the rebel Prime Minister concluded: 'We have struck a blow for the preservation of justice, civilization and Christianity.' Government censorship had just been imposed and the already existing state of emergency was now further embellished by eight additional arbitrary regulations.

Some two hours before, Smith had gone to Government House to advise Rhodesia's Governor, Humphrey Gibbs, of the imminent broadcast and the rupture with Britain. Gibbs, utterly loyal to the Queen who had appointed him Governor of the British colony of Rhodesia, told Smith he was making a great mistake. From a nearby table he picked up a copy of the October 1965 issue of the Rhodesian journal, *Property and Finance*. Leafing through its record of the country's economic progress, the Governor warned him that all this would be sacrificed if Smith were to promulgate a U.D.I. The abbreviation for a 'unilateral declaration of independence' had become a household word in Rhodesia in prolonged anticipation of the event.

The Governor had been forewarned of the illegal act, which in prospect he had both feared and condemned, eight days before when Smith had paid him an earlier visit. It was the evening of 3 November. Smith had brought for the Governor's signature an order declaring a state of emergency throughout Rhodesia. It was a peculiar matter because Rhodesia for some weeks had been extremely quiet. The crime statistics hardly justified exceptional measures. Accordingly, the reason for the emergency order, as disclosed in an affidavit drawn up by Police Commissioner F. E. ('Slash') Barfoot, was not domestic unrest at all, but the alleged assemblage of Rhodesian African guerrillas in Zambia to the north. The Governor signed the order but failed to date it or to keep a copy. Strangely the following day the order was not gazetted. Angry inquiries from the Governor's office revealed that the document had been placed under lock and key by Smith.

The manœuvre was now becoming transparent. If there had been need for a state of emergency, the order would have been promulgated immediately and regulations issued under it. Clearly it was part of a larger plan in the service of which the Governor's signature on a state of emergency order would be highly useful when the right time came. The Attorney General now advised that if not promulgated

right away the order would lose efficacy. By this time two days had elapsed since Gibbs had signed the document. Smith and his colleagues, noting the Attorney General's judgement, dated the order 'November 5' and it came into effect forthwith.

It was under this order that censorship was imposed just prior to Smith's U.D.I. proclamation. A counter-proclamation made immediately by the Governor was caught by the censor and received almost no notice in Rhodesia. Prepared weeks before and held for just this contingency, Gibbs's message, 'in command from Her Majesty the Queen', dismissed the members of the Rhodesian Government and called upon Rhodesian citizens to refrain from any acts that would help the illegal Government in pursuing its illegal objectives, but otherwise to maintain law and order.

The balance of the day passed without event. The vast African townships west of Salisbury seemed numb. Representatives of the United Peoples Party, the small all-African opposition in Rhodesia's Parliament, had presented a memorandum that afternoon to the British High Commissioner in Salisbury expressing opposition to U.D.I. and allegiance to the Queen. It was an undemonstrative gesture. (Leaders of the mainstream African nationalist movements of Rhodesia were under Government restriction or in exile.) That evening Salisbury was quiet, more empty than usual. British High Commissioner Jack Johnston and American Consul General Ross McClelland, who together had listened to Smith's broadcast in Johnston's office, were at home finishing their packing. Each had been recalled.

◇   ◇   ◇

The Salisbury sun contrasted with London's chill grey sky. So too was Salisbury's introspective almost torpid mood at variance with the dramatic tension in Whitehall and Westminster when at 11.15 a.m. G.M.T. (two hours behind Salisbury) the B.B.C. broke into its morning broadcast. It was Ian Smith's voice announcing U.D.I.

Parliament sat at 2.30 p.m. The customary prayers were said. From the packed visitors' gallery a number of intent African faces fixed upon the figure at the dispatch box. Prime Minister Harold Wilson began: 'Mr. Speaker, with your permission, I should like to make a statement on Rhodesia. The House will have heard with deep sadness of the illegal declaration of independence by the men who until that declaration constituted the Government of Rhodesia.' Wilson recalled the interminable year-in and year-out negotiations to break the Rhodesian impasse, seeking a workable balance between Britain's responsibility for effecting ultimate majority rule and white Rhodesia's fear of it – negotiations which had persisted to the last

possible moment. The Prime Minister described an incredible telephone exchange he had had with Smith at six o'clock that morning: a final effort to demonstrate that there were no procedural differences between the two sides and culminating in an offer to fly one of his Ministers to Salisbury for further clarification. Smith said he would take Wilson's message to his Cabinet but added, 'It looks as though this thing has gone too far.'

Wilson dismissed, as he had often before, the use of military coercion against the rebellious white Government of Rhodesia, then turned to a staccato account of the economic penalties to which these 'lawbreaking men' were immediately to be subjected: trade was to be restricted including a ban on tobacco and sugar purchases which constituted 70 per cent of Rhodesia's exports to the United Kingdom; arms exports were to cease; all aid was to be terminated; Rhodesia was to be removed from the sterling area, exchange controls applied, export of British capital and access to the British capital market disallowed; credit guarantees were no longer to be available; and Rhodesia was to be suspended from the Commonwealth preference area.

Moreover, Wilson continued, Britain had asked the United Nations Security Council to meet the following day in support of British action. (Within hours, in fact, the United Nations General Assembly would interrupt its general debate to adopt a resolution condemning U.D.I., urging the United Kingdom to take the necessary steps to end the rebellion and recommending that the Security Council consider the issue as a matter of urgency.) Britain's Foreign Minister was already en route to New York.

Across the aisle, speaking for the Conservative Opposition, Edward Heath noted 'how deeply we on this side of the House also deplore the unilateral declaration of independence by the former Government of Rhodesia today'. He emphasized 'the importance at this time, in every action which is taken and every word which is spoken, of maintaining our own national unity and thus helping to maintain the unity of the Commonwealth, to which we hope that at some future date an independent Rhodesia will be able to return'. Nevertheless, many Tories seemed restive as Wilson revealed his arsenal of sanctions, and some openly protested against his initiative at the United Nations.

There were rustlings of discontent also from those who wanted more action, not less. Liberal Party Leader Jo Grimond raised the question of curtailing oil supplies to Rhodesia and was told swiftly, 'We have no proposals to make on this subject.' And when the following day a Member of Parliament inquired what steps Her Majesty's Government was taking to protect loyal Rhodesians, the Attorney

General Sir Elwyn Jones replied grandly that the protecting arm was that of Governor Gibbs – the Queen's arm and voice.

Back at Rhodesia's Government House, Gibbs, lonely and power-less, was about to begin a frustrating tour of duty which would run for forty-four months, while in London H.M. Government assumed the uncertain mandate of Rhodesia's 'government-in-exile'. But for the moment drama conjured its own reality. The Rhodesians, as Harold Wilson explained to a national television audience on the evening of 11 November, had put themselves 'beyond the pale of world society'. It was a ponderous peroration faintly reminiscent (as Wilson no doubt hoped it would be) of Churchill's style. 'At this anxious time I hope that no one in Rhodesia will feel that Britain has forgotten them or that we are prepared to yield up the trusteeship which is ours – trusteeship for the welfare of all the peoples of Rhodesia. Whatever the cost to us, we shall honour that trusteeship until we can bring the people of Rhodesia, under God, once again, back to their true allegiance, back to the rule of law, and forward to their true destiny in the family of nations.'

ᘓ   ᘓ   ᘓ

During these events, Sir Richard Luyt found himself in the Colonial Office in London and, by chance, in conversation with Britain's Commonwealth Secretary Arthur Bottomley. Before his appointment as Britain's last Governor in Guyana (negotiations for whose new constitution had brought Luyt back to London from Georgetown), he had served as Chief Secretary and on occasion Acting Governor in Northern Rhodesia, now Zambia. Luyt knew Central Africa inti-mately, both black and white, and had won the lasting friendship of Zambia's first President, Kenneth David Kaunda. Luyt and Bottomley talked of the disturbing news from Salisbury. 'But the real tragedy of U.D.I.', Luyt said, 'will be Zambia.'

There was reason for apprehension concerning the newly in-dependent country located on Rhodesia's northern boundary. Zambia's African-controlled Government relied upon a substantial community of more than 70,000 whites for technical skills both in the Government and in the huge copper industry. According to the 1961 census, 63 per cent of the whites living on the Copperbelt (Zambia's Ruhr) were natives of Southern or Central Africa. It was inevitable that many would be sympathetic to Smith – and hardly enthusiastic when Kaunda, the passionate advocate of majority rule and non-racialism throughout Southern Africa, declared in a nationwide broadcast on 11 November that Zambia was determined that treason should not be permitted to prosper and that the rebellion be brought to an end.

In the white communities on the Copperbelt, sentiments were running strong. At Chingola, white locomotive engineers working the still unified rail system that linked Zambia and Rhodesia celebrated the announcement of U.D.I. by prolonged blasts on their whistles. A white labour union meeting at Mufilira mine turned into a 'bloody independence celebration' according to a union leader who was present. A more provocative situation was difficult to imagine in a sensitive African state still aching from the discriminatory practices of the recent colonial past. No one could predict the flow of African emotion. At the offices of the British High Commission in Zambia's capital, Lusaka, workmen were labouring to install a heavy wrought-iron security grill.

Zambia's plight arose even more from its continuing reliance on the rebellious colony with which it shared a long border at the Zambezi River. Transport links, communications networks, power supplies and trading patterns joined the Zambian and Rhodesian economies as inextricably as Siamese twins. Britain had announced that it would respond to Rhodesia's rebellion with economic sanctions. The implications for Zambia were obvious and ominous: to punish Rhodesia was automatically to penalize Zambia.

So, on 11 November 1965, Kaunda appealed for calm – and declared a state of emergency. Carriers were made ready to transport some three companies of Zambian troops to the border in answer to Rhodesia's deployment made in preparation for U.D.I. More than two battalions of Ian Smith's troops were positioned along the southern bank of the Zambezi River.

◇   ◇   ◇

Elsewhere in Africa, and in many other parts of the 'coloured world' – Asia, the Middle East and the Caribbean – emotions rose. Particularly concerned were members of the Commonwealth, linked by their colonial history to Britain, and hence by association to one another. As a self-governing British colony, Rhodesia had until 1964 enjoyed the status of an observer at meetings of Commonwealth leaders. U.D.I. now made Rhodesia a Commonwealth pariah.

After his appointment as Commonwealth Secretary-General in June 1965, Arnold Smith, a skilled and respected diplomat of the Canadian service, placed the mounting Rhodesian crisis at the head of his agenda. On 11 November he was travelling in Africa, urging that in the event of U.D.I. Commonwealth states should not withdraw from the organization in protest against what they might consider to be an inadequate British response. For, Smith argued, the Commonwealth would then more than ever need their support to

Environment (margin annotation)

exert constructive influence. The Canadian Secretary-General was working hard to disentangle the Commonwealth from its uniquely British past, and one suspects that 'constructive influence' meant among other things keeping pressure on the British Government. Returning to London, Arnold Smith sent cables to the leaders he had been visiting further emphasizing his concern. Demonstrations against the British, meanwhile, were erupting in a number of Commonwealth states. The leaders of Kenya, Uganda, Tanzania and Zambia, all members of the Commonwealth, convened in Nairobi and talked about the possible need 'to take the matter out of British hands'.

11 November 1965 sent an equally strong tide coursing through the Organization of African Unity. Meeting in Nouakchott, the heads of four French-speaking African states, Mali, Senegal, Guinea and Mauritania, called on every African state to consider itself at war with Rhodesia. In Accra President Kwame Nkrumah called for the immediate creation of an O.A.U. military force. In Cairo President Nasser declared that the United Arab Republic was in a state of war with the illegal Government of Rhodesia and had a right to seize all Rhodesia-bound goods in transit through Suez. Congo (Brazzaville) announced it was ready to place volunteers at the disposal of the O.A.U. for service in Rhodesia. A few days later the O.A.U.'s Defence Committee met in Dar es Salaam where a senior Tanzanian Minister vowed: 'No power on earth will stop us from a final duel with the forces of white racism in Southern Africa.'

Dr. Hastings Kamuzu Banda, Prime Minister of Malawi and the irrepressible curmudgeon of the O.A.U. who delighted in outraging his colleagues at every opportunity, was not so sure. 'Ten Rhodesian mercenaries', he told his Parliament shamelessly, 'will whip 5,000 so-called African soldiers; the Rhodesian army if Smith pushed could conquer the whole of East and Central Africa in one week.' As to the threats of certain African states to leave the Commonwealth and withdraw bank accounts from London, he demanded to know: 'What money? What accounts? Their overdrafts?'

On the day of Rhodesia's U.D.I., South Africa's Prime Minister, Dr. Hendrik F. Verwoerd, observed privately, 'I have offered advice to three Rhodesian premiers. The first two were wise enough to take it.' A leading South African newspaper predicted that the gravest trouble would come to white-ruled South Africa from 'this hot-headed and ill-considered action by Mr. Smith'.

But most whites in South Africa were not so restrained. Students in the port city of Durban climbed a tower of the university and unfurled a banner proclaiming 'Rhodesia'. At Bloemfontein the United Party, representing most of South Africa's whites of British heritage, was holding a convention. News of U.D.I. was read to the congress from the platform. Someone shouted, 'Three cheers for Smith!' The entire congress echoed its approval. Head of the United Party and political opposition leader Sir de Villiers Graaf won an ovation when he declared that the future of South Africa and the future of Rhodesia were closely linked and there should be white control over the whole of Southern Africa. With an eye on South Africa's coming election he urged Pretoria to grant diplomatic recognition to Rhodesia thus indicating 'the sympathy we feel for them'.

The following day Dr. Verwoerd was also on the hustings attending a meeting of his National Party at Pietermaritzburg. He said that South Africa would pursue a policy of non-interference in the dispute between Britain and Rhodesia. At the same time it would not participate in any boycott of Rhodesia. Both intervention and boycotts were wrong. Rather South Africa wished to maintain 'normal and friendly relations with both countries'. 'We intend', he said in a phrase which was perhaps purposefully vague, 'to preserve friendship with whatever Government the Rhodesian people see fit to choose.'

Verwoerd's instinct for caution was explained in an editorial that same day in the influential South African daily, *Die Burger*. Predicting that South Africa would be accused of helping to subvert the economic blockade of Rhodesia and thus might itself become the object of attempts to expand the sanctions campaign, the editors concluded that 'the fate of the whole of Southern Africa is concerned with what was decided in Salisbury yesterday. . . . What is clearly foreseen is that South Africa (possibly together with Portugal) will increasingly have to share the intensified international anger against Rhodesia.'

As *Die Burger* suggested, Portugal, through its control of Mozambique abutting Rhodesia on the east and Angola adjacent to Zambia in the west, also had a direct interest in Smith's act of rebellion and would be equally affected by the pressures now arising with the U.N., the O.A.U. and the Commonwealth. But the initial reaction from Portugal was enigmatic. In New York at the United Nations, Lisbon's Foreign Minister Franco Nogueira was noncommittal about recognizing the rebel regime or participating in sanctions against it. In Lisbon there was no official comment. It was noted by observers, however, that economic agreements arrived at the year before had further tightened relations between Rhodesia and Portugal. Meanwhile in Salisbury a spokesman at the Portuguese Consulate said:

'We see no reason for closing down the Consulate. We will keep it open as we always have.'

◇   ◇   ◇

Izvestia was on sale in Moscow only two hours after the news broke in Salisbury. Under the headline, 'Independence – Racist Style', the Soviet paper censured U.D.I. as a monstrous crime and an impudent challenge to world opinion. Radio Moscow announced that the Soviet Union would 'back the decisive steps of the African countries against the Rhodesian racialists. We believe the Africans will win.'

President Lyndon Johnson received the news from Salisbury at the Texas White House on the Pedernales. After a special meeting of the Cabinet, Secretary of State Dean Rusk speaking for the President deplored the 'illegal seizure of power by the white minority Government in Rhodesia'. Immediate action was taken to stop the sale to Rhodesia of thirty-six heavy diesel locomotives involving some $10 million. State Department contingency plans, long in preparation and designed to help salvage Zambia in the event of Rhodesian retaliation against its northern neighbour, seemed suddenly relevant.

Besides condemning U.D.I., the Cold War capitals agreed on a second point. Rhodesia was a British responsibility. A spokesman at the Department of State indicated that the United States would 'be in consultation with the British Government'. Rusk said that he had been instructed by the President to inform the United Kingdom that the United States 'in no way recognizes the rebel regime'. Meanwhile the United Kingdom closed the Rhodesian Affairs Department of its Embassy in Washington informing American officials that its five officers no longer enjoyed diplomatic status. As for the Russians, British responsibility was ascribed somewhat differently. *Izvestia* said curtly that U.D.I. 'took place with the clear connivance of England'.

◇   ◇   ◇

Rhodesia was an evocative issue. It aroused emotion and inspired superlatives. Wilson once called it 'the most difficult and complicated problem which any British Government have had to face'. His Foreign Secretary believed the Rhodesian crisis affected 'the whole of mankind and the peace of the world'. A former Prime Minister, Sir Alec Douglas-Home, found that Rhodesia raised 'issues as momentous as any that have ever occupied this House in its history,' and concerning which, he added, 'emotions will run strong and deep and tensions will be taut'. On 11 November 1965, no one would have gainsaid that.

Why should a dispute between a metropolis and a remote remnant of a dismantled empire have provoked such a response in so many capitals? The question is still intriguing even though now, seven years later, the Rhodesian problem commands almost no notice, having long since been overwhelmed by a crowded international agenda and by its own interminableness. The central issue had to do with the allocation of power in a situation where the contending sides were sharply demarcated by colour. In the simplest terms U.D.I. and the uproar accompanying it sprang from the question: who would rule an independent Rhodesia, the black majority (95 per cent) or the white minority (5 per cent)?

Compromise solutions – power shared between racial communities or power allocated on the basis of criteria divorced from race – were unlikely given the history of racial rule and the stark racial stratification of Rhodesian society. White was synonymous with relative privilege and power; black was synonymous with neither.* Within each group there were just enough exceptions to prove the rule. Looking towards the future, whites recoiled at what they saw (or thought they saw) in newly independent black-ruled countries to the north, insisting that 'civilized standards' (often a code name for continued white rule) could be lowered only at the risk of chaos. The dynamics of African nationalism tended equally to produce all-or-nothing positions as African leaders, fearful of being outflanked by the more militant, refused to put forward anything other than unobtainable demands.

Granted, as Harold Isaacs reminds us, that race adds its own 'peculiar accretion of greater glandular involvement' to all other forms of conflict, one may still ask why the self-assertive act of a racial minority in a country of less than five million inhabitants located in the hinterland of Africa should have created such commotion. It was surely because the answer to the question, Who rules in Rhodesia? had significance, again by virtue of the racial factor, for Southern Africa generally. Trouble in white-controlled Rhodesia resounded within a huge region where approximately four million whites (in South Africa, South-West Africa, Angola, Mozambique as well as Rhodesia itself) exercised absolute control over approximately thirty-one million non-whites. Wedged into Southern Africa and contiguous to black Africa (Zambia), Rhodesia provided a potentially formidable fulcrum for change. If an African government could be brought to power there, new leverage would be gained for an eventual transition to black rule in adjacent white-ruled areas. If on the other

---

* In 1965 non-Africans constituted 12 per cent of the labour force but earned 95 per cent of total income from employment. White Rhodesians enjoy one of the highest living standards in the world, higher even than white South Africans.

hand white rule were consolidated in Rhodesia, prospects for change within the region would correspondingly be diminished for a long time to come.

Thus, added to the racial character of the confrontation there was the strategic significance of Rhodesia within white-ruled Southern Africa, itself the last remnant of white western colonialism, and (particularly South Africa) the universal symbol of racial oppression. In equal measure, then, U.D.I. fanned the emotions of coloured leaders everywhere, and brought into play the vital interests of the white power structure of the region. The operative view throughout the 'coloured world' was preferably that force be used against Rhodesia, or alternatively that massive economic sanctions be imposed on *all* of white-ruled Southern Africa, most particularly on powerful South Africa itself. If Afro-Asians pressed for radical change in Rhodesia, the white rulers of Southern Africa were of course equally determined to prevent it. In Pretoria and Lisbon, declaratory policy coolly acknowledged that U.D.I. was a matter of domestic jurisdiction to be handled between Britain and its colony without outside intervention. Action policy, on the other hand, was directed toward assuring that coercive measures designed to oblige change in Rhodesia would fail.

The nature of Britain's own response to the problem also helped to 'internationalize' it. London wished to effect change – but at tolerable cost. The object was ambitious: to end the rebellion and to restore legitimacy under circumstances which would assure a transition to ultimate rule by the African majority. Britain, however, was hobbled by Rhodesia's peculiar status as a fully self-governing colony, which meant that London had no established means for exercising direct control over Salisbury. For this and other reasons which will be examined in due course, Britain decided not to rely on direct intervention (force) but on indirect pressures (diplomatic isolation and economic sanctions).*

To succeed, such a policy would have to convince Rhodesia's white élite that the loss of power inherent in a return to legality and an expanding political role for Africans were preferable to the alternative: economic constraints arising from sanctions, international ostracism,

---

* The distinction between 'direct' and 'indirect' measures is that the former would establish British authority on the ground in Rhodesia, while the latter would impose penalties from the outside for Rhodesian non-compliance with British terms. Structurally, it is the difference between effecting change through British initiatives (obliging compliance) or through Rhodesian initiatives (under pain of penalties). Operationally, it is the difference between positioning oneself to *execute* terms or to *negotiate* them.

an increasing reliance on South Africa and the possibility one day of an African uprising. These penalties were not convincing for they were either speculative or remote, while the risks of submission and sharing power were real and immediate. Such perhaps is always the problem of attempting to manipulate another polity at a distance, for it is difficult to make credible the threat attending non-compliance with one's demands.

In short, British policy suffered from a radical disparity between legal jurisdiction and operative authority, between responsibility and power, between stated objectives and the capacity to achieve them within the limits imposed by the use of indirect measures, all of which only added to the alarm of Third World nations seeking swift and effective change in Rhodesia. Beyond this, the actual implementation of British policy threw the dispute between metropolis and colony immediately into the international arena. For the use of indirect means to achieve policy ends invariably makes action multilateral. This is not simply because the responsible party compensates for his own incapacity by recruiting the efforts of others, but because the mechanisms of indirect pressure (sanctions, for example) require concerted rather than unilateral effort.

Certain results flow from the indirect exercise of power and from a disjunction between objectives and capabilities. For Britain these conditions created an unending round of problems. First, London found itself to an alarming degree dependent for the execution of its policy (that is, the actual implementation of sanctions) on numerous actors not all of whom by any means shared Britain's interests, and some of whom in fact were intent on subverting and disrupting those interests. Additionally, the application of international sanctions inevitably entails for the participants different levels of sacrifice and of risk (as Zambia shortly would discover), raising serious questions as to the viability, even the justice, of such a policy.

Second, the indirect exercise of power tends to aggravate the disparity between policy objectives and the capacity to achieve them, as the lamentable history of international boycotts and economic sanctions has demonstrated repeatedly. Moreover, there arise in these situations immense possibilities for miscalculation. Discipline and thus the predictability of results are reduced as the number of participants upon whom policy implementation depends increases. The reaction of the target society to economic pressures is equally problematic. There are additional difficulties in estimating the impact of policy in situations when power is exercised indirectly and at a distance, but where at the same time formal jurisdiction is not in question. (No one doubted Britain's legal responsibility for granting or withholding Rhodesia's independence except those who seized it.) Under these circumstances the distinction between formal jurisdiction and operative authority is on occasion blurred, further distorting the realistic assessment of capabilities. In any event, as we shall see, bad estimates became the stock-in-trade of policy-makers in London.

Finally, the disparity between objectives and capacities must lead either to a downgrading of objectives to make them more consonant with available means, or to a fixation on short term expedients to minimize losses consequent on a bankrupt policy. In fact both of these developments characterized Britain's policy toward Rhodesia, giving it an insubstantial and frenetic quality, and adding further to the tensions between Britain and its antagonists.

These tensions were acted out in numerous bilateral settings, but most importantly in two international bodies, both of which suffered as a result: the United Nations and the Commonwealth. The politics of policy-making in these international arenas at times bears little relationship to the purposes for which the organizations were formed or indeed their capacities to achieve designated objectives, as the Rhodesian crisis would demonstrate time and again. In its effort to make sanctions multilateral, Britain turned repeatedly to the U.N. Security Council and gained unprecedented decisions under the debatable assumption that the Rhodesian situation constituted a threat to international peace. But because these actions could not be enforced, short of imposing a blockade on South Africa and Mozambique which neither Britain nor other Western powers were willing even to consider, U.N. actions were bound to be unavailing. Initiatives at the U.N., however, often served more parochial British purposes, frequently pre-empting militant proposals urged by the Afro-Asian bloc, or sometimes offering a useful diversion when the heat in some other theatre tended to become overbearing, or perhaps providing a means for implicating other powers in Britain's Rhodesia policy so that blame could be dispersed should that policy fail.

In the art of tactical manœuvre, Britain was equalled by its adversaries of the Afro-Asian bloc, not only in the U.N. but in the Commonwealth. The abiding purpose was to force Britain's hand, on occasion by threatening to leave the Commonwealth or more frequently by mobilizing maximum pressure at the U.N. on behalf of resolutions calling for measures which Britain had precluded and which the Afro-Asian states had no ability themselves to undertake, such as the use of force against Rhodesia or sanctions against South Africa. As was true of Britain respecting Rhodesia, so it was true of militant Third World states respecting Britain. Each had grand objectives and impoverished means. Frequently it was a formula for irresponsibility.

The final result, while discomfiting to Rhodesia, has not dislodged the rebels nor surely has it dissuaded South Africa and Portugal from pursuing their interests in sustaining white control in Southern Africa. 'We should not intervene in these matters,' said Winston Churchill speaking of the League of Nations' futile efforts on the occasion of Italy's campaign against Ethiopia, 'unless we are in earnest and prepared to carry out intervention to all necessary lengths.' Strangely enough, Harold Wilson publicly endorsed Churchill's observation shortly after U.D.I. when it was already apparent he had foreclosed the possibility of intervening decisively. How Britain, on 11 November 1965, found itself in this predicament relates importantly to Rhodesia's unique history.

II

Prelude to Rebellion

Of Pioneers and Imperialists

A scant seventy-five years separated Ian Smith's U.D.I. and the beginnings of the Rhodesian story. On 12 September 1890 the earliest white settlers, members of the so-called Pioneer Column, raised the Union Jack in a simple ceremony near a small hill named Harari in the highlands of Central Africa. They named their newly founded community Fort Salisbury and at the point where the flag was hoisted they established in time a park which they called Cecil Square. Both city and square were named after the British Prime Minister of the day, Robert Cecil, the third Marquess of Salisbury.

It was not Lord Salisbury, however, who had arranged this modest imperial venture. Rather it was the man who subsequently gave his name to the area lying north of the Limpopo River and traversed by the Zambezi, known until then simply as Zambezia. Cecil John Rhodes, from his home at Groote Schuur under Table Mountain at Cape Town, presided over a fortune dug from the diamond pipes of Kimberley and over the government of Britain's Cape Colony, of which he had become Prime Minister only two months before the pioneers arrived at Fort Salisbury. Rhodes was a man whose vision was bounded by no horizon – an Elizabethan, someone described him, 'the endless rolling plains of Africa his sea'. His resources, will and nerve were proportionate to his grandiose schemes. He once tried to buy outright from Lisbon the Portuguese province of Mozambique. He dreamed of a 'red route' (British Imperial Red) from Cape to Cairo and might have succeeded in constructing that fabled continental rail link if the Boer War and his own untimely death had not intervened. The move into Zambezia was the indispensable first step in translating these sweeping plans into reality. For its accomplishment Rhodes turned his attention both to Salis-

bury's Government in London and to the paramount chief of the
area, an imposing African leader called Lobengula.

Lord Salisbury concurred in Rhodes's schemes only reluctantly,
not wishing to involve London in costly new imperial ventures. But
there were possible commercial advantages (rumours had long
circulated of the gold fields of Mashonaland in Zambezia), and the
encroachment of the German, the Portuguese and the Boer needed
containment or deflection. Most important, Rhodes's Cape Colony
was a vital link with India, the centrepiece of Britain's empire, and it
was prudent to mollify the impatient genius of Groote Schuur.
Accordingly, in the fall of 1889, Queen Victoria granted a Royal
Charter to Rhodes's British South Africa Company authorizing on
behalf of the Crown the right to administer the territory north of the
Limpopo.

Towards the African chief, Lobengula, Rhodes directed an
offensive different in style but no less artful than that which had
won the consent of London's establishment. Lobengula ruled the
Matabele, an offshoot of the Zulu nation under whose formidable
king, Chaka, Lobengula's father, Mzilikazi, had served as an
eminent warrior. To escape the advancing Boers, Mzilikazi had led
his people north of the Limpopo where, by occupation and conquest
(not unlike that of the Europeans who would follow), he quickly
established ascendancy over the scattered Mashona tribes. Rhodes,
using both blandishments and guile, now extracted concessions from
Lobengula which progressively denied the African leader the right to
enter into agreements with other parties without British consent,
won for the concessionaires the right to exploit mineral deposits and
finally gained for them the additional right to make grants of land to
whites. These concessions were then used without the slightest legal
justification as the basis for the assumption of a sovereignty which
Lobengula never meant to surrender and which under the Queen's
Charter Rhodes's Company was authorized to exercise.

By these presumptuous events the twig was bent, and so would the
tree grow. Three features deserve particular mention. Rhodesia was
established by the right of occupation exercised by a small white élite;
Rhodesians from the outset were never ruled from London and as
time passed came to enjoy virtual autonomy; Rhodesia and South
Africa were linked in a special (though seldom positive) relationship.

The 200 white 'pioneers' who raised the Union Jack at Fort
Salisbury in September 1890 and who were the vanguard of the
settlers had in fact been carefully recruited by Rhodes, and had each
been promised fifteen gold claims and 3,000 acres of land. Thereafter,
the anniversary of the arrival of the Pioneer Column was celebrated
with disarming candour as Occupation Day until a more discreet

generation (in 1961) changed the name to Pioneer Day. In the early years there was, predictably, trouble between the settlers and the indigenous Africans, but by 1897 the Maxim gun had subdued even the formidable battalions of the Matabele, and Lobengula, having taken flight, lay in an unmarked grave somewhere in the hinterland of his occupied country. Rhodes in his generation was hardly alone in believing in the innate superiority of Nordic peoples, foremost among them the English. 'We are the first race in the world,' he once said, 'and the more of the world we inhabit the better it is for the human race.'

The occupation of Rhodesia by the racially elect took place in the name of Queen Victoria whose Government promptly delegated authority to Rhodes – 'that most autonomous of all men' as Margery Perham once described him. When Salisbury's Cabinet acceded to Rhodes's request for a Royal Charter, a Colonial Office minute recorded with precision that Rhodes's British South Africa Company 'which is to enjoy the profits . . . shall also discharge and bear all the responsibility of Government'. So from the beginning it was the settler and the Chartered Company, not the Colonial Office, which opened up the resources of the country, collected the taxes, built the roads and railroads, recruited the administrators and maintained order. In a word, Britain assumed nominal responsibility but never real authority.

That disjunction was of no consequence in 1890, just as the occupation of alien lands by a white minority raised scruples in only the most idealistic circles. The indifferent legacy of 1890 had by 1965, however, become Britain's most difficult problem, not because Rhodesia or the Rhodesians had changed so much, but because the world had, and Britain's role in it. Latter-day notions of self-determination and human equality defied the right of occupation and the privileges of a racially defined élite. These revolutionary doctrines nurtured, and then in turn were strengthened by, the anti-colonial convulsions that swept the world following Europe's decline in the two World Wars. Consistent with the new doctrines, Britain had disassembled an empire until virtually all that was left was Rhodesia, for which responsibility remained but effective power on the ground, as it had been from the start, was absent. 'Independence', wrote Patrick Keatley in his study, *The Politics of Partnership*, published two years before U.D.I., 'is not just a catch-phrase among the settlers. . . . It is, in very large measure, a political condition which the settlers of Rhodesia have enjoyed from the start.'

Rhodesia was shaped by the fact of occupation and the condition of autonomy, and also by its relationship to South Africa. Rhodes had prudently seen to it that his hand-picked Pioneer Column and its accompanying escort included a good many men of British stock from Natal and the Cape, assuring a South African lobby for British intervention had anything gone wrong. (A minority of Afrikaners were included giving Dutch-descended South Africans a small stake in the enterprise as well.) Tangible links to the south accumulated over the years. The Roman-Dutch law of South Africa prevailed in Rhodesia. Virtually all of Rhodesia's early legislation and many of its policies, particularly native policy, derived from the Cape or Natal, as did its administrators. In the development of infrastructure, mining and commerce the role of South Africa was important, often predominant.

The significance of these links was obscured, however, by the animus between Briton and Afrikaner, etched deeply by the Boer War, and the desire of the Rhodesian to remain outside the South African orbit. When in 1922 the mandate of the Chartered Company was about to lapse, a referendum was held to determine whether Rhodesia would unite with South Africa as a fifth province. The proposal lost by 8,774 votes to 5,989 and Rhodesia in 1923 was officially annexed to the Crown as a self-governing colony under a constitution which further assured Rhodesia's internal autonomy. The link to London served to offset the powerful pull of nearby Pretoria and was kept vigorous by a self-conscious devotion to things 'British', exemplified by Rhodesia's contribution to the Mother Country not only in the Boer War but in the trials of 1914 and 1939.

Only in the fifties when Britain could no longer ignore the demands of black nationalism did serious strains appear in the favoured relationship between Salisbury and London. With the trauma of U.D.I. and its aftermath, sentimental attachments withered and the realities of common interest with the kindred white minority of South Africa revived; and one remembered again the artful Rhodes who had sought to link South African interests to his imperial venture north of the Limpopo. The great imperialist would have been appalled to learn, however, that the Rhodesia established by his pioneers, rather than sealing off Boer expansion to the north and thus consolidating Britain's control of Central Africa, was eventually to move into the orbit of a South Africa now fully in the control of the Afrikaners themselves.

Collision Course

For Rhodesia's settlers, as has been suggested, relations with both Britain and the indigenous inhabitants were relatively trouble-free for the first half of the century. The constitution of 1923 which gave self-governing status to Rhodesia, reserved to Britain certain functions the most important of which was the right to veto legislation discriminatory against the African. While quiet consultation with London preceded many legislative enactments and probably helped to modify some of their worst features, Rhodesia nonetheless developed over the years a body of laws which not only protected white interests but generally inhibited Africans from developing their skills or demonstrating their capabilities, and during the entire period Britain never once exercised its legislative veto. Centrepieces of discriminatory legislation were the Land Apportionment Act which demarcated separate areas for white and black ownership and usage (a device at first protective of the African, but later the bedrock of racial segregation and discrimination), the Industrial Conciliation Act which barred Africans from specified jobs and excluded them from wage and industrial agreements negotiated under it, and the Native Registration Act which further limited black economic and social opportunity and mobility. Only the franchise was colour-blind, based on income requirements irrespective of colour; by 1939, seventy Africans had qualified in an electorate of 28,000.

In short, Rhodesia's autonomy in developing discriminatory institutions was more apparent than Britain's surveillance in the interests of 'native' rights. Many years before U.D.I. was ever contemplated, a Rhodesian Prime Minister, Sir Godfrey Huggins (later Lord Malvern), exchanged views on Britain's reserve powers in Rhodesia with the Colonial Secretary of an earlier Labour Government, Arthur Creech Jones. The brief report of their conversation (even though it was probably much improved in the telling by Huggins) informs us of everything we need to know about the character of the problem Britain eventually was to face. Huggins called attention to the fact that constitutionally legislation differentiating between the races in Rhodesia was subject to the consent of a British Secretary of State.

Mr. Creech Jones (with feigned innocence): 'What happens if the Secretary of State does not agree?'
Mr. Huggins: 'Well that depends on the substance of the law in question. If the Prime Minister and his colleagues consider the matter of major importance and are satisfied with their local knowledge that it is reasonable, just and fair, the Prime Minister would appeal to the country for a mandate.'
Mr. Creech Jones: 'He would come back with an overwhelming majority?'
Mr. Huggins: 'Probably, yes.'
Mr. Creech Jones: 'And what happens then?'

Mr. Huggins: 'If the Secretary of State has a spare Army Corps available for active service in Africa, he might insist on his disapproval. If not, he would have to change his mind and compromise if possible or agree.'
Mr. Creech Jones: 'Exactly, the safeguards are of no worth.'

The statement was exaggerated and Huggins's account may have misrepresented Creech Jones. The point is, however, that Salisbury's control of its own affairs was virtually unrestricted, inspiring confidence that one day Rhodesia would progress, as had other British settled communities, to full independence under Dominion status. Already its affairs were handled through the Dominions Office (later the Commonwealth Relations Office), with which its ties were quasi-diplomatic and processed by High Commissioners located in the respective capitals. The Governor performed honorific functions. From 1933, Rhodesia's head of government was called a Prime Minister and was invited to attend Commonwealth meetings. Rhodesians made their own laws, were judged in their own courts, raised their own revenues, recruited their own civil service, mobilized their own defence forces, were under the jurisdiction of their own police, travelled on their own passports and controlled their own foreign commerce. Full independence, however, together with admission to the state system, was a matter of expectation, not accomplishment. Rhodesians not only raised the Union Jack and sang 'God Save the King' (or Queen), but did not question that formal and residual (as opposed to operative) authority rested with London.

The African population remained largely passive, overwhelmed physically and spiritually by the European occupation and by the sheer magnitude and omnipresence of European culture. However, the war and post-war years stirred new forces in Rhodesia as elsewhere. To the white community this period brought an industrial and agricultural boom and a considerable population explosion, from 70,000 in 1945 to 135,000 in 1951. To the Africans it brought new awareness. Many had seen service in the war, and the thrust for self-determination which emerged in Asia at the end of the conflict began in time to be reflected in Africa too. An African general strike in Rhodesia in 1948 sent tremors of anxiety through the white community, a foretaste of things to come.

The war which had stimulated economic activity throughout the region had also heightened administrative collaboration between Rhodesia and Britain's two other Central African colonies, Northern Rhodesia and Nyasaland, both of which (unlike Southern Rhodesia) were administered in typical colonial fashion. While permitting increasing internal autonomy in the two northern areas, Whitehall retained responsibility for defence and foreign policy, and lines of authority ran from London through a British-appointed Governor to the security services and to the civil service. A project long mooted to bring the northern territories into formal association with Rhodesia was, in 1953, consummated by the British Parliament, and the Federation of Rhodesia and Nyasaland came into being. Several aspects of this undertaking are worth noting. It appeared to validate Rhodesia's expectations that Dominion status lay ahead, now within the framework of a vastly expanded jurisdiction of significant economic potential and, within its region, of strategic importance. It provided scope for Rhodesia's energetic entrepreneurs by opening access to markets north of the Zambezi and to revenues for development purposes generated on Northern Rhodesia's lucrative Copperbelt. Finally, it seemed to offer a formula for progress in race relations compatible with demands that were sure to grow in a turbulent post-war world whistling with 'the winds of change'. At the same time, the Federation carried within itself contradictions which were bound to undo it, and in turn to overwhelm the political life of Rhodesia generally. These last points deserve further examination.

The Federation broke precedent. Under its constitution, six Africans sat in the Federal Parliament and as time went on an African came to hold the rank of junior Cabinet Minister while a few Africans were appointed to serve in relatively senior posts in the Federal civil service as well as in the Federation's external service. Though the basic pattern remained rigorously segregative, there were emergent modifications in behaviour and a certain relaxation of social barriers, permitting Africans access to many public facilities. The new non-racial University College of Rhodesia and Nyasaland, for example, was opened to black and white alike. The phenomenon was called 'partnership'. But as might be expected, the ambivalences were profound. Sir Godfrey Huggins (Lord Malvern), first Federal Prime Minister and predominant political power in Rhodesia for a score of years, once defined partnership as the relationship between horse and rider. Africans readily perceived which was which. Sir Roy Welensky, the pugnacious, colourful figure who succeeded Malvern, expostulated that the African 'can achieve equal standing but not go beyond it'. Even thus qualified it was an astonishing doctrine in white Rhodesia in the 1950s. The revolutionary force of Welensky's proposition was slightly attenuated, however, when Sir Roy allowed that the process for achieving parity would take 100 or perhaps even 200 years.

At first, some Africans responded favourably to these tentative overtures. Men who later would lead campaigns of violent protest

stood for African seats in the new Federal Parliament and held
offices in burgeoning associations dedicated to improving race relations. But white ambivalence was in fact more than matched by black
doubts, nurtured by deep frustrations and the obvious lack of real
progress. By 1956, African militancy had surfaced. The following year
the Southern Rhodesian African National Congress (S.R.A.N.C.)
was founded with calculated provocation on 12 September, Occupation Day. The cycle of demonstrations leading to riots leading in turn
to the banning of organizations and the restriction of leaders began in
1959, in which year too there were serious disruptions in Nyasaland.
Mass demonstrations in Salisbury in July 1960 immobilized African
townships, then spread to the industrial city of Bulawayo where
eleven Africans were killed, the first blood spilled in large-scale
clashes between whites and Africans since 1897.

For Britain, too, the experiment in Central Africa was creating
mounting problems. Federation if anything had stimulated nationalist
movements in Northern Rhodesia and Nyasaland where Federal
authority was seen, not as a cautious experiment in multiracialism,
but as the attempt of Rhodesia's whites to extend their sway north-
wards and as a prelude to independence for the entire region under
white control. A special commission appointed in 1960 under Lord
Monckton examined the future of the Federation and fixed upon the
right of constituent territories to secede if they wished, having in
mind of course the growing nationalist agitation north of the
Zambezi. At the same time, the Commission urged racial parity in
the Federal Legislative Assembly and more power for the territorial
governments as the only hope for breaking through to genuine multiracialism. Concerning these matters, a Federal legislator by the name
of Ian Smith said in a Parliamentary debate that he rejected all
proposed concessions to African nationalists, wanted 'continuous
control in civilized hands for all time' throughout the Federation, and
accused Britain of a 'scandalous betrayal'.

The governance of Rhodesia itself revealed in even more marked
degree the tension between African assertion and what Frank
Clements, a former mayor of Salisbury, had called white 'paternalistic
reformism'. The latter phenomenon came to a climax under the
premiership of Sir Edgar Whitehead (1958–62) when the Rhodesian
Parliament passed an unprecedented body of social and economic
legislation improving African wages, education and amenities, and
encouraging a fair measure of multiracialism. But these efforts,
laudable in the context of white Rhodesia, did not blunt rising
African militancy. They were too little too late; and historically-
rooted mistrust ran too deep. To handle the recurrent problems of
disorder, repressive laws went hand in hand with reforming legisla-

tion: the Unlawful Organizations Act and the Preventive Detention Act of 1959 and the Emergency Powers Act and Law and Order Maintenance Act of 1960. These measures made available virtually all the instruments of arbitrary government. Political parties could be banned by executive action; freedom of assembly was abolished; the police were given arbitrary powers of arrest, while individuals, guilty until proved innocent, could be detained without trial.

In 1961 a new constitution was hammered out under the guidance of the British Commonwealth Secretary, Duncan Sandys, in a conference representing all Rhodesia's major groups. Two features of the 1961 constitution require particular attention. First, Britain gave up its right of surveillance over discriminatory legislation, thus rounding out Rhodesia's autonomy and moving the self-governing colony a step closer to full independence. As a substitute for Britain's vacated responsibility, a Declaration of Rights was written into the constitution, permitting aggrieved individuals the right of appeal to the High Court and beyond that to the Privy Council. The Declaration however was not retroactive, and thus had no effect on legislation already on the books. A limited watch-dog function over new legislation contravening the Declaration was vested in a multiracial Constitutional Council.

Second, African representation in the Rhodesian Parliament was for the first time assured by a complex franchise which would result immediately in up to fifteen African seats and potentially could have led many years hence to majority rule. Two electoral rolls were created each based on property, income and educational qualifications, an 'A' or Upper Roll for which principally Europeans would qualify and a 'B' or Lower Roll which would be African-dominated. In simplified terms, 'A' roll voters would elect fifty members to the Legislative Assembly while 'B' roll voters would elect fifteen. An intricate cross-voting system gave each 'A' roll voter a quarter vote in a 'B' roll electoral district, while each 'B' roll voter received a quarter vote in an 'A' roll constituency. Thus each roll had a marginal impact on the other, a device which, it was hoped, would mitigate the *de facto* racial character of the two-roll system. Amendments to the so-called 'entrenched' (or particularly important) sections of the constitution, including the franchise requirements just reviewed, had to be approved either by the British Government or by each of Rhodesia's four communities – African, white, Asian and coloured (or mixed-blood) – voting separately in a referendum.

The 1961 constitution represented significant concessions from the point of view of the white community, and Joshua Nkomo, leader of the National Democratic Party (N.D.P.) which had succeeded the Southern Rhodesian African National Congress following its banning early in 1959, initially gave it his support. But he soon reversed himself under pressure from militants both at home and abroad. To Africans, the constitution looked like a quarter loaf, and a step closer to full independence under white minority rule. In 1961, it was perhaps not difficult to believe that more might be gained from total opposition than from qualified support for white-initiated and white-controlled multiracial schemes. Independence under majority rule was spreading like a contagion as France, Britain and Belgium withdrew from the continent. An anti-Portuguese insurrection in Angola had just erupted and South Africa was still reeling from the international repercussions to the Sharpeville massacre the year before. North of the Zambezi, African rule seemed assured in both Northern Rhodesia and Nyasaland. A little more pressure in Southern Rhodesia, it was thought, particularly if it endangered foreign investment, would elicit British support for further demands, or perhaps outright British intervention. It was a tragic miscalculation.

Whitehead meanwhile had become utterly dependent upon gaining support from moderate Africans. For he had to demonstrate to a sceptical and anxious white electorate that it was possible to achieve a multiracial solution which would defuse African extremism while maintaining white control over the pace of African advance. Yet, the voice of the African militant was becoming more strident and so too was that of the white extremist, narrowing further Whitehead's ability to manoeuvre. William Harper, who soon would play a leading role in Rhodesia's shift to the right, argued with Sir Edgar in Parliament (23 August 1960) that if Africans were seated in the Legislative Assembly 'they will share the restaurant with us and they will share the bars with us. We will be living cheek by jowl with them and what sort of legislation can the people of this country expect when we ourselves are being conditioned to living cheek by jowl with Africans.'

Whitehead's effort to win African support led him to promise the repeal of the repugnant Land Apportionment Act following the first election under the new constitution, now scheduled for the end of 1962. In October of that same year, he told a U.N. committee that he expected Africans would constitute a majority on the voting rolls within fifteen years, an unrealistic estimate but hopefully as reassuring to Africans as it was doubtless alarming to whites. Yet, all Sir Edgar's blandishments and his insistent efforts to register Africans under the new electoral laws and to gain African membership for his party failed disastrously. The African nationalists, having rejected reform within the system, committed themselves to agitation outside the system. Still hoping for the support of the moderate black élite which he assumed had been intimidated by extremists, Whitehead moved repeatedly against the militants only to find at the end of the process that the moderates had disappeared. Thus, reform and repression continued to go hand in hand, the former alienating whites, the latter alienating blacks, and the resulting militancy in each community only excited extremism in the other.

Now for the first time African violence was directed toward white property. Forests and crops were burned; cattle were maimed; and railway lines were blown up. The agency was the so-called Zimbabwe Liberation Army, an underground arm of the Zimbabwe African Peoples Union (ZAPU) which had emerged to take the place of the N.D.P. when it was banned in December 1961.* Domestic disorders combined with events north of the Zambezi to emphasize white anxiety further. Earlier it had been the Mau Mau in Kenya. Now it was violence in the Congo. Belgian refugees streamed south from Katanga and their stories of a new African nation in disarray embellished already rising fears in Rhodesia. (Somewhat later, the Congo experience also demonstrated to fascinated Rhodesians that some 200 white mercenaries could conrol vast areas of the country.)

Moderation and gradualism declined as issues affecting both race and politics polarized. African extremism was now matched by its white counterpart. The vehicle was a new amalgamation of conservatives, dissidents and eccentrics organized in March 1962 and known as the Rhodesian Front. The key statement in its election manifesto read, 'The Front recognizes that inherent in the new constitution there is the intention to ensure the dominance by the African of the European before the former has acquired adequate knowledge and experience of democratic government. The Front believes this must be avoided.' It was an appealing sentiment to increasing numbers of whites – and only partially revealed the Front's reactionary and deeply racist hard core which in fact was insisting that multiracialism must give way to separate development, and that Africans must never rule in Rhodesia.

These doctrines were laced with the most extraordinary theories of worldwide conspiracy and self-indulgent notions of Rhodesia's worldwide importance. Rhodesia was an island of sanity in a world gone berserk, a bastion in defence of Western civilization and Christian standards against (depending upon the speaker) world communism, liberalism, Leftists, 'political internationalism', international financiers, and the 'forces of evil'. These had seized control (again depending

---

* Zimbabwe is the name of an impressive monumental ruin in the southern part of the country built by a pre-European culture and thus the symbol of both past African accomplishments and future aspirations.

upon the speaker) of the Kremlin, Wall Street, Washington, London, the State Department, the U.N., UNESCO, the World Council of Churches, the media and seats of learning. Clifford Dupont, soon himself to be deeply involved in conspiratorial planning against Great Britain, once told the Legislative Assembly (13 March 1963) that 'Southern Rhodesia today is in the front line: but we are fighting not only our battle for existence but [that of the United States and Britain]. . . . We are the keystone, and I have no hesitation in saying that if we go the way of Central and East Africa then it is only a question of time before Western civilization also has to go.'

After years of uncertainty, change and sporadic disorder, fearful of the future and convinced more than ever that strong measures would be needed to stabilize the country and to disentangle it from waning British authority, the Rhodesian electorate at the end of 1962 turned government over to the Front. African nationalists had assured this outcome by their boycott of the elections and by their violent tactics. No more than one-fifth of those entitled to a 'B' roll vote had registered and of these only one-fourth had cast ballots. According to Sir Edgar's later estimate, an additional 5,000 African 'B' roll voters exercising their cross-voting privilege could have changed the results. But Africans clearly had rejected 'partnership' and their leaders actually welcomed the Front's victory, hoping to demonstrate to the world how serious the situation was in Rhodesia and thereby stimulate external intervention. It was another bad miscalculation.

We can only guess what the outcome would have been had Joshua Nkomo tipped the balance to Sir Edgar Whitehead and entered Parliament himself at the head of a deputation of fifteen African nationalist representatives. Certainly in Parliament Nkomo would have enjoyed substantial tactical advantages: a platform of national and even international prominence; a degree of leverage on Whitehead; and the possibility of legitimizing his claim for further African advances which, at the very worst, would have placed the onus for failure on a recalcitrant white establishment rather than on rebellious African leaders. In view of the alternatives and with the benefit of hindsight, Nkomo was foolish to have denied himself these opportunities. At the same time, given the depth of black frustration and white fear, one suspects that racial confrontation would only have been postponed, not averted. In his book, *African Nationalism*, the Reverend Ndabaningi Sithole (later to lead a faction of the nationalist movement) observed quite accurately that multiracialism and partnership really meant that 'other races are allowed to participate in government affairs so long as they are satisfied with a secondary place in the whole scheme, while the first place is reserved for whites only'.

In any event, there was about these developments, as so frequently would be the case throughout the Rhodesian story, a fateful sense of inevitability. Each effort by white gradualists to win African support was met not only with understandable suspicion by African leaders but with renewed efforts to spark African resistance, leading to intimidation and violence, evoking further repressive measures by the whites, and creating still further alienation among the Africans. In this process the leaders on each side quickly became the prisoners of their followers. It is moot whether in broad outline this progression could have been avoided, or once started, reversed.

Despite the eccentricities of many of its supporters, the Rhodesian Front for the moment was cast in the comforting image of its first leader, Winston Field. He was a solid man of cautious instinct, profoundly conservative but fair-minded, and he commanded wide personal respect. He was also an anachronism in the increasingly bizarre world of Rhodesian politics, and in a sense his qualities were his undoing. Mandated by his Party to remove the threat of African nationalism and gain independence from Britain, he found neither could be achieved quickly. A Party cabal, some sixteen months after he had taken office, unseated him in mid April 1964. Four months prior to that, on 10 January 1964, Field's Deputy Prime Minister, Ian Smith, had announced in Parliament that 'whatever they [the British Government] say or do will not make the slightest difference to our intention to get independence'. It was to Smith that the Party leadership now turned.

Mr. Smith Goes to London

Ian Douglas Smith was once described as the most improbable rebel in British history – a man utterly lacking in flamboyance, with an unsmiling countenance (war wounds had stiffened his facial muscles), a monotonous speaking voice and a plodding mind. But he had in him a stubborn combative streak, the gift of political cunning, and the commanding virtue of being Rhodesian-born – the first Southern Rhodesian Prime Minister of that distinction. His route to power was not Eton, Oxford, the professions or international commerce as had been true of most members of Rhodesia's white establishment, but local schools, Rhodes University in South Africa, the R.A.F. and a career in farming. He was born in 1919 in the tiny rural town of Selukwe, the son of a Scots immigrant who arrived in the country in 1898, not long after Rhodes's vanguard. From the grass roots himself, Smith possessed a canny sense of how grass-roots opinion was developing. And in time he was to become the very embodiment of

conservative reaction to the modest multiracialism of Sir Edgar
Whitehead and the white Rhodesian establishment.

He was by his own account a 'strong right-wing man'. In fact, he
resigned as Sir Roy Welensky's chief whip in the Federal Parliament
in protest against the 1961 constitution, which for the first time
allowed Africans to sit in the Southern Rhodesian Parliament. Yet,
his own views were often in some doubt for he was quite capable of
devious ambiguities, obfuscation or even taking (or appearing to
take) more moderate positions on particular issues – generally for
reasons of tactics. Moreover he had a penchant for eliciting and then
articulating a consensus rather than building it. Still, for those who
took the trouble to probe, his opinions were available and un-
varnished. 'The white man is the master of Rhodesia,' he once said.
'He has built it and intends to keep it.' Conviction as well as expediency, then, aligned him with the more intransigent views of his
colleagues. And his inflexible mind and constrained vision, liabilities
in other contexts, became the source of towering strength in the
strange, insulated and increasingly paranoid world of Rhodesia.

Politics in that country was now dominated by race. Increasingly,
white politics became preoccupied with the need to assert unquestioned and unfettered white control. A precondition was independence from Britain, without which, it was thought, white control at
some point in the future would be likely to be compromised. This was
what the selection of Ian Smith was all about and his mandate from
the Party would remain valid only as long as he showed tangible
progress toward these ends. In his first press conference Smith said
he hoped independence could be achieved by negotiation, 'but we
have made it quite clear that we can visualize circumstances which
might drive us to do something else'.

The preoccupation with independence arose too from other concerns. One was economic. Uncertainties relating to Rhodesia's future
were drying up the flow both of investment and white immigrants.
The white population had shown a sharp drop from 222,000 as of
30 June 1962, to 209,000 as of 30 June 1964. Rhodesian Fronters
argued that these problems would be set right once independence was
achieved, no matter how. Stories circulated of major investors
poised to come in as soon as Rhodesia's sovereignty was assured.
Another reason related to both Rhodesian pride and frustration as
other countries, particularly Northern Rhodesia and Nyasaland,
achieved independence after only the briefest apprenticeship in self-
government, while Rhodesia was denied similar status after forty
years of responsible home rule. But far and away the most important
reason was fear that as long as 'even the thread of an apron string
attaches us to the British Government', as Smith once put it,

Rhodesia would be subject to intervention and external manipulation. The avenues of possible intervention were many. It was frequently argued, for example, that until Rhodesia ruptured its formal links to Britain, African nationalist politicians would continue to appeal to London to exert influence on the Salisbury Government. Smith repeatedly insisted that this was truly a 'life and death' question for Rhodesia, that independence was necessary to restore the authority of the tribal system and to convince the African nationalists that they had no alternative but to return to obedience under the constitution, and that without independence white Rhodesians would feel there was no future for them in the country. The Commonwealth too was a source of increasing anxiety. The British Government had suggested that discussions with Commonwealth leaders might help break the deadlock and assure a solution which would permit Rhodesia to assume full membership in that organization. Rhodesians bristled at this 'unprecedented' proposal. When Britain agreed to establish a Commonwealth Secretariat, fears began to spread that new and unpredictable initiatives would ensue. The Commonwealth meeting scheduled for mid 1966 was viewed by some (however irrationally) as the occasion when members would agree to impose a new majority rule constitution on Rhodesia, and a Rhodesian 'pre-emptive strike' prior to that date came to assume inordinate importance for a number of anxious leaders in Salisbury.

Nor was intervention at the instance of the United Nations to be lightly dismissed. Beginning early in 1962, various organs of the U.N. passed resolutions calling upon Britain *inter alia* to convene a new constitutional conference leading to immediate majority rule, to gain the release of detained African nationalist leaders, and to refuse to transfer military aircraft to Rhodesia following the dissolution of the Federation and its armed forces. All such measures, of course, involved not the exercise of existing executive powers on the part of Britain, but the outright subjugation of Rhodesia. With the advent of a Labour Government, fears only increased that Britain would find some way to intervene – 'legislating' for Rhodesia in contravention of existing conventions, or unilaterally altering the constitution, or interposing its will by some more explicit means. Viewed from the closed ambit of that isolated society, the image of a socialist administration sitting in London activated in some Rhodesians the most eccentric notions, that the British Government was now working hand-in-glove with Moscow as a part of a world-wide communist conspiracy an important target of which was the bastion of Western Christian values in Central Africa.

In the pursuit of independence, Ian Smith picked up where Winston Field had left off. As early as March 1963, once London had made clear that Northern Rhodesia as well as Nyasaland would be allowed independence under African rule outside the Federation (a decision which of course sealed the fate of that entity), Field had formally applied to Britain for independence for Southern Rhodesia. The stalemate which quickly emerged turned on the role of the African in an independent Rhodesia. Salisbury insisted on the 1961 constitution as the basis for independence – something of a contradiction because the Front's leaders at the time and thereafter were resolutely against its multiracial features. Britain wanted changes in that constitution to diminish racial discrimination and to enhance the Africans' role. Specifically the Conservative Government in London insisted on repeal of the Land Apportionment Act, a strengthened Declaration of Rights, lowered franchise requirements on both electoral rolls enabling more Africans to register, and an increase in the number of 'B' Roll seats sufficient to give Africans a veto over amendments to the constitution which required (except for the 'entrenched clauses') a two-thirds majority of the Legislative Assembly. Respecting these requirements, Field went part of the way, but not far enough. When Rhodesia accused Britain of unfair treatment, Duncan Sandys replied (on 7 December 1963), 'the present difficulty arises from your desire to secure independence on the basis of a franchise which is incomparably more restricted than that of any other British territory to which independence has hitherto been granted'.

Nonetheless the Rhodesians increasingly felt misused. Britain's approval of the 1961 constitution, they argued, represented an 'implied contract' to grant independence under it in due course. After all, Field insisted, had Rhodesia not joined the Federation, it doubtless would have gained independence as a separate entity years before. The break-up of Federation, which took place at the end of 1963 and which positioned the northern territories to move rapidly towards independence, emphasized the anomaly. It was argued in Salisbury (though totally unsupported by the facts) that Britain had committed itself to grant Rhodesia its independence under the 1961 constitution if the Federation were dissolved.* Mistrust of Britain

---

* There was also a variation on this theme. Prior to the conference at Victoria Falls where the dissolution of Federation was agreed upon in June 1963, Rhodesia's Minister of Internal Affairs, John H. Howman, had private conversations in London with R. A. Butler who was charged with Central African affairs by the Conservative Government. Field had insisted publicly that he would not attend the Victoria Falls conference without assurance that Rhodesia would subsequently be granted independence. Howman later claimed that Butler had given him that assurance, but there was no written record

grew rapidly throughout 1963 and 1964. Only a few short years before, white Rhodesians had believed themselves to be linked to Britons, not only by history and culture, but in common cause. Their rejection now was viewed as a betrayal. Rhodesia's 'standards' and 'way of life' were to be sacrificed so that Afro-Asians within the Commonwealth and the United Nations might be appeased.

White Rhodesian and British interests had indeed diverged. For Britain had legitimate concerns in these wider theatres which from the narrower Rhodesian perspective were both incomprehensible and dangerous. Canada's Prime Minister Lester Pearson put the matter succinctly after the Commonwealth Conference in 1964: 'If we can solve the Rhodesia problem, the Commonwealth will grow greater still in world importance. If we cannot, then the future of the Commonwealth is dim indeed.' In any event, assuming Britain had wished to support the Rhodesian position, for example by maintaining the Federation, it would have been obliged to commit ever greater resources to the area in order to resist the rising tide of African nationalism in the northern territories. Such a course was made difficult by rapidly changing attitudes towards empire and a corresponding sharp decline of imperial will, accelerated by the Suez fiasco of 1956. Beyond these considerations were simple matters of equity which had assumed new importance in the more democratic and egalitarian milieu of the post-war world. To grant independence to a government totally controlled by a tiny white minority without guarantees for rapidly expanding participation by the overwhelming mass of the population in the management of their own affairs was to fly in the face of even the most rudimentary of democratic ideals.

In September 1964, Ian Smith went to London for another round of exchanges on the independence issue with the British Prime Minister, Sir Alec Douglas-Home, and the Commonwealth Secretary, Duncan Sandys. The positions of both sides were reviewed. Renewed attention was given to the threat of a unilateral declaration of independence, about which there had been increasing talk in Salisbury as frustration and disillusionment steadily increased, resulting from the dissolution of the Federation and subsequent exchanges with London about preconditions for independence. In previous correspondence Sandys had outlined the weighty consequences of U.D.I. Sharp reactions could be expected from Africa, the U.N. and the

---

of it. Butler, a courteous man and on occasion a sibylline speaker, may well have left this impression in Howman's mind, but it clearly did not represent British policy.

Commonwealth, resulting in Rhodesia's diplomatic and economic isolation, and making it the object of boycott and subversion. For its part Britain could not accept the legal validity of such an act. H.M. Government would be pressed to regard Rhodesia as being in a state of revolt. The Queen could not continue to be the Sovereign of Rhodesia under such circumstances. There would be heavy pressure to withdraw Commonwealth preferences and Rhodesia's membership in the sterling area. Rhodesian Ministers who were parties to an illegal action 'would be acting unconstitutionally and in breach of the obligations they assumed on taking office'.

At the London talks, however, Ian Smith suggested that the danger of U.D.I. had sharply decreased. For the first time, the two sides gave detailed consideration to procedures for ascertaining the views of all Rhodesians on settlement terms. Smith argued that he was certain the terms of the 1961 constitution were in fact 'acceptable to the people of the country as a whole', to use the phrase of the final *communiqué*. The British remained equally certain that more widely representative institutions would be demanded by a majority of the Africans prior to independence. But if Smith could demonstrate the contrary, a new situation would have arisen. When Smith proposed, however, to ascertain African opinion by putting the question to an *indaba* or council meeting of Rhodesia's chiefs and headmen, the British flatly refused. These traditional officials in no sense represented the urbanized Africans and moreover received both their appointments and their salaries from the Rhodesian Government. Smith in turn rejected a comprehensive referendum (fearing both the outcome and the precedent) and said he would consider what other methods might be used.

On returning home, the Rhodesian Prime Minister professed optimism that independence could be negotiated by the year's end, then proceeded to organize the *indaba* which Sir Alec had unequivocally turned down. The British Government was informed of these plans on 14 October 1964, and invited to send observers. It was the eve of a British General Election. Just conceivably, with Britain's politicians caught up in the climax of an electoral campaign, Smith might be able to slip his plans through without serious objection from London. On 15 October, however, a message was flashed back from the Commonwealth Office strongly reiterating that the *indaba* 'would not provide conclusive evidence of the wishes of the people' and refusing to name observers. The next afternoon the election returns were in, and by the narrowest of margins, Labour had unseated the Conservative Government.

Mr. Wilson Goes to Salisbury

On top of Harold Wilson's in-tray when he assumed office was a red-flagged file on Rhodesia. He was not unfamiliar with the problem. In Parliament, he had opposed the Federation of Rhodesia and Nyasaland in 1953 along with a majority of his party. Labour had also opposed the 1961 Rhodesian constitution for granting too little to the Africans. In March 1963, after he had assumed the leadership of the Labour Party, Wilson censured that constitution: 'A Labour Government would . . . alter it – let me make that very, very plain.' During the election campaign of 1964, Wilson responded to a request for his views on Rhodesia from Dr. E. Mutasa of the Rhodesian Committee against European Independence. He wrote: 'The Labour Party is totally opposed to granting independence to Southern Rhodesia as long as the Government of the country remains under a white minority.' As soon as Labour had taken office, Mutasa gave the letter to the press.

It is not certain, however, whether the new Prime Minister fully understood just how difficult and intractable was the problem he had inherited from (and himself six years later would bequeath to) the Tories, and even less clear that he appreciated Britain's meagre leverage. For Wilson had almost limitless confidence in his own ability to manipulate political situations. This, combined with his pragmatism and his rather romantic views concerning Britain's role as a world power and his own role (which mixed Kennedyesque and Churchillian images), all seemed to contribute at the outset to a certain optimism that, with the proper application of wit and energy, the matter would in fact be quite manageable. In any event, his political virtuosity tended towards a preoccupation with the short term. He often seemed more concerned with packaging policy than with its content and was quicker to estimate the immediate impact of actions than to analyse their longer-term consequences. Similarly it was a concentration on style and energy and approach, certainly not a careful scrutiny of the problem, that must have led to the judgement rendered by the left-wing *Tribune* on 6 November 1964: 'In Harold Wilson, Ian Smith has met his match.' More than his predecessors, perhaps, Wilson would have a bad time taking the measure of his opponents, or of his own capabilities.

His policy was marginally tougher and much more public than that of the Conservatives, but it followed the same general lines. Sir Hugh Foot (later Lord Caradon), who in October 1962 had resigned as British representative on the Trusteeship Council in protest over the Conservative Government's refusal to declare that independence would not be granted on the basis of the 1961 constitution, was now named British representative to the United Nations. Hardly had the Labour Party assumed office when rumours began flying that Rhodesia would declare U.D.I. on 24 October 1964, during Zambia's (Northern Rhodesia's) independence celebrations. Wilson sent a stiff note to Smith which he shortly made public. He reiterated many of the points earlier made by Sandys concerning penalties which would follow U.D.I. He left no doubt that that event would be an act of rebellion, that steps to give it effect would be treasonable, that financial aid or access to the London money market would be denied, that trade relations with Britain would be jeopardized – in short, that U.D.I. 'would inflict disastrous economic drainage upon her, and would leave her isolated and virtually friendless in a largely hostile continent'. In the months to come, these prospective economic sanctions were given greater precision and stressed with increasing urgency. At the same time, however, Wilson's Government made clear that the use of military force was not contemplated.

Similarly respecting the conditions for independence, Wilson took the themes already established under the Tory Government and gave them greater precision. These were set forth as five, somewhat repetitive principles which had come to achieve considerable consensus in the Westminster Parliament:

1. The principle and intention of unimpeded progress to majority rule, already enshrined in the 1961 constitution, would have to be maintained and guaranteed.
2. There would also have to be guarantees against retrogressive amendment of the constitution.
3. There would have to be immediate improvement in the political status of the African population.
4. There would have to be progress towards ending racial discrimination.
5. The British Government would need to be satisfied that any basis proposed for independence was acceptable to the people of Rhodesia as a whole. . . .

Meanwhile, in Salisbury, preparations for a final break moved ahead. It was important that the political climate in Rhodesia be made as favourable as possible. At Smith's *indaba*, held towards the end of October 1964 at Domboshawa, the chiefs not surprisingly supported without dissent immediate independence under the 1961 constitution. The *indaba* was followed by a referendum of all voters held on 5 November. In response to the (too simple) question, 'Do you want independence under the 1961 constitution?' almost 90 per cent of the respondents, who were overwhelmingly white, voted 'yes'. A General Election was called in May 1965. Smith avowed that it had nothing to do with U.D.I. Rather, it was to be an affirmation of unity to strengthen his hand in negotiations with Britain. He also suggested that if he could gain a two-thirds majority in Parliament, he would introduce amendments aimed at reducing the influence of African elected members to the Legislative Assembly. By now the white opposition had fragmented. Smith won every 'A' Roll constituency, controlling fifty of sixty-five seats in Parliament.

Measures against the African nationalists were similarly decisive, aided in this case by a serious split in the movement. It occurred in July 1963 when part of the leadership rallied to the Reverend Ndabaningi Sithole to form the Zimbabwe African National Union (ZANU). Nkomo's ZAPU, like the S.R.A.N.C. and N.D.P. before it, had been banned the previous September and, though the organization continued to function in exile, guidance for the movement within Rhodesia was placed in the hands of a so-called People's Caretaker Council (P.C.C.). New violence now flared, sparked in substantial measure by repeated head bashings between the contesting adherents of ZAPU and ZANU. It was a disgraceful episode bringing great discredit to the nationalist cause, not only among non-Africans and foreign observers but among Rhodesian Africans themselves. By the end of 1964 the unrest was crushed, both the P.C.C. and ZANU having been banned and most leaders who had not fled the country placed in custody.

Plans meanwhile were put in train to develop an effective propaganda arm headquartered in the Government's Information Department. Gradually in turn the Rhodesia Broadcasting Corporation was also brought under political control. Civil servants of doubtful loyalty throughout the administration were identified and isolated from sensitive discussions bearing on preparations for U.D.I. In a few notable cases senior officials were replaced. Smith ascertained that, though Governor Gibbs strongly opposed any illegal action, he was most unlikely to place himself at the head of an opposition movement to the Government.

Fully aware of the dangerous drift within Rhodesia, Harold Wilson probed incessantly for terms of settlement consistent with his five principles, or at the very least for delaying actions. Lengthy exchanges of correspondence, two visits to Salisbury in February and July 1965 by British Ministers and a second visit to London by Smith in October produced no progress whatsoever. With the evidence of an imminent illegal action by Rhodesia now overwhelming, Wilson suddenly announced his intention to fly to Salisbury for an eleventh-hour attempt to avert U.D.I. He arrived on 25 October 1965 for six gruelling days of consultations and bargaining.

Wilson said that he placed no time limit on majority rule.

Unimpressed by African leadership and its fratricidal conflicts, he tried to make clear that progress towards African rule should not be measured by clock or calendar but by achievement and by progress in making democracy work. Still, that process would have to be accelerated and safeguarded by guarantees that it would not be reversed. Yet, virtually every proposal to forward these ends was turned aside by Salisbury. To constitutional amendments designed to expand the franchise, the Rhodesian response would if anything have slowed down the process. The Rhodesians talked of eliminating cross-voting and 'fading out' 'B' Roll seats as Africans won 'A' Roll constituencies. Britain had offered financial aid to speed African education and thus to qualify Africans more quickly for the franchise. Salisbury was not interested. Indeed while in London, Smith had stated with surprising candour that 'the Government Party in Rhodesia did not believe in majority rule. They accepted that the 1961 constitution would eventually bring it about, but they would not take any action to hasten the process.'

It was the same with remedies for discriminatory practices. The Land Apportionment Act would not be repealed. Nor could agreement be reached on mechanisms to assure an African veto over retrogressive amendments to the constitution. Only respecting a device to test the acceptability of any agreed formula to the people of Rhodesia as a whole was a breakthrough achieved. Near the end of his visit to Salisbury, Wilson suggested that a three-man Royal Commission be established for this purpose with a mandate to devise procedures for the approval of the two Governments. Respecting the terms of the settlement itself, however, the gap remained unbridgeable. As a last desperate manœuvre, it was agreed that the Royal Commission should attempt to ascertain the views of the Rhodesian people on the 1961 constitution as a basis for independence. But procedural differences immediately emerged to hobble the attempt, despite a torrent of ideas from Wilson's fertile mind, until at last the situation was overtaken by Rhodesia's unilateral declaration on 11 November.

U.D.I., as James Barber has suggested in his study, *Rhodesia: The Road to Rebellion*, was entirely consistent with the 'all or nothing' mood prevailing in Rhodesia. Joshua Nkomo had already been restricted by Rhodesian authorities for over a year when in mid 1965 he again insisted to a visitor that there could be no compromise: 'Power must be handed over to us, who represent the majority of the people.' He was no less insistent on majority rule when Wilson saw him during his Salisbury trip. So too was Sithole. Nor could the Rhodesian Front envisage any essential compromise with white rule. As Wilson later put it to Commons (21 December 1965): 'They were obdurate because they were determined men utterly resolved on one proposition, and that was that we should not seek majority rule in Rhodesia in their lifetime. It was as simple as that. . . .'

The gradualism implicit in British policy was an echo of the ephemeral era of 'partnership' which had disappeared as politics polarized on the race issue. British policy – it made no difference whether it was Tory or Labour – had been caught and would continue to be for years to come in a vain effort to recreate the incipient moderation of that fleeting period. Extremism was a function of deep

mistrust, even fear – African of white, and white of African. Just
before leaving Salisbury, Wilson told a press conference:

> 'There can be no doubt, I am afraid, that the situation is
> hyper-charged with emotion; and that is not conducive to
> getting the right answer for, among those emotions,
> predominant is the emotion of fear, with the attendant
> emotions of distrust and suspicion and of unfounded rumour.
> And fear is a bad counsellor. . . .'

III

Issues and Instruments

All things considered, there was impressive unity in the Commons in the days immediately following 11 November 1965, so much so that Reginald Maudling, Deputy Leader of the opposition Conservative Party, could state publicly that Wilson had handled himself with dignity, and he could think of no major thing the Prime Minister had done wrong. All members regretted Smith's rebellion; most recognized the importance of maintaining consensus within the House and responsibility in the hands of H.M. Government; and all but a handful opposed military coercion while favouring in some degree British-initiated economic sanctions to bringing about a return to constitutional government in Rhodesia. The principal argument turned, not on whether to impose sanctions but how tough they should be, not on whether to effect change in Rhodesia through sanctions but how dramatic the anticipated change would be.

Tory Leader Edward Heath said he was worried by the notion of 'punitive' sanctions. If sanctions were too tough they would consolidate the European community behind the rebel regime forcing Rhodesia 'further into rebellion' or, worse, precipitating 'a gradual slide into chaos'. One member thought sanctions should be 'reformative', not 'punitive'. The point became almost metaphysical as other members talked about a sanctions programme so delicately modulated as 'to encourage men of good will in Rhodesia to bring Rhodesia back to the privileges of the Commonwealth'. Sanctions were to persuade, not to force.

'I am puzzled,' responded Jo Grimond, Leader of the Liberal Party. 'If these sanctions are not punitive, what are they?' He feared not chaos so much as 'a very long trial of bitterness and disillusion'. Sanctions must be 'short, sharp, effective'. He pressed immediately for sanctions on oil.

Humphry Berkeley, a Conservative member who stood well to the left of Tory leadership (differences on Rhodesia within each party were generally more pronounced than differences between the opposing front benches), maintained flatly that the objective of sanctions was to inspire 'a loss of European confidence in the leadership of Mr. Smith who has put the Europeans in this parlous position'.

Those who advocated what Grimond called 'gentle' sanctions were already veering towards a negotiated settlement with Smith and his Rhodesian Front. Sanctions were to afford just enough pressure to induce a return to the negotiating table. Harold Wilson would have none of it: 'There can be no truck with this illegal regime or any compromise with it.' His object was to unhorse Smith – but not to create chaos in Rhodesia in the process nor to press sanctions to the point of losing consensus with the Opposition front bench. (Ironically he would later introduce stronger sanctions endangering consensus with the Conservatives while at the same time moving to adopt the position implicit in Conservative policy from the start – to negotiate a compromise with the rebels he now excoriated.) All in all, however, there was more that united Government and Opposition views than divided them. Both Wilson and Heath believed it was possible to project British influence into Central Africa, and at long distance through economic manipulation to effect favourable political change. In short, most Members of Parliament believed in the efficacy of economic sanctions – most, but not all.

Those who did not stood outside the consensus either to the right or to the left, anathema to one another but somehow sharing a canny awareness of the factors of power. In the light of what was to transpire, their views are worth noting carefully. Reginald Paget was a Labour maverick whose differences with his Party's policies on Rhodesia would finally prompt him to leave the fold for a period of time. Sanctions, he said plainly, would accomplish nothing except to bring misery to the African population in Rhodesia and to impose added strains on Britain's hard-pressed economy. 'Whether we like it or not,' he warned, 'the point will come when we shall have to deal with Mr. Smith, because there is nobody else there to deal with. . . . These things which we have done', he said referring to British sanctions, 'are going to hang like a dead chicken around our necks and our problem will be how, saving our faces, we can get rid of it.' His Labour colleagues hissed as he sat down.

John Biggs-Davison was active in the pro-Rhodesia lobby of the Monday Club, a gathering place for the right wing of the Conservative Party. During the debate he recalled a phrase from Lord Chatham, who was no friend of the American revolution, spoken in Parliament in 1777. 'You may ravage,' Chatham said of British efforts to suppress the colonists' revolt. 'You cannot conquer.'

Biggs-Davison predicted that British sanctions would not stifle the Rhodesian rebellion either, but would accomplish the incorporation of Rhodesia within the South African system.

On the left judgements about objectives could not have been more distant from those held by the right, but the opposing positions shared a tough-minded scepticism about the effectiveness of economic measures. Michael Foot, member of the left-wing Tribune group and brilliant younger brother of Britain's representative to the U.N., Lord Caradon (Sir Hugh Foot), listened carefully as Harold Wilson quoted Churchill's words about carrying intervention 'to all necessary lengths' or else not intervening at all – spoken almost thirty years before when Italy was the object of sanctions resulting from its invasion of Ethiopia. 'I think that is right,' Foot agreed. 'When I vote for the bill [enabling sanctions to be imposed], that is what I think I shall be voting for – all necessary lengths to insure that the rebellion is put down.' A member interjected, 'Including military force?' 'An Honourable Member opposite interrupts me and asks, "Including military force?" My answer to him would be, yes.' On another occasion Foot made his position still clearer: 'If we are not prepared to face these consequences – the most severe economic sanctions ... with the possibility that later we may have to use military force – we would be better never to have started on the enterprise.'

But for Wilson 'all necessary lengths' stopped short of military force. 'I think what the whole House will feel', Wilson said, 'is that we should not consider sending what would have to be a major military invasion for the purpose of imposing a constitutional solution on Rhodesia.' Obviously the use of force was not part of the consensus. Confidence in economic sanctions was.

The Matter of Force

No decision made by Britain concerning the Rhodesian issue was more pivotal than the decision not to use military force. On the face of it, the choice, as the Afro-Asians at the United Nations pointed out, was almost inexplicable. 'How is it possible not to use force against a people in a state of rebellion?' the delegate from Mali demanded to know. Britain's capability seemed beyond question. Its military budget was 400 times that of Rhodesia's. Only twenty years before, Britain was still governing a quarter of the world's population. In 1965 it deployed 58,000 troops east of Suez, 62,000 in Germany, 23,000 in the Mediterranean area, and 9,000 in other parts of the world. 'From the military point of view,' declared Jeremy Thorpe from the floor of Parliament, 'it would be a fantastic position if this country were incapable of putting down a rebellion of a population the size of that of Portsmouth – for this country with its tremendous imperial past and its present Commonwealth tradition.'

However, when the military chiefs of staff drew up their assessment of the situation, together with contingency plans for various kinds of military initiatives or responses, the Rhodesian case began to take on a different and difficult quality. Rhodesia was distinctive among Britain's colonial problems. It had financed and developed its own security forces and command structure. Thus, as Wilson once put it, 'it would not be a case of arresting a subversive individual. It would mean a bloody war – and probably a bloody war turning into a bloody civil war.' How bloody and how divisive were crucial questions of judgement. The facts were as follows.

The Rhodesian forces included an army of 3,400 men, 1,000 of whom were Africans officered by Europeans. The Army possessed little artillery and no armoured vehicles other than armoured cars. The Rhodesian Air Force consisted of close to 1,000 men and six squadrons of aircraft, including forty to fifty operational Hunter and Vampire fighters and Canberra light bombers, as well as a squadron each of French-produced Alouette helicopters, Dakota transports, and armed Provost reconnaissance aircraft.* The armed forces were supported by the British South Africa Police (B.S.A.P.), whose misleading name derived from the days when Rhodesia was run by Cecil Rhodes's British South Africa Company. The active strength of the police was approximately 6,400, two-thirds of whom were Africans. It included armoured vehicles and a small para-military force.

Beyond the regular units were a conscripted Territorial Force and the Territorial reserves. All Rhodesian residents between the ages of eighteen and twenty-three, except Africans, were liable to four and a half months (later extended to nine months) of full-time military training and weekend service for another three years thereafter. During this period each man was assigned to one of four active battalions of the Territorial Force. Approximately four more battalions could be mobilized from men who had completed their

---

* When the Federation of Rhodesia and Nyasaland was disbanded in 1963, the Air Force reverted to Southern Rhodesian control. With some justification, the African states viewed this as an act of British irresponsibility, if not perfidy, for it placed in Rhodesian hands a significant weapon bound to make much more difficult the subsequent fulfilment of Britain's responsibility to achieve majority rule in its colony. A Security Council resolution calling on Britain not to transfer the Air Force was vetoed by Britain on 13 September 1963.

regular training and were now enrolled as reserves. The B.S.A.P. too had its reserve arm. Taking these several units into account, there were as many as 20,000 Europeans who could be mobilized at any one time, though the effect on the economy of maintaining such a force in being for more than a brief period would of course have been extraordinarily severe.

Loyalty and morale defy precise measurement under most circumstances. This was particularly true in Rhodesia in late 1965. Smith had forced the retirement of Army Chief, Major-General John Anderson, in October 1964. Brigadier Rodney Putterill and Air Vice-Marshal Harold Hawkins had been placed in charge of the Army and the Air Force presumably to assure loyalty to the regime at the top and hopefully throughout the officer cadre. Even so, it was far from certain that, had Britain decided to use force shortly after U.D.I., either man would have swung his full support behind the rebel Government. In those early weeks of the crisis, the force commanders in Salisbury through one means and another maintained contact with London. Both refused to move against Governor Gibbs who, representing the Queen, was their military superior and Rhodesia's Commander-in-Chief.*

Even after a 'purge' of top officers, the question of loyalty within the officer corps remained moot. Substantial numbers of men, in some units up to 25 per cent, had actually been recruited from Britain; many among them would have been reluctant to have made a final break with their homeland. The performance of the African police and police reservists and African army personnel would at best have been unpredictable in the event of a head-on clash with Britain. The rebel Government had already taken the precaution of disarming some of these units. On the other hand, the 2,000 Europeans in the police force together with their leaders were, from the outset, more sympathetic to Smith's Government. The same could be said of the Territorials and reservists who probably reflected more accurately than did the professional forces the prevailing mood of the European population in general. The Territorials and reservists in numbers and determination, though not in quality, were men to be reckoned with. They were the potential Minutemen of the rebel regime.

There was of course no easy way to make a final judgement from

---

* Significantly, Putterill, upon his retirement, joined Rhodesia's opposition Centre Party and declared himself vigorously opposed to the new Rhodesian (1969) constitution and against the regime's determined effort to make Rhodesia a republic. The case of Hawkins on the other hand was more problematic. On retiring he became Salisbury's Diplomatic Representative to South Africa.

these disparate observations as to Rhodesia's will to resist. With the benefit of hindsight it seems reasonable to assume that had a British military response been swift and decisive, filling the vacuum of Rhodesian self-doubt and confusion immediately following U.D.I., resistance would have been minimal and certainly manageable, despite much braggadocio to the contrary. Protracted guerrilla warfare in the rural areas was unlikely for a predominantly urban white community of little more than 200,000 people, three-quarters of whom lived in four cities. It also seems likely that South African intervention could have been avoided had London advised Pretoria that a swift military solution was essential to British interests, and a prelude to direct British rule in Rhodesia leading to a gradual transition over a number of years to responsible government by the African majority. In all events, the key elements were immediacy and swiftness. A delayed or protracted engagement might well have produced the situation described by a British parliamentarian upon his return from South Africa where he had been told that following an invasion of Rhodesia 'there would be only generals left in South Africa because everyone else would be gone over the border in plain clothes'.

The question is raised, then, as to why Britain did not establish itself in Rhodesia by a *coup de main* – a sudden air invasion staged from, say, Nairobi 1,200 miles distant. Not inconceivably it could have been handled by a few companies of paratroopers supplemented by appropriate psychological fanfare involving prestigious representatives of the Queen and perhaps, as one observer suggested, the band of the Grenadier Guards parading in the main streets of Salisbury! Though this possibility might well have existed, the dramatic *scenario* it suggests ignores an essential military reality. No responsible commander would have embarked upon such a risky venture without a substantial reserve force at the ready. It was here – the estimates of troop strengths necessary to assure swift success and to handle all contingencies, as well as the painstaking analysis of myriad logistical difficulties – that the real problems emerged.

To disarm the Rhodesians and control the country thereafter with minimal risk, troop estimates ran from approximately three brigade groups up to two divisions (roughly 15,000 to 25,000 men). Not much more than two battalions were immediately ready from the Strategic Reserve. One unit made to order for this operation was virtually disqualified for reasons that illustrate once again the uniqueness of the Rhodesian problem. The Special Air Service (S.A.S.), a battalion-sized regiment, had all the capabilities for deep penetration. But ironically this unit was psychologically poorly equipped for such a mission. It had a sister unit in Rhodesia, the Rhodesian S.A.S. The two units ran exercises together and frequently exchanged personnel. For a military operation, troops would have to have been brought from other theatres. With Aden, Cyprus and Malaysia active trouble spots, the most likely source would have been the British Army of the Rhine, Britain's chief contribution to NATO's defence forces. Units could have been 'borrowed' as the French had done for their Algerian operations some years before. Raising troops, then, would have been difficult but not impossible.

Problems of logistics were more formidable. Rhodesia enjoyed a highly favourable strategic location, South Africa protecting its rear and Mozambique its eastern flank. Bechuanaland on the west was still in British hands but the area was utterly dependent upon South Africa. Thus the only route by land into Rhodesia was through Zambia. The gorge of the Zambezi and Lake Kariba formed a natural frontier bridged at only three points. For ground fighting the terrain was favourable to defensive action. An invasion would have to depend upon aerial assault. Carrier-based helicopters operating from the Mozambique Channel were in short supply, of limited range, and would have had to cross Mozambique – without doubt evoking the most strenuous Portuguese protests if not actual physical resistance. Aerial envelopment would have to rely on Zambia as an advance staging area.

Kaunda had frequently offered, even urged upon Britain, Zambian facilities for just this purpose. Even so the problems were staggering. Conceivably the R.A.F. Transport Command could have staged troops to Dar es Salaam, though to move one brigade group 5,000 miles would have taken a week to ten days, and to move much larger numbers would have meant commandeering civilian aircraft or soliciting aid from other governments, most likely the United States. From Dar es Salaam to Lusaka, short-haul aircraft like the Argosy could have been used. And from Lusaka airborne operations could then have been launched, though with equipment then available not more than 800 men could have been dropped at any one time.

Air support to cope with Rhodesia's small but efficient Air Force would have been vital, and defence against attacks on Zambia, which was peculiarly vulnerable to sabotage, would have been indispensable. Mounting and maintaining enormously long supply chains anchored at Zambia's small and inadequate airfields would have been costly in men and money. The Rhodesians on the other hand would have enjoyed the considerable advantage of operating from their own bases and enjoying great mobility within their own country, able to concentrate forces at the relatively few targets of recognized strategic importance. In short, the operation would have been extremely difficult – but not impossible.

Nonetheless, the upshot of the staff studies was to leave the military chiefs opposed root and branch to any military solution. There were not only the problems of finding adequate forces and overcoming logistical hurdles, but just as tricky, insisted the chiefs, was the problem of morale, or the 'kith and kin' factor as it was popularly known. Everyone knew of Rhodesia's contribution to the Allies in two World Wars – the regime in Salisbury saw to it that this was not overlooked. Relations between the R.A.F. and the Rhodesian Air Force were particularly close – Mr. Smith, himself an ex-R.A.F. pilot who had suffered extensive facial injuries in a wartime accident, helped to nurture the importance of this liaison. Many Britons had 'cousins' or 'someone they knew' who had gone to Rhodesia in recent years, and the propaganda machine in Salisbury spewed out thousands of postcards to the United Kingdom with reassuring messages about developments below the Zambezi.

Stories were circulated of discreet samplings of opinion among British units as to whether they would be willing to go to Rhodesia to fight; the results purportedly were largely negative. On everyone's lips was the precedent of Curragh where in 1914 certain elements of Britain's Regular Army refused to coerce the citizens of Ulster. Stories circulated concerning resignations at high levels in the Armed Forces if the decision were made to invade Rhodesia. 'It was unthinkable to ask United Kingdom soldiers to go to Rhodesia and shoot Britishers,' reminisced a leading Conservative. 'We were in fact', said a senior civil servant reflecting on these decisions, 'kithier and kinier than anyone realized.'

No one could deny that this was a serious problem. But in military terms it was hardly determinative. The kith and kin factor was a two-edged sword, cutting in Britain's favour in so far as Britons in Rhodesia were concerned, particularly if a British 'police action' had been launched with instructions to fire only if fired upon. Professional units within the British Army surely were available to mount such an expedition against a European population, as was proved by more recent 'police actions' in Ulster itself. Resignations might have been submitted, but probably not including (contrary to some reports at the time) that of Lord Mountbatten, Chief of the Defence Staff and Chairman of the Chiefs of Staff Committee. In fact, certain army commanders were incensed at the stories circulating in the early months after U.D.I. that the armed services could not or, worse, would not undertake a military operation against Rhodesia. If the Government had decided to use military force, the great weight of law, constitution and custom over countless generations would certainly have leaned heavily in the direction of faithful execution by the Armed Forces. To assume the contrary was, on reflection, almost inconceivable. One suspects that the kith and kin factor was inflated to cover a general aversion to a military solution arising from other more compelling reasons.

There was also the parlous state of the economy which was so delicate that when, shortly after the election of October 1964, the new Labour Government declared its intention to increase old age pensions, the announcement alone was enough to cause a run on the pound. A memo prepared for the new administration disclosed an anticipated £800 million ($2,240 million) deficit in overseas payments for 1964, with prospects for the coming year not much brighter.* When Wilson declared 'no force in Rhodesia' he was talking as much to Britain's financial creditors as to any other audience. Related was the fear of becoming mired down indefinitely in Central Africa. Memories of the Boer War died hard. Great Britain had committed nearly 450,000 Britons and took almost 43,000 casualties in that disaster. 'It could be done,' Wilson confided to a friend in the early days after U.D.I. as they discussed the use of force, 'but I don't know how large the war would be.'

Still more uncertain was the aftermath in Rhodesia. Following a British invasion of Rhodesia, how many whites would have fled the country, with what impact on the economy, the security forces and the administration? Would the operation prompt an African uprising and if so what would race relations be like and how long would Britain have to garrison the area? What would the final bill come to, including perhaps restitution to Zambia if that country were seriously damaged by sabotage or by overt Rhodesian reprisals? It was indeed to expect a great deal of a government in the waning days of its imperial rule and crippled by an ailing economy to accept an indeterminate colonial responsibility at a quite unpredictable cost for an area where it had never before exercised direct control.

If anything, the political factor weighed even more heavily than the economic. Wilson won the Election of October 1964 with a slender overall majority in Parliament of only five seats. Before four months had gone by, Labour's lead had been shaved to a paper-thin three

---

* Significantly, the first sentence (and subsequent *leit-motif*) of Wilson's memoir, *The Labour Government 1964–1970: A Personal Record*, reads: 'This book is the record of a Government all but a year of whose life was dominated by an inherited balance of payments problem which was nearing a crisis at the moment we took office. . . .' (We shall be using pounds sterling throughout this book, indicating U.S. dollar equivalents in parentheses. The rate was £1 = $2.80 until Britain's devaluation of 18 November 1967. Thereafter the rate used in the text is £1 = $2.40.)

seats.* At one point, on 7 November 1965, only four days prior to
U.D.I., the margin shrank to one seat. Had Labour lost both by-
elections then pending, it would have lost its absolute majority in
Parliament. Governing under such circumstances was terrifying.
'One spent every night in Parliament,' a Minister later recalled.
'Government feared for its life on every important vote, and practi-
cally every vote was a three-line whip.' It was a situation bound to
hone to a fine edge the instinct for political survival, which in Wilson
was in any case a sharply defined urge. He would do nothing to
jeopardize Labour's chances at the polls when the right time came.

Public opinion samplings among the electorate had consistently
shown a strong aversion to the use of force in Rhodesia, indeed to
any punitive actions. There was in fact a fair measure of sympathy
for the Rhodesian Prime Minister. During Smith's visit to London in
early October 1965, Gallup found only 41 per cent of its sample
approved the British Government's handling of the situation. At the
same time the British public overwhelmingly felt that independence
should be granted only on conditions acceptable to the Rhodesian
people as a whole and recognized that in the event of U.D.I. 'something' would have to be done.

Wilson read the indicators like a book. Responding to the British
Prime Minister's indefatigable efforts up to the eleventh hour to avert
the illegal declaration and his seemingly firm unharried reaction once
U.D.I. was promulgated, the polls in mid November showed an
unbelievable leap from 41 to 68 per cent approving the Government's
performance. (It fluctuated in ensuing weeks but almost invariably
stayed well above the 50 per cent mark until the end of February.)
Wilson played his role with consummate skill. He appeared to stand
firm against both left and right. With fine finesse he used the Queen's
personal role to authenticate the Government's position on the
constitutional issues involved. In television orations, public appearances and on the floor of the Commons he posed as a statesman of
world stature, referring to Rhodesia as 'my Cuba'. He took the
matter to the United Nations, discomfiting his Parliamentary
Opposition but not the electorate which surprisingly, before U.D.I.,
had indicated overwhelming support for such a move. He reacted in
measured terms. And he abjured force. After trailing the Conserva-

---

* Patrick Gordon Walker had been defeated in October but
nonetheless was named Foreign Secretary pending the first by-
election. A seat became available when Labour M.P. Reginald
Sorensen was given a life peerage. In the ensuing by-election on
21 January 1965, Mr. Walker was defeated by the Conservative
candidate, Ronald C. Burton.

tives in the polls the previous August, he watched with evident pleasure as Labour jumped eighteen points ahead of the Opposition shortly after the rebellion.

Equally, Wilson must have appreciated the grave political risks had force been attempted. A *coup de main*, over within forty-eight hours, was one thing. But the build-up of sizeable forces capable of handling every contingency was quite another. It could be done neither quickly nor inconspicuously. The dreadful image of the Suez fiasco less than a decade before must have haunted both Whitehall and Downing Street. Then, the military build-up leading to the invasion of Egypt had triggered an angry outcry in the U.N. while public opinion at home with equal vehemence turned upon Nasser. Now, it would be the inverse – a sort of internalized 'Suez' reaction, and even more dangerous for the Government. While world public opinion would heartily support a military sweep into Rhodesia, British opinion, possibly favouring Smith in such an eventuality almost as much as it had once reviled Nasser, would be overwhelmingly against it. The political risks at home were very real. Before the operation could be got under way, Wilson might have to face a vote of confidence in Parliament. Five, possibly six, Labour members could not have been counted upon to vote with the Government to use force. There might have been a few abstentions from the Opposition benches but exactly how many would have depended upon circumstances impossible to predict. Wilson could have counted on most but not all of the ten Liberal votes. The odds were that Labour would have won, but it would have been a near thing. Should anything subsequently have gone wrong preventing rapid military success, it would have spelled certain political disaster for the Labour Party.

More difficult to understand was Wilson's repeated public declarations long before U.D.I. that force would never be used, 'One of the greatest blunders any government could make', President Kaunda once observed privately, since it unnecessarily removed an element of doubt as Salisbury attempted to calculate Britain's response to U.D.I. When, for example, the military correspondent for the London *Times* published an analysis on 4 August 1965, under the headline, 'Police Action Plan for Rhodesia Considered', Lord Shackleton, Minister of Defence for the Royal Air Force, went out of his way to brand the article inaccurate and in no way based on official sources (which is not true). Denis Healey, the Minister of Defence, condemned the report as 'irresponsible speculation'. In Salisbury, these protestations were carefully noted.

It is of course impossible to know whether official silence on this sensitive subject might have deterred the Rhodesian leaders, or indeed what the impact might have been had Britain deployed a small contingent of troops to Zambia prior to U.D.I., as both Presidents Kaunda and Nyerere had urged. The fact that these deterrents were not introduced arose again from overriding considerations of domestic politics. It was in fact an issue difficult to side-step as the Parliamentary Opposition repeatedly pressed for a clarification of the Government's views on the use of force. Also critically important was the Prime Minister's determination to negotiate a settlement with Salisbury, thus avoiding U.D.I. London seemed to fear (though exactly why is not clear) that prospects for a settlement would be diminished if it were thought that Whitehall was considering recourse to force or the actual deployment of troops to Zambia.

The announced policy not to use force and London's unwillingness to deploy a deterrent force to Zambia were of course secondary decisions, derivatives of the central policy not to invade Rhodesia. All of the considerations set forth above – the scarcity of troops, the logistical difficulties, the kith and kin factor, the economic crisis, the unpredictable character of an involvement in Central Africa, and the political hazards of a threadbare majority in Parliament – had weighted the scales decisively against invasion. With the military chiefs and the Ministry of Defence ranged strongly against it on military grounds, it is unlikely that the military option ever came to a full-scale debate or was put to a formal vote in Cabinet. There were moreover few, if any, 'hawks' within the Cabinet ready to press the case for force.*

Each of the arguments was impressive; in combination they were the more so. None however was necessarily determinative; nor were all taken together. Force could have been used. The fact that it was not suggests that the issues at stake – reversing U.D.I. and assuring ultimate majority rule in Rhodesia with all that that entailed for the evolution of affairs in Southern Africa and Britain's position in Black Africa, the Commonwealth and the United Nations – were not worth the economic cost and political risk involved in applying force. There was here a question of priorities, and beyond that a question of values and leadership. But of course it was never quite that clear-

---

* Barbara Castle was probably an exception. In late 1966 three junior Ministers (Judith Hart, Lord Walston and Maurice Foley) tried to get the question looked at again, but there was no sign that senior Ministers were interested. While the possibility of a military solution to the rebellion was probably never seriously contemplated, military planning for lesser contingencies was undertaken. Wilson himself repeatedly made clear that Britain would respond to a request from the Governor for troops 'to restore law and order' within Rhodesia. (For contingencies relating to Zambia, see Chapter IV.)

cut. For Wilson and his associates seemed certain, possibly because the military route was indeed so hazardous, that there must be an alternative, a reasonable prospect that the rebellion could be ended and Rhodesia set irreversibly on the road to African rule without recourse to military action. There was here a question of the adequacy of information and analysis, and beyond that a question of political judgement and wisdom. In any event, Wilson was not a man to take a tough decision today if by postponing it there were some chance it might not be there tomorrow. Once again, his instrument would be economic sanctions.

The Sanctions Arsenal

At two hours past midnight on 16 November 1965, the Clerk of the Parliaments intoned the Norman French phrase signifying the passage of a bill: 'La Reyne le veult.' The Southern Rhodesia Bill was enacted. It would enable the Government to make any Order in Council regarding Rhodesia (subject to Parliamentary approval within thirty days) thought to be necessary in consequence of the illegal seizure of independence.

A stack of Orders had already been drawn up in anticipation of the Act. These and numerous subsequent ones covered an amazing and often esoteric subject matter. The legal centrepiece in Britain's response to U.D.I. was an Order amending the provisions of the 1961 Southern Rhodesian consitution while voiding the new constitution which the rebel regime had promulgated on 11 November 1965, as the legal instrument for severing its remaining ties to London. The British Order invalidated laws passed by the Rhodesian Parliament and enabled the United Kingdom Government to legislate for Rhodesia; it freed the Rhodesian Governor from his obligation to act only in accordance with the advice of Rhodesia's Ministers; and it gave to the Secretary of State for Commonwealth Relations the power to exercise executive authority in Rhodesia. In a word it technically reduced Rhodesia to Crown Colony status, governed now from Whitehall and Westminster.

There was a curious through-the-looking-glass quality about all this. Obviously one was dealing more with form than substance. Britain might propose in London but had no capacity to dispose in Rhodesia. The Zambian Ambassador at the United Nations two days after U.D.I. drew a cruel literary parallel between Britain's assertion of nominal authority and the deranged King Lear, 'who, after giving away his kingdom, imagines in his insanity that he is still the sovereign ruler'. A mirror was held up to the embarrassing truth by Miss Judith Todd, a very young and courageous critic of the rebellion, who announced her intention to return to her home in Rhodesia and to join her father, Garfield Todd, a former Rhodesian Prime Minister of liberal persuasion now under house arrest. She wrote a letter asking H.M. Government to afford her protection as a British subject returning to a British domain, and equally to extend protection to her fellow citizens 'who are demonstrating their opposition to the regime of Mr. Smith at a great personal cost'. Michael Foot read the letter to a sobered House of Commons on 24 November, reminding the members that she too was 'kith and kin'.

The question of loyalty was vexing and anomalous like everything else. On the one hand, Wilson said it was the duty of everyone owing allegiance to the Crown to refrain from all acts which would assist the illegal regime to continue in rebellion against the Crown. On the other hand, he made clear that public servants in Rhodesia must carry on with their jobs presumably to avoid any breakdown in public order. It was difficult to know what other advice could have been given in a situation where one claimed responsibility but had no commensurate power to punish the disloyal or to protect the loyal or indeed to prevent disorder from sliding into chaos. The anomalies were easily exploited. 'We talk about treason,' said the puckish Mr Paget in the Commons the day after U.D.I. 'It is an odd sort of treason when one of the traitors, the [Rhodesian] High Commissioner, is not arrested but sent back to join his fellow conspirators in rebellion.' Paget asked whether those who assisted the High Commissioner's 'escape' would be prosecuted. He might also have called attention to the fact that, while each side withdrew its High Commissioner, each retained an office staffed by its own nationals in the other's capital.

The fantasy created when Britain asserted the right of formal governance while unable (or unwilling) to execute the responsibilities of true governance was epitomized in a Parliamentary exchange on 14 December concerning the powers and responsibilities of the new Board of the Reserve Bank of Rhodesia. London had 'dismissed' the members of the old Board and named as their replacements six Britons under the chairmanship of Sir Sydney Caine, the Director of the London School of Economics. The point was to gain a legal hold on Rhodesian Bank assets located in countries willing to recognize the mandate of the reconstituted Board. At issue however was whether this new British-controlled entity would assume responsibility not only for the assets but for discharging the Bank's liabilities, particularly the payment of interest on Rhodesian loan stock. Obviously, the fulfilment of Rhodesia's financial obligations would not have served the purpose of Britain's sanctions programme, but in public debate the matter could not be stated so directly and the result was sheer mystification. The protagonist, Mr. John Diamond, was Chief Secretary to the Treasury.

Mr. Diamond: 'The Secretary of State [for Commonwealth Relations] has power to give the Board directions. But that does not make the Bank the Secretary of State's agent so as to attract to him the liabilities of the Bank. Nothing like it.'

Mr. Thorpe: 'Are we to assume that the Secretary of State is to give directions that these liabilities are not to be shouldered by the Bank . . . ?'

Mr. Diamond: 'The Secretary of State cannot give directions to a bank that it should not shoulder responsibilities which it has. If a bank has responsibilities, it has responsibilities.'

Mr. Paget: 'Is it not the position that the liabilities for Rhodesian debts are the responsibility of either the bank or the Rhodesian Government? If we take over the bank and are the Rhodesian Government it does not seem to matter much.'

Mr. Diamond: 'I can only repeat . . . that the appointment of directors is not and bears no resemblance to taking over liabilities.'

Mr. Paget: 'We are the Government of Rhodesia. As a result of these orders we have in our hands the reserves of the Government of Rhodesia. Are we proposing to pay the debts of the Government of Rhodesia?'

Mr. Diamond: 'It is absolutely inaccurate . . . that we, the British Government, own the assets or funds of the Reserve Bank of Rhodesia. The assets and funds of the Reserve Bank of Rhodesia belong today exactly where they belonged before the order was introduced. It has not affected that position one iota. . . .'

Mr. Paget: 'I desire, Mr. Deputy-Speaker, to ask the Chief Secretary who is the customer of the Reserve Bank of Rhodesia? Is that customer the Governor of Rhodesia? Are we the government of Rhodesia?' [He never got an answer.]

In all this apparent madness there was nonetheless a certain method. To discern it, several assumptions underlying British policy have to be understood. It was Rhodesia's close ties with Britain that in part made the problem so difficult to handle by direct intervention. Wilson would now use these same sentiments to call into question the wisdom of Smith's action. Through a range of psychological ploys and material pressures, he would discredit Smith and bring into power a more tractable government in Salisbury. He spoke of 'very many people in Rhodesia' who wanted a return to legality, of people who were 'only too anxious to make themselves known at the right moment and identify themselves with constitutional rule'. The purpose of the new legislation and its accompanying orders and executive actions was to facilitate this transition by arousing and giving focus to the feelings of unease which many Rhodesians must have felt following their government's illegal action. For example, the majority of Rhodesians genuinely wished to maintain their links with the Crown. Accordingly, the Southern Rhodesia Act would dramatize the fact that by her own Order Rhodesia remained a part of Her Majesty's dominions and that the Government and Parliament of the United Kingdom had responsibility and jurisdiction in respect of it.

Governor Gibbs, in Wilson's strategy, would play an important part in this psychological offensive. No move was missed to add stature to his position as 'Her Majesty's representative to the people of Rhodesia', as he pointedly referred to himself. The Queen conferred upon him the singular honour of Knight Commander of the Royal Victorian Order, while the leaders of all three parties in a virtually unprecedented move tabled a motion in the Commons expressing admiration for Sir Humphrey's courage and loyalty. Since censorship in Rhodesia concealed these and other actions from the population, Wilson arranged for special B.B.C. broadcasts to beam the news into the rebel colony pending the opening of a special transmitter for this purpose which was rushed to completion at Francistown, just over the border from Rhodesia in British-controlled Bechuanaland.

London would also exploit internal cleavages in Rhodesia and seek opportunities to challenge the authority of the illegal regime on its home ground. The first of many such efforts came shortly after the seizure of independence with an Order in Council revoking censorship in Rhodesia. On the face of it, it was just another act of whimsy since Britain had absolutely no power of enforcement. But some of Rhodesia's editors had shown spirit in resisting censorship. The British Order gave them a legal basis for carrying the issue to Rhodesia's courts which in turn might precipitate a confrontation between the judiciary (which was notably cool to U.D.I.) and the regime – and again provide a focus for the latent sense of uneasiness which Wilson hoped would quickly spread throughout the European community.*

---

* In this particular instance the court dismissed the case arguing that it lacked the necessary jurisdiction. Britain continued to try, though with singular lack of success, to excite a crisis which would prompt the courts to find the regime illegal (see particularly Chapter IX).

Apart from this presumed battle for men's minds and loyalties, real deprivations would also be an essential part of the external pressure which would lead to internal change in Rhodesia. The single most important purpose of the many British enactments was to create a legal base from which H.M. Government could prosecute sanctions. As it turned out, these were introduced gradually, not becoming complete as far as Britain was concerned until the end of January – a sort of sanctions programme on the instalment plan. Most of the measures announced on 11 November 1965 were of marginal value. But many believed that the financial measures – exchange control and denial of British capital – would hurt; and that the boycott of tobacco and sugar would raise serious problems. Together these two commodities represented nearly three-quarters of Rhodesia's exports to the United Kingdom, or £22 million ($61.5 million) out of £31 million ($87 million) in 1964.

Tobacco would be crucial, Wilson thought, and sanctions against it might alone tip the scales against Smith. It constituted by value almost 30 per cent of Rhodesia's exports. Britain took more than 40 per cent of the crop and would prevail upon other purchasers to co-operate in the boycott. Tobacco moreover was a politically potent target, for tobacco farmers were a pillar of the party and had contributed heavily to the Rhodesian Front's campaign chest. But more than that, tobacco was assumed to be the pillar of the economy. 'The whole financial and banking structure of Rhodesia', Wilson told Parliament confidently, 'revolves around tobacco financing in such a way that this decision will have a pretty serious and pretty speedy effect.'

Serious perhaps, but surely not speedy. It is hard to know why Wilson should have thought otherwise. At the time of U.D.I. the new crop was already financed and would not be ready to market until the end of March. Smith had chosen carefully the time for his act of rebellion. Rhodesian exports were annually at low ebb in the period beginning in mid November, leaving time to make new trading arrangements before the flow began again four months later.

The second instalment of Wilson's sanctions plan was announced on 1 December, the embargoed items now accounting for more than 95 per cent of Rhodesia's exports to the United Kingdom.* Wilson told Parliament that Britain was in 'close touch' with other countries which provided significant markets for Rhodesian goods in an

---

* The new list included in addition to tobacco and sugar, asbestos, copper and copper products, iron and steel, concentrates of antimony, chromium, lithium and tantalum, corn, meat and a range of other foodstuffs.

effort 'to deny Rhodesia, as far as possible, the export outlets on which the finances of the illegal regime depend'. A few days later a Government Minister confidently announced that as a result of British approaches to other trading nations the tobacco ban alone would be 90 per cent effective. This was to be the mainspring of the sanctions strategy – to squeeze Rhodesia's earnings from exports and thus to create a foreign exchange crisis, making it impossible for the regime to buy the imports necessary for economic viability, or at least for maintaining the comforts to which the affluent white population had become accustomed.

In addition further measures were introduced to put a stop to virtually all current payments from the United Kingdom to Rhodesian residents, reinforcing the earlier embargo on capital transfers and making it illegal for British firms or banks to transfer funds to subsidiaries or branches in Rhodesia. Restrictions on travel to Rhodesia were stiffened. Finally there was the move to gain control of Rhodesian assets held abroad by reconstituting the Board of the Rhodesian Reserve Bank. But the provident Rhodesians by this time, of course, had moved many of their holdings to invulnerable Swiss accounts.

The third instalment was announced by the British Government on 17 December when an Order in Council was put forward prohibiting the import of petroleum products into Rhodesia. The Conservative Party found itself in disarray when it came to vote on the Order. The leadership decided to abstain. Fifty Opposition members, the 'Rhodesia Lobby' as Government members now called them, bolted and voted against the Order. In reaction, thirty-one members of the Conservative Party known for their strong views against Smith and U.D.I. voted with the Government. Wilson noted that Heath had had a difficult passage, adding: 'We have only had to handle the problem – he has had to handle his party.' These three tendencies within the Conservative Party have persisted more or less intact throughout the Rhodesian affair.

At the end of January a final flurry of enactments virtually completed the process of cutting off all Rhodesia's imports from and exports to Britain. To make it more difficult for Salisbury to raise credit at home or abroad, London announced that it reserved the right following the conclusion of the rebellion to repudiate any debts incurred by the Smith regime. Orders in Council were also introduced making it illegal under both Rhodesian and British law to sell such Rhodesian products as chrome, tobacco or sugar – at first sight another whimsical move, but in fact designed (under the doctrine of *force majeure*) to release foreign importers from contractual obligations to Rhodesian exporters, and thus hopefully to make it possible for them to comply with the requests of their home governments to cease trade with the rebel territory.

These then were the instruments of persuasion and pressure to work upon the 'loyalist' sentiment of the Rhodesians, to discredit Smith and the Front, and to raise very real threats to an economy inordinately dependent upon international trade and foreign investment. (Rhodesian exports constituted nearly 40 per cent of the Gross National Product.) Sanctions presumably would also shrink Smith's support by driving off substantial numbers of whites. A sizeable proportion of Rhodesian whites were working class, able to live in Rhodesia on middle-class standards. This was the reason they had emigrated to Rhodesia in the first place, largely since the Second World War. (In 1961, for example, only 15 per cent of Rhodesia's whites were native-born.) Threaten their affluence, reasoned the planners in London, and they would emigrate again, probably to South Africa where there were jobs in abundance. This would squeeze out large numbers of those who had provided fervent support for the Front.

At the proper point in this unravelling process, the Governor would be able to call forward new political leadership from among the many known loyalists in Rhodesia. There would follow a brief period of 'direct rule' under the Governor who would be advised by Rhodesians of all races and who with Britain would then prepare the way for a rapid return to full constitutional rule. At the same time the Governor would appeal to the armed forces to rally to himself and to the Queen. He would talk with General Putterill, the Governor said, when the time came. Possibly British forces in small numbers might then, at the invitation of the Governor, move to Salisbury to stiffen his hand and to help Rhodesian security forces maintain order during the transitional period to follow. This of course was very different from direct intervention by force. Indeed even to talk about 'force' would compromise the *scenario*. The Governor himself was resolutely against it, and almost certainly would have resigned had he thought Britain intended military intervention. London believed this attitude was shared by many Rhodesians potentially loyal to Britain who would be deeply alienated if they thought force were in prospect.

Wilson may have had private doubts about all this but if so they were well concealed. His public confidence was amply supported at every turn by the most prestigious British publications. On 2 December, *The Times* noted that the new financial measures could be expected to bite quickly and should show the Rhodesians the real nature of the road their government had chosen. On 8 January *The Economist* reported ecstatically that 'everything now points to the ultimate defeat of the Rhodesian rebellion'. A few days later, on

13 January, an article in *The Times* surveyed the security requirements of the post-U.D.I. period, never questioning the capacity of British policy to end the rebellion and establish a period of direct rule.

There were of course many who did raise questions. Liberal Party Leader Jo Grimond accused Wilson of a failure to plan ahead and said that no Prime Minister had ever required 'so many cuffs for playing off' as had Harold Wilson. Others wondered about piecemeal and graduated sanctions. Why had the boom not been lowered at once? Confronted with this question on one occasion the Attorney General replied candidly, 'It was hoped that the earlier sanctions would have had the necessary effect. That has proved not to be the case and so the enforcement of further sanctions has been necessary.' There were other reasons. Much of the staff work had indeed been faulty.* Even so, volumes of contingency papers had been written by officials prior to U.D.I. outlining a wide variety of sanctions that Britain might apply, but government is a ponderous thing and Ministers tend to defer difficult decisions until there seems to be no other choice. One suspects too that Wilson may have been searching for the proper level of punitive measures: too little and the threat is unreal; too much and the result is alienation of those you seek to win over, with the added risks of economic chaos or South African intervention.

Finally, Wilson wanted to maintain consensus with the Tory Opposition in Parliament as long as possible and enhance his political appeal in anticipation of a new election – while at the same time not allowing adverse reactions to get out of hand in the United Nations, in the Commonwealth and in Africa. All of these considerations generally jibed with his inclination to escalate sanctions experimentally and by stages.

It was all rather neat and pat, this confident manipulation of political forces at a distance of 6,000 miles. Conservatives objected with increasing heat to many of Wilson's formulations, but they too were certain that Rhodesia could be returned to constitutional government and ultimate majority rule by a combination of external pressures and persuasions. A former Rhodesian Prime Minister scrutinized the central assumption underlying policy and put down

---

* One critic claimed that the professional economists within the Government were largely ignored. In *Crisis in the Civil Service* (edited by Hugh Thomas), Dr. Dudley Seers notes that 'the staff work was almost unbelievably bad. At no time was there any serious effort to search for the weak points of the regime. . . .' Seers, until recently the Director of the Institute of Development Studies at Sussex University, was at the time of U.D.I. head of the economic planning staff at the Ministry of Overseas Development.

his conclusions in an article for the *Spectator* of 28 January 1966. Sir Edgar Whitehead was no apologist for the Rhodesian Front which had defeated him at the polls in December 1962, in part because Whitehead had told the Rhodesian electorate to expect African rule within fifteen years. Now in retirement in the United Kingdom, he warned flatly that 'the basic error in British official thinking is that they believe political and racial attitudes can be altered by economic pressure'. Sanctions were no more likely to produce political change in Rhodesia than in Cuba. The two major political parties, in their bipartisan imposition of sanctions, 'have forgotten what they would have done to anybody in 1940 who had suggested that they must give in to Hitler because otherwise they would be subject to sanctions and short of petrol'.

Problems at the U.N.

At the United Nations the Rhodesian issue became a *cause célèbre* overnight. Most of the Afro-Asians who commanded the debates (though not the votes) in the Security Council insisted not only that economic sanctions would not work, but that military force would have to be used. Knowing this, Wilson's decision to take the matter immediately to the United Nations was curious. Britain's consistent position since 1962, when the issue was first raised at the U.N., was that constitutionally Rhodesia was a fully self-governing territory. The U.N. had no jurisdiction, and Britain had neither the responsibility nor the capacity to respond to those provisions of the Charter requiring administering powers to transmit regular reports on non-self-governing territories under their aegis. Britain had even refused to participate in votes on resolutions concerning Rhodesia. Lady Tweedsmuir twitted the Prime Minister on the incongruity of now rushing to the U.N. The position had been changed, he answered, by the illegal declaration of independence. The Rhodesians had torn up their constitution and 'altered the whole situation'.

Perhaps more to the point, Wilson knew that if he did not go straight to the United Nations others would, with considerably less respect for Britain's interests. He spoke in Parliament of 'the tremendous passions' that had been aroused in Africa and Asia and the need to take the lead in demonstrating that 'we ourselves mean business and are carrying out effective measures'. In the absence of such initiatives, warned the Prime Minister overdramatically, Britain might finally face in Rhodesia 'a Red Army in blue berets'. Wilson was also anxious to gain U.N. support for his limited and voluntary sanctions programme. This too was odd. Britain had been arguing for years that sanctions, long advocated by the Third World against South Africa and Portugal, would be unavailing. But overnight times had changed. So Michael Stewart, Britain's Foreign Secretary, was sent to New York where he stepped into a maelstrom of invective.

The fury of the Afro-Asians was of course responsive to the arc lights focused on all U.N. debates. But their reaction went deeper than that. It was prompted by an awareness of the strategic importance of Rhodesia. Abutting South Africa's northern flank and lodged between Angola and Mozambique, Rhodesia was viewed by many as the keystone of a developing redoubt of white-controlled states. This awareness inspired apprehension. Rhodesia's flagrant, almost flippant, seizure of independence dramatized the racism and domination of Caucasian peoples which had been a part of the experience of most Afro-Asian states, and even worse, it highlighted the impotence of the non-white world before an unconscionable act of usurpation by a tiny white enclave in a black country. This condition inspired anger. Rhodesia finally was a self-professed British problem for the solution of which Britain claimed to have only limited capabilities. This admission inspired the deepest scepticism and ridicule.

One African delegate after another suggested that a conspiracy was afoot to create a consortium of racist states in the very heart of Africa. But a greater danger (more felt, perhaps, than reasoned) was that these racist states would soon threaten the rest of the continent. The weakness and uncertainty of Africa's new states and the recency of their emergence from European rule understandably gave rise to the gravest anxieties. So it was not surprising that U.D.I. and the growing consolidation of racist forces should have been seen as 'a matter of life and death for the African continent' or as the 'new colonialism of white supremacy' extending 'into the heart of Africa'.

From the Afro-Asian point of view there was no question but that the situation created by U.D.I. clearly constituted a 'threat to the peace' of the kind that permitted the Security Council under the Charter to take the most far-reaching measures. The Council was warned of the storm 'that is now gathering over all of us', the prospect of imminent race war. Others predicted that racial war would be ignited by the efforts of African populations within and around the racist redoubt to undo this rebellion which violated everything the U.N. Charter stood for. Only a little over a year before, whites had rescued whites from blacks in the besieged town of Stanleyville in the Congo. That incident, Ambassador Arsene Usher of the Ivory Coast told the Council on 13 November, had current relevance:

'Gentlemen and members of the Council, you have admitted

that the Americans, the Belgians, the British were entitled to go to free their white brothers taken as hostages by other rebels in Stanleyville. Do you believe in your soul and conscience that the Africans have not the right to free their brothers taken as hostages by white rebels under a regime condemned by you and considered by world public opinion as illegal, in a country described as being without law or legal order by the Administering Authority, which admits that it is incapable of administering because it has no physical presence in that country? . . . All the conditions for a racial war to break out in the centre of Africa have been created.'

When Michael Stewart for Britain responded that Britain was prepared to broaden its economic sanctions, but would not use force to impose a constitution, the Afro-Asians argued in turn that it was not to impose a constitution that force must be used, but to defeat a rebellion. Britain had used force innumerable times in other colonial situations which had invariably involved suppressing non-Europeans – in India, Malaya, Borneo, the Gold Coast, Nigeria, Nyasaland, Kenya, British Guiana, British Honduras and Aden. But now faced with a rebellion among settlers of British stock in Rhodesia the United Kingdom abjured force, valuing, it seemed, 'white blood more than black blood'.

There is a special optic through which the Afro-Asian states view the U.N. They see it as an instrument to strike down colonialism and racial domination, and to elevate formerly oppressed peoples. They see it as a means for rectifying the historical injustice arising from a colonial system imposed from Europe by Caucasians. In identifying the purposes of the organization, the Charter speaks of 'respect for the principles of equal rights and self-determination of peoples' and of 'promoting and encouraging respect for human rights'. And in defining the responsibilities of members having authority for non-self-governing territories, the Charter requires recognition that 'the interests of the inhabitants of these territories are paramount'.

These were 'the basic principles of our Charter' to which the Afro-Asian delegates now referred and which the Rhodesian rebellion, they claimed, had defiled. Left uncorrected, the rebellion would of course become a threat to international peace, for who could doubt that men would assert their rights now enshrined in the Charter? The machinery of the United Nations was designed to secure the peace, but surely to do so consistent with the principles of human rights and self-determination inscribed in its purposes and principles. According to this view, the cause of the threat to peace in the Rhodesian case was the unjust imposition of minority rule and the

justifiable grievances of the racial majority. If the situation were
likely to disturb the peace of the region, it was the cause that must be
attacked and not the manifestation of discontent that must be stifled.
The Charter under such an interpretation became a prescription, not
for maintaining the status quo but for change, and if need be revolutionary change. It is only from within this frame of reference that one
can understand the assertion of the Pakistani delegate that 'Southern
Rhodesia is one of the eventualities for which Chapter VII of the
Charter was drafted.'

Chapter VII contained the most august provisions and powerful
measures in the Charter. It permitted the Council to treat with
threats to the peace, breaches of the peace or outright acts of aggression by applying measures ranging from non-military sanctions to
the actual use of military force. Even more important, under Chapter
VII the Security Council had the right to make its decisions binding
on the membership of the whole organization. Britain on the other
hand was advocating a limited and voluntary programme of economic
sanctions not under Chapter VII at all. The Ethiopian delegate
responded poignantly: 'I need no further proof', he said, 'that
diplomatic and economic sanctions are doomed to failure, since I
represent the state which was the first victim of collective security by
a similar Council only three decades ago.' At issue was not only a
lesson of history but of geography. The Afro-Asian spokesmen found
it unimaginable that Rhodesia's neighbours to the east and south,
Portuguese Mozambique and South Africa, would permit sanctions
to succeed. Virtually all the Afro-Asian states heard at the Council
table urged the use of military force, or at least contended that it
must not be ruled out. Most urged Britain itself to apply force.

All these concerns found expression in a tough draft resolution
introduced by Africa's spokesman on the Council, the articulate
Ambassador from the Ivory Coast, Arsene Usher. Invoking the
language of Chapter VII, the resolution determined that the Rhodesian crisis constituted a threat to international peace and security and
called for total sanctions and military force. There was of course no
chance that this resolution could gain the required number of votes,
nor that among the permanent members of the Security Council
Britain (and almost certainly the United States) could have been
prevailed upon to do other than vote against it, causing it to fail
automatically since the negative vote of any permanent member
constituted a veto. On the other hand, a draft resolution introduced by
Britain was too bland to command the support necessary for adoption
and it began to look as though no resolution would be passed.

While wishing to avoid any Security Council action which would
force its hand or take matters out of its control, Britain also wanted

to avoid a display of U.N. ineffectiveness which would only have served to give comfort to Rhodesia. On the issue of force Britain was prepared to give no ground. But it was willing to accept a call to U.N. members 'to do their utmost in order to break all economic relations with Southern Rhodesia, including an embargo on oil and petroleum products'. The language was cast in terms of a recommendation presumably under Chapter VI of the Charter. But while Britain could not accept that the Rhodesian issue now constituted a threat to the peace, it did agree to a rather odd formulation – that 'its continuance in time constitutes a threat to international peace and security'.*

Malaysia complained that this language, the result of five weary days of debate, was bad English, bad grammar, and bad idiom. The Bolivian representative was then serving as President of the Council. Speaking as a member of the Spanish Academy, he apologized for the awkward phrase but speaking as President of the Council he was, he said, glad of it – quite happy to have an effective compromise clothed in inelegant language. On 20 November 1965, the resolution was passed by ten votes to zero with only France abstaining, declaring that the Rhodesian issue was solely within Britain's domestic jurisdiction and therefore beyond U.N. competence.

For Wilson the outcome was reasonably satisfactory. It strained his consensus with the Conservatives, but not to breaking point. Britain remained in control of the action while gaining U.N. support for voluntary economic sanctions. But clearly indicated were all the pressures from the Third World that would come to preoccupy Wilson in the near future. As it happened, the day before the resolution was passed Princess Margaret and Lord Snowdon were feted at the U.N. by the Secretary-General. All the invited African delegations boycotted the event in protest against British policy in Rhodesia.

The Rebel Response

Once independence had been announced, the champagne sipped and the telegrams read, Ian Douglas Smith turned his attention to

---

* In a subsequent Parliamentary debate on 23 November 1965, Wilson argued that the wording was a compromise and that the resolution might 'be interpreted as something between Chapter VI and Chapter VII'. In fact no one presumed that the economic sanctions called for in the resolution were mandatory. By recognizing, however, that there was a prospective 'threat to the peace', Britain had nudged ajar the door to Chapter VII – which would be thrown wide open later on.

consolidating his position at home and defending it from harassment abroad. An immediate problem was Governor Gibbs, who was the very embodiment of the danger of divided loyalties. Smith and his associates pressed the Governor to resign. But Gibbs had a keen sense of duty and would not budge. A tall, greying man of quiet dignity, educated at Eton and Oxford, he had the respect and affection of many Rhodesians. Thousands now lined up to 'sign the Governor's book' (a rather archaic courtesy in British colonies) as an indication of their loyalty. On 15 November, the Rhodesian Cabinet sat late considering the problem. There was speculation that Gibbs might be removed physically from Government House despite a stern warning issued the previous day from 10 Downing Street that anyone forcibly expelling Gibbs or otherwise assaulting him, or anyone usurping or seeking to usurp his authority, would commit an act of treason.

Smith now issued a statement betraying a measure of anxiety. He warned Rhodesians that they would be subjected to pressures and flattery designed to sow doubts and undermine their loyalty. He was particularly concerned about the security forces. 'I remind everyone in the Services that first and foremost he is the servant of Rhodesia – his country – and its Government. This you must put foremost in your mind whenever you see suggestions and insinuations that there is some other authority either within or outside the country which claims your allegiance.' As to Gibbs, the Cabinet settled on an enveloping tactic rather than direct confrontation. His official Rolls Royce was removed as well as the ceremonial Askari Guard. His Government-paid staff was dismissed obliging the Governor to place the management of Government House in the hands of his personal staff aided by voluntary assistants, the whole enterprise financed by private funds. Even the Governor's telephones were cut off. For some seven months personnel at Government House used a neighbour's phone or a call box down the street. Typewriters and office furniture disappeared and the regime finally tried to charge Gibbs $700 a month for rent – at which he firmly balked. Writing to the editor of the *Rhodesian Herald*, an official of the Ministry of Information confirmed 'that censor officers have received instructions to delete any reference to Sir Humphrey Gibbs'. He was to be a non-person.

Meanwhile on 17 November, Clifford Walter Dupont resigned his post as Minister of External Affairs to receive the cumbersome title of Officer Administering the Government. He was sworn in by a justice of the peace as no judge of Rhodesia's High Court was willing to administer the oath. Somewhat later Smith wrote a personal letter to the Queen, who was still acknowledged under the new (1965) constitution to be Rhodesia's sovereign, submitting Dupont's name for appointment as Governor-General and 'praying your Majesty may be pleased to appoint him to that office'. Not surprisingly the Queen directed that no action was to be taken and that Gibbs himself be asked to pass this word back to the rebel regime.

Dupont, a tiny, frail, bird-like man, whom the British came to refer to as the 'mini-Governor', had settled in Rhodesia only seventeen years before, one of those latter-day Rhodesian converts whose passion for his adopted country seemed related inversely to the length of his residence. He was a leading right-wing figure in both party and government circles, and had long been an advocate of U.D.I. A gambler by nature, he had dismissed the careful reports prepared by the civil service predicting severe damage from sanctions, and had played a role of no little importance in evicting the cautious Winston Field from the Prime Minister's chair. Government House being otherwise occupied, Dupont was now assigned an official residence three miles out of Salisbury. He would have to wait more than three and a half years to gain access to the home reserved for Rhodesia's first citizen. During that long span Gibbs tried, as he put it in an early press conference, to 'provide the link which will make a satisfactory settlement of the present situation possible'.*

There was no more articulate spokesman against the rebellion in all Rhodesia than Dr. Ahrn Palley. A balding Irishman with penetrating, intelligent eyes, Palley was trained as both a doctor and a lawyer, and sat in the Rhodesian Parliament as an independent member for the African township of Highfields in Salisbury. Parliament convened for the first time after U.D.I. on 25 November to hear a report from the Minister of Law and Order, Desmond Lardner-Burke, pursuant to the declaration of the State of Emergency which Gibbs had approved in those bizarre events of 3 and 5 November. After prayers and a brief point of order put by an African member, Dr. Palley rose and called upon the Speaker to suspend the sitting of the House. 'Since the House last met,' he went on, 'certain Honourable Members have, in collusion, torn up the valid Constitution under which this House meets and they have seen fit to produce a document which they have purported to issue as a new constitution for this country. Those people who accept that document . . . I submit to

---

* Gibbs, representing the Queen, was the only symbol of legality the British managed to contrive, apart from the judiciary which ultimately succumbed to the regime. Years later, a senior Cabinet Minister in the Rhodesian regime speculated privately on what might have happened had the Queen immediately after U.D.I. named from within Rhodesia a new Prime Minister and Cabinet. Conceivably, he said, it would have led to a genuine 'civil war'. As it was, the person of Gibbs provoked a degree of divided loyalty but the problem proved entirely manageable for the regime.

you, are acting illegally and on their own conscience must face in due course what the law demands.' A member interjected: 'The law is an ass.'

The Speaker then made clear that the new Rhodesian constitution of 1965 was binding on proceedings of Parliament and that members presuming otherwise ought to withdraw. Palley protested, 'I will not obey any order which to me is illegal.' There were cries of 'order' and 'sit down'. Palley refused. The Speaker cited his disorderly conduct and ordered him to withdraw. Palley persisted in his objections. The Minister of the Interior rose to move Palley's suspension which was quickly approved. A half step ahead of the Sergeant at Arms, Palley retreated. His voice was barely audible over the din: 'I accept no ruling from this House . . . (Interruptions) . . . I leave this House . . . (Interruptions) . . . Long live the Queen!' Nine African parliamentarians followed him out. Four Africans and one Asian remained in their seats, to be congratulated by members on the Government front bench. It had been a splendidly defiant – and altogether fruitless – gesture.

Potentially the strongest bastion of European resistance was the Church. Leaders of the Anglican communion, the Roman Catholic Church and the Christian Council of Rhodesia, which gathered together a number of denominations, were at one in their repudiation of Smith's rebel Government. The Christian Council urged all Christians to support the Governor, regretted the blow which had been delivered to constitutional law and advised those opposed to U.D.I. to speak out as a matter of principle. None of this was permitted to appear in the censored news media. In Salisbury's Cathedral on the Sunday after U.D.I., the Anglican Bishop of Mashonaland said Christians need not be morally obliged to obey laws which issued from an illegal government. When printed by the *Rhodesia Herald*, the report of his sermon was so censored that it was almost unintelligible. The Roman Catholic Bishops of Rhodesia issued a hard-hitting pastoral instruction:

'Vast numbers of the people of Rhodesia are bitterly opposed to the Unilateral Declaration of Independence. . . . They are particularly angered that it should be stated publicly that this action was taken in the name of preserving Christian civilization in this country. It is simply quite untrue to say that the masses are content with this recent decision or that they have consented by their silence. Their silence is the silence of fear, of disappointment, of hopelessness. It is a dangerous silence; dangerous for the Church, for all of us.'

Ecclesiastical unity was impressive – but equally so the gap between the hierarchy and the laity. The Church's voice was muffled by censorship and its message dulled by the repeated contention that it should not meddle in politics. The majority of white Rhodesians seemed largely unconcerned about the clash between their Church and their State, as indeed about growing infringements on civil liberties. Censorship was the most obvious of these invasions. The courageous editor of the *Rhodesia Herald*, Malcolm Smith, responded to censorship by leaving large white spaces wherever the censor's blue pencil had struck out copy. As the white spaces grew in size the newspaper became known as the 'Government White Paper', infuriating the regime which however never succeeded in putting a stop to Malcolm Smith's act of quiet defiance. Allegations of phone taps and tampering with the mail were frequently made and never officially denied. Penalties were imposed for listening to 'subversive' broadcasts from abroad, and security procedures surrounding measures to overcome sanctions were progressively tightened.

From time to time rustlings of discontent were heard from the University College of Rhodesia, located on a rise on Salisbury's outskirts. But student demonstrations were sporadic, often involving only a small minority of the student body, and any disloyal group could be hived off. Its multiracial clientele and its occasional 'radical' (by Rhodesian standards) pronouncements were convenient targets for Front spokesmen who referred to it as that 'Kremlin on the hill'. As an institution, however, the University was hardly a serious threat to the rebel regime.

Among those who served the state, the judiciary were among the most reserved about U.D.I. Shortly after the rupture with Britain, the judges of Rhodesia's High Court announced they would 'continue to perform their duties in accordance with the law'. Which law under which constitution was not specified, though it became clear as time went on they meant that of 1961 and not the constitution introduced by the illegal regime. Indeed, Sir Hugh Beadle, the Chief Justice, moved into Government House with Sir Humphrey Gibbs, and the regime decided to postpone as long as possible any cases which might test the loyalty of the judges. Though there were a few resignations of highly placed civil servants, most Government employees stayed on at their jobs, as did the officers of the several security forces. After all Wilson had not instructed them to do otherwise. But there was more to it than that. Sir Roy Welensky, former Prime Minister of the Federation of Rhodesia and Nyasaland, expressed the mood of many. 'I am an opponent of U.D.I.,' he said, 'but I love my country.'

As the weeks wore on, initial doubts began to ebb. Businessmen who had opposed the Front and had considered U.D.I. a disaster now found themselves administering Government controls and staffing new boards and committees attempting to overcome the hazards of sanctions. There might have been reservations about the regime in Salisbury, but to more and more Rhodesians Wilson, not Smith, was anathema. Smith warned of a dark plot to divide Rhodesians and clamp upon the country direct administration from Whitehall, reversing more than forty years of progress under self-rule and paving the way for a rapid transition to an African government. In a statement to the Lisbon *Diario Popular*, Smith went further, accusing the United Kingdom of wishing to sacrifice Rhodesia and of 'playing the Communist game'. For its part, Smith continued, Rhodesia meant to guarantee 'the integrity of what is the ultimate bastion against communism on the African continent'. Somewhat later, in an assessment delivered three months after U.D.I., Smith posed an astonishing rhetorical question: was Wilson perhaps a 'fellow traveller'? After all, he concluded blandly, Britain assisted the Viet Cong and Cuba and encouraged the 'communist' states of Africa.

Stickers on car windows and bumpers appeared in profusion as individual Rhodesians broadcast their loyalties. Gibbs's supporters, who remained stubbornly faithful though few in number, announced their allegiance by displaying a phrase cut from the carton of a toothpaste in local use called conveniently, 'Gibbs SR'. More popular by far was a sticker disseminated by supporters of the Front which proclaimed, 'Forward Rhodesia!' And even more popular for a time was one reading, 'I hate Harold.' Even opponents of Smith admitted that upwards of 90 per cent of the white population had concluded that the only way to salvage something of 'their Rhodesia' was to close ranks against external pressures. The traditional parochialism of Rhodesians now mixed with their deep anxieties to make perfectly believable any scurrilous charge against Wilson, and entirely plausible the extraordinary claim that white supremacy in Rhodesia was consonant with Christianity, civilized standards and indispensable to the West's fight against world communism.

Resistance to the rebel regime within the African community was also sporadic and easily manageable. After numerous and often isolated incidents in several areas, a general strike got under way on 22 November focused primarily on the industrial city of Bulawayo. African organizers toured the townships urging participation, then set up picket lines and used in some cases more direct means of intimidation to bar workers from the factory areas. A police-escorted bus carrying workers was badly damaged. There were noisy demonstrations by some 2,000 African strikers in Mpopoma township. The following day the strike expanded; it was 60 per cent effective. Violence continued. An African was killed. Some 170

Africans were picked up under the Law and Order (Maintenance) Act on suspicion of fomenting trouble. Warnings were issued that all absentees from work the following day would be dismissed instantly. With that the strike ended peremptorily.

One month after U.D.I. unrest had virtually ceased. Smith was in full control. Random acts of disorder would continue to occur. But these were maintained at a tolerable level and the regime spoke incessantly and not without some justification of the high level of law and order which prevailed. Those in detention or under restriction probably numbered no more than four to five hundred – though it should not be overlooked that they included the senior echelon of African nationalist leaders, apart from those who had fled the country.

In the opening months of the crisis, the impact of sanctions was surely more serious than Smith had predicted. It would be 'a three-day wonder', he had once said of British efforts to thwart U.D.I., suggesting that independence might be declared on a Friday with all the excitement (if any) ended by Monday morning. During his speech on 11 November, he spoke of 'short-term economic disadvantages' but in the longer run he saw a 'prosperous and better future for everyone'. 'I cannot conceive', he continued, 'of a rational world uniting in an endeavour to destroy the economy of this country'. Immediately after U.D.I. South Africa announced a temporary suspension of transactions involving Rhodesian currency, creating consternation when Rhodesians on holiday in the Republic discovered they could not buy traveller's cheques. Within a few days, however, these restrictions were lifted and Pretoria permitted the exchange at par of Rhodesian for South African currency. Trade between the two countries continued and would soon increase.

Even before U.D.I., Salisbury had introduced import controls to assure that purchases abroad did not exceed foreign exchange holdings, which were bound to contract under the weight of sanctions. Excise and customs duties went up; so too did the price of sugar. Rhodesian gold production, about £7 million ($20 million) a year, was held off the world market and used to strengthen Rhodesian reserves. Meanwhile the search got under way for outlets for the embargoed tobacco and sugar crops.

Wilson's second round of sanctions, particularly the 'take-over' of the Rhodesian Reserve Bank under the chairmanship of Sir Sydney Caine, caught regime leaders unawares. The 'great Caine robbery', they called it. Minister of Finance John Wrathall said on the evening of 6 December that Rhodesia was 'at war' and 'fighting for survival'. The following day the Government assumed power to prevent strikes, to give directives to the management of banks, commercial concerns and industries and if necessary to sequestrate firms. In a broadcast on 8 December, Smith admitted that the seizure of Rhodesian funds in London (estimated at about £9 million or $25 million) was injurious and created temporary embarrassment. At the same time, he said, 'these deceitful Wilsonian actions' absolved Rhodesia from obligations to pay interest, rents, dividends, profits and capital from Rhodesia to United Kingdom nationals, thus significantly easing Rhodesia's balance of payments position. Nor would Rhodesia honour its debts to the British Government or the World Bank. 'As Mr. Wilson has filched our bank reserves,' Smith continued, 'I am sure he will accept the responsibility attached thereto, and meet our international financial obligations.'

Smith also announced plans to meet the problems of unemployment arising from the application of sanctions, and to raise further revenues. A credit squeeze had been anticipated accentuated by demands from farmers for overdraft facilities prior to the next harvest. But the squeeze kept receding into the future as credit requirements continued to be met somehow from well-subscribed independence bond sales, a lowering of the liquidity requirements of commercial banks, lower import levels and United Kingdom funds trapped in the country after U.D.I.

The future nonetheless remained uncertain. From pre-U.D.I. levels external reserves shrank by 25 per cent in approximately one month. An oil embargo imposed in mid December raised new hazards. The pipeline carrying crude oil into Rhodesia stopped pumping by the end of December, the refinery closed down in mid January, and petrol allowances were progressively reduced. The Rhodesian Iron and Steel Company was forced to close two of its three blast furnaces toward the end of January. Automobile assembly plants began laying off workers, mainly Africans. The Dunlop tyre factory changed to a four-day week largely due to the loss of East African and Zambian markets. Smaller concerns were also beginning to retrench. To make matters worse a severe drought, which had denied rain to parts of the country for over fourteen months, was approaching the proportions of a national disaster. The Chairman of Barclays Bank predicted considerable deterioration in the Rhodesian economy, while the President of the Associated Chambers of Commerce of Rhodesia speculated that 4,000 Europeans might soon be out of work.

At Christmas, 1965, Ian Smith sent an open letter to the people of Britain. He tugged at shared memories of the war, of a time when 'we stood with Britain and faced an awful future'. He then appealed for an end to measures levied against kith and kin which 'will not beat us to our knees, but will only cause bitterness and lasting resentment'. Defiantly he concluded, 'We will never surrender to force and intimidation.' Another Christmas letter travelled in the other direction. To Sir Humphrey Gibbs, the Queen of Britain – and of Rhodesia – expressed admiration for the steadfastness and dignity with which the Governor had upheld constitutional government. She deeply regretted the events which placed under strain the loyalties of Rhodesians. 'It is in the hope of a speedy ending of this unhappy situation and an early return to constitutional rule that I send my good wishes for the coming year to all my loyal subjects in your country.'

Even as this was being written Wilson was planning new moves to achieve that 'speedy ending'. His attention now fixed upon Zambia.

IV

Zambia and the 'Quick Kill'

Long before U.D.I., it was obvious that the Rhodesian crisis might overwhelm Zambia. Inextricably tied to the Rhodesian economy, Zambia depended upon that country for its very survival. Hit Rhodesia with sanctions and Zambia must flinch.

The danger to Zambia arose from other sources too. Britain's hard-pressed economy depended on imports of Zambian copper amounting to some 300,000 tons per annum, more than half of Britain's total consumption and conveniently available from within the sterling area. Zambian copper could not be produced and marketed without coal, hydro-electric power and transport, all controlled by Rhodesia. Why then would not Rhodesia hit back at Britain through Zambia, holding Zambia 'at hostage', as an early Government brief had put it, 'to prevent British policy from causing a breakdown of the Rhodesian economy'? A confrontation with Rhodesia also raised the most serious risks for stability within Zambia. Though now ruled by a popularly elected African Government, Zambia continued to depend for technical expertise on a large white community with substantial links with white-controlled Southern Africa. In a showdown between Rhodesia and Britain many would sympathize with Smith. And how black Zambians would respond to that was anyone's guess.

No one was more aware of these dangers than Zambia's first President, Kenneth David Kaunda. An act of rebellion in Salisbury answered by British sanctions would place him in an appalling quandary. He could not believe that sanctions alone would do the job. More than most, he had known at first hand the tough resourcefulness of the whites who ruled Rhodesia. And given Zambia's own economic dependence on Rhodesia and susceptibility to rebel counter-attack, how could Wilson expect to bring down Smith without first shattering Zambia? U.D.I. was a time bomb. The mechanism was triggered in Salisbury; but the explosive was in Lusaka and on the Copperbelt.

Zambia might be released from this quandary in either of two ways. London could use force which Zambia together with other Afro-Asian states insisted in any event was the only realistic answer to rebellion. Or Lusaka could refuse to participate in sanctions, conducting business as usual with the rebels. Wilson's policy foreclosed the former. And Kaunda's principles precluded the latter. This son of an African minister of religion had been formed in the struggle to gain dignity and rights for his own people and burned now with the desire to rid Southern Africa of racism; more than most leaders, he would do all he could to make the slender resources of his country serve this end. Just conceivably there was a third possibility. Careful advance planning might prepare Zambia for the U.D.I. contingency by reducing its reliance on Salisbury and thus its vulnerability both to British sanctions and to Rhodesian counter-attack. But this would require massive external assistance, for which Zambia understandably turned to the British Government.

What happened thereafter constitutes one of the most incredible episodes in the U.D.I. story, revealing not only Wilson's political virtuosity but his basically flawed policy – for which Zambia was to pay dearly.

Dealing with 'Hypothetical Situations'

In November 1964, shortly after Zambia's independence, President Kaunda travelled to London. With him was his economic adviser, Gordon Goundrey, a Canadian professor engaged the year before through the United Nations at Kaunda's behest. Goundrey was responsible for Zambia's first efforts at planning for contingencies that might arise from the Rhodesian situation. He had prepared for the President a working paper outlining the problem and some recommended initial actions. At 10 Downing Street, President and Prime Minister, both having acceded to their present positions the previous month, had a few minutes alone before dinner. Wilson agreed that Kaunda faced real difficulties and later asked his new Commonwealth Secretary, Arthur Bottomley, to convene a meeting to examine the situation while the Zambian team was still in London.

This first venture in contingency planning left something to be desired – a foretaste of chronic and increasing difficulties in British–Zambian relations as the Rhodesian problem intensified. The Zambians had expected to confer at the ministerial level. When it became apparent that the senior British representative, who was to chair the meeting, held the rank of Deputy Under-Sectetary in the Commonwealth Office, Zambia's Ministers of Finance and Foreign

Affairs quietly withdrew leaving the discussions to their officials. Other than providing an opportunity for Goundrey to air his estimates and recommendations little was accomplished.

By the end of January 1965, Kaunda went to London once more. Quite at the last minute he decided to attend Churchill's funeral. A contingency paper was again prepared containing estimates of required tonnages of vital supplies, identifying ways in which these requirements might be met, and singling out priority projects that ought to be got under way. Kaunda found Wilson sobered by an encounter he had had with Ian Smith, who like Kaunda had used Churchill's funeral as an opportunity to work in a private talk at Number 10. The Zambian President again raised the danger of Rhodesian retaliation against Zambia and was encouraged by Wilson to continue examining ways in which Britain might help maintain the copper industry if Rhodesia tried to force Zambia to the wall. Some weeks after Kaunda's return, a telegram arrived in Lusaka asking if Goundrey could come to London to discuss his estimates of Zambia's contingency requirements. Serious planning now appeared to be getting under way in the British capital as well.

In March, at the instance of both the British and the Zambians, a working group on contingency planning was formed in Washington. By May the British and American planning teams were ready to compare notes. They convened in the American capital. A representative of the Canadian Government sat in and Goundrey joined the group for the final two days of the talks. For the purpose of the exercise the planners assumed the very worst. In confrontation with Rhodesia, Zambia would no longer have access to coal from Rhodesia's colliery at Wankie. Coal imports for smelting copper, running the railways, firing thermal power stations and servicing industry were running at well over one million tons per year. Nor would Zambia under these circumstances any longer receive hydro-electric power from turbines at Kariba Dam. Though jointly owned by Rhodesia and Zambia and built under World Bank financing, the power station had been carved out of bed-rock on the southern (Rhodesian) bank of the Zambezi River. Zambia's annual intake from Kariba was roughly 70 per cent of its total power requirements.

Again assuming the worst the planners posited that Zambia would be denied access to the railway line running through Rhodesia to Mozambique and South African ports. All Zambia's copper exports and 95 per cent of its imports including virtually all of its petroleum products made their way by rail across the dramatic span high above the gorge at Victoria Falls which linked Zambia to Rhodesia and through Rhodesia to Southern Africa and the world beyond. Zambia's gross annual imports approached two million tons, and exports nearly one million. Knit tightly into the economic structure of the white-dominated areas to the south, Zambian industry and trade had developed no alternative sources of supply. Even stocks of indispensable items were virtually non-existent, for Rhodesia next door traditionally had served as Zambia's warehouse.

Calculations also had to reckon with Katanga's needs. Neighbouring the Zambian Copperbelt, the Congo's southernmost province produced 275,000 tons of refined copper a year which, together with Zambia's 700,000 tons, constituted 25 per cent of free-world copper production. In 1963–4 some 145,000 tons of Katangese minerals were sent by rail to ocean ports through Rhodesia while over 300,000 tons of Congolese imports (mostly coal from Wankie) were moved into the area over Rhodesia Railways. These requirements too were in jeopardy and the contingency planners had to take account of Katanga's needs in their proposals together with those of Zambia.

No alternative – it did not matter how bizarre – escaped review at this or subsequent sessions, or at similar exercises in Lusaka involving Zambian officials and planners from the copper companies. Why not substitute locally produced charcoal for coal in the smelters? (One calculation found it would take 40,000 workers for the scheme to be of real value. It was quickly dropped.) What about opening up coalfields in southern Tanzania? (The quality was found to be below that of Rhodesian coal though still passable, but problems of accessibility and transport finally defeated the idea.) Then why not exploit Zambia's own coal deposits in the Gwembe valley north of Lake Kariba? (The quality was even worse but with enormous effort the coal could be, and ultimately was, made accessible.) Could coal not be replaced by fuel oil which produced more copper by weight than did coal? (The answer was, yes – given time to install new furnaces.) Was it possible to develop bulk storage depots for petrol on short notice? (A scheme was developed to fly in collapsible rubberized bags with capacities running close to 100,000 gallons.)

What if the United States Government were to release refined copper from its strategic stockpile to meet the requirements of Zambia's customers while acquiring title to equivalent amounts produced in Zambia, thus eliminating the problem of transporting Zambia's production during the emergency? (The response was predictable: U.S. title to a copper stockpile located in the middle of Africa could hardly be regarded as a strategic asset in the event of the U.S. being involved in hostilities.) And if the worse came to the worst why not sustain Zambia with a massive airlift? (One estimate found that an airlift of only 200,000 tons of copper exports per annum with a backhaul of 200,000 tons of coal would involve thirty-seven flights a day for planes with pay loads of fifteen tons each, for a grand total of 94,500 flying hours and with costs running as high as £30 million or $85 million a year!)

Even more important was the identification of alternative transport routes not dependent on Rhodesia.* The principal ones bore exotic and misleading names. The Great North Road was a euphemism for the most important section of an endless gravel track winding more than 1,100 miles from central Zambia to Dar es Salaam, the Tanzanian capital on the Indian Ocean. It was soon to become the famous 'hell run', a vital and dangerous truck route for the import of fuel oil. The Great East Road (another bit of hyperbole) joined central Zambia to the rail head at Salima in Malawi from which a railway line ran due south through Mozambique to the port of Beira. A complex road-lake-rail route ran from the Copperbelt to the un-developed port of Mpulungu at the foot of Lake Tanganyika which was linked by boat to the Tanzanian lake port of Kigoma, and thence by rail to Dar es Salaam. (The largest of the vessels was the *Liemba* a steamer of *African Queen* vintage. It had been assembled by the Germans on the lake prior to the First World War, sunk during the hostilities and resuscitated later by the British.) Finally there was the Benguela railway line, owned by British-controlled Tanganyika Concessions, running from the port of Lobito on the Atlantic through central Angola to Dilolo, then over the Chemin de Fer du Bas-Congo et Katanga (B.C.K.) through southern Katanga to the Copperbelt.

There were lesser routes even more remote and exotic, involving virtually impassable mountain escarpments, river barges and little used rail spurs. One enterprising planner proposed hacking a new route through virgin territory in northern Zambia across a river basin and over a mountain range to Lake Malawi. Transit across the lake to gain access to a road leading to the Tanzanian port of Mtwara involved not only the construction of landing stages on either side but the acquisition of large, roll-on roll-off landing craft which after delivery to the port of Beira would have to be cut up and shipped by rail to the south end of Lake Malawi where they would be welded back together again.

For each component of each of these routes extra transport capacities had to be calculated – road, rail, transhipment points, harbours. What was at issue was not simply how many trucks could be run over a road or trains down a track or ships brought along a quayside. 'Capacity' was a function of the availability of equipment, of fuel needed to power equipment, of facilities needed to maintain equipment. 'Capacity' related to the experience and the skills and the

---

* See the map opposite.

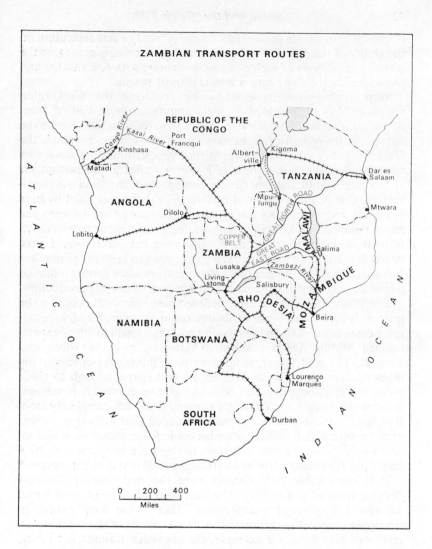

ZAMBIAN TRANSPORT ROUTES

REPUBLIC OF THE
CONGO

Congo River

Kasai River

Port
Francqui

Kinshasa

Matadi

ANGOLA

Dilolo

Lobito

ATLANTIC OCEAN

Albert-
ville

Kigoma

TANZANIA

Dar es
Salaam

Mpu-
lungu

GREAT NORTH ROAD

Mtwara

COPPER
BELT

ZAMBIA

GREAT
EAST ROAD

MALAWI

Salima

Lusaka

Zambezi River

Livingstone

Salisbury

RHODESIA

Beira

MOZAMBIQUE

NAMIBIA

BOTSWANA

Lourenço
Marques

SOUTH
AFRICA

Durban

INDIAN OCEAN

0   200   400
Miles

efficiency of available personnel. 'Capacity' rose or fell depending on the ability of the different companies and governments managing the several components of each route to co-operate with one another and to rationalize the route into a true transport system.

Surprisingly, given these staggering problems, the Washington review of May 1965 yielded a mildly optimistic result. Cut off from Rhodesia, Zambia could survive. Alternative routes would have to be improved, many more freight cars and road vehicles acquired, the Gwembe valley coal-field brought into production, coal stockpiles established, and possibly some of Katanga's mineral production left at the mines until the emergency passed. Zambia could survive – survive, that is, on a 'care and maintenance' basis sustained by bare essentials and generating only enough thermal power to keep the mines pumped out. This alone constituted an enormous requirement. If hydro-electric power from Kariba were cut off it would take nearly half a million tons of coal a year simply to keep the mines dry! Just conceivably under these adverse conditions some copper might be mined and processed, say roughly 30 per cent of normal production.

The Washington review also disclosed how much still needed to be learned before these crude estimates could be refined and approximate costs calculated. In the ensuing months a small army of experts roamed Middle Africa examining harbours, railways, roads and airfields. The data they produced were complex, subject to varying interpretations and despite best efforts still sparse enough to elude precision. But the more that was learned the narrower, it seemed, became the margin for Zambia's survival if cut off completely from Rhodesia. At last planners grimly concluded that following a complete rupture with Rhodesia, Zambia could be sustained at minimum levels only if the alternative surface routes were supplemented by a major airlift running perhaps at 100,000 to 200,000 tons per annum.*

It is remarkable how slender were the real accomplishments deriving from all this activity. The Zambians might be excused for an occasional display of exasperation. There were long delays in developing and vetting reports. The formal results of the Washington review of May 1965, for example, did not reach Kaunda until July. Each study, rather than spurring commitments, spawned yet more studies. In October 1965 a small team of Zambian officials, led by Cabinet Secretary Valentine Musakanya, travelled to London to

---

* The Katanga case, never studied with as much care, was more tractable. It had its own hydro-electric supply and first option on rail links to the Atlantic. The loss of Rhodesian coal would have created serious industrial problems but nothing approaching in scale the difficulties facing Zambia.

review with the British where things stood. Musakanya explained that the Zambian Government was committing itself to projects within Zambia which under normal circumstances would be considered uneconomic, perhaps even unnecessary. Would the British help fund projects outside Zambia necessary to prepare for emergencies that might arise from U.D.I.? Of particular concern were improvements on the Tanzanian side of the Great North Road and at the harbour of Dar es Salaam, for which the Tanzanian Government clearly had no resources. The British officials explained they had no authority to commit funds. In any event it was difficult to consider, as they put it, 'hypothetical situations'.

Almost a year had passed since Kenneth Kaunda and Harold Wilson first discussed Zambian contingencies. British-Rhodesian relations were skidding towards a crisis. And Britain still had committed itself to nothing more tangible than surveys. Nor indeed had the Americans. Kaunda had approached the United States Government as early as May 1965 requesting assistance in constructing a rail link running more than 1,000 miles through Tanzania to Dar es Salaam, thus bypassing Southern Africa's white-controlled rail outlets. A team of surveyors from the People's Republic of China had just arrived in Tanzania, precursors of a generous offer to construct the strategic rail link (which no less an imperialist visionary than Cecil Rhodes himself had projected some three-quarters of a century earlier). Communist initiatives not withstanding, President Johnson was reluctant to undertake a major new venture in East-Central Africa the cost of which alone (somewhere around £140 million or nearly $400 million) would have stirred up a storm in Congress. Foreign aid in general was coming under increasing attack and, largely as a result of the seemingly interminable series of crises in the neighbouring Congo, interest in Africa had plummeted. In any event, Rhodesia and the problems emanating from it were viewed as a British responsibility. So, overriding the advice of the State Department's Bureau of African Affairs which was strongly supported by dispatches from the field, Johnson vetoed direct American assistance for what was to become one of Africa's largest and politically most potent aid projects. Instead the Americans offered Kaunda a comprehensive economic survey of the road link to Dar es Salaam, while the British, with Canadian support, agreed to finance yet another study of the economic feasibility of the projected railway.*

The problem in London was simply that contingency planning for U.D.I. was at cross purposes with increasingly frantic efforts to

---

* In Washington and London, it was hoped that once the Zambians viewed the results of the two surveys side-by-side, they would opt for

avoid U.D.I. So long as this remained the prime objective, the British reasoned, nothing must be done to provoke Salisbury into seizing independence. Major projects designed to disentangle Zambia from Rhodesia might provide just such a provocation. From the outset London pursued contingency planning with secretive caution and Wilson no doubt warned Kaunda to do the same. Beyond this there were considerations of cost for the tightly stretched British economy coupled with increasing concern, as the sobering results of the many surveys were analysed, that Zambia probably could not in any event be salvaged in an all-out economic conflict with Rhodesia. Strangely enough this view was soon to be abandoned as the United Kingdom a few weeks after U.D.I. moved to involve Zambia in its sanctions programme against Rhodesia. And even before U.D.I. there were some British officials who took the sanguine view that the rebellion, if it could not be avoided, would quickly crumble under the weight of sanctions – again making expensive contingency preparations in Zambia hardly justifiable. 'Don't you believe it,' Musakanya said at one point to his British colleagues. 'Just as you underestimated the force of black nationalism you are underestimating the force of white nationalism. It will be a long drawn-out affair.'

But the Zambians too were ambivalent about contingency planning. They were convinced that a rebellious Rhodesia, not quickly invested by British forces, would one way or another strike out at their new black state located on Rhodesia's northern flank. Advance preparations were therefore vital. Most priority projects, however, depended on outside assistance and this was painfully slow in materializing in both London and Washington. Yet all things considered not much was accomplished prior to the rebellion within Zambia either. Schedules were somewhat advanced in expanding the hydro-electric power station at Livingstone. Plans were sketched out to develop harbour facilities at Mpulungu on Lake Tanganyika, to upgrade the Zambian end of the Great North Road running to Dar es Salaam and to stockpile coal from Rhodesia at Livingstone. Potential suppliers of trucks and railway wagons were identified. Most important, work in the Gwembe valley to open up Zambia's own coalfields actually got under way with impressive speed. Nonetheless when the rebellion came, Zambia still had only a marginal stockpile of coal and virtually no stocks of petroleum, and the essential task of

---

the far less expensive and in many ways economically more versatile road. In fact they opted for both. American assistance was eventually forthcoming to help construct a segment of the road in southern Tanzania.

developing alternative routes and new sources of supply had only just begun.

The hard fact was that all contingency planning projects took resources away from Zambia's new development plan. Not surprisingly each Minister resisted cuts in his department. The intricate calculations for alternative routes and emergency schemes did not exactly command the attention of politicians and officials gripped with the challenge of plotting a new nation's course and anxious to use every spare unit of currency and every extra ton of carrying capacity to build new institutions and to supply new programmes. Contingency planning suffered too from the secrecy surrounding it. Zambia had inherited from the colonial government a large cadre of white civil servants. Many of them had close ties with Rhodesia. So the whole planning operation was kept under wraps. The result was not only that things were left undone but that officials and political leaders were often never informed as to why these preparations were important.

There was, too, the frankly awkward problem for Zambia of dealing with the Portuguese Government, a colonial power which nonetheless was of great importance in these matters, controlling as it did indispensable alternative routes to the sea. Perhaps even more distasteful was the need to deal with Moise Tshombe, former leader of the Katanga secession of 1960 to 1963. Though now the Congo's Prime Minister and thus an important participant in many plans affecting the region, he remained in Kaunda's view the white man's stooge and the black man's burden. But more basic, one suspects, than all this in explaining the Zambian attitude toward contingency planning was the conviction that Rhodesia after all was Britain's responsibility, that British talk of sanctions toppling the regime was fatuous, and that preparations in Zambia to neutralize the fall-out from Britain's coming economic contest with Rhodesia might be viewed as Zambian acquiescence in British irresponsibility.

Still, as with Britain, Zambia's view remained ambivalent to the point of apparent contradiction. It would not be long before Zambia too would be talking of participating in sanctions against Rhodesia.

The Crisis of Confidence

With the possible exception of Ian Smith himself, no one studied Wilson's catalogue of sanctions, issued immediately after U.D.I., more carefully than did President Kenneth Kaunda.* Almost

---

* See above, p. 18

immediately he let it be known that London's response to the rebellion was hopelessly deficient. Britain's limited sanctions programme could not bring Smith down quickly – not unless oil were effectively embargoed, which would entail, Kaunda believed, a naval blockade of the Portuguese port of Beira and the sternest warnings to South Africa; and not unless, however dangerous, Zambia itself participated in the sanctions effort. So Kaunda appealed again for swift and sizeable British aid to get Zambia ready.

His urgent recommendations were in a way prophetic. Britain did in fact introduce oil sanctions, but more than a month after U.D.I. Britain also gained a U.N. mandate to interdict tankers putting into the Mozambique port of Beira with petroleum products destined for Rhodesia, but that was five months after U.D.I. For the Zambian President, the time was now. If Smith were not down within three months, Kaunda astutely predicted, he would not be downed at all. The sanctioners would lose interest and potency, while the Rhodesians would devise ways of circumventing the embargoes. For Zambia in particular, Kaunda reasoned, the longer the rebellion continued, the greater was the risk of racial strife at home and the danger of economic strangulation by a racist and rebellious regime deeply antithetical to everything Zambia stood for.

Wilson must have been astonished by the vigour and swiftness of Kaunda's riposte. He knew well enough that Zambia wished Britain to use force. At the Commonwealth Prime Ministers' meeting in London the previous June, Kaunda had urged Wilson to position troops in Zambia as a deterrent to illegal action. Less than three weeks before U.D.I. and on the eve of Zambia's first anniversary of independence the Zambian President, while addressing a mass rally in Lusaka, had warned that should U.D.I. occur, British force would have to be applied – not, he stressed, African, U.N. or great-power force, as these would risk racial or ideological war. Repeatedly Wilson had told Kaunda that British force would not, and could not, be used. No doubt he stressed this again when briefly, less than a fortnight before, the two leaders had met at Livingstone airport immediately following Wilson's last minute mission to Salisbury trying to avert the rebellion.

Thus rebuffed, Kaunda turned his attention to sanctions which previously he had scorned as ineffectual, and subsequently would again. But it now seemed the only tactic available. In a speech delivered only four days before U.D.I. he suggested that Zambia would not be 'an easy country for [the Rhodesians] to handle' representing a £35 million (close to a $100 million) a year market for Rhodesian goods. 'Without this', he said, 'their foreign exchange position is very shaky.' Pondering the situation Zambia would face,

Foreign Minister Simon Kapwepwe concluded that just as you could not be half in rebellion so those resisting rebellion could not afford to take half measures.

The Zambians had suddenly reversed the assumptions underlying all contingency planning, sweeping aside at least for the moment their earlier ambivalence on the subject. Britain and the United States premised their involvement on a willingness to examine what could be done to rescue Zambia in the event of hostile action from Rhodesia. Kaunda was now suggesting that the object of contingency planning was to do everything possible to position Zambia to take hostile action against Rhodesia. It was apparent that Zambia was going to push the British hard to move swiftly and decisively against Rhodesia, even at some considerable risk to Zambia itself.

Wilson saw matters differently. To escalate sanctions would imperil the consensus he was working to sustain in Parliament. Nor did he wish to alienate potential support within the Rhodesian white community by pressing any harder than necessary. Most important, according to the rapidly accumulating evidence from the numerous contingency planning surveys, Zambia remained mortally vulnerable. With all the help in the world, Wilson told Kaunda, Zambia's economy could not be maintained following a complete rupture with Rhodesia. (This concern was shared by the American Government.) The economic measures Britain had devised, Wilson said, would have a steady cumulative effect, though almost certainly it would take considerably longer than three months to end the rebellion. Nor were these measures dependent on Zambian participation which Wilson felt would lead to dangerous complications. Meanwhile if Rhodesia without provocation should take punitive measures against Zambia, Britain would do its best to help. As to defraying the costs of such contingency preparations as might now be put under way, Wilson remained silent. He promised, however, to send to Lusaka his special emissary, Malcolm MacDonald, Britain's adroit, experienced and deeply sympathetic Special Envoy to East and Central Africa.

Kaunda remained sceptical. The urgency of the problems he faced seemed to make quite irrelevant the repeated counsels of caution and the talk about the steady cumulative impact of sanctions. There were racial flare-ups in Livingstone serious enough to evoke from Kaunda an appeal to Zambian Africans not to see 'a Smith in every white face'. Two hundred white railwaymen, virtually all of them Rhodesians, went on strike bringing Zambia's rail traffic almost to a standstill. Within the Zambian Government, white technicians understandably were advising the Zambians to act with care. But equally understandably the notion rapidly incubated in Zambia's troubled environment that the 'expats' (as expatriate or foreign employees were called) were buying time for Smith rather than protecting the interests of Zambia. Relations between Zambian and expatriate civil servants deteriorated.

On the Copperbelt saboteurs felled a 110 foot power pylon cutting the main power line to Zambia's vital industrial complex. A second pylon was mined but the charge failed to go off. The culprits were never found. In a desperate frame of mind Kaunda found himself telling a press conference on 25 November, 'I do not know how many people realize how close we are to World War Three.' A senior Minister epitomized the mood with less drama but even greater force. Zambia wished simply to know what its friends would do by way of tangible contingency preparations. 'Our queries are met with a conspiracy of silence,' he said sadly.

Malcolm MacDonald, as Wilson had promised, arrived in Lusaka on 22 November. Kaunda's rising anxiety had now come to focus on the extraordinary fact that Smith's soldiers were in full control of Zambia's power supply from the jointly owned Kariba Dam, as both the generators and the switching gear were conveniently located within Rhodesia itself. At the airport MacDonald was asked if he were prepared to discuss a request Kaunda had made a few days before for British troops to guard the Kariba facilities, on which occasion the Zambian President also had implied that other powers had offered troops and that under certain circumstances these offers might be acted upon. 'What I have to say about that,' MacDonald replied, 'I will say to the President.'

Wilson's emissary met with Kaunda and his Ministers several times over the next few days and came away impressed with the courage and responsibility of Zambia's leaders in the face of the most appalling uncertainties. MacDonald was also sobered. There was in Zambia a profound crisis of confidence in British intentions. Zambia had asked for swift aid to enable it to join in sanctions against Rhodesia only to be told this was both unnecessary and imprudent. Even contingency aid to reduce Zambia's reliance on Rhodesia had not materialized. Meanwhile fears continued to run deep that Smith sooner or later would lash out against Zambia. If British troops could not occupy Salisbury, the Zambians argued, they must at least control the power house on the south bank of Kariba. And if Britain could not be responsive, experienced observers in Lusaka conjectured, pressures would surely increase to bring in African contingents from member states of the Organization for African Unity (O.A.U.) with incalculable consequences for the entire region. Egypt seemed a possible source. Ghana was agitating for military action. On 25 November President Nkrumah announced the cancellation of all military leave and talked about plans for mobilization. O.A.U. Foreign Ministers were scheduled to meet soon in Addis Ababa. The pressure on Britain seemed almost palpable as MacDonald hurried back to London convinced that Britain's time-table was too relaxed, that Zambian anxieties were not entirely unfounded, and that contingency assistance to Zambia must now quickly be forthcoming.

On the evening of 28 November, MacDonald delivered to Wilson Kaunda's formal request for British troops. It was a meeting as auspicious as the subject matter was grave and delicate. Present were George Brown, Deputy Prime Minister; Michael Stewart, Foreign Secretary; Denis Healey, Defence Secretary; James Callaghan, Chancellor of the Exchequer; and Arthur Bottomley, Common-wealth Secretary. For two hours the Ministers weighed the risks of outside intervention should Britain fail to accede to Zambia's request, and the danger of provoking a rash reaction from Rhodesia if Britain were to send troops to be stationed in Zambia. A well-timed inter-view with Ian Smith had just appeared in the West German publica-tion, *Der Spiegel*. Rhodesia, the rebel Prime Minister avowed, would not hesitate to fire on the Union Jack if British troops entered the country. Britain's policy, so it was believed in London, needed above all time for sanctions to take their toll without simultaneously wrecking the Rhodesian economy or throwing Rhodesia's administra-tive apparatus into chaos. It was precisely Kaunda's objective to deny this time and to force the pace of Britain's response.

The following day, 29 November, MacDonald was dispatched back to Lusaka with Britain's proposal. A battalion of troops and a few R.A.F. aircraft would be deployed. The troops were not, however, to be sent to the Rhodesian side of the Kariba Dam as that would trigger the military confrontation which Britain was as anxious to avoid as Zambia was determined to see joined. They would remain solely under United Kingdom command, while Zambia would assure that offers of further military support from other states would be turned aside. Zambia's Cabinet pondered these conditions at two long meetings. It was obvious that the British proposal was run-ning into difficulties. At this point, on the evening of 29 November, Wilson sent Commonwealth Secretary Arthur Bottomley to Lusaka with plenary powers.

Both Zambia and Britain had now arrived at an extremely delicate pass. Kaunda's position was made no easier by two gratuitous com-ments from questionable sources. In a broadcast originating from Salisbury at about the time Bottomley was taking off from London, Ian Smith said that Rhodesia welcomed the dispatch of British troops to Zambia – to keep order there! And on the floor of Parlia-ment the day Bottomley began his conversations in Lusaka, Julian

Amery, a Conservative M.P. and a well-known advocate of white rule in Southern Africa, dismissed the possibility that troops were needed to defend Zambia against Rhodesia. Rather they would be used to defend Zambia against African extremists. 'It is not uninteresting to note', he concluded, 'that the only way in which the democratically elected Government in Zambia can be maintained in a crisis may be by the intervention of British military forces.' In Lusaka Kaunda fumed!

Wilson was afraid that time was running out. The Committee of Five of the O.A.U., charged with advising on military initiatives in Rhodesia, was about to meet in secret session in Addis Ababa preparatory to a meeting of Foreign Ministers scheduled for 3 December. Chairman of the Committee, Tanzania's Foreign Minister Oscar Kambona, had earlier announced that U.D.I. had to be met with the 'greatest force'. There were rumours that the Soviet Union might be invited to give logistical support to an O.A.U. military effort in Rhodesia. (These rumours were never substantiated. Somewhat later Wilson was to confess in the Commons, with considerably more drama than the facts could support: 'We have been within inches of a very serious intervention by other countries.')

Accordingly on 1 December, as we have already seen, the British Prime Minister in Parliament announced new initiatives. The sanctions noose would now be pulled still tighter. New exchange control measures would make transfers of funds to the rebel colony virtually impossible while 95 per cent of Rhodesia's exports to the United Kingdom would be placed under boycott. Wilson then turned to the problem of Kariba. After re-emphasizing that British troops would not invade Rhodesia, Wilson added with measured emphasis that 'If Mr. Smith uses his illegitimate control over this international project, the Kariba Dam, to destroy the economy of Zambia, and indeed very seriously to disrupt our own economy, we cannot stand idly by.' He suggested that British troops stationed in Zambia would constitute a deterrent. 'It is no good talking about a deterrent unless you are prepared to make it effective. . . .' he said looking across the aisle at Mr. Heath. 'If that did mean a limited operation we should be prepared to undertake that operation.' As if to underline his determination, Wilson noted that the aircraft carrier H.M.S. *Eagle* was cruising off the coast of Tanzania. (It had been deployed by the Admiralty from Singapore prior to any Cabinet consideration of such a move. The naval staff was anxious to demonstrate the swift reaction time and general all-round utility of its carriers, which had been under political attack.)

The Prime Minister declared that Britain was now prepared to fly to Zambia a squadron of Javelin aircraft complete with radar environment and a detachment of the R.A.F. regiment to protect installations and aircraft at all three of Zambia's major airports. He laid down that the R.A.F. could not be used as air cover for an invasion of Rhodesia and insisted that, consistent with Britain's assertion that Rhodesia was a British responsibility, 'We should do everything in our power to prevent the stationing of other air forces in Zambia, wherever they may come from . . . ' which suggested that one of the conditions of the offer was that Zambia would agree not to invite in other air units. The Zambian Cabinet once again retired for intensive deliberations.

The following day during Question Time in the Commons, Wilson was handed a message from Lusaka which had just been deciphered and rushed to Parliament. Kaunda and the Zambian Cabinet, Wilson was able to announce to the House of Commons, had accepted the terms of Britain's offer to send the R.A.F. squadron. Meanwhile discussions concerning the disposition of ground troops continued. The Royal Scots of the Strategic Reserve stood by for immediate departure. But there was no sign in Lusaka that the deadlock on conditions for deploying troops would soon be broken.

On 3 December Kaunda convened a press conference and again insisted that British forces must agree to occupy the dam on both sides of the Zambezi to ensure that Smith did not cut off power. A British refusal, he suggested, might lead to a call for United States or Soviet troops. Even allowing for the calculated militancy of any political statement issued as the O.A.U. convened in Addis Ababa, it was becoming perfectly clear that Kaunda would not, and perhaps could not, entertain a British battalion except en route to Rhodesia. Anything less would be viewed within Zambia as an army of occupation, and hardly relevant to the urgent business of unseating Mr. Smith. London's *Sunday Times* of 5 December recorded Kaunda's mood in a revealing interview: 'I must be frank,' the Zambian President said. 'It is a terrible problem for the Zambian Government and me to decide whether Mr. Wilson is determined with sufficient single-mindedness to carry this through to the end. Mr. Bottomley explained to me at length the difficulties of the Labour Government with their tiny majority. I understood that difficulty. But what is good politics in England may be bad politics in Africa. Let us say I still remain to be convinced that Britain will be absolutely committed to help us.'

Pressure from the O.A.U.

Wilson's aim was to pre-empt military aid to Zambia before the O.A.U. Foreign Ministers could convene on 3 December, thus keeping the O.A.U. out of a volatile area and maintaining in London control over the pace and outcome of the Rhodesian crisis. By sending in the R.A.F. squadron he had only partly succeeded in reaching that objective for the stalemate concerning the deployment of British ground troops persisted. As for Kaunda, he had already made clear the dangers likely to follow an O.A.U. engagement on the very frontier of white-controlled Southern Africa. The answer was effective British action against Rhodesia. This was not materializing. Kaunda appeared caught between British reticence and O.A.U. rashness.

No one was more determined that the O.A.U. should seize the initiative, leaving it neither to Britain nor Zambia, than its restless and highly political Administrative Secretary-General, Diallo Telli. He took the lead, in collaboration with radical delegations like those from Ghana and Guinea, in pressing for O.A.U. military action. In the lobbies of Africa Hall where the O.A.U. convened, the word was that Zambia, like it or not, would have to play host to an O.A.U. force. The martial air in Addis Ababa intensified as delegations poured in. Ghana's Kojo Botsio said on arrival that if the United Kingdom would not move, the O.A.U. would, and called for immediate military action against Smith. Foreign Minister Mongi Slim of Tunisia said his country favoured effective action by the O.A.U. if the United Kingdom did not bring down Smith. Mahmud Riad of Egypt announced tersely that economic sanctions were of no use at this stage. When the delegates and their advisers from thirty-five African nations (only Gambia was absent) assembled around the enormous horseshoe table in Africa Hall, it appeared that almost half of them were in uniform. Emperor Haile Selassie opened the proceedings by condemning Smith's rebellion as a 'cancer deadly to human liberty and equality'. He called upon the African states to rise above their differences and rescue their brethren in Rhodesia. Ethiopia, he declared, was ready to make the needed sacrifices in a joint effort.

Despite the heady rhetoric, however, most delegations were not at all ready to commit the organization and even less their own countries to a martial adventure, and Britain's pre-emption of the vital field of air cover in Zambia was probably greeted by many African states with silent relief. Attention turned instead to consideration of non-military measures against Rhodesia, where consensus formed quickly, and to pressures against Britain, where agreement could be hammered out, though with greater difficulty. Concerning Rhodesia, O.A.U. members called for a complete suspension of communications and all economic and commercial relations, appealed to all nations to refuse to Rhodesia oil and fuel deliveries, pledged to press the U.N. to take similar actions, and determined to use all media at their disposals to support and encourage the Rhodesian African nationalists.

As to Britain the delegates took their guidance from the resolution passed in Ghana the previous October. There the Assembly of Heads of State and Government had decided in the event of U.D.I. 'to reconsider all political, economic, diplomatic and financial relations with the Government of the United Kingdom'. The conference drafting committee now brought forward a resolution calling for the withdrawal of ambassadors as a punitive measure against Britain if the Rhodesian question were not resolved satisfactorily. Senegal immediately pointed out that this was worthless. The *chargé d'affaires* would simply fill in behind the departed ambassador and everything would go on as before. If O.A.U. states wanted to take a truly effective step they had better threaten a complete break in relations.

Curiously, the proposal took hold most emphatically among some of the more moderate French-speaking states. They had little to lose in breaking relations with Britain, unlike members of the Commonwealth. Some delegations seemed to have found in the proposed action against Britain a basis for arguing against military action which an increasing number of states now wished to avoid. Various deadlines were proposed for giving effect to the ultimatum. During the debate, Foreign Minister Ketema of Ethiopia left the hall presumably to inform the Emperor, the only Chief of State available for consultation. When he returned Ketema recommended 15 December. The date was accepted. If, by then, 'the United Kingdom does not crush the rebellion and restore law and order,' the final draft read, 'and thereby prepare the way for majority rule in Southern Rhodesia . . . the Member States of the O.A.U. shall sever diplomatic relations . . . with the United Kingdom.' It was passed without a dissenting vote, though Malawi and Libya abstained. The once vaunted military initiative which had attracted so much attention prior to the meeting received short shrift. The Ministers requested the Committee of Five to reconvene with military advisers from Member States 'to study and plan the use of force to assist the people of Zimbabwe'.

Once the Foreign Ministers left Addis Ababa to report to their Chiefs of State, the consensus which had congealed so rapidly began to dissolve. Upper Volta, Tunisia, Niger and Liberia were among the first to express doubts about the desirability of implementing the break with Britain. Emperor Haile Selassie clearly had second thoughts. A story went the rounds in Addis Ababa that the Emperor could not possibly break relations with London for the Queen had just been to the Ethiopian capital as his guest. Be that as it may,

Selassie concluded that the decision was imprudent and appealed to the British Government to take some (unspecified) action to solve the predicament, while the Ethiopian Foreign Minister tried to delay the fulfilment of the ultimatum. President Kenyatta made it clear to his Parliament that Kenya had no intention of breaking relations on 15 December. He subsequently called for a meeting of the U.N. Security Council hoping that the British would acquiesce in a resolution under Chapter VII providing for mandatory U.N. sanctions against Rhodesia. If so, he reasoned, the African stampede to break with Britain might be halted. But the idea aborted.

Even such radical states as the U.A.R. expressed misgivings. Debates arose as to whether the resolution demanded that Britain actually terminate the rebellion by 15 December or only take effective steps toward that end; or whether the Ministers had the power to commit their governments acting on the strength of the resolution already approved by the O.A.U. Chiefs of State the previous October, or could take positions only *ad referendum*. For Zambia in particular the decision to break with Britain, which was concurred in by Foreign Minister Simon Kapwepwe, raised the most difficult problems. Kapwepwe suggested that the resolution must be understood in a special sense. It was what the O.A.U. would like to do if it could, even while knowing it could not. Therefore it measured the depth of African feeling.

Sensing a critical turn in the Rhodesian affair a number of international newsmen travelled from Addis Ababa to Lusaka with Kapwepwe following the O.A.U. meeting. Zambia's fiery Foreign Minister had no sooner disembarked when he was telling the assembled journalists at Lusaka's airport that Britain had cheated Zambia by sending inferior aircraft. The Javelins, he complained, were no match for Rhodesia's Hunters. Kapwepwe, who had picked up the story from a misleading article he had been shown en route to Lusaka and which ironically had appeared in a decidedly pro-Smith London newspaper (the *Daily Telegraph*), contributed to the atmosphere of contention already gathering in the Zambian capital. Journalists began filing accounts of violent debates in the Zambian Cabinet pitting President Kaunda against his Foreign Minister and sometimes against a majority of his Cabinet on such admittedly controversial issues as the British military presence in Zambia, an O.A.U. initiative in Rhodesia, or the decision just reached in Addis Ababa to break relations with Britain.

At one point Kaunda was reported to have warned President Nyerere in neighbouring Tanzania not to break with Britain and to have written to all African heads of state expressing his reservations about the O.A.U. resolution. The matter was finally clarified when

Kaunda told a press converence on 8 December that his purpose was 'not to tell other nations whether they should break ties with the United Kingdom or not, but . . . [to] explain to fellow leaders the difficult position in which Zambia would find itself in circumstances which would follow such action'. On 11 December, only four days before the ultimatum was to come into effect, Kaunda and Nyerere met at the hill town of Mbeya in southern Tanzania. The two found full agreement. Their differing strategies arose from differing circumstances, but aimed at a common goal. Zambia's special position, involving among other things a continuing effort to get from London contingency aid and a commitment to prepare to move troops to Rhodesia from Zambia, argued against a diplomatic break; Tanzania on the other hand would persist in putting maximum pressure on the British, abiding faithfully by the O.A.U. ultimatum.

At midnight on 15 December, Tanzania broke relations with Britain. A last-minute message from Wilson failed to turn Nyerere aside. 'Unfortunately, as always,' said the Tanzanian President, 'it was ambiguous in its phraseology.' He went on to say that he would be very pleased to be proved tomorrow the greatest fool that Africa has ever produced, but London's record in Rhodesia, he noted, was not good enough to give her the benefit of any doubt. Following Tanzania's action, the O.A.U. diplomatic assault on Britain largely frittered away, as had the vaunted military initiative before it.* Only Ghana among the African Commonwealth states joined Tanzania in breaking relations. Seven other states sporadically followed suit. There, the bandwagon was brought to a stop owing in large part to the efforts of Kenyatta of Kenya, Obote of Uganda and the Emperor of Ethiopia.

All in all, the O.A.U. intervention was a fractious and melancholy affair. Still, it had a pronounced impact on Harold Wilson – whose reaction in turn brought new danger to Zambia.

---

* Nothing more was heard of an O.A.U. military effort after the visit to Zambia in February of a military mission headed by Major General Aferi, Ghana's Chief of Staff. Nigeria and the U.A.R. were also represented. They stayed long enough to become impressed with the difficulties of a military venture launched from Zambia across the Zambezi, then retired to Addis Ababa for further consultation. On 22 February, President Nkrumah stopped in Cairo and exchanged views with President Nasser on how Africa might mobilize for military action against Rhodesia. Nkrumah was on his ill-fated mission to North Vietnam. Two days later, with the military mission still in consultation, a coup in Ghana rendered homeless and impotent Africa's most vocal advocate for an O.A.U. military solution.

Zambia at the Brink

When he decided that he would fly to New York on 15 December and address the United Nations the following day, Wilson could not have known precisely how far Britain's position in Africa and possibly within the Commonwealth would deteriorate. He needed a bold new move to stop the rot. His consternation must have increased with his virtually unprecedented reception, for when he mounted the rostrum to address the General Assembly some one hundred delegates from a score of African countries ostentatiously left the hall. Of the African Commonwealth countries only the delegation from Malawi remained in its place. Zambia meanwhile was calling again for military intervention in Rhodesia. Kaunda announced he was sending top-level missions to Washington and Moscow. And when Cledwyn Hughes, Britain's Minister of State for Commonwealth Affairs, arrived in Lusaka on the very date the O.A.U. had designated for severing relations with Britain a diplomatic chill gripped the Zambian capital and Kaunda remained unavailable for four days. 'If they have come', Kaunda told the *Guardian*'s Commonwealth correspondent, referring to Hughes's team, 'to give us the answer we need on Kariba that is fine, but if [Hughes] avoids facing up to the problem of securing the south bank and the power station then there is nothing to discuss.'

Immediately following his encounter at the U.N., Prime Minister Wilson hurried to a meeting with President Johnson in Washington. The time had come, he told the American President as the two men conversed at the White House, to carry out the oil embargo against Rhodesia alluded to in the security Council resolution passed almost one month before. But, Wilson explained, Britain needed American support not only to help stop the flow of oil to Rhodesia but to assure continued supplies for Zambia. The latter could only be done by airlift. For Wilson, American participation was highly desirable to help defray costs, mobilize equipment, and make British policy more palatable to Zambia. Just as important, U.S. involvement would also strengthen Wilson's position in facing hostile Opposition benches in Parliament. At that very moment, Conservative M.P.s were circulating a motion censuring Wilson for his Rhodesia policy. It would attract 100 signatures.

Johnson was impressed with Wilson's presentation, and with the British Prime Minister's apparent vigour and imagination in attacking a most complex issue. Rhodesia was clearly a British problem. Nonetheless the American President was inclined to join the oil blockade and participate in the Zambian airlift. These actions would

be consistent with the general pattern of Anglo-American co-operation and Johnson, for his part, no doubt hoped that he could continue
to count on Wilson to curb the most extreme demands of Labour
backbenchers who were by now openly opposed to U.S. policies in
Vietnam. In addition, the Zambian airlift would demonstrate American sympathy for that sensitive African state. It might also help to
mitigate President Kaunda's disenchantment occasioned by the
obvious disinterest of the White House in the Tan-Zam rail link.

In Lusaka, Cledwyn Hughes waited impatiently for word from
Washington. On 17 December, George Brown, Britain's Acting
Prime Minister in Wilson's absence, telephoned from London to the
British High Commission in Zambia. Hughes was summoned to the
phone. The connection was poor and the two men had to shout so
loud as to make the intervening apparatus almost unnecessary.
Through the static Brown explained that word had just been flashed
from across the Atlantic: Britain and America had agreed to an oil
embargo against Rhodesia and an oil airlift for Zambia, subject to
Zambia's concurrence.

Kaunda earlier had urged a tough sanctions policy including oil.
But it was then assumed that sanctions affecting Zambia and British
material assistance would go hand in hand. Though Britain over the
last several days had indeed assumed a much more positive position
on preparing Zambia for 'contingencies', Zambia remained
appallingly vulnerable.* If oil were cut off to Rhodesia, Rhodesia
would in turn cut off oil to Zambia. Approximately seventeen oil
wagons a day rumbled across the bridge at Victoria Falls carrying
fuel from Rhodesia to meet Zambian needs. No other source or
transport route could fill this requirement except of course an airlift.
The prospect suddenly filled the Zambians with alarm.

The Zambian Cabinet, confronted with the imminent embargo,
called in the Secretary-General of the newly formed Zambian
Contingency Planning Organization, Kenneth Knaggs. He reviewed
the grim facts. There was no more than 8,000 tons of fuel (petroleum,
oil and lubricants) in the entire country, less than two weeks' supply
under normal consumption. Experts had advised that a viable
rationing system should be based on a minimum of two-month
stocks held in reserve. According to projections rationed use would
continue to outstrip the build-up of supplies during the dangerous
period when both the airlift and the new surface routes were being
developed to the point where by mid January stocks would have fallen
below 1,000 tons – less than two days' consumption! Everyone
around the Cabinet table knew that at stake was not only the intricate

* See above pp. 86–92.

industrial mechanism of the Copperbelt, but the willingness of already edgy whites to stay on at their jobs. A disabling petrol ration over an extended period of time might cause an exodus of expatriates from both government and industry. The Cabinet decided that Zambia's minimal monthly requirements under rationing must be set at 14,000 tons, not at 10,000 tons as proposed by London. (Normal consumption ran to about 17,000 tons.) The British representatives agreed to make a 'best endeavour' to meet the expanded goal. The embargo was announced that night in London. The next day, 18 December, Rhodesia cut off oil to Zambia. Kaunda in the meantime himself conveyed to President Johnson the urgency of American participation in the oil airlift which shortly was to become an airborne lifeline sustaining the economy of the young African nation.

It was an extraordinary situation. Not only the economy of a country but quite possibly its political viability were placed in jeopardy in order that a rebellion in a neighbouring country might be defeated and the rights and duties of a third country might be upheld. In all of this Zambia was an innocent bystander. It was of course also an interested party, for Kaunda considered the Rhodesian rebellion a moral affront to the African people and a grave danger to Zambia. It entrenched a regime determined to maintain in perpetuity the rule of a tiny white minority in a preponderantly black state which sat astride Zambia's vital transport links to the sea. If Rhodesia in rebellion were a threat, corresponding risks must be run to help put the rebellion down. Kaunda and his Cabinet, however, had no great confidence that oil sanctions unaccompanied by other means would realize anything more than hardship for Zambia. 'Slow torture,' Kapwepwe called it. But Britain offered nothing else. Zambia could hardly afford to say 'No', Kaunda reasoned, as this might tempt Britain to lay the failure of its policy at Zambia's door. So Kaunda went along – deeply angered that his friends in London should have placed him in such an unenviable position.

⌒　　　⌒　　　⌒

Cledwyn Hughes stood at Lusaka airport on 19 December when the first two R.A.F. Britannias arrived, each carrying 3,000 gallons of oil. One plane swung too sharply from the runway to the parking apron and mired a wheel in the soft surface. It was an inauspicious start of a difficult, dangerous operation. Over the next weeks the build-up was painfully slow. Airport facilities were inadequate and soon began to deteriorate under the constant stress. Following the arrival of the last flight each day, labourers spread out over the runways working at night to repair cracks that had opened under the wheels of planes, the weight of whose precious cargo sometimes exceeded by double the rated capacity of the tarmac strips. Before the end of December a Royal Canadian Air Force C-130 arrived with a token load of oil. Soon four of these huge cargo carriers from Canada began shuttling between the Congolese capital of Leopoldville (later Kinshasa) and Zambia. Early in the new year, America joined the effort. Two cargo-carrying Boeing 707s, each capable of handling close to 30 tons in pay load had been hired by the U.S. Government. No airport in Zambia could receive jet planes of this size and they had to fly to nearby Elizabethville (later Lubumbashi) in Katanga and the drums of fuel were then transported overland to the Copperbelt.

The airlift was meant to bridge the gap until alternative surface routes could be developed. Now at last plans drawn up long before began to be put into action. Rented lorries started moving south over the Great North Road, renamed the 'hell run', filled with drums of petrol and diesel oil. Oil tankers were ordered from Britain, and oil wagons from Japan. Locomotives were needed to move oil products by rail from Beira to the rail head in Malawi, from which the fuel would be trucked into Zambia. Nigeria had five locomotives on order and agreed to release them to service Zambia's emergency. A storage depot had to be established at the Malawi rail head at Salima. The Malawi Government gave the contract to a South African firm. Zambia paid the bill. Work moved painfully forward at the tiny port of Mpulungu at the foot of Lake Tanganyika. Giant deflatable rubber and nylon tanks with capacities of nearly 100,000 gallons were flown in by chartered aircraft to establish an instant storage depot for fuels transported by lake steamer and barge. Somewhat later hundreds of smaller collapsible rubber tanks would be fitted like huge black sausages on trucks and trailers. Carrying fuel from the Tanzanian capital into Zambia it was inevitable that they would be called 'Dar es Salaamis'.

At the outset problems accumulated faster than solutions as the staff of the Zambian Contingency Planning Organization laboured around the clock to keep fuel supplies from falling dangerously behind tightly curtailed consumption. Tens of thousands, then hundreds of thousands, of steel drums had to be brought to dispensing depots in the coastal cities which were attempting to service Zambia's needs. The first emergency supply came down from Aden by a British naval frigate, creating near panic among politically sensitive Tanzanians as Her Majesty's warship arrived in Dar es Salaam harbour. Drums were purchased as far away as India and as close at hand as South Africa. Tanzania refused to unload any South African products, however, and the drums had to be sent to the Portuguese port of Beira for delivery to Zambia through Malawi – only then to be shipped on return trips to Tanzania for refilling.

Everywhere along the complex routes crises emerged and brushes with disaster became an everyday occurrence. As the precious petrol jostled over the week-long trek to Zambia down the 'hell run', seams in the steel drums opened causing a loss of as much as 50 per cent of the cargo. Crashes often resulted in a fiery pyre for the unfortunate drivers, close to 100 of whom lost their lives before the operation was done. At the Isoka fuel dump in northern Zambia on the Great North Road, management at one point broke down entirely. An official from Lusaka flew in to find dozens of lorries waiting to unload at the chaotic depot. Each driver was crouched by the side of his loaded vehicle cooking his breakfast over an open fire on the oil-soaked ground. Some 20,000 drums of petroleum products were piled nearby!

At the beginning the ration in Zambia was less than a gallon a week for the average private motorist. Some thirteen commercial passenger flights were cancelled to save fuel. Bicycle sales increased fourfold. Diplomats curbed their cars and began pedalling. Nonetheless the supplies dwindled faster than the still tiny airlift and the primitive surface routes could bring in the fuel. By the end of the first week in January, petrol pumps in Zambia went dry and the country's stocks fell to the predicted 1,000 ton level a full week early. This, however, proved to be the low point. Supply routes, both air and land, gradually developed momentum and stocks slowly began to accumulate. The American and Canadian airlifts did not terminate, however, until 30 April 1966;* the British continued for some months after that. Nor was rationing formally lifted until Zambia had completed an oil pipeline running 1,049 miles from Dar es Salaam to the Copperbelt. It was built by an Italian firm (having first been turned down by the British as 'unrealistic') in an unbelievable seventeen months and a cost of £16 million ($45 million). At the end of August 1968, the first oil through the pipeline reached Zambia, thirty-two months after the embargo began.

ᵔ   ᵔ   ᵔ

---

* Some idea of the scope of the operation may be gained by citing statistics from the American lift. Two Boeing 707s, often making three round trips a day and carrying nearly 30 tons in pay load, transported a total of 68,921 drums, amounting to 12,115 short tons or 3,639,028 U.S. gallons. For the air transportation alone, costs ran close to 40p (or well over $1.00) a gallon. More fuel was actually consumed by the planes than was transported by them. Since however the aircraft were fuelled on the coast for their round trip, there was no drain on Zambia's scarce reserves.

Britain's oil embargo against Rhodesia whiplashed Zambia in another respect. Not only did Smith immediately stop the movement of petroleum north of the Zambezi but on 19 December he announced a hundredfold increase in taxes on coal shipped out of Rhodesia. The tax jump was from 5p to £5 (14c to $14) per ton! Smith estimated that from sales to Zambia and the Congo the tax would bring in a whopping £7 million ($20 million) per year in new revenues. He said that he regretted that this action brought hardship to Zambia rather than to the real culprit, Great Britain, even though Zambia had foolishly allowed itself to be talked into supporting Britain's punitive sanctions programme. 'If it has not been appreciated up to the present,' the rebel Prime Minister declared, 'I hope it will be now, that the more we are attacked the more determined, indeed the more defiant, we become.'

Kaunda was convinced that Rhodesia would now do everything possible to destroy Zambia. His first reaction was to give no ground. If Smith persisted in thus holding Zambia to ransom, Zambia would respond by imposing a total embargo against Rhodesia. It was learned that Kaunda would give his answer to Smith in a broadcast at 10.00 p.m. on 22 December. Again advice from London was filled with caution. The Americans, who had been working closely with Zambian planners on the airlift and overland supply routes, were equally apprehensive. For Zambia was in no position to cut all economic and commercial ties with Rhodesia unless it wished to commit economic suicide. At State House in Lusaka attention turned to the precise form Zambia's retaliation might take. There was the possibility, not of a total embargo, but of curtailing all copper shipments. But it seemed likely that only one-third of Zambia's production could exit by alternative routes. The balance would have to be stockpiled, valued at well over £100 million (or approximately $300 million) per annum at current market prices, whereas the denial to Rhodesia of copper traffic would cost the regime only £5 million ($14 million) in rail carrying charges. Also considered was the possibility of diverting, say, 20 per cent of Zambia's copper traffic, or cutting Zambia's imports from Rhodesia by an amount equal to the new tax on coal. But either of these expedients might set in motion a ruinous round of economic retaliation with Zambia almost certain to be the loser.

As the time for Kaunda's broadcast approached it was not clear – perhaps not even to the President himself – what he would say. He arrived at the studio at 10.05 p.m. and took his seat before the microphone. 'Should [Smith] persist in trying to collect these illegal extra charges,' he told the nation at the close of his brief message, 'we shall, as and when appropriate, take further measures in order to show that the Smith efforts to threaten and blackmail us will fail utterly.' It was an ultimatum without a time limit and a threat without a penalty.* Kaunda had no choice. And Zambia's very impotence added to his frustration and his inner fury. Oil supplies were cut. Coal supplies were threatened. All in the interest of a sanctions programme of questionable effect.

The U.D.I. time bomb, its explosive lodged in Zambia, continued to tick. From Kaunda's perspective, the situation was surely critical. But 'our friends reply "caution",' he confided sadly. 'Time is running out; let all our friends get together, crush the rebels and, if in the process Zambia is hurt, help Zambia afterwards.'

Deeply disturbed, he pondered on another occasion Zambia's efforts to construct a non-racial society on the borders of white-ruled Southern Africa. With careful preparation and great exertion the experiment had a good chance of success. Now, however, U.D.I. brought to the surface the old antagonisms. Many Zambian ex-patriates were sympathetic to Smith. African emotions were aroused. Racial violence lay just beneath the surface. The slightest spark could ignite this emotional dry tinder. He had appealed to leaders of the white community within Zambia to publish a statement in support of the Government. No one had stepped forward. Poignantly Kaunda concluded that if Harold Wilson 'could sit in my chair for only five minutes' he would fully understand the urgency of the issues at stake.

In London, as it happened, policy toward Zambia was taking a remarkable turn. At the height of the coal tax crisis Britain urged not only patience and caution but stressed that the timing of Zambia's response was all-important. Wait until sanctions have begun to bite in Rhodesia, London insisted, and until preparations were more advanced in Zambia. Co-ordination with Britain was indispensable and premature action would be dangerously abortive. *But at the right time Zambia might deal a 'lethal blow' to Smith.* It was vaguely suggested that the right time might come around the end of January or shortly thereafter. Among the *cogniscienti* in London an inelegant phrase was coined to describe the new British policy.

---

* Zambia's only direct countermove to Smith's coal tax came two days later when Lusaka announced it would require advance payment in dollars for all Zambian exports to Rhodesia. A similar exaction by Rhodesia on Zambia had been imposed a few days before. Zambia also announced that henceforth payments to the Central African Power Corporation which ran Kariba and to Rhodesia Railways would be remitted to their offices in Zambia and that the Zambian Government would permit the release to Rhodesia of monies only to cover operating expenses, not profits. This was soon to precipitate a new crisis in Zambian–Rhodesian relations.

'The Quick Kill'

On 6 January 1966, the London *Sun* carried on its front page an 'exclusive' headline, 'Wilson's Timetable for Defeat of Rebel Regime'. The story said that H.M. Government was confident that it could destroy the illegal regime by the end of March when oil sanctions would have brought the country virtually to a standstill, at which time Zambia would deliver the 'final blow' – a complete ban on imports from Rhodesia. Secret plans were under way to tide Zambia over a 'few weeks' until normal conditions were restored. As the Smith regime began to crumble, the Governor, Sir Humphrey Gibbs, would order Smith to leave his official residence. If Smith refused, a 'police operation' might become necessary and Sir Humphrey would seek assurances from the Rhodesian Army that they would not resist a token British force.

The new policy, described by the *Sun* with considerable accuracy, had begun to emerge within the offices of the British Prime Minister more than a month before. In the opening weeks of the crisis Wilson had moved cautiously, abjuring force and seeking consensus in Parliament. By the end of November it was apparent that the initial measures were inadequate respecting not only the Rhodesian crisis but, more immediately important, the crisis created by Rhodesia for Britain's relations with Zambia, the Commonwealth and Africa in general. Accordingly, sanctions would now be stiffened. A small military unit would be positioned in Zambia. Certain contingency preparations at last would get under way. Quite possibly Zambia itself could be positioned to join the sanctions club, imposing severe new pressures on Rhodesia. The British Prime Minister was heard to say something about a 'quick kill'.

Meanwhile, officials in London were developing an elaborate organizational structure for handling operations and plans respecting Rhodesia and attendant problems in Zambia. It was capstoned by what the press referred to as the 'Rhodesia Group' in the cabinet, the membership of which generally included the Prime Minister, the Foreign, Defence and Commonwealth Secretaries, the Chancellor of the Exchequer, the Minister for Economic Affairs, the President of the Board of Trade, the Lord Chancellor (Leader of the House of Lords), and the Attorney General. Sir Burke Trend, Secretary to the Cabinet, and Sir Saville Garner (now Lord Garner), Permanent Under-Secretary of the Commonwealth Relations Office and head of the British Diplomatic Service, also sat in. Under this ministerial group there was convened the Official Committee on Sanctions against Rhodesia, known to the bureaucracy by the initials 'R.S.'.

Though chaired by a Minister (the Minister of State for Common-wealth Affairs, Cledwyn Hughes and later Judith Hart), it was composed only of civil servants who were drawn from a number of Ministries representing a wide range of competences. The 'R.S.' was answerable directly to the Prime Minister, not to the senior Minister in the Commonwealth Office, Arthur Bottomley, whom Wilson had bypassed. A third committee chaired by Sir Saville was designed to process policy recommendations on purely political matters which then went before the Rhodesia Group in the Cabinet.

The foregoing were all 'talks' or policy committees. There was in addition an operational committee called the Rhodesia Unit which was responsible for executing policy. Assigned to this group were officers representative of all Ministries concerned with the development, implementation and impact of sanctions against Rhodesia as well as contingency preparations for Zambia. It was chaired by William (later, Sir William) Nield who for this purpose had been moved from the Department of Economic Affairs (D.E.A.) to the Cabinet Office at the Prime Minister's elbow. The D.E.A. had earlier assumed a prominent role in these matters in part because George Brown, then Secretary of State for Economic Affairs as well as Deputy Prime Minister, fancied himself as a Czar in the field of economic warfare. Also Wilson thought this assignment too much for the Commonwealth people to handle. Through Nield the influ-ence of D.E.A. staff remained substantial. As time went on, Nield became perhaps the single most influential official helping to develop Wilson's policies, including now the 'quick kill'.

The new strategy, which evolved in London during the first half of December, would enable Zambia to invoke an embargo against Rhodesia after about six weeks of intensive preparations and then would sustain the Zambian economy on a 'care and maintenance' basis for possibly as long as six months (this estimate was later reduced to two or three months) while Ian Smith's regime was battered under the combined weight of Zambian, British and hope-fully worldwide sanctions. Zambia's contribution was considered critically important because 30 per cent of Rhodesia's foreign revenue derived from the sale of goods and services to Zambia, some £35 million (or almost $100 million) a year.

It was an audacious even reckless *scenario*, so incredible as to raise the most serious questions as to why it was considered at all, let alone accepted at the highest levels in London. Underlying it were the following assumptions, each subject to grave doubt. First, sanctions against Rhodesia would constitute a psychological wallop sufficient to call some alternative political grouping quickly into being. Eminent personalities in Salisbury including the Governor were indeed predicting that if Britain hit hard enough an opposition would build up and Smith might well be out in three months. Second, South Africa and Portugal would not intervene to salvage the Rhodesian economy. Third, and most astonishing of all, Zambia could quickly be positioned to withstand the shock of cutting all economic links to Rhodesia, and could then be mothballed with its imports reduced to about one-quarter the normal flow while the corrosive effects of sanctions took their toll in Rhodesia. It was a little as if Kaunda and Smith were to see who could hold his breath the longer, a rather one-sided contest since no one believed that Zambia could be held on 'care and maintenance' longer than three months at the most. (The planners also noted that if the contest lasted longer than that, Britain too would be in trouble as British copper reserves would run out and the flow of copper from Zambia would remain curtailed.) What in the meantime would have happened to Zambia's already skittish white population and to an incendiary racial situation was evidently not examined.

The plan belied all the sober evidence collected by survey teams and contingency planners as to the time-consuming difficulties of disengaging Zambia from dependence on Rhodesia. It was at cross-purposes with Wilson's earlier concern to keep Zambia from a high-risk confrontation with the rebel regime. It may have occurred to him that the best way to prevent an irrational Zambian move was to include Lusaka in some grand strategy which at the right moment would permit Zambia to play its appropriate role. This would have been logical, even desirable. But the 'quick kill' went well beyond such a measured approach. In the excitement of the moment, Wilson seemed suddenly to be gambling on long shots. His experts, in some cases perhaps chosen for this purpose, told him what he most wanted to hear: force would not have to be used; economic pressures would achieve political results; oil sanctions could be enforced; Zambia with a minimum of preparation could deny Rhodesia 30 per cent of its export trade, finishing off the rebellion swiftly.* To their credit, high ranking American officials scoffed when presented with this fanciful picture. It was a classic instance of the policy wish fathering the intelligence estimate.

When Cledwyn Hughes arrived in Lusaka in mid December to implement the oil embargo and start the airlift, he brought with him a

---

* Dr. Dudley Seers in his contribution to *Crisis in the Civil Service* (edited by Hugh Thomas) writes: 'I was present when the official who had been largely responsible for some of these phantasies [about 'quick kill'], rather steeply told an official committee that he prepared them because this was the picture he thought the Ministers wanted!'

formidable team of officials captained by a Parliamentary Secretary in the Department of Economic Affairs, Maurice Folcy. An engaging and deeply concerned Irishman, Foley had been a close friend in happier days of many Zambian Cabinet Ministers including President Kaunda. Hughes and Foley were determined not only to win Zambia's agreement to the oil embargo but now at last to get on with contingency preparations. Zambia must be put into play quickly. 'Some corners must be cut,' they said. 'Some risks must be run.' In the nature of the situation the risks appeared to be more Zambian than British.

When the Zambians pointed this out and asked for guarantees that Zambia would emerge from the contest with its economy fully intact, the British demurred, stating that it was not certain how serious the impact of economic warfare would be on their own already ailing economy. Nonetheless they made clear that Britain was determined to do everything possible to assist Zambia. An agreement was reached on the division of costs for contingency preparations, Zambia covering 'internal' and the United Kingdom 'external' expenditures. Foley then began signing a wad of vouchers, by some reports totalling some £3 million (or over $8 million) in two days. The funds were mainly to cover the purchase of British rolling stock to service Zambia's alternative transport routes and otherwise to improve their capacities as quickly as possible. A joint statement at the end of the Hughes–Foley mission committed the United Kingdom to £3.5 million ($9.8 million) for contingency preparations in addition to bearing the cost of the British airlift.

It was a gung-ho performance. On 18 December the *Times of Zambia* ran a heady account of things to come based on an 'authoritative source', which of course was Cledwyn Hughes himself.

> 'The Anglo-American embargo on the oil supply for Rhodesia will be followed by a mass airlift of fuel and other essential supplies [including coal] for Zambia. . . . The airlift . . . will involve scores of heavy cargo aircraft flying round the clock into Zambia's three airports.
>
> 'The Benguela railway will be boosted to its maximum capacity together with emergency surface routes to Tanzania and Malawi, to keep enough essentials coming for Zambia's copper mines and other essential industries in production. . . .
>
> 'Britain is convinced, the *Times of Zambia* was told, that the new tough barrage of sanctions will begin to show its effect in Rhodesia during the next crucial three weeks. By March, say sanctions experts, visible cracks which might admit "a Governor's party" to oppose Smith will appear. . . .'

Gradually London's new energetic approach both to sanctions and to contingency preparations restored somewhat Kaunda's confidence in Britain's intentions. This was apparent in his press conference of 30 December which presented a careful balance between Zambia's preference for United Kingdom military action and Zambia's prospective participation in Britain's economic sanctions effort. To the newsmen the President said he was still convinced that the Rhodesian situation could be solved only by a military operation. But in this instance Britain had chosen economic sanctions. Zambia could not sit down and say it would not participate. He would be happy if sanctions alone would do the job. Zambia would give all the help it could to make them a success. But if sanctions failed, Kaunda stressed, let military operations take place.

There was also beinning to be apparent in Lusaka a growing sense of confidence in Zambia's own position particularly *vis-à-vis* Rhodesia. On New Year's Day Ian Smith offered to accept crude petroleum for Zambia at Rhodesia's refinery, process it and ship it north. (While the offer was not made contingent on providing a share for Rhodesia's own use, it is hard to see how this could have been avoided.) Smith also said he would suspend the coal tax. Kaunda scorned the oil offer, but Smith nonetheless retracted the surcharge on coal which Kaunda interpreted as a sign of weakness – wrongly as it turned out. But the psychological impact in Lusaka for the moment was great. The oil airlift also helped. As the oil drums began to roll into Zambia, Salisbury announced petrol rationing and it began to look at least momentarily, that the pinching shoe might soon be on the Rhodesian foot.

In London the Whitehall strategists were brimming with optimism as the new year opened. Their plans they said were realistic. The possibility that Smith might survive was incredible. The question was not whether the rebel regime would succumb but only when. H.M. Government was fully committed. Oil sanctions were going well. Reserves in Rhodesia were put at eight to ten weeks, perhaps stretched to twelve to fifteen weeks by rationing. Acute transportation and distribution problems in the rebel territory could be expected soon; increasing shortages and unemployment would be likely to arise in February; and the period of maximum pressure would begin with the opening of new tobacco sales in March. Zambia's contingency preparations and the closing of the Zambian–Rhodesian frontier would have to be geared to this schedule.

Time then was of the essence. South African and Portuguese neutrality could not be expected to last indefinitely. Pressures would rise in both Lisbon and Pretoria to support Smith if it appeared he had any chance of success. Moreover, London planners re-emphasized, both Zambia and Britain would be badly hurt if Smith were not brought down in two or three months after Zambia joined the sanctions effort and was placed in its 'care and maintenance' limbo. The first priority was to increase the capacity of the alternative surface routes to the point where, combined with the airlift and whatever coal could be mined in the Gwembe valley, they could meet Zambia's minimum needs set at about 45,000 tons of imports per month.

It did not seem to matter that President Kaunda had said that even a limited moratorium on economic activity in Zambia would be catastrophic; nor that an American economic survey team had just calculated that necessary minimum improvements on the Great North Road alone would take four to six months; nor indeed that Zambia even then was in a headlong race with disaster straining every transport resource simply to meet its needs for oil imports.

From Lagos to Lusaka

One major complication remained in orchestrating these finely drawn and delicately balanced plans. The Commonwealth was about to convene in the Nigerian capital of Lagos to discuss the Rhodesian crisis. For Britain the outcome was unpredictable as with all such meetings where emotions were highly charged. The proposal for a Commonwealth conference had originated with Nigeria's talented Prime Minister, Sir Abubakar Tafawa Balewa. Sir Abubakar was deeply disturbed by the O.A.U. resolution to break relations with Britain and wanted to devise a way to allow the African states to extricate themselves from their predicament. A timely Commonwealth initiative might do the trick. He flew to London on the night of 13 December and lunched with Wilson the next day. The Nigerian's plan broke precedent. He wanted the Commonwealth to meet solely to discuss the Rhodesian issue. It had never before been convened to deal with one specific political issue. And he wanted the conference located not in the British capital, where it had invariably met in the past, but in Africa – specifically in Lagos on 10 January.

Wilson's reaction was mixed. Until now he had taken the view that no useful purpose would be served by a Commonwealth conference on Rhodesia. He could not afford to be placed in the dock pilloried by African Ministers. That would hardly go down well with the British electorate and the desirability of holding a new election as quickly as possible was never far from the Prime Minister's mind. Nor did he wish to run any risk of losing control of the Rhodesian issue for which Britain alone had constitutional jurisdiction. Out of

London, he would not be in the chair and the course of the debate would be hard to control. At the same time he recognized that Sir Abubakar's device might prove useful in attenuating the effect of the unfortunate O.A.U. resolution and there was point in giving support to the Nigerian's effort to placate Commonwealth Governments in Africa. On 6 January, four days before the conference opened, Wilson announced that he personally would attend. His decision was surely influenced by the fact that the oil embargo seemed to be working well. As *The Times* put it, 'the United Kingdom has nothing to hide and something to report. . . . Sanctions, without destroying Zambia, may force a change of opinion in Rhodesia soon.'

Commonwealth Ministers converged on Lagos to find strict security precautions in force. There was violence in the Western Region of Nigeria and the distant crackle of gunfire was in the air. The conference opened with Sir Abubakar in the chair. It was his last function as an international statesman. He would shortly be lost in the convulsion which would rack his country for the next four years.

Wilson must have been relieved that at Lagos two of the Commonwealth's most militant voices were still. Neither Kwame Nkrumah of Ghana nor Julius Nyerere of Tanzania were at the conference table, having only just broken diplomatic relations with Britain. Sir Albert Margai, Prime Minister of Sierra Leone, had, however, stopped in Accra to consult with Nkrumah en route to Lagos. He now thundered militant denunciations and demands for the immediate use of force. With less bombast so too did Uganda's Prime Minister Milton Obote and Vice President Reuben Kamanga of Zambia. (President Kaunda had remained in Lusaka.) The majority, however, held to the more moderate line set forth by Sir Abubakar's opening speech which placed emphasis on planning for the post-rebellion phase in Rhodesia.

Wilson himself, in top parliamentary form, put forward his view of the harsh realities of going to war with Rhodesia and gradually appeased African impatience and suspicion while winning a grudging reprieve for his policy of sanctions. The meeting ended with an agreed *communiqué* and an accolade from the new Commonwealth Secretary-General, Arnold Smith, who described the issue as 'the Commonwealth v. Ian Smith' and the outcome as a 'great success'.

So it was, surely from Britain's point of view. There had been no walk-outs. No deadlines had been established, though it was agreed that a new meeting would be convened in July if the rebellion were not ended before then. No requirement to use force had been imposed, though it was accepted that its use could not be precluded if this proved necessary to restore law and order. Britain's jurisdictional authority was not called into question, though the delegates acknowledged at the same time that 'the problem was of wider concern to Africa, the Commonwealth and the world'. And efforts to invoke mandatory sanctions at the U.N. were for the time being turned aside. Two continuing committees were established, the first to monitor the effects of sanctions and the special needs of Zambia with the right to recommend reconvening the Prime Ministers' conference or recourse to the United Nations, and the second to co-ordinate assistance in training Rhodesian Africans.

Famous Last Words?

RHODESIA
'It will be over in weeks . . .'

Beyond this, Wilson made two statements which were duly recorded in the *communiqué*. He said that following the termination of the rebellion 'a period of direct rule would be needed' in Rhodesia. (How long a period was hotly debated without reaching agreement.) This would eventuate in a fully representative constitutional conference 'for the purpose of recommending a constitution leading to a majority rule on a basis acceptable to the people of Rhodesia as a whole'. Also noted was a statement made by the ebullient Mr. Wilson which took even some of his closest advisers by complete surprise.

On the expert advice available to him, the British leader said, 'the cumulative effects of the economic and financial sanctions might well bring the rebellion to an end within a matter of weeks rather than months'. More than three years later, speaking on a B.B.C. television newscast at the close of another Prime Ministers' conference where yet again the still unresolved Rhodesian rebellion had been debated, Wilson said of his statement at Lagos: 'One always regrets being wrong. It was wrong, yes, but it was not wrong on the basis of the evidence available at that time.'

Wilson boarded his plane at midnight in Lagos and flew directly to Zambia. Kaunda and his Ministers were on the tarmac when the R.A.F. Comet touched down in Lusaka shortly after daybreak. It was now 13 January 1966. Following his success at Lagos Wilson was determined to maintain his stride. He was moving now more boldly and quickly than perhaps even his most enterprising planners. In the bureaucracy his rapid pillar-to-post actions and decisions were being described as 'instant Wilson'. So far it had been a virtuoso performance, bringing along the British public and (however reluctantly) the Parliamentary Opposition, containing frontal assaults in the U.N. and the O.A.U., mollifying the Commonwealth – and now he had come to sensitive, critical Zambia. The short figure moved purposefully to greet the graceful and handsome Zambian President, then passed along the hastily assembled reception line to the waiting motorcade.

Soon Wilson's party had settled down on one side of the cabinet table in Kaunda's office in State House. Opposite them were the most senior members of the Zambian Government. As he had in Lagos, Wilson reviewed for Kaunda the worsening situation in Rhodesia and said that there was a good prospect there would be no fuel by the end of February. It was now important to agree on a cut-off date for Zambia. It would be a knock-out blow delivered when Smith was already wobbling. Following the cut-off, everything would stop except coal. An airlift for coal was impossible, Wilson said.

Then, once more surprising some of his most senior advisers, Wilson put forward 15 February as the target date for Zambia to implement the final phase of the 'quick kill' policy. It was barely a month away. Zambia was still reeling under the impact of oil sanctions. Kaunda and his colleagues were openly sceptical. Wilson however was adamant in his estimate of the coming distress in Rhodesia, saying in effect, 'You can take it from me.' Kaunda replied that in that case Zambia would design its policies accordingly and do what it could to get ready. Kaunda insisted that the United Kingdom must take responsibility for returning Zambia's economy to its pre-U.D.I. status. Wilson promised that Britain would help in so far as it could. At this point Wilson returned once more to the desirability of positioning a small British military contingent in Zambia. Kaunda demurred as he had before. British forces would be permitted into the country only en route to Rhodesia. The two however agreed that staff talks would be useful and for this purpose Wilson quickly arranged for Major-General John Willoughby, British Commander in the Middle East, to visit Zambia.

To the press before departing Wilson said 'our joint efforts can be planned in such a way as to intensify [*sic*] the end of the illegal regime,' to which Kaunda added at a separate press conference that Zambian and British policies were now closer than ever before. For the British Prime Minister it was another notable success. He had at least partly broken through the barrier of Zambian distrust. Back on board the Comet, however, many of Wilson's most senior officials now expressed consternation about the imminent cut-off date. Despite earlier optimistic estimates, they had come to fear that Zambia could not be got ready in time. Wilson dismissed the matter. He had announced his policy and they were now to work toward it.

'The Long Haul'

Throughout the better part of January oil sanctions seemed to be holding firm. Wilson was confident. He had repeatedly and defiantly refused to consider talks with the rebel regime. 'Rhodesia's future course cannot be negotiated with the regime which illegally claims to govern the country,' he told the House of Commons on 25 January.* Mr. Heath took vigorous exception to this formulation, calling it a demand for 'unconditional surrender' and unrealistic.

The surrender Wilson had in mind was not to be accomplished by military means even though attention continued to be given to positioning a small military force in Zambia. Such a force was seen as an adjunct to the 'quick kill' strategy. The military contingent would add a further dimension to psychological pressures on Rhodesia. Moreover it would be useful to have it at the ready to help the Governor maintain order during the period following the collapse of the rebel regime when a new government was being formed. The

---

* On the other hand, while in Lusaka on 13 January, Wilson had telegraphed Governor Gibbs that Commonwealth Secretary Arthur Bottomley was ready to fly to Salisbury and to meet with Smith under the Governor's aegis. Smith made it clear, however, that Bottomley could come only as a private citizen enjoying no special security protection. The initiative was dropped.

possibility was even entertained that the Governor at the right moment could negotiate with senior Rhodesian military officers the peaceful entry of a small British force. Beyond this it might well be necessary to maintain a small number of troops in Rhodesia for the duration of the transitional period when an interim government would be preparing for a return to constitutional rule.

Whatever merit the idea had, Britain never succeeded in gaining Kaunda's acceptance. Major-General Willoughby flew in with his team on 19 January – and out again on the 24th. He had staff talks with his Zambian counterparts, visited Livingstone and stood on the Zambian shore at Kariba where he examined through his field glasses a Rhodesian gun emplacement on the opposite side of the dam wall. Given the pre-emption of airlift capacities by Zambia's oil supplies, and numerous additional logistical difficulties, it was hard to see how more than a single battalion could be maintained. After Willoughby returned to London the proposal quietly disappeared from view.

Nonetheless Wilson confidently elaborated on the transition he envisaged in Rhodesia following the collapse of the rebellion. Gibbs would be asked to form an 'interim Government', Wilson told Parliament on 25 January. It would be responsible to the Governor and would represent 'the widest possible spectrum of public opinion of all races'. Security forces would become the direct responsibility of the Governor. Those under political restriction would be released provided they ensured that their political activities would remain within constitutional bounds. The economy would be restored; educational and training programmes pursued; and procedures introduced to consult the views of the entire population on changes necessary to the resumption of full constitutional government consistent with the five principles – to which Wilson now added a sixth, 'namely, the need to ensure that, regardless of race, there is no oppression of majority by minority or minority by majority'. Pressed by Heath on the delicate question of direct rule, Wilson said 'it was never intended to be direct rule from Whitehall or from Westminster'. Rather the Governor was to be in charge. The newly formed interim Government representative of Rhodesian opinion was to be responsible to him.

It was difficult to make this square with what Wilson, with manifest approval from the African Commonwealth Governments, had said a few days earlier in Lagos, that 'a period of direct rule would be needed'. However the discrepancy did not seem to bother President Kaunda who accepted the Prime Minister's Parliamentary statement as a real step forward and an act of political courage. Preparations in Zambia for the break with Rhodesia were pressed forward. The Contingency Planning Organization prepared an extensive memo on

Zambia's essential requirements for consideration by the Commonwealth Continuing Committee on Sanctions which held its first meeting in London on 25 January. The document, however, indicated that road and truck capacity would not be adequate to move Zambia's essentials, following a complete rupture with Rhodesia, until about mid April. Even that projection, which assumed full Commonwealth support, was wildly optimistic. Nonetheless, Zambian official policy continued to look forward to a cut-off long before April. This made the continuation of the airlifts all the more indispensable as Kaunda now emphasized in diplomatic correspondence.

Still doubts about 15 February were beginning to accumulate. At high levels of the Zambian Government there was increasing talk of the need for some fail-safe system – full assurance that alternative sources for all vital supplies would be forthcoming; or that minimal needs as outlined in the paper sent to the Sanctions Committee would be met; or that force would be used if, following the cut-off, the rebel regime survived long enough to threaten Zambia's economy. But these apprehensions did not yet affect the pace of planning in Zambia. On 5 February the Government approved a proposal put forward by the Contingency Planning Organization for stockpiling essential dry cargo imports. A special committee was formed to examine how copper could be exported by air and surface routes should the rail link through Rhodesia be cut. The United States had offered Zambia the use of its aircraft to carry copper on return trips from Katanga to Leopoldville. On 10 February, President Kaunda told a press conference that 'the deadline' (which had never been announced publicly) still existed. *The Times* of the same date reported that the British Government continued to believe that the oil embargo would topple the regime by the end of March or early April.

Suddenly however headlines in the Zambian press announced that gaping holes were opening in the sanctions dike and fuel began to flow north across the Limpopo River from South Africa. Disillusionment rose almost as rapidly as estimates of Rhodesia's remaining oil reserves. On 14 February Kaunda in a B.B.C. interview noted that 'formidable aid' sent to Rhodesia from South Africa augured poorly for the success of sanctions. It was difficult to see, he concluded, how any means other than military force could reverse U.D.I. 15 February arrived – and nothing happened, to the obvious relief of the British who in the preceding fortnight had had second thoughts about the readiness of Zambia for a rupture and the efficacy of Zambian sanctions against the Smith regime, but were reluctant to reopen the question with Lusaka. Enough aid was now filtering into Rhodesia from South Africa to make the outcome of even a massive Zambian effort uncertain.

London's hopes for swift and massive Zambian participation in sanctions were false hopes, for London's policy had been based on a contradiction. The only way quickly to bring the full force of sanctions into play against Rhodesia was to give Zambia a guarantee that *in extremis* if sanctions were found not to work quickly enough there would be recourse to force – which the sanctions policy was devised in the first place to avoid. Much depended also on the willingness of Rhodesia's white-controlled neighbours to maintain the oil embargo. From the outset British policy as a whole towards the Rhodesian rebellion, and most especially the 'quick kill', had been an intricately designed, delicately balanced house of cards. South Africa had just flicked the bottom one. A bright young planner in the Commonwealth Office, sceptical from the outset about Zambia's capacity to break away from its rebellious neighbour, suggested a new tag for the Rhodesia policy of H.M. Government. Call it, he said, 'the long haul'.

5

Oil 'Spills' in Southern Africa

In rejecting direct intervention against Rhodesia, Harold Wilson made his policy hostage to the actions (and interests) of others. This is the corollary of power exercised indirectly. It is multilateral and collaborative in character. He had hoped for massive Zambian participation in his sanctions programme. That had proved both reckless and unrealistic, though the project, suitably modified, would be mooted again in due course. He had hoped too for tacit support from both South Africa and Portugal, without which his all-important oil embargo would certainly fail.

It would seem essential in this business of organizing the efforts of many participants to accomplish one's own policy objectives that one should know at the outset who is playing on which side. To say the least, South Africa and Portugal were unlikely collaborators in a venture aimed at pushing Rhodesia towards African rule through the application of international sanctions. Once Wilson found this out, he would rush to the United Nations for an unprecedented mandate aimed at Portugal, thereby deeply implicating the world body in his efforts to make sanctions work while at the same time raising some fundamental questions of international law and practice. The upshot was to curtail but not to cut off oil supplies to Rhodesia. To have accomplished the latter would have involved a direct confrontation with South Africa which Wilson was as unwilling to undertake as he was determined to avoid using force against Rhodesia.

All of this was not immediately apparent, however, for at the outset Pretoria and Lisbon masked their interests behind behaviour marked by caution. This aroused intense curiosity as the oil embargo against Rhodesia began to take effect, particularly on the part of South Africa-watchers.

Beit Bridge on the Limpopo

One of these was Laurence Gandar, the courageous editor of the South African *Rand Daily Mail*, an anti-Government paper known throughout the world for its opposition to apartheid. When fragmentary reports began to accumulate that fuel might be starting to move north from South Africa to Rhodesia, Gandar sent one of his most enterprising young journalists, Peter Hazelhurst, to see what was happening.* Hazelhurst disappeared into the Northern Transvaal. At Beit Bridge, the road north crosses the Limpopo River and enters Rhodesia. The *Mail* reporter repeatedly checked all the feeder roads leading to the bridge, keeping track of suspect traffic in oil products. After a time it became clear that efforts were under way to establish a regular petroleum shuttle service to Rhodesia on a commercial basis. Conversations were reported to be taking place between oil company representatives and Government officials. A premium was placed on keeping the matter quiet.

On 5 February, after an intensive two-day surveillance, the *Mail* reported that three to four vehicles a day were making the trip. A picture of a Rhodesian fuel tanker was published with the story. Faintly visible through a thin coat of grey paint was a large 'P', part of the insignia 'B.P.' – the British Petroleum Company, in which H.M. Government held 51 per cent of the shares.† Over the days that followed, the *Mail* continued to report lorries and tankers moving north, their ownership and origins a secret and the depots where

---

* Hazelhurst subsequently became *The Times* correspondent in India.

† B.P. was first into the breach to be followed shortly by Shell and subsequently by other international oil companies. When asked why Britain could not then and there have stopped the traffic, official spokesmen stressed that B.P. in South Africa was registered under South African law and thus was a South African company beyond the reach of British law; the British Government had always scrupulously avoided using its controlling interest to dictate policy to the company, for B.P. would not be permitted to operate in many areas of the world if it were thought to be an agent of the British Government; and if Britain were to have succeeded in shutting down B.P.'s supply operation into Rhodesia other companies would immediately have filled the vacuum. At stake however was the credibility of British intentions and Britain's will. London's failure to use effective pressure against B.P. at the very outset carried far-reaching consequences. (Within Rhodesia, B.P. like many other companies was operating under *force majeure*.)

they had taken on fuel unknown. The flow was small, but disturbing.

Officers in the British Embassy in Pretoria were incredulous. Repeatedly they rang the *Rand Daily Mail* questioning the basis of the stories which in turn they discounted in their dispatches to London. On 12 February, the Embassy established its own observation post at Beit Bridge. Officers maintained a round-the-clock surveillance from a parked car a few yards from the border gate, exciting the displeasure of the South African Government.

Meanwhile Hazelhurst persisted in his investigation. On 16 February a major story broke under the headline, 'Secret Fuel for Smith'. The article estimated that 35,000 gallons of petrol, oil and kerosene were now flowing across Beit Bridge daily. The same tanker that had been pictured on 5 February was back in the news again, though this time the 'B.P.' insignia had been painted out completely. The *Mail* story identified in some detail the vehicles and their routes (they travelled principally at night), the place and method of taking on fuel (huge closed furniture vans, for example, picked up sixty to seventy oil drums each at a depot in Pietersburg) and the general *modus operandi* (the drivers of the big lorries were instructed 'to speak to no one and "at all costs" not to disclose their destinations'). An oil supply scheme was also operating from Mozambique, according to the *Mail*; if true (it was at this time unconfirmed), Rhodesia was receiving about 70,000 gallons a day, or almost enough to meet its rationed consumption. Before long other South African papers were running similar accounts of fuel-running into Rhodesia.

In London, many had argued that South Africa's politically astute and cautious Prime Minister, Dr. Hendrik F. Verwoerd, would stand aside, permitting oil sanctions to take their toll. This was precisely the basis on which Wilson at Lagos had told the Commonwealth that the matter might be dealt with 'in weeks, not months'. During the period following U.D.I., exchanges at high levels between Britain and South Africa confirmed privately what South Africa had been saying openly, that it did not wish to become involved in a dispute between the United Kingdom and Rhodesia, that it wanted to maintain to the fullest degree its relations with both sides including what Verwoerd called 'normal trade', and that it would follow a policy of non-interference avoiding public judgements as to the rights or wrongs of the parties involved. Beyond this Whitehall believed that neither South Africa nor Portugal wished to be implicated in a dispute which Rhodesia might lose. Thus neither had been as forthcoming economically or financially as Rhodesia might have hoped. An assessment published on 25 November by the influential Afrikaans daily paper, *Die Burger*, was very much in this vein. It warned Rhodesia against over-reliance on South Africa. No one yet knew, the editorial noted, what the effect of sanctions would be. 'The Rhodesian economy as it exists today is certainly not designed for prolonged resistance against efforts to break it.' Based on all available evidence *The Times* thought it detected in South Africa an attitude of 'aloof non-interference'.

From the outset however there were other voices which, had they been listened to, might have suggested that South Africa would be inclined to a less precise interpretation of such key phrases as 'non-interference' and 'normal trade'. A few days after U.D.I. (21 November 1965) the Johannesburg *Sunday Times* warned flatly that South Africa could not stand by and see Rhodesia collapse. 'We need to save Rhodesia because in doing so we go a long way to saving ourselves.' A matter of equal importance was stressed by *The Transvaler*: 'Should Rhodesia be able to withstand the application of economic sanctions, it is highly doubtful whether this weapon will ever again be made use of in the future.' For a government apprehensive that one day the U.N. might try to apply sanctions against it, the implication was inescapable.

In point of fact Verwoerd's own statements were open to widely varying interpretations. His New Year's message was a case in point. As always he attacked sanctions, reaffirmed that South Africa would not join in, and spoke once more of maintaining normal relations with Salisbury. At the same time he made no overt declaration of support for Smith's Government. Enigmatically he said only that U.D.I. had created a situation from which South Africa could not escape. Yet, at the end he talked of South Africa's blood relations across the border. 'However others may feel or act toward their kith and kin when their international interests are at stake,' he declared, 'South Africa, on the whole, cannot cold-shoulder theirs.' He went on to say that if black supremacy should be established in Rhodesia, it would endanger the peace and harmony of all Southern Africa. Analysing the speech South African commentators differed markedly. Stanley Uys, an influential columnist for the opposition *Sunday Times*, concluded that there would be only 'routine relations – and no special help' for Rhodesia. *Die Vaderland* on the other hand was certain that Smith's Government would welcome Verwoerd's statement. Obviously it could be played either way.

Verwoerd's caution arose from South Africa's acutely visible position in the world arena. One thing that Verwoerd no doubt meant by 'non-interference' was to do nothing that would invite international interference in South Africa's internal affairs. Despite strong sentiment among many South Africans for a more forthcoming approach to Rhodesia, there had been no diplomatic recognition, no economic missions to Salisbury, no assurances to exporters that earnings in

Rhodesian pounds would be recoverable in South African currency (that would come later), and least of all no sweeping endorsements of white solidarity throughout Southern Africa. While it could be argued that Verwoerd could not afford to see sanctions succeed against Rhodesia (for U.N. pressures might then have become overwhelming to apply sanctions to the heartland of apartheid), neither did he wish to appear the direct cause of their failure. This too might lead to the extension of U.N. sanctions to South Africa, and a possible confrontation with Britain and the United States. Discretion was the better part of valour, even though for the moment Verwoerd opened himself to political attack at home.

It was not long in coming. The Opposition Party's campaign reached its high-water mark when, on 21 January, the South African Parliament opened its final session before General Elections. Almost immediately United Party Leader Sir de Villiers Graaf introduced a motion of no confidence in Verwoerd's Rhodesian policy which, accused Graaf, had failed to grant *de facto* recognition or practical support to Smith's government. 'Are we prepared to stand by and see Rhodesia forced to her knees and chaos created?' Graaf wanted to know in a bitter debate on 25 January. Verwoerd replied that nobody was more sympathetic towards the whites of Rhodesia than was the South African Government. Nonetheless, national interest dictated that the Republic should not be drawn into the conflict if this could be avoided. South Africa should not create unnecessary enemies. Furthermore a non-aligned South Africa would be of more value to Rhodesia than a South Africa directly involved which would then be made a joint target of sanctions and other actions by the adversaries of the Salisbury regime.

Verwoerd then proceeded to introduce a brief gloss on the often-stated policy of non-interference. His declaration revealed a discreet middle ground between open support and no support at all. 'If there are producers or traders', he said, 'who have oil or petrol to sell whether to this country or to the Portuguese, Basutoland, Rhodesia or Zambia, then it is their business and we do not interfere. We do not prevent them from selling. Because, Sir, if we tried to prevent them we would then be participating in a boycott.' Nor would the Government, Verwoerd made clear, prevent South Africans from sending gifts of oil, petrol or other goods to Rhodesia, because that too would be participating in boycotts.

Voluntary-aid organizations were in fact springing up all over South Africa. Verwoerd's own brother, Dr. Len Verwoerd of Stellenbosch, was one of the prime movers. So too was one of the Prime Minister's former Secretaries, Fred Barnard of Pretoria. Coupons were sold in petrol stations throughout the country and the proceeds were used to purchase drums of fuel for Rhodesia. Early in February the first load of free petrol from South Africa (as distinct from the commercial flow mentioned earlier) crossed Beit Bridge and rolled into the Rhodesian industrial city of Bulawayo. It was a modest 6,000 gallons but the psychological impact was real and far-reaching. That evening Wilson's sanctions co-ordinator, Cledwyn Hughes, was at the Commonwealth Office. Working alone into the night, he was brought news that the first voluntary consignment of petrol had reached Rhodesia from South Africa. His heart sank.

Hughes's private pessimism notwithstanding, Britain's public posture remained astonishingly buoyant, kept afloat in part by the sceptical reports that continued to be filed by the British mission in Pretoria. Hughes's senior Minister, Arthur Bottomley, declared on 9 February, 'We are confident that whatever petrol is getting in – and some is getting into the country – it is not enough to enable the economy to survive.' But by mid February, following the *Rand Daily Mail*'s *exposé* and the British Embassy's own surveillance at Beit Bridge, the situation could no longer be dismissed. Britain's Ambassador, Sir Hugh Stephenson, was instructed to call on Foreign Minister Hilgard Muller. They conferred on 16 February. Three days later Harold Wilson called in South Africa's Ambassador, Dr. Carel de Wet, for an interview. In both meetings the British expressed their concern over reports of increased movements of fuel to Rhodesia. Such traffic was inconsistent, the British argued, with the notion of normal trade. Should the abnormal traffic continue, it would be difficult to resist the pressures of those advocating mandatory economic sanctions. Still the public position in London remained optimistic. Reports that Rhodesia was getting nearly enough fuel to break the siege were dismissed as wild exaggerations and 'very clearly highly coloured'. Even at this late date some in Whitehall were disposed to think that many of the stories about oil leaks were fabricated in Salisbury to give the impression abroad that the embargo had failed. During the last week of February, however, press reports from several sources put the average quantities passing Beit Bridge at 40,000 gallons a day.

If doubt remained as to South Africa's policy, it was finally dispelled by Prime Minister Verwoerd when on 28 February he opened his election campaign with an address to a National Party rally in Johannesburg. Turning to the one question which had become central to the whole debate – the definition of normal trade – the Prime Minister asserted flatly that if South Africa had commodities to trade, it would do so regardless of the quantity. He regretted, he said, that his earlier reference to normal trade had been misinterpreted. It did not mean selling only those commodities one had sold before. 'Normal trade means that everyone in competition tries to sell as much as he can. . . . If one sells more, it is not abnormal trade, but better trade.' 'It is no longer clear,' said an editorial in the Johannesburg *Star* on 1 March 1966, 'in what respect the Government's policy differs from that urged upon it by the [opposition] United Party. It has from the start given implicit *de facto* recognition to Mr. Smith's Government by maintaining normal relations with it. It is now prepared to give Rhodesia unlimited trade and aid.'

Meanwhile in neighbouring Mozambique Britain's oil embargo was about to be put to an even more excruciating test.

Tankers Away!

On 29 March 1966, a nondescript oil tanker of Greek registry and modest size, named the *Joanna V*, heaved into view on the front pages of the world press. Dead ahead lay a kind of bathtub nautical drama and an unprecedented action by the United Nations.

The *Joanna V* was the object of one of those labyrinthine commercial intrigues in which the canny and hard-pressed Rhodesians with the help of South African commercial interests came to specialize. In January 1966, an agent for A. G. Morrison Ltd. of Cape Town, contracted with Mr. Nicos Vardinoyannis of Athens for the delivery of a number of cargoes of crude oil to customers to be specified by the South African company. The contract was later expanded to include a total of twenty-seven cargoes, approximately 400,000 tons or about one year's fuel supply for Rhodesia.

On 7 February Vardinoyannis arranged for the charter of a tanker, the *Arietta Venizelos*, from the firm of Venizelos S. A. with port options to be determined once the tanker was at sea. A contract was drawn up between Venizelos and A. G. Morrison on 16 February for the tanker to load 14,000 tons of crude oil at Bandar Mashur in the Persian Gulf and to proceed through the Mediterranean to Rotterdam. As required by the Greek Government and consistent with the Security Council resolution of 20 November 1965, a clause in the contract forbade transshipment of the fuel to Rhodesia. The vessel loaded and set out to sea on 23 February. Rhodesia's hand in these manœuvres was suggested two days before when the Minister of Commerce and Industry in Salisbury, Mr. Bernard Musset, announced that a tanker with oil for Rhodesia would arrive at Beira 'in the foreseeable future'.

While the *Arietta Venizelos* was at mid passage on 8 March Vardinoyannis arranged with Venizelos to purchase the tanker for £400,000 (or $1,120,000, which was almost twice its market value) and the ship passed into the ownership of a Panamanian firm controlled by Vardinoyannis, the Varnicos Corp. Venizelos reportedly was mystified as to who were the real buyers, but 'for money like that who asks questions?' The transaction was closed in New York City on 16 March with an irrevocable letter of credit from Johannesburg. Meanwhile A. G. Morrison, to whom the tanker remained chartered, ordered her to proceed to South Africa. En route she put in at Dakar in West Africa on 15 March, changed her name to the *Joanna V* and was boarded by a new master, one George Vardinoyannis, younger brother of Nicos. By 31 March, having all but circumnavigated the African continent, she found herself 600 miles south of the Mozambique port of Beira and steaming north at five knots an hour. There seemed little doubt that she meant to off-load at Beira where workmen, labouring around the clock, had just finished constructing two new oil storage tanks conveniently located near the terminus of an oil pipeline which ran 189 miles inland to Rhodesia's oil refinery.

Britain's oil embargo depended upon closing three principal routes, the road over Beit Bridge, the rail line through Mozambique originating either in South Africa or the port of Lourenço Marques, and the pipeline at Beira. Portugal controlled the latter two and so became as much the object of British attention as did South Africa. Portuguese interests in the Rhodesian affair were not dissimilar to South Africa's. No more than Pretoria did Lisbon welcome U.D.I., let alone encourage it. One suspects the Portuguese were doubly upset by the rebellion for, unlike South Africa, Portugal had hoped that Rhodesia might in time move towards multiracialism Portuguese-style – a lowering of the colour bar in the social and economic, though not necessarily the political, spheres. For Lisbon U.D.I. meant not only additional unwelcome attention for Southern Africa, but the entrenchment of conservative interests within Rhodesia likely to move that country decisively into South Africa's orbit.

The Portuguese had other concerns. Angola and Mozambique were contiguous to black independent African states. Portugal was already waging a low-level but protracted and expensive campaign against black African guerrillas infiltrating from neighbouring African territories, though not yet from strategically placed Zambia. The Portuguese had good reason to try to develop better relations with independent Africa, and particularly with Kenneth Kaunda. The Rhodesian rebellion would only complicate this effort. For Portugal, like South Africa, could not afford to see sanctions against Rhodesia succeed.

All these considerations for Portugal, as for South Africa, dictated a policy of professed neutrality in Britain's 'domestic' conflict with Rhodesia. In the Portuguese case refuge was sought in Portugal's 'responsibilities' under international law as a seaboard entrepôt to all those land-locked states that depended on its lines of communication. These are 'the geographical realities which cannot be removed', said Foreign Minister Franco Nogueira in a press conference two weeks after U.D.I. Portugal would respect the rights of transit of these states and would refuse any involvement in sanctions. In any event, Nogueira added, you cannot blockade Rhodesia without blockading Zambia, Malawi and the Congo. To those who argued, as did the United Kingdom repeatedly, that sanctions against Rhodesia would succeed only if Portugal collaborated, he fired back, 'We reject all responsibility in the matter, because it is not our responsibility.' Portugal would look to 'the just equilibrium of the collective needs of all'.

For Zambia, Portugal would co-operate in moving oil supplies by rail from Beira to Malawi and copper exports over the Benguela line to Lobito Bay.* 'Neither the International Press,' the Lisbon Government once announced petulantly, 'nor the United Nations, nor the British Government which have been so concerned with the interests of the interior countries, have ever made a single reference to the decisive service which Portugal is rendering to those countries. . . .' One of 'those countries' was of course Rhodesia. Two days after Britain had announced the oil embargo, an 'informed' Portuguese source told a London *Times* correspondent: 'I imagine that if any oil reaches Beira, we shall pump it the 180 miles to the Umtali refinery [in Rhodesia]. If it does not arrive it is nothing to do with us.' Nor was the bleakness of that prediction relieved by the frequent queries, probes and protests which the British lodged periodically with the Portuguese Government, attempting without success to gain Portuguese compliance in an effort to deprive the rebel Government of oil.

There was however more than one way to stop the flow and London now systematically worked over each link in the complex supply chain which brought oil to Rhodesia's refinery. There was first the refinery itself, controlled by a London-based company

---

* What the Zambians (and British) wanted however was to anchor a fuel airlift in Beira (only 600 miles from Lusaka). When the Portuguese learned it would be a military lift staged by the R.A.F. they would have none of it. In fact, as the crisis developed the Portuguese believed Britain might attempt a military operation against Beira in connection with the oil blockade or perhaps even an invasion of Rhodesia. Anti-aircraft guns were installed at the Beira airport and for a period vehicles were left parked on the runways and removed only when authorized aircraft were about to land.

known by its acronym, CAPREF. Shares were held by several international oil giants: British Petroleum, Shell, Mobil, Caltex, Total,
Aminoil and Kuwait oil. But the writ of CAPREF's international
directorate, as Britain learned on more than one occasion, no longer
ran to its operation in Rhodesia. Registered under Rhodesian law,
the refinery together with its local management were subject to the
rebel Government's regulations concerning the oil industry. It was
much the same with the Mozambique–Rhodesian Pipeline Company
(or C.P.M.R.). Though 62 per cent of the shares of C.P.M.R. were
directly or indirectly British owned, Portuguese directors under
Portuguese law had control of that part of the pipeline traversing
Mozambique. Neither the pressure of the British Government nor
the persuasion of the British directors won from Lisbon any assurance that oil, once available, would not be pumped through it. The
answer, said Alan H. Bell, Chairman of Lonrho, the British company
which held the largest block of C.P.M.R. shares, was to keep the oil
from coming in in the first place.

That might be done if the storage facilities at Beira were denied
to oil destined for Rhodesia. Since the tank farm was controlled by
the international marketing companies, these facilities were in fact
placed out of bounds for Rhodesian oil as soon as the companies
acquiesced in the embargo. Not long thereafter, however, construction began on six new prefabricated tanks each with a capacity of
3,000 tons. When asked about these, the Portuguese explained that
they were being built by private Portuguese interests. No assurance
was forthcoming however that the tanks would not be used to handle
Rhodesian oil. That this in fact was envisaged was strongly suggested
when early in March the Rhodesian Secretary for Transport arrived
in Beira to inspect the construction work which was then in progress.
His colleague, the Minister of Commerce and Industry, announced at
about the same time that 'the day our first tanker arrives in Beira we
shall have won this economic war'.

The tanker of course was the final link in the supply chain.
Systematic surveillance of the Mozambique Channel by the British
began early in 1966. The aircraft carrier H.M.S. *Eagle*, later relieved
by H.M.S. *Ark Royal*, was deployed together with escort frigates.
Gannet aircraft equipped with early-warning radar monitored the
sea lanes assisted later by Shackleton Maritime Reconnaissance aircraft using facilities at Malagasy's Majunga Air Base. The surveillance
brought protests against British planes 'buzzing' merchant ships
when attempting to read their names and ports of origin, and
alleged violations by Britain of national waters and air-space.
Verwoerd said that the activity did not accord with 'international
usage'. Portugal complained of 'a powerful British air and naval

concentration' and made it clear in repeated notes that Britain's surveillance of shipping was unwelcome. One out of every four ships passing through the Channel was in fact a tanker and the rumours multiplied that some were en route to Beira with oil for Rhodesia. Between 7 January and 1 March some thirty-two 'phantom tankers', as British diplomats referred to them, were investigated and found innocent or non-existent. But the suspense increased until in Beira there appeared to be almost as many journalists as stevedores on the piers. Then towards the end of March the *Joanna V* rounded the Cape of Good Hope and began moving north into the Mozambique Channel.

In Beira the two newly completed storage tanks were tested with water under pressure, while elsewhere frantic diplomatic manœuvres sought to assure that they would never be used. Britain's Ambassador in Athens, Ralph Murray, who had been in almost constant contact with Greek authorities, succeeded in getting the Greek Government to signal both the *Joanna V*'s master and its owners ordering that the vessel must not be unloaded. To do so would violate a Greek Royal decree issued by King Constantine on 12 March which forbade ships under the Greek flag to deliver cargoes of liquid fuel for Rhodesia. As the pressure mounted the *Joanna V* reduced its speed to two or three knots awaiting further instructions in the waters off Lourenço Marques. Britain asked Greece for permission to use force if necessary to prevent the tanker from entering Beira. Athens refused, then again warned the owners and the master that a violation of the Royal decree would involve disciplinary action including heavy fines.

On 4 April the British escort frigate, H.M.S. *Plymouth*, acting on secret orders, intercepted the *Joanna V* on the high seas heading for Beira. The ship's master refused to accept the *Plymouth*'s warning not to proceed to the Mozambiquan port, stating that he had instructions to put in at Beira for bunkering and provisions, then to proceed up the coast to Djibouti in French Somaliland to discharge his cargo. (Djibouti, it might be noted, has no refinery.) The *Plymouth*'s captain claimed his action in intercepting the Greek tanker conformed to the 20 November resolution of the U.N. Security Council which had recommended oil sanctions, and was taken with the knowledge of the Greek Government. He was constrained however from using force and despite further efforts in Athens the *Joanna V* by 5 April had dropped anchor one mile from the tanker off-loading berth at Beira.

A frenzy of activity ensued. In Lisbon the British Ambassador, Sir Archibald Ross, reiterated Britain's view to Foreign Minister Nogueira that Portugal would be responsible if the oil were pumped to Rhodesia. In London, Michael Stewart emphasized the same point to the Portuguese *chargé d'affaires*. Greece instructed its consul in Beira to take legal action the moment it was established that the *Joanna V*'s cargo was being discharged into the Rhodesian pipeline. Whereupon the owners of the vessel applied for her removal from the Greek shipping register. Spokesmen for the owners said the *Joanna V* would hoist the Panamanian flag. Athens responded that this was of no concern. Formalities for removing a ship from the register took about a week. She was still considered Greek and liable to penalties if found to be in violation of the Greek Royal decree. Matters were further complicated when it was learned that another tanker had loaded some 14,000 tons of crude oil in the Persian Gulf and was proceeding to Beira. She had been purchased on 4 March by the same Nicos Vardinoyannis for a new Panamanian affiliate, the Varnima Corporation, and renamed the *Manuela* (after Mrs. Vardinoyannis). Formerly under the Liberian flag she was now, like the *Joanna V*, registered in Greece and owed flag allegiance to that country.

On 6 April, the Greek Government suddenly reversed itself, taking the drastic action of striking the *Joanna V* off the Greek register and making it, Greek authorities said, a 'pirate' ship. At the same time they revoked the master's licence for life and committed him to trial for ignoring six wireless signals from the Ministry of Merchant Marine ordering the ship to stay away from Beira. The owners were now liable to a fine of up to £30,000 ($84,000). In Piraeus, outside Athens, Vardinoyannis fumed: 'This is like the gambler who loses at poker with a hand of four aces because his opponent has two guns.' The *Manuela*'s master meanwhile was advised by the Ministry of the penalties to which he too would be subject if he put into Beira. In London a message received from H.M.S. *Eagle* put the *Manuela* 600 miles north of the Mozambiquan port.

While these events were unfolding, directors of the pipeline company, having been summoned with twenty-four hours' notice, were convening in Lisbon to decide what to do if the *Joanna V* off-loaded. Three British directors flew in from London. On the same plane was the Parliamentary Under-Secretary of State from the Foreign Office, Lord Walston, who on arrival promised he would stay in Lisbon as long as necessary to resolve the problem. But according to an official Portuguese Government release issued on the day of Walston's arrival, there was no problem to be resolved. Lisbon again argued that Portugal was the object of groundless discrimination: no one suggested that Greece whose flag the *Joanna V* displayed, or Britain whose 'aero-naval concentration' had failed to prevent passage, or South Africa whose nationals (the A. G. Morrison firm of Cape Town) owned the cargo should be held culpable if the *Joanna V* broke the embargo. Why then should Portugal be considered responsible simply for 'doing its duty' in assuring 'the free access of landlocked countries to the sea' and in refusing to interfere in the activities of privately owned companies? At the same time, the Portuguese Government said it would take no 'initiative tending to ensure supplies of oil to Rhodesia'.

It was this last point that Walston now seized upon. In two long talks on 6 and 7 April, he evidently received assurances from Nogueira that the new oil tanks would not be used to take oil for Rhodesia. It was technically possible, however, for the tanker to be linked directly to the pipeline, bypassing the storage tanks. To do so would require traversing a few yards of Portuguese territory. For Portugal to permit such a link to be put in place would constitute the 'initiative tending to ensure supplies' which the Government's statement had pledged it would not take. Nogueira replied vaguely that no request to build such a link had been received. Moreover he could give no assurance that oil entering the pipeline would not be pumped insisting again that the company was private. Portugal would in fact have to indemnify the C.P.M.R. if it enjoined the company from pumping oil.

In London meanwhile the Cabinet was labouring not only with the problem of the *Joanna V* but with a rapidly maturing Afro-Asian effort to convene the Security Council and to ask for sanctions binding on all U.N. members. The situation called for a dramatic new move by London. Walston meanwhile was still in Lisbon. Little did he realize, until actually hearing the news on 7 April over the B.B.C., that H.M. Government would decide to table a resolution in the United Nations Security Council authorizing what amounted to a limited naval blockade of the Portuguese port of Beira. That evening Nogueira arrived for dinner at the British Ambassador's residence furious that Walston had made his approach to Portugal on this most sensitive matter while, simultaneously and without consultation, Britain was asking the U.N. to take binding decisions that would, as he put it, 'restrict the free action of private companies on Portuguese territory'.

Walston may have noticed hanging in the Foreign Minister's waiting room at the Palacio de Necessidades which houses the Foreign Ministry in Lisbon, an etching of rather considerable symbolic significance depicting the battle of Rolica in 1808 when Wellington, commanding combined British and Portuguese forces, defeated the French. It was evident that Britain's oldest alliance had fallen upon hard days. In its official statement issued on 8 April, the Portuguese Government expressed 'profound astonishment' at what had just transpired. Portugal then accused Britain of attempting again to make Portugal responsible for the existing situation. On the contrary, Portugal argued, Britain could have prevented the *Joanna V* from proceeding to Beira. But Britain deliberately abstained from doing so for reasons which were 'certainly open to serious doubts'. In diplomatic parlance that was pretty strong language.

The Beira Resolution

Franco Nogueira felt misused. Britain had gone behind his back to the Security Council and in its effort to punish Rhodesia was now singling out Portugal, suggesting that British relations with Lisbon were more expendable than with Pretoria. Nogueira's point, however, that Britain had done less than it might have done in denying passage to the *Joanna V* was disingenuous.

When Britain urged Greece to permit the use of force to divert the tanker the Greek Foreign Under-Secretary replied that no Government would consent to a foreign power intercepting merchant shipping under its flag. After a further appeal from London, he added on 4 April that 'if the U.N. authorizes the British Government to intercept the vessel, we shall respect the decision. However we cannot give our permission without a U.N. ruling.' International law left no doubt on this point. The 1958 Geneva Convention of the High Seas declares that the state with which a ship is registered must grant permission to any other nation wishing to intervene. Acts of intervention have been excused as self-defence. But self-defence was clearly not in question. The Security Council resolution of 20 November 1965, had 'recommended' oil sanctions, not required that members comply. The resolution might have provided a certain aura of legality but hardly a firm legal base on which Britain might exercise extraordinary authority, recognizing that a case against it under international law might have been carried to the World Court at The Hague – and that as a seafaring nation Britain had a special interest in scrupulously maintaining the codes that assured freedom of the seas. Britain could have argued that under international law nations are enjoined from assisting an unrecognized government in its rebellion, but Britain itself was enjoined under the Charter from 'unilateral forcible self-help' in such situations. If shipping crude oil to Beira was to be stopped, the Security Council mandate would have to be strengthened.

The British resolution tabled on 7 April 1966, called upon the Portuguese Government neither to allow oil to be pumped through the pipeline nor to receive at Beira oil destined for Rhodesia, and upon the government of the United Kingdom 'to prevent by force if necessary vessels reasonably believed to be carrying oil destined for Rhodesia' and to 'arrest and detain' the *Joanna V* upon departure from Beira in the event of her discharging her cargo there. Britain found the justification for these unprecedented actions in the language of Article 39 of the United Nations Charter. Citing the arrival of the *Joanna V*, the approach of the *Manuela* and the possible transit of oil through the pipeline, the British draft resolution declared that the resulting situation would constitute a threat to the peace. According to the Charter, that phrase was the key which unlocked the many punitive measures available to the Council in Chapter VII and which enabled the Council to make decisions binding on the organization's membership. Whether or not the successful delivery of oil through Beira, or for that matter the larger issue of the Rhodesian rebellion itself, was a threat to the peace would be argued for years.

Britain's immediate objective, however, was simply to gain Security Council agreement for these extraordinary yet precisely limited measures as quickly as possible. When the Council sat on 9 April, Lord Caradon pleaded for swift action to deal with the matter at hand, not a wide-ranging debate on the whole question of Southern Africa. 'Let us stop it now,' he said referring to the slowly approaching *Manuela*. 'If we do so, we shall sustain the authority of the United Nations. . . . I cannot believe that any member of this Council, by obstruction or procrastination, wishes to frustrate that purpose.' For the African states the intention was not to frustrate the oil 'blockade' of Beira, but once again to use the occasion to press for a comprehensive Security Council involvement in the Rhodesian affair – to go to the root of the problem, as the Uganda delegate put it.

The three African members of the Council,* Mali, Nigeria and Uganda, introduced amendments to the British draft resolution calling on the United Kingdom to use force to prevent the entry into Rhodesia of all goods over all routes, not just oil and not just through Beira. However, by the end of the day, these and similar amendments had been defeated and the draft resolution passed. No one voted against it, but five members abstained including two of the Council's permanent members, France and the U.S.S.R. France persisted in the view that the Rhodesian problem was an internal British affair beyond the purview of the Security Council. The Soviet Union abstained in protest against the inadequacy of the British resolution and in doing so probably expressed the views of Jordan, Nigeria and Uganda even though these three had reluctantly cast consenting

---

* African representation rose from one to three following the expansion of the Council from eleven to fifteen members which took place on 1 January 1966.

votes. Inadequate it may have been, but it was historic nonetheless. It was only the second occasion in the United Nations' twenty-one years when the sanctions provisions of Chapter VII of the Charter had been invoked, the first having been the resolution of 27 June 1950, at the onset of the Korean War. It was the first time that a member of the U.N. had been authorized on behalf of the Council to use 'armed force if necessary' to carry out the will of the Council.

The unprecedented Beira resolution provided a textbook account of the differing interpretations of the three protagonists – Britain, the militant Afro-Asians and the Portuguese (whose position was similar to that of South Africa) – respecting the purposes and procedures of the United Nations as these related to Rhodesia. Britain's appeal to the Security Council was carefully hedged, designed to pre-empt unwanted initiatives by militant Afro-Asians and to gain only that increment of pressure believed useful at the time, in this instance the interdiction of oil supplies to the pipeline terminating in Beira. Chapter VII was invoked as the only means available to authorize the use of force against blockade-running tankers. Justifying this action, the British Attorney General argued in the Commons on 27 April 1966, that 'the loss of control of the situation which would have resulted from a major breach of the oil embargo, the assistance which it would have afforded to the illegal regime, the diminution of the prospect of an outcome acceptable to world opinion, might well have led others, in this highly explosive situation, to despair of peaceful solutions and to demand resort to action which would have had grave and incalculable consequences for the peace of Africa.' The argument was at best questionable. If Britain's invocation of a threat to the peace had been logically sound, within its own terms of reference, South Africa would had to have been as much the object of the proposed blockade as Portugal.

This was precisely the position of the more militant Afro-Asian states. Their approach to Security Council action was as sweeping as Britain's was circumscribed. The object was to use Council debates and resolutions for mobilizing maximum pressure on Britain either to use force against Rhodesia or to engage in a major confrontation with South Africa. 'Why does Britain', pursued the delegate from Uganda, 'only concern itself with tankers and not with oil coming in from South Africa?' Sierra Leone's outspoken Ambassador Collier, in mock pity, sympathized with 'poor Portugal' which seemed to be the sole object of British coercive attentions, while not even mentioned was South Africa which harboured some £1.1 billion (approximately $3 billion) in British investments. If the United Kingdom were willing to ask for the use of force in this isolated case, why should it not use force in a wider context as prescribed by

Articles 41 and 42 of the Charter (those calling for the imposition of economic and military sanctions)? The Afro-Asian position had the advantage of consistency (it never varied), and a line of logic which flowed devastatingly from Britain's own original objective: to defeat the rebellion and to assure ultimate African rule. Yet in its way, this position too was irresponsible. The Afro-Asians lacked the required capability and hence would not be called upon to make the sacrifices entailed in implementing the policies they demanded. Only Zambia was the exception and it was nearly undone in the attempt.

As was true of the Afro-Asians and of the British, Portugal's position also flowed from Portugal's interests, which were to frustrate international efforts to coerce the regime in Salisbury. In practice Portugal has never breached the Beira resolution. But neither has Portugal ever accepted it, and the thrust of its argument was to cast as much doubt as possible on the validity of all Security Council actions respecting Rhodesia. Like South Africa (and France), Portugal insisted that the United Nations had no business involving itself in a domestic dispute between metropolis and colony.

A complex battery of other questions was raised as well in correspondence directed by Foreign Minister Franco Nogueira to Secretary General U Thant at the United Nations. They included the following. First, as to voting requirements in the Security Council, Nogueira called attention to the provision under Article 27, Paragraph 3 of the Charter, that decisions of the Council are to be made with the concurring votes of the five permanent members (the United States, the Soviet Union, Britain, France and China). He said he recognized that in practice a doctrine had been admitted according to which the abstention of a permanent member was not considered a veto. But this doctrine obtained in past cases which had not involved Chapter VII decisions and when the Council's membership was only eleven in number, not its present fifteen – an expansion which had taken place shortly before the Beira resolution. Since under the new voting procedures only nine affirmative votes were needed to take decisions in the Council, it would now be possible, according to the previous doctrine on abstentions, for the Council to adopt substantive resolutions in cases where all five of the permanent members had abstained. Was it then to be understood, asked Nogueira, that the non-permanent members of the Council had the right 'to take decisions concerning the peace, war and world security, and to formulate and put into execution policy which affect[ed] the entire community of nations, without the votes of all or some of the permanent members?'

Second, as regards international law, Nogueira noted that the Beira resolution constituted a denial of the principles of freedom of the seas and the rights of free access to the sea by land-locked countries. Was international law respecting these matters now to be regarded as repealed? If not, the resolution was invalid. If so, when could the Council violate international law and when could it not do so? Finally, as to the matter of jurisdiction, Nogueira recalled the vehemence with which prior to the rebellion the United Kingdom had argued at the United Nations its exclusive jurisdiction for Rhodesia, even to the point of refusing to participate in the voting. Now Britain had taken the initiative in submitting the issue to the Security Council under the terms of the Charter's most potent injunctions. Was the matter of Rhodesia still to be considered within Britain's jurisdiction or had jurisdiction now passed to the Council? The point was important, Nogueira argued, because if the Beira resolution were to be regarded as binding on all United Nations members (a point which he did not concede), it must be made clear who was authorized to supervise compliance and to call to account possible offenders. Was it the Council itself, in which case British jurisdiction had fallen away, or was it Britain, in which case the Council would have abdicated part of its responsibilities, conferring on a single member the power to supervise at its discretion the performance of all other members?

These inquiries (which have never been answered) were of course self-serving, but no more than were the positions of the other protagonists. However, the problem was not really the legality of Security Council actions as the Portuguese position implied. It had long been established that the Council was autonomous, the master of its own house. It had the right and the duty under the Charter to determine 'in accordance with the purposes and principles of the United Nations' (Article 24, Paragraph 2) whether or not a threat to the peace existed, and if so what actions were called for. That determination, or lack of it, was essentially a political act representing the coalescence of interests on the part of the required number of Council members, or to the contrary the failure of interests to coalesce in which case no action materialized.

The problem was essentially one of political judgement. Was it wise and was the precedent thus established useful to engage the United Nations, under the gravest provisions of the Charter, in a course of action which closed off only one of the routes by which oil was reaching Rhodesia – that is, which committed the organization in all probability to ineffective action? Britain believed so, in part because the resolution mitigated or postponed pressures for more militant actions, and in part because just conceivably the hint of a wider threat inherent in the Beira resolution might make the South Africans somewhat more responsive to Britain's request to put pressure on Salisbury. The Afro-Asians permitted the resolution to pass simply because half a loaf was better than none, particularly if there were any prospect that Britain, step by step, could be drawn toward a real confrontation with the white Southern African power structure. As it turned out, neither expectation was remotely realistic.

'One Miserable Tanker . . .'

With the resolution in hand, the United Kingdom lost no time. Early on 10 April the Commander-in-Chief of the British Forces in the Middle East was instructed to stop all ships going into Beira with oil for Rhodesia. At 7.30 a.m. G.M.T. on the same date the *Manuela* was intercepted by H.M.S. *Berwick*, 150 miles south-east of Beira where she had been cruising as if headed for Durban. A young lieutenant, accompanied by a second officer as a witness and two armed men, presented to the master of the *Manuela* an order signed by the *Berwick*'s Commander: 'Acting on instructions of my Government in conformity with the resolution of the United Nations Security Council that force may be used to prevent tankers carrying oil to Beira, I have been authorized to use force as necessary to implement this instruction.' When the *Manuela* failed to give a clear undertaking not to proceed to Beira the boarding party was strengthened. Thus persuaded, she set a course for Durban and eventually sailed off the pages of the world press.

The *Joanna V* meanwhile moved from her off-shore anchorage into Beira harbour early on 11 April. To the accompaniment of cheers from Portuguese onlookers and Rhodesian holiday-makers and with her whistles blaring she nudged into an oil berth no more than thirty feet from the terminus of the C.P.M.R. pipeline. Her papers were confiscated by the Greek Consul and her master officially informed that the vessel had been struck from the Greek register. Captain Vardinoyannis almost immediately left for South Africa 'on business'. Soon the *Joanna V* was flying a Panamanian flag, her Greek name having meanwhile been painted over and her English one substituted. It was said that a search was under way for a 'reduction valve' that would permit a direct connection between the *Joanna V*'s six-inch off-loading pipe and the ten-inch pipeline. Britain once again stepped up its diplomatic pressure. The Government of Panama announced that if the *Joanna V* broke the embargo it would cancel her provisional registration, and then did so anyway the day after awarding it, no doubt considering the case too hot to handle. The Portuguese authorities then placed the tanker under restraint while at the same time taking measures to guard the pipeline with a contingent of paratroopers flown in from Lourenço Marques for that purpose.

In Salisbury the rebel Cabinet was meeting daily. Early on 16 April, Ian Smith who had earlier called the whole affair a bit of a joke, announced that Rhodesia would not be using oil from the *Joanna V*. Although the oil had been meant for Rhodesia, he explained, his Government had decided against accepting it in order that other countries should not be drawn into the dispute between Rhodesia and Britain. (It is reasonable to assume that the Portuguese Government had something to do with Smith's quite remarkable statement.) He chastised London for its 'cowardly and despicable actions'. For expenses involving the *Joanna V* and the new storage tanks, the 'despicable actions' had probably cost the Salisbury regime somewhere between £0.5 and £1 million (roughly $1.5 and $3 million). From that time until the present no oil has been offloaded at Beira for Rhodesia. The Rhodesian refinery has been idle and the oil in the pipeline, some 14,000 tons of it, has lain dormant since January 1966 when the pumps stopped for the last time.

Wilson had won the battle of Beira but was losing the oil sanctions war. The U.N. resolution gained for Britain the sole right to act forcibly against the blockade-runners. But while world attention had been riveted on the *Joanna V* and the *Manuela*, more fuel than that carried by either tanker flowed into Rhodesia from South Africa each month. So the press continued to report, including the *Rand Daily Mail*. Noticing a change in the pattern of traffic north to Beit Bridge, Laurence Gandar's enterprising reporter, Peter Hazelhurst, again scouted the countryside. There runs south-east from Pietersburg through the Transvaal a railway line that traverses the famous Kruger Game Park before crossing into Mozambique just north of Lourenço Marques. There it connects with the main line running north through Malvernia to Bulawayo in Rhodesia. The *Mail* reporter positioned himself in Kruger Park and again began counting, this time oil wagons and flat trucks carrying oil tankers. The story broke under a banner headline on 10 March: 'Fuel for Smith – By Rail'. The *Mail* estimated the daily flow at 140,000 to 160,000 gallons, roughly equalling normal Rhodesian consumption. Most of it originated in South Africa's Transvaal and travelled the long devious route through Mozambique before arriving in Bulawayo and Salisbury.*

---

* Later the Sonarep refinery outside Lourenço Marques was able to handle Rhodesia's requirements and rail transport from South Africa ceased. In fact prior to the development of Rhodesia's own refinery and the oil pipeline from Beira, Rhodesia had drawn its oil

London continued to believe the figures were inflated, but was deeply concerned nonetheless. As we have seen, Wilson hoped that renewed United Nations involvement would exercise some restraint on policies in Pretoria as well as in Lisbon. The door to Chapter VII sanctions had been opened, only a crack to be sure to deal with the limited problem of oil supplies through one transit point, but it could be widened to encompass more than oil and more than the Beira route. The pressures within the U.N. were already great and would undoubtedly become greater to do just that, unless oil sanctions were seen to be working effectively.* The risks seemed to be rising steadily. In Lisbon on 13 April Portuguese Prime Minister Antonio Salazar warned that 'all may be lost if passion is heard above reason. . . . The situation might kindle a vast fire with risks for all who believe that they can remain immune because they are far from the flames.'

In Pretoria too one sensed that things were moving into a more critical period. 'Is it not, in fact, the oil supplied by South Africa that is defeating sanctions at its most critical point, the oil embargo?' asked the *Rand Daily Mail* on 21 April. 'And if the oil lift is "normal trade" why have the tanker cars had their identification marks painted out. . .? We are systematically and deliberately helping to break the U.N. oil embargo against Rhodesia and therefore run the

---

needs from Sonarep. The effort to break the Beira blockade, as it turned out, was not related to Rhodesia's immediate survival, given the alternative sources of fuel available through South Africa and Mozambique. Indeed only 27 per cent of Rhodesia's energy requirements derived from fuel oil, a figure which could have been reduced further if necessary. Rather, breaking the blockade would have meant a quite sensational psychological victory over Britain's entire sanctions programme. Also, for economic reasons, the Rhodesians wanted to reopen their own refinery. The haulage of oil products by road was exorbitantly expensive, the South African Government even charging taxes on the fuel. And refined products purchased from Sonarep cost considerably more than processing their own crude oil within Rhodesia.

* After the Beira resolution the General Assembly's Special Committee on Colonialism continued to meet. A resolution calling for force was passed on April 21. Following the initiation of 'talks' between British and Rhodesian representatives (see Chapter VI) some thirty African members of the U.N. on May 10 called for an immediate meeting of the Security Council to consider a resolution calling for comprehensive mandatory sanctions and the application of force under Chapter VII. The Council met from 17 May to 23 May 1966. The proposed resolution, lacking nine affirmative votes, was defeated. Britain and the United States, together with six others, abstained.

grave risk of this oil embargo and perhaps general sanctions being extended to us.' The South African Government had made known its concern about Britain's appeal to the Security Council under Chapter VII, and even before the Council convened Verwoerd had expressed the hope that Britain and the United States would not allow themselves 'to be drawn into imprudent action' against South Africa. That had been avoided – for the present. Perhaps Verwoerd, who had won an impressive mandate at the polls on 30 March, would now quietly co-operate in placing pressure on the rebel regime in Salisbury by reducing the flow of oil, and thereby avoid 'imprudent actions' in the future. So Wilson must have hoped.

Diplomatic pressures, however, run in both directions when risks are mutual. It was not only South Africa which would find an expanded U.N. role awkward. Further U.N. involvement carried for Britain the liability of decreased control over the outcome of the Rhodesian issue, for which London nonetheless continued to claim responsibility, and indeed for which it would continue to be held responsible. Further U.N. involvement presented, too, the possibility of sanctions against South Africa which would have had a disastrous impact on Britain's already badly deteriorated export and balance of payments positions. And further U.N. involvement would finally create a furore within Britain, with consequences not as profound as would have obtained before the Election of 31 March when Wilson had stretched his overall majority in Parliament from a slim three to a substantial ninety-seven seats, but serious nonetheless. When risks are reciprocal the advantage lies with the side which can demonstrate the greater credibility in applying or resisting pressures. Often this is a simple function of the extent to which critical interests are perceived to be engaged. For Britain the defeat of the rebellion through sanctions was surely important. For South Africa the defeat of sanctions was absolutely vital. The disproportion between an 'important' interest and a 'vital' interest now became fundamental.*

---

* An interest earns the adjective 'vital' if it affects the continued existence of the society which propounds it. It could hardly be argued that the existence of British society would be endangered by the failure of British policies in Rhodesia; it could however quite credibly be argued that the future of South African white society would be affected adversely, and might well be affected vitally, should sanctions in Rhodesia succeed. This critical disparity existed throughout the entire affair, determining the level of energy and the willingness to run risks in assuring the defeat of sanctions by South Africa, Portugal and most especially Rhodesia, as opposed to the much less constant and vigorous efforts applied by Britain, and even less so of course by its associates.

In the ensuing diplomatic debate with South Africa, Wilson pressed again the notion of normal trade, by which he meant maintaining oil sales at pre-U.D.I. levels. Abnormal trade was not consistent with neutrality, but rather constituted support for the rebellion. Inevitably if the oil flow could not otherwise be curtailed the issue would return to the Security Council and demands would be lodged for mandatory sanctions against South Africa. A United Kingdom veto under these circumstances would open the way to communist influence and jeopardize important British collateral interests in and beyond Africa, including the future of substantial British communities elsewhere on the continent. Wilson also stressed that Britain's objective was to establish stable government in Rhodesia effecting a transition to majority rule only gradually with progress in that direction measured, not by the clock or calendar but by African achievement. Reduced to its essentials Wilson was asking Verwoerd once again to help Britain in defeating the rebellion by tacitly collaborating in an embargo on oil.

Verwoerd, for his part, said that Britain was wrong to have taken a domestic issue to the Security Council. He could not accept that the Council should underwrite a policy including the use of force which compelled governments in no way involved (and in some cases wishing to remain neutral) to give support to a member government in its handling of a domestic situation. South Africa recognized full well that this could escalate to the point where stronger measures would be attempted against both Pretoria and Lisbon. Equally South Africa could hardly ignore the frequent public declarations by many countries that successful application of sanctions against Rhodesia would have future significance *vis-à-vis* South Africa itself. Throughout the debate Verwoerd made it clear that his Government would not be a party to Britain's dispute with its self-governing colony and that if the oil embargo were extended to South Africa it would be resisted by all possible means, not excluding in extreme cases resigning from the U.N.

The South African Prime Minister discounted the possibility of a gradual and orderly transition to African rule in Rhodesia, noting that a chaotic situation on its northern frontier was hardly in South Africa's interest. Verwoerd acknowledged the mutual economic advantages that South Africa and Britain enjoyed, while underlining in particular Pretoria's contribution to the stability of the sterling area. But he also made it clear that the interests at stake in Rhodesia were for South Africa truly vital. In short, though it would wish to avoid such stark alternatives, South Africa might be obliged to choose between maintaining its present relations with Britain and the United Nations on the one hand, and its very existence on the other.

Whether it was to come to that was not for South Africa alone to decide. After all, Britain and the United States, not South Africa, had the right of veto in the Security Council.

Although Britain repeatedly in the years to come would seek South African support for its Rhodesian policy (generally without the slightest success), it never seriously considered actions in the U.N. aimed at forcing South African compliance with sanctions – nor Portuguese compliance either, except for the Beira resolution. And so the oil 'spill' continued despite prodigious diplomatic efforts in numerous capitals and the hollow victories of the Mozambique Channel. Zambia's Foreign Minister, Simon Kapwepwe, after returning from the Security Council session and surveying the disappointing results, added a bitter postscript. 'A great power mobilizes the formidable resources of the world organization – and succeeds in stopping one miserable tanker.'

VI

Talks about Talks

Turning Point

In the development of a crisis there will sometimes occur a turning
point which everyone immediately recognizes to be important, but
the true significance of which is revealed only with the passage of
time. What happened in Britain's Parliament on 27 April 1966 was
just such an event. Harold Wilson announced to an unsuspecting
House of Commons that talks would soon begin with representatives
of the rebel regime. 'I make it plain that these are not negotiations,'
he insisted. 'Her Majesty's Government are not negotiating with the
illegal regime. These are informal talks to see whether there is a basis
on which proper negotiations could take place. . . . They are without
commitment on either side.'

Many Labour back-benchers, tight-lipped with apprehension,
feared a sell-out. So too did more than one Labour Minister. Some
wondered if talks would not seriously diminish the impact of sanctions. Only a few Ministers closest to Wilson knew in advance of this
surprising development. Most Conservatives on the other hand
applauded Wilson's initiative, welcoming his 'belated' decision which
they hoped would lay the groundwork for a sensible settlement. In
African and U.N. circles Wilson's statement stirred emotions and
precipitated a call for new Security Council action by thirty-two
African states. It wounded relations with Zambia, which to this day
have not healed. And it was the prelude to a confrontation which
almost dissolved the Commonwealth.

The deeper significance of Wilson's new move, however, was not
that it would lead to a settlement or to a sell-out. Though it was the
precursor of the most extraordinary and prolonged negotiations,
Wilson's new policy would not much affect the outcome of the
Rhodesian affair. Subsequent negotiations in fact proved futile, but
even had they succeeded, they probably would not have resulted in
lasting changes, so compromised were the settlement provisions.
The real significance of 'talks about talks' (as R. H. Turton called

them during a Parliamentary debate) was that, in retrospect, they signalled the end of Mr. Wilson's attempts to deal in any meaningful sense with the Rhodesian problem as such, that is, to achieve his prescribed outcome: to remove Ian Smith, to return the situation to legality and to effect a gradual and guaranteed transition to majority rule.

Unwilling to intervene directly Wilson had had to rely on the efforts of others to supplement Britain's own sanctions programme. His initial attempts had failed to place much additional pressure on Rhodesia by recruiting Zambian and South African assistance. He would make further efforts but the evidence was already irrefutable that the level of risk was too high in the case of Zambia and the compatibility of interests too low in the case of South Africa to make either one a viable collaborator. More and more, thus, he would be reacting not to the problem itself; rather he would be reacting to the reactions to the Rhodesian impasse in an effort to minimize British losses.* But few knew that now, possibly not even the Prime Minister himself.

Talking About 'Talks' in Britain

Wilson described for Parliament what had happened. He had received a report from Governor Gibbs the previous week indicating that Smith was prepared to talk without preconditions. In fact the initiative for this move had come largely from Gibbs himself who had been anxious from the outset to promote negotiations. Using as a go-between a Rhodesian Front businessman for whom Gibbs had regard, the Governor urged Smith to start a dialogue with the British. Smith finally concurred and met Governor Gibbs on 19 April 1966, informing him that he would be willing to enter into talks 'to settle the present situation'. The message which Gibbs then sent to the British Prime Minister arrived just after a member of Wilson's secretariat, J. Oliver Wright (later named Ambassador to Copenhagen) had departed for South Africa where he was to assist in delicate negotiations then under way with Prime Minister Verwoerd. Wilson cabled Wright to stop in Salisbury for a few hours en route to Pretoria. Wright had a discussion with Gibbs, then advised Wilson

---

* To a fair degree this already had been the case. The incremental tightening of sanctions, the sending of Javelins to Zambia, the oil embargo and even the Beira resolution were all in part efforts to contain reactions damaging to British interests among Commonwealth nations, in the O.A.U., at the U.N. and in Zambia.

that the matter was indeed worth pursuing. After a brief stay in Pretoria, Wright under instructions returned to Salisbury where he met with Smith on at least two occasions, once at Government House for a session which was in effect chaired by the Governor.

On 26 April the Rhodesian Prime Minister told Parliament in Salisbury that he was prepared to reopen unconditional negotiations with the United Kingdom. He stressed that he had never laid down preconditions and never closed the door. 'I have made it clear that talks may start at any level, at any place, at any time.' What Wilson found of particular significance, however, was that Smith had been willing to make his approach through Governor Gibbs who from Britain's point of view remained the only constituted authority. Equally significant, Wilson thought, was the fact that Smith seemed willing to enter into preliminary talks at the official level without insisting upon British recognition of Rhodesian independence. It was clear, Wilson said, that sanctions and the Beira resolution had been 'decisive' in producing this new development. 'I think the Commonwealth countries, particularly those which were represented at Lagos, will now recognize, as I said at Lagos, that the economic sanctions work.'

The flow of oil by now reaching Rhodesia from South Africa argued strongly to the contrary. Nor was it at all certain that the Rhodesian rebel leader had made a radical turnabout. It is true that he had earlier left the impression that Rhodesia's independence must be recognized before talks could begin. Indeed as late as 20 April, Rhodesia's diplomatic representative in South Africa, John Gaunt, declared in an address to a business luncheon in Johannesburg that there was no chance of British–Rhodesian negotiations as long as Harold Wilson refused to acknowledge Rhodesia's independence. Still, in the past months Smith had referred repeatedly to the desirability of constructive talks with the United Kingdom to end the impasse. On 6 March he had said: 'The only thing now standing in the way of open talks is the obstinate attitude of the British Prime Minister himself. He appears to be the only man in the world who doesn't want to talk to me.' Less than a month later Smith declared, 'The door is open for any talks. It is still open.' The fact was of course that conversations involving officials of Britain and Rhodesia, no matter how informal or preliminary the contacts might be, could be construed as a rudimentary form of recognition redounding to Smith's advantage. From this point of view the change of policy announced by Wilson on 27 April was far more decisive for Britain than for Rhodesia, despite the British Prime Minister's argument to the contrary. The point was made with force by the Conservative Opposition.

For some months Conservative leadership had been increasingly restive with Wilson's policy. They had supported sanctions as an inducement to reopening negotiations. Wilson on the contrary, they believed, saw sanctions as a means for toppling Smith or gaining his capitulation. 'We cannot negotiate with these men,' declared Wilson on the floor of the Commons on 10 December 1965, 'nor can they be trusted, after the return to constitutional rule, with the task of leading Rhodesia in the paths of freedom and racial harmony.' In a subsequent debate, Wilson talked of the repugnance of negotiating with the illegal regime and expressed amazement that anyone might have thought that Britain could ask the nations of the world to reverse the policies now being carried out at Britain's request and to stay their hand while H.M. Government entered into a parley with Smith and his associates. Edward Heath once again noted that Wilson was insisting upon 'the complete, absolute and unconditional surrender of everybody in the present illegal regime'. But, Heath insisted, there was no group ready to accept Wilson's offer of unconditional surrender. If one were to wait to start negotiations until the Smith regime had collapsed it would mean creating a political vacuum which could only be filled by direct rule from London, a prospect that aroused the most basic fears on the part of even moderates in Rhodesia.

In February 1966, Heath asked Selwyn Lloyd to undertake a trip to Rhodesia and to prepare a first-hand assessment, on the basis of which the Opposition might establish more precisely its attitude toward Wilson's policies. Lloyd, Foreign Secretary from 1955 to 1960, was then the Conservative spokesman on Commonwealth affairs. Ten days and 300 interviews later, Lloyd emerged convinced that there must be talks. He had told the Rhodesians that U.D.I. was wrong, that they must tackle the problem of racial discrimination, and that the European minority could not rule a large African majority indefinitely. If these principles were accepted, talks could be useful. Lloyd dismissed as nonsense the possibility of an alternative government emerging in Rhodesia. British actions had if anything consolidated Rhodesian opinion behind Smith who was in firm control. In short, there was no alternative to talking to Smith. There must be, Lloyd insisted, 'negotiations without preconditions'. Forthwith six leading members of the Conservative Shadow Cabinet signed a motion on 24 February 1966, calling upon H.M. Government 'to initiate talks with Mr. Smith and his colleagues with the aim of achieving a constitutional settlement in Rhodesia'. Language to this effect was then introduced into the Conservative Party's manifesto preparatory to the elections scheduled for the end of March.

The differences of view between Heath and Wilson were now

expressed with increasing vehemence. 'So long as the Prime Minister is there', said Heath in the Commons on 31 January, 'there can be no honourable settlement in Rhodesia.' To which Wilson retorted: 'The only thing in Rhodesia standing in the way . . . of a diminution of the right-wing and semi-fascist resistance there . . . was their belief that because of the arguments of the right honourable gentleman, delivered with increasing heat every time he gets to his feet on the Rhodesian question, the Conservatives were taking a different view from that of the Government in this country.' During the election campaign Heath accused Wilson of making Rhodesian policy a personal issue between himself and Smith. His handling of the crisis had been 'disastrous'. Wilson shot back that the Tory position was 'irresponsibility without parallel'.

It was understandable, then, that after Labour's victory at the polls when Wilson announced 'talks' would take place, Tory gratification was mixed with cynical amusement at his inconsistency and increased bitterness at his tactics. Wilson had excoriated the Conservatives in the election campaign for their irresponsible advocacy of talks with rebel spokesmen. But no sooner had he reorganized his new Government than the Prime Minister fully incorporated into his Rhodesian policy Selwyn Lloyd's proposals for 'negotiations without preconditions'.* It was not only the Conservatives in Britain, however, who took note of Wilson's astonishing reversal.

Listening to the News in Lusaka

At 6 p.m. on 27 April 1966, President Kenneth Kaunda, as was his habit, switched on the portable transistor radio which he always kept nearby for monitoring major newscasts. The headlined item was Harold Wilson's announcement in Parliament that afternoon that talks with representatives of the rebel regime were about to begin. Kaunda was dumbfounded. Equally surprised was Sir Leslie Monson, Britain's High Commissioner to Zambia, who heard the same broadcast at his residence nearby.

Though Wilson had explained to Parliament that his Government

---

* It was hardly an unpopular step with the British electorate. The *Daily Express* on 24 February 1966, published the results of a public opinion poll which found that 71.5 per cent of the sample favoured immediate negotiations with Ian Smith with a view to a satisfactory solution to the Rhodesian problem. Eighty per cent of the Tory, 64 per cent of the Labour and 73 per cent of the Liberal voters were in favour.

had taken steps that morning to inform all concerned Commonwealth states about this latest development, Monson received no word from London until midnight (six hours after Kaunda had heard the news by wireless) when a telegram arrived giving background to be used for briefing the Zambian President. Monson waited until 6.30 a.m. before calling Michael Talmage, Kaunda's Personal Private Secretary, only to learn that the President was already on the Copperbelt and not expected back until evening. When Kaunda refused to grant Monson an appointment, the gist of Whitehall's tardy briefing was included in a memo which Monson sent to State House.

Kaunda was not only angry, but felt deeply misused. Shortly after the 15 February 'quick kill' deadline had passed by default, Wilson sent word to Kaunda in confidence that British elections would be called for 31 March 1966. It was presumably an earnest of his continuing concern that the British Prime Minister should have given the Zambian President several days advance notice before publicly announcing the new elections on 28 February. He promised Kaunda another communication in due course which would advise him of British plans once the Labour Party had won a substantial majority in the election. There was in Wilson's message the intimation of a tougher policy, and to Kaunda it must have suggested the strong possibility that force would not be ruled out. The Zambian President was pleased with the news but nonetheless firm in his response. He would advise his Ministers to hold their fire during the election campaign, doing nothing to make Wilson's position more difficult. He realized that Wilson would need a suitable period after the elections to reorganize his Government and establish his policies. Thereafter Zambia would use all possible pressures to gain the swiftest action against Rhodesia. If H.M. Government was then not forthcoming, Kaunda declared, Britain would be 'finished in Africa'.

When news of Britain's election returns reached them on 1 April, Kenneth Kaunda and his Foreign Minister, Simon Kapwepwe, were attending a summit meeting in Nairobi of eleven East and Central Africa states. Wilson had won an impressive overall majority in Parliament of ninety-seven seats. It was 'an answer to a prayer', Kapwepwe declared. Kaunda told the assembled heads of state that the Labour Government would now face stronger African pressures over Rhodesia; in turn, he expected Wilson to take stronger action. In a brief congratulatory note to Wilson, Kaunda sounded the same theme. He now settled back to await Wilson's promised response, inquiring from time to time of the British High Commissioner as to whether word had not yet been received from the British Prime Minister in London. But the message which was promised 'in due course' advising Kaunda of Wilson's new strategy was carried by the newscast announcing 'talks about talks'. Kaunda's relationship with Wilson was never to be the same again.

The Zambian President wrote to the British Prime Minister expressing his surprise and shock at this sudden turn of events. His own views about negotiating with the rebels were well known. During the British election campaign, Kaunda had granted an interview to the London *Financial Times*. Noting the insistent urging of Conservative leaders to begin negotiations with the Salisbury regime, Kaunda allowed that such negotiations would be a moral outrage. It would mean 'sacrificing all principle to accommodate a handful of rebels', and would be 'the end of the Commonwealth'.

Replying to Kaunda, Wilson said that he was not at all optimistic that a negotiated settlement could now be achieved with Rhodesia consistent with Britain's six principles. That being the case, not only were sanctions to be maintained, but Britain was determined to intensify them. It was hoped accordingly that Zambia might scale back its imports from Rhodesia as quickly as possible and perhaps achieve an effective cut-off by the end of June, barring only coal, power and the use of the railways. Zambia had already cut its imports from Rhodesia by some 30 per cent. On a world-wide basis Britain estimated Rhodesia's exports had now been cut by 58 to 60 per cent. (The figures turned out to be hypothetical, and highly inflated.) Once Zambia had completed its cutback, sanctions on Rhodesian exports would be 75 per cent complete. Wilson now suggested that working-level discussions get under way immediately to identify the sectors where further trade reorientation might take place and to decide upon assistance which Britain might be able to offer to reduce further Zambia's reliance on Rhodesia.

Despite his sense of betrayal Kaunda agreed to further talks with the British and instructed the Secretary-General of his Contingency Planning Organization to take the necessary steps. Still there was no great enthusiasm for these renewed contacts with Britain and more than three weeks were to go by before they actually began. Kaunda no doubt was eyeing the other 'talks' then getting under way in London.

The Talks with Salisbury Begin

The principal reason, of course, for talks with Rhodesia was not at all that sanctions had succeeded, but that they had failed to work as decisively as Wilson had expected. The 'quick kill' had been attractive because it permitted the rapid intensification of sanctions, underlining Britain's determination and the efficacy of British policies. It had been deemed essential partly as a response to Zambian exuberance but also to protect Britain's flank from African detractors, to soften up the Rhodesian population quickly enough to avoid doing irreparable harm to Rhodesia's economy, and to convince both Pretoria and Lisbon that Smith was a non-starter. The foregoing points in turn became an inventory of difficulties Britain faced in managing a sanctions programme over the long haul. Sanctions success depended upon maintaining momentum and the programme was now levelling off. The United Nations had endorsed voluntary sanctions and more than fifty nations had signed on. The United Kingdom had imposed a total embargo, including oil, and with United Nations concurrence, had even imposed an oil blockade on the port of Beira. Short of risking a direct economic confrontation with South Africa, which Wilson was determined to avoid, there were few arrows left in his quiver.

Britain now had to await the results of its policy of 'protracted kill' in a situation where the Rhodesian economy was still intact, morale was still relatively high, and Smith was able to mount new efforts to crack the sanctions dike. Under these circumstances both South Africa and Portugal would increasingly be tempted to give aid to Rhodesia in the belief that Britain's policy was no longer viable. Available options were rapidly narrowing. Wilson would either have to move to mandatory sanctions under Chapter VII of the United Nations Charter with all of the attendant dangers of a show-down with South Africa and a diminution of Britain's capacity to maintain control of its Rhodesian policy, or begin talks with the rebel regime, hopefully leading to a negotiated settlement while most certainly intensifying Britain's problems within the Commonwealth and at the U.N.

Wilson chose the latter, even though there was not the slightest indication as yet that Rhodesia was interested in accepting any of the principles which both Conservatives and Labour had endorsed – the guarantee of an unimpeded advance to majority rule; progress toward ending racial discrimination, together with the immediate improvement of the political status of the African people; and assurance that any settlement leading to independence would be acceptable to the people of Rhodesia as a whole. In fairness, Wilson at this time was not particularly optimistic, as he had made clear to Kaunda, that the 'talks' would get very far very fast. But he still hoped that over the ensuing months the sanctions bite, particularly with Zambia's increasing participation, would become more effective, producing in turn enough concessions from the Rhodesians to make possible a settlement minimally consistent with the above principles – though most certainly not satisfactory to Kaunda.

For the moment, however, all the signs were decidedly unfavourable.

On the very eve of the talks Rhodesian television and radio were fiercely attacking Wilson. The Chairman of the Rhodesian Front, Colonel Matt Knox, made a special point of assuring Rhodesians that Smith would not let them down and would never surrender independence. Reviewing the prospects for settlement, The London *Times* observed on 2 May 1966 that agreement, though not easy, need not be impossible if one assumed that the argument would be about the pace of development rather than the direction. But for many, *The Times* noted, including powerful elements in the Front, the argument was about direction and not pace. They would wish to move away from the British position on such critical issues as racial discrimination and effective African political representation. Those representing these reactionary views constituted, after all, the wing of the Rhodesian Front responsible for putting Smith in office in the first place. In Salisbury many assumed that it would be, not Rhodesia, but Britain which would be forced into major concessions in order to stop the damaging erosion of sanctions on its failing economy. Some believed that the British position had already moved significantly towards the Rhodesian position since November, and one report suggested that the Rhodesian Treasury was preparing a reparations bill to present to London!

On 8 May 1966, the Rhodesian officials arrived at London Airport and were whisked off amidst a fleet of police escorts. It was a strong team including Sir Cornelius Greenfield, Chief Economic Adviser to Ian Smith and formerly Permanent Secretary of the Rhodesian Treasury; Gerald Clarke who since 1955 had served as Secretary to the Rhodesian Cabinet; and Stanley Morris, Chairman of the Public Services Board and a man who had had long experience concerning internal affairs. The British team included Noel Duncan Watson, an Assistant Under-Secretary in the Commonwealth Relations Office; J. Oliver Wright, whose clandestine mission had preceded Wilson's announcement about 'talks'; Charles Martin Le Quesne, later Ambassador to Algeria but then the head of the West and Central African Department of the Foreign Office; and Kenneth J. Neale, head of the Rhodesia Political Department of the Commonwealth Relations Office. A secret meeting-place had been chosen. It turned out to be the council chamber of the old India Office in King Charles Street just off Whitehall. Both sides agreed to work out of the lime-light and avoid all leaks to the press concerning either progress or difficulties. No time-table was set; the meetings were left to their own pace. There were no formalities, no social gatherings of any kind. The Rhodesian officials were treated with civility, but also as men representing an illegal regime who had come to Britain under safe conduct.

For a dozen days each team examined in detail the position of the opposing side and then adjourned the talks 'for a period of reflection and consultation'. At the end of May the British team left for Salisbury and talks reopened there on 2 June. In public, the participants were as laconic as ever. Greenfield who captained the Rhodesian team, told the press that he was like Old Man River: he would not say anything, but would just keep moving along. There was one swift and tangible result, however, when the talks moved to Salisbury. On 3 June Governor Gibbs's telephone was reconnected. Otherwise, there was little to show for the effort. Jeremy Thorpe, soon to become Leader of Britain's Liberal Party, returned from a private visit to Rhodesia and insisted that the talks had become a farce and should be broken off. 'Unless they are archaeologists', he said, 'there can be nothing left to explore.'

In point of fact each side had wrongly estimated the willingness of the other to give ground. Neither side, however, wished to bear the onus of ending the talks. The British moreover were under pressure from Governor Gibbs to keep the dialogue going. A faint hope remained that the present and prospective pressures of sanctions would finally extract concessions. Rhodesian businessmen clearly wanted a settlement and felt it was important to gain an understanding with Britain before committing the economy to a new tobacco crop while the fate of the current crop was still unknown. These concerns were expressed to Smith by a group of leading businessmen in a long interview on 19 June. A few days before, the outgoing President of the Rhodesian Associated Chambers of Commerce had painted a bleak picture of Rhodesia's economic prospects. But, as always, Smith was under even greater pressure from his party caucus, many of whose members would find any conceivable settlement to be unacceptable. Accordingly Smith's line hardened. 'The last thing we are going to do is throw in the sponge,' he told the annual Congress of the Rhodesian National Farmers' Union in Salisbury on 21 June. He pointedly reaffirmed his allegiance to the principles of the Rhodesian Front, an elliptical way of saying he had no intention of relaxing restrictive legislation respecting the African population.

On 5 July 1966, Prime Minister Wilson announced another pause in the talks for further consideration of the respective positions. The impasse had come to turn on a rather basic 'cart and horse' question: which was to come first, a 'return to legality' (Wilson's euphemism for the abandonment of Rhodesia's claim to independence), or agreement concerning the shape of the constitution under which Rhodesia's independence would be recognized? Somehow, of course, both cart and horse would have to be pulled along together in the exploratory talks; that is, the procedures for ending the rebellion and the elements of a constitutional settlement would have to be considered jointly. But once the broad outline of such an agreement was reached, Britain insisted that the rebellion must end – the claim to independence must be abandoned – before the final step could take place which was to put the agreement to the Rhodesian people as a whole to see if it met with their approval. Only thus could one assure that the test would be pursued with maximum objectivity.

Here the Rhodesians balked. They wanted to settle with Britain the shape of the constitutional solution. Once that was accomplished the question of a return to legality could be considered, according to Salisbury, 'providing adequate assurances were forthcoming that effect would be given to the shape [of the constitution] so devised'. In other words the rebellion would end only when it was certain that Britain would grant independence on the basis of the new constitutional formula. The Rhodesian *scenario* left no room for the testing of opinion under an authority other than that of the rebel regime. The point was fundamental and would prove persistent.

It was obvious that the talks had already foundered on these basic disagreements when the two sides met again in Salisbury on 22 August 1966. Indeed, the regime's attitude had hardened further. A fortnight before Smith had told a meeting of party members that 'we will continue to work things so that, as long as is necessary – and there is no time-limit on this – civilized hands will hold the reins.' ('Civilized' of course was a code word for 'white'.) The British Prime Minister said this would suggest that Smith was going back to the old notion, 'No majority rule in my lifetime.' Wilson was openly disturbed.

Behind Smith's unyielding statement was not only the weight of Rhodesian Front sentiment but the relative buoyancy of European morale which persisted despite the warnings of the business community. Moreover, Finance Minister John Wrathall had on 21 July 1966, introduced a remarkably optimistic budget. Anticipated expenditure for the financial year ending 30 June 1967 would be up slightly, while revenues would fall by only £2.5 million ($7 million). All but £400,000 ($1,120,000) of the anticipated deficit would be covered by carrying forward a previous surplus. Income taxes would not be increased. Tobacco support prices were to be continued. The pessimism expressed at the beginning of the year had not yet borne fruit. Alternative markets and sources of supply were quietly being arranged by Rhodesian commercial interests and middlemen working behind the scenes. Sanctions were hurting, but the country was surviving. In Britain meanwhile the economic situation had gone from bad to worse. A crippling seaman's strike had choked British exports for seven weeks in May and June, setting off repeated speculative raids on the pound. In mid July the Government enacted a set of ruthless deflationary measures including a six-month wage-price freeze. And by mid August, the sterling crisis had drained one-fifth of the Government's reserves.

Almost immediately after the talks reopened, the Rhodesian Minister of Law and Order, Desmond Lardner-Burke, asked the Rhodesian Parliament to approve a constitutional amendment which would enable the Government to introduce legislation permitting preventive detention. The amendment affected several provisions of the Declaration of Rights which had been carried over to the 1965 'rebel' constitution from the constitution of 1961. The 1965 constitution had vastly simplified the amendment procedures which would now involve no more than a two-thirds concurrence of the Rhodesian Parliament voting twice in separate sittings. The British officials in Salisbury warned that this step towards preventive detention would have an adverse effect on the talks then in progress. The Rhodesians decided to press forward with the enabling amendment nonetheless. Without hesitation, Wilson ordered his team home.

Commonwealth Prime Ministers were about to converge on London. It might be just as well in any event to adjourn the talks during the difficult period about to begin. Wilson had had a foretaste of Commonwealth troubles in his rapidly worsening relationship with Lusaka where a second series of negotiations important to his strategy had also fallen on hard times.

Another Look at Zambian Sanctions

There had been from the first persistent and profound differences of view between Zambia and Britain respecting the Rhodesian problem. These had largely been resolved only during January with the apparent and unexpected success of the oil embargo which had made the sanctions policy for the first time credible to the Zambians. However by early February, when it was clear that South Africa and Portugal were going to sustain Rhodesia and when the full range of difficulties surrounding Zambia's contingency preparations became clear to the Cabinet, the Zambian Government began to lose interest in any major participation in British sanctions, returning to the recurrent theme that force was the only answer. Now with 'talks' between the British and the Rhodesians actually under way, Zambia was less inclined than ever to take risks with its economy when at the end of the road the United Kingdom might well decide upon some accommodation with the Rhodesians totally unsatisfactory to Lusaka.

This was the dilemma facing Judith Hart in London when she took over Cledwyn Hughes's responsibilities as Minister of State for Commonwealth Relations in the cabinet reshuffle following Britain's elections. She plunged immediately into the closest examination of the Zambian question. Within the Official Committee on Sanctions against Rhodesia she established a separate group of economists to focus exclusively on the impact of sanctions on Zambia and the consequent need for further contingency assistance. It was 23 May 1966, when Mrs. Hart and her team arrived in Lusaka – just three days after the first round of 'talks about talks' had adjourned in London. The British Minister of State was met unceremoniously at the airport by two junior Zambian officials from the Protocol Office. It was an unenviable assignment. The Zambians were less than impressed by a junior Minister who carried the added liability of being a woman. Kaunda was still smarting from his treatment by Wilson. In a radio broadcast that took place about the time the British–Zambian talks got under way, Kaunda breathed contempt for Britain's handling of Rhodesia, accusing the United Kingdom of connivance with conspirators and insisting that the 'talks' constituted *de facto* recognition of the rebel regime.

Mrs. Hart also walked into a rapidly maturing crisis over the Rhodesia railway system. For a number of weeks Lusaka had been retaining all revenues for rail traffic originating in Zambia, refusing to forward them to the central railway office located in the Rhodesian town of Bulawayo. The sector of the railway passing through Rhodesia was accordingly running an acute deficit, for Zambian copper was a major earner for the unified rail system.* When it was apparent that the Zambians were not going to forward remittances, the Rhodesians announced that they would accept in transit no goods originating in Zambia unless paid for in advance in designated currencies. The Zambians refused. Traffic was interrupted shortly after Mrs. Hart's arrival and came to a standstill a few days later.

It was a paradoxical situation. Zambia's exports were now cut off while Zambian imports from Rhodesia continued – the exact reverse of what the United Kingdom was after. If the situation persisted, it would result in some harm to Rhodesia, great damage to Britain and catastrophe for Zambia. The Zambians were reluctant to forward revenue to the rebel regime in part because they erroneously thought

---

* In the previous financial year Zambian copper exports earned almost 25 per cent of the revenue of Rhodesia Railways. It was estimated that approximately £1 million ($2.8 million) a month had to be transferred from Zambia to Rhodesia to keep the system financially viable.

that the railway deficit within Rhodesia was evidence of a sudden and unexpected financial crisis about to overwhelm the rebel economy. Beyond this, the Zambians hoped that their action would excite greater activity in the development of alternative routes. This it did, but after weeks of labour and experimentation it was apparent that no more than one-third of Zambia's normal copper production could be transported over them.

Most important of all, the Zambians assumed that by threatening to cut off the copper which was vital to Britain's economy, they could press London to take more decisive action against Rhodesia. Approximately half of Britain's copper needs were provided by Zambia, payable in sterling. If the supply were cut and not replaced, there would be two million people thrown out of work in Britain within a matter of months, as Harold Wilson later acknowledged in his memoirs. The world price of the metal, already at an astronomical £600 (almost $1,700) a ton, would be forced still higher. The short fall in Britain's supply, assuming it were available at all, would have to be obtained from outside the sterling area, paid for probably in dollars. The cumulative impact on Britain's limping economy would be severe indeed. Within the Zambian Cabinet, which held interminable discussions on the railway crisis, the view was expressed frequently, 'If Britain wants its copper, let it solve the whole issue.'

Britain's response to these pressures remained cool and firm. If the result of the railways impasse were to interdict copper exports but leave imports from Rhodesia intact, the British Government would not feel obligated to assist Zambia. If on the other hand the result were to reduce or stop imports from Rhodesia, thus squeezing Smith's income, the British Government would within reason be responsive to Zambia's needs. In either case, Mrs. Hart made it clear that in Britain's view the first requirement was progressively to cut trade with Rhodesia – not the use of the rail link. Britain's calculated response took the Zambians by surprise. And it made no easier Judith Hart's task of negotiating expanded participation in Britain's sanctions effort.*

---

* The rail crisis persisted for almost seven weeks during which stocks of refined copper accumulated in Zambia valued at some £20 million or close to $60 million at then current (and highly inflated) world market prices. At this point a compromise formula was worked out according to which copper consumers made their own arrangements with the Rhodesian regime for rail charges south of the Zambezi River. British importers arranged transfers to Salisbury through Swiss middlemen, which nonetheless was an unlawful breach of currency regulations under Britain's own sanctions programme. But copper flowed again to the mutual benefit of the

As the talks progressed in Lusaka, it indeed became clear that Zambia was less and less interested in sanctions, as narrowly defined. Zambia's scepticism was strengthened by the difference of view between London and Lusaka as to what finally would constitute a legitimate 'end of the rebellion and restoration of constitutional rule in Rhodesia' as it was phrased in the joint *communiqué* which concluded the first round of negotiations. The Rhodesian–British 'talks' had assumed the greatest significance for the Zambians. They were certain these presaged a sell-out – an unacceptable end of the rebellion. The Zambians thus were wary of accepting London's sanctions formula, which still turned on the idea of selected emergency preparations leading to a fairly rapid decrease of Zambian imports from Rhodesia, because they lacked confidence both in the efficacy of sanctions *and* in British intentions to effect a satisfactory settlement. This being the case, the objective, as the Zambians now began to redefine it, was slowly and steadily to build up a satisfactory and safe alternative to present reliance on Rhodesia, an alternative which would sustain them, not for some months, but for an undetermined period of time. The notion of short-run contingency preparations linked to British sanctions was thus gradually transformed into the concept of full disengagement over the long run as the Zambians instinctively began to feel that they would be confronted with a hostile regime on their southern boundary for the indefinite future.

Mrs. Hart quickly grasped the essentials of the Zambian outlook, for which she developed considerable sympathy. As a result she gradually won the confidence of her Zambian counterparts. She was prepared to recommend in London that the guidelines for contingency aid be expanded to include support for longer term projects as well as short-run contingency preparations. When she arrived in London Judith Hart reported to the Prime Minister, then went to work to gain greater understanding within the Government and among the British public of the unique difficulties Zambia faced. This was critical for there was in Britain little awareness of and even less sympathy for Zambia's awkward and vulnerable position in the Rhodesian affair, and growing impatience with Kaunda's frequent outbursts. Zambia's press in the United Kingdom during this period was particularly bad – 'a calculated campaign to undermine the integrity and strength of Zambia,' Finance Minister Arthur Wina once put it on returning from the British capital. And even British officials who should have known better talked critically of Kaunda's 'bloody-mindedness'.

Zambian and British economies, while Rhodesia had won a new source of foreign exchange.

Within the British Government, Judith Hart's labours were partially rewarded. She left London for Lusaka on 17 June 1966, with an offer of aid amounting to £7 million (nearly $20 million). The assistance Britain now proposed would enable a start to be made on longer-term projects involving the development of overland transport routes and fuel and power supplies.* It would continue to the end of 1966 or to the end of the rebellion, whichever came first. If the rebellion had not ended by the close of the year, London would continue aid under an agreement to be negotiated at that time. The 'end of the rebellion' was again defined as the return to constitutional rule, together with the restoration of normal traffic. Since Rhodesia was in rebellion against the United Kingdom it was up to London to determine the content of 'constitutionality'. But for British aid, there was to be a *quid pro quo*: London wanted Zambia to scale back its imports from Rhodesia by 90 per cent from pre-U.D.I. levels in approximately three months.

It was a small step in the right direction, but still far from adequate insurance against the risks entailed, as Dominic Mulaisho, the head of Zambia's negotiating team, made clear. The anticipated cutback of imports would almost surely mean that the use of the rail line through Rhodesia would be denied. Even under the most optimistic estimates, Zambia envisaged that copper production would fall by one-third and that national income would decline by one-fourth. Here we are, Mulaisho said to Judith Hart's team, contemplating measures at your behest that will do calculable harm to our country while you speak of expenditure ceilings. 'This is like quibbling over the cost of a blood transfusion. . . . We cannot accept the principle that lies behind your offer – that of limited commitment. Our commitment is not limited. Our risks are open-ended. We know that you are reluctant to use force to embark upon military war to end the rebellion in Rhodesia, but we had understood you were prepared to use the weapons of economic war. But, if this is a war of any kind, let us not hear of limited commitments or we shall conclude that it is a war waged with limited determination and with limited sincerity.'

If the United Kingdom were to agree to defray the cost of

---

* British proposals included *inter alia* contributions to the improvement of the Great North Road through Tanzania and the port facilities at Dar es Salaam; improvements at Mtwara airport and harbour, a potentially important outlet in southern Tanzania; the purchase of additional vehicles; and the extra costs involved in the emergency exploitation of Zambian coal deposits and in completing, again on an emergency basis, the link from the Victoria Falls power station to the Kariba power grid.

developing the alternative routes, to maintain its aid until the rebellion had ended, and to assure the restitution of the economy to its pre-sanctions level, it would be quite a different matter. The Zambian team then set forth estimates of required cargo capacities necessary to permit a phased reduction of Rhodesian imports and services. Twenty-eight thousand tons a month would have to be allocated for the importation of petroleum products, including ten thousand tons of furnace oil for smelting copper and a large increase of diesel fuel to run expanded truck fleets. In addition forty-one thousand short tons of carrying capacity would have to be developed within about three months for general cargo, expanded to sixty thousand short tons within six months. While building up to the sixty-thousand-ton level, the short fall would be met from stocks which Zambia had been accumulating over the previous months. Once assurances were in hand that these capacities could be developed Zambian officials said they would be in a position to recommend to Ministers to proceed with a phase down of Rhodesian imports.

This was of course a gigantic order. No government, unless its vital interests were directly and massively engaged, could have given the open-ended commitment the Zambians sought, least of all Britain labouring under a major economic crisis, which Mrs. Hart pointedly called to the Zambians' attention. At the same time, it was foolish and irresponsible to have asked that Zambia assume the risks of cutting its ties to the south without something approaching a full guarantee. The two positions were inherently irreconcilable, providing further arresting evidence of the impracticality of British policy. Judith Hart left the British offer on the table while the Zambians insisted they would move forward on their own without British help to do what they could to bring Smith down, while at the same time protecting their own vital interests.

The Commonwealth Affair

One more matter now arose to complicate relations further between London and Lusaka. At the Lagos Commonwealth meeting in January it had been agreed that the Prime Ministers should next convene in July if the rebellion by then had not been brought to an end. As July approached the British Government suggested postponement until September, having in mind its continuing talks with the Rhodesians. The Commonwealth Secretariat polled the Commonwealth Presidents and Prime Ministers as to their preferences. To Kaunda, who wished the full weight of the Commonwealth to be brought to bear upon Wilson as quickly as possible, the postponement was a breach of faith for which he held Wilson personally accountable. He insisted that the meeting be held as scheduled in July and be moved from London. He pressed for New Delhi. The Secretariat found that many members did not care which date was selected; some in fact preferred September, and that month was finally settled on.

Early in July a directive circulated within the Zambian Government making clear that, with the exception of the Foreign Minister and the Minister of State for Commonwealth Affairs, no Minister, junior Minister or Permanent Secretary was to travel to the United Kingdom or to any other Commonwealth country until further notice. Official visits already laid on for senior members of the Government were peremptorily cancelled. On 12 July Kaunda in a speech on the occasion of his installation as Chancellor of the University of Zambia threatened to pull Zambia out of the Commonwealth entirely. He had earlier suggested organizing a move to expel Britain! Two days later it was announced that Zambia would not participate in the Commonwealth Games soon to take place in Jamaica. On 15 July the Minister of Information announced that B.B.C. relays to Zambia would be terminated. Viewing these developments with considerable apprehension, Canada's Prime Minister, Lester Pearson, sent a message to Kaunda asserting that the Commonwealth was not a British club and advising Zambia not to bolt. Arnold Smith, the Commonwealth Secretary-General, encouraged Kaunda to come to the September summit meeting in order to assure that Zambia's concerns about U.D.I. be presented as effectively as possible.

These developments now became enmeshed with the unsolved problem of contingency aid. At the beginning of August Malcolm MacDonald came to Lusaka with another proposal, more flexible than the earlier one. The original offer of £7 million for the balance of the 1966 calendar year still stood but restrictions on its utilization were now considerably loosened. If the rebellion had not terminated by the year's end Britain promised another meeting with the Zambian Government in December for the purpose of pledging close to another £7 million for the first half of 1967. The total package then would come to just under £14 million or approximately $39 million. In return for this London expected that Zambia would further reduce imports, but with great realism specified neither amounts nor time schedules. London did ask for assurances that Zambia would do its utmost to permit the maximum shipment of copper. Finally, the British Government made clear that it would have to reconsider its offer were Zambia to break diplomatic relations with Britain or to leave the Commonwealth.

Several strings had thus been disentangled from the earlier offer.

But several more were entwined around it. It was a generous proposal presented at a time when the United Kingdom was retrenching its commitments throughout the world. On 20 July Wilson had in fact announced a major austerity programme which included cuts in overseas expenditures by at least £100 million ($280 million) annually. Still, the British offer to Zambia did little to abate, as officials in London hoped it might, the prevailing notion in Lusaka that British talks with the rebel regime were a prelude to a sell-out. British policy was caught once more in a contradiction. Talks worked against the efficacy of sanctions, certainly in the case of Zambia; and it was upon the anticipated impact of sanctions that the talks depended for success.

For President Kaunda, contingency aid and an accompanying Zambian commitment to expand sanctions could not be disassociated from Britain's ultimate objectives in Rhodesia; nor could they now be disengaged from the forthcoming Commonwealth meeting. He decided not to accept the British offer until the results from that meeting were in. If the results were negative Zambia presumably would leave the Commonwealth 'in great sorrow for I believe in the Commonwealth', he said. Aid arrangements, if still applicable at all, would then have to be renegotiated. If the results were favourable Zambia would then doubtless sign an agreement with Britain, placing its seal upon the British offer while remaining in the Commonwealth. So, instead of making himself beholden to the United Kingdom prior to the conference, Kaunda brought double pressure to bear on the British: a threat to leave the Commonwealth and an unwillingness to participate in an accelerated sanctions squeeze. It was hard to know at the time whether this was a master stroke – or a futile gesture costing the Zambians almost £14 million.*

Beyond all doubt, however, was Kaunda's now quite unreserved disdain for Wilson, a clever showman, he said, in an article published in London early in September, who approached the coming Commonwealth conference 'like an over-exposed actor seeking a few quick rounds of applause rather than a statesman working for a just settle-

---

* It was not until February 1967 that a British-Zambian 'Memorandum of Intention and Understanding' was signed allocating £13,850,000 ($38,780,000) for contingency aid. By this time, however, the Zambians clearly viewed the funds as no more than partial 'compensation' for damages incurred by U.D.I. and certainly not as 'aid' on behalf of a joint British-Zambian sanctions effort. Britain probably viewed the transaction in much the same light, an attempt to mollify the irate Zambians while hoping that the impasse with Rhodesia might one day be settled by a negotiated compromise.

ment of a major international conflict.' Showmanship could not be a substitute for action and Kaunda said he would refuse to attend a 'repeat performance'. *The Times* noted that in the history of Commonwealth relations there had been few parallels of the 'crisis of distrust' that now characterized the Zambian President's attitude toward the British Prime Minister.

The whole affair had about it the ineluctable quality of Greek tragedy as the two Commonwealth partners, who at the outset of the Rhodesia crisis appeared to need each other most, seemed fated to fall out. Zambia more than most was able to measure the chronic short fall between London's ambitious objectives in Rhodesia and the inadequacy of its means to fulfil them. This was because Zambia knew its own vulnerability in applying sanctions and because Zambians had had long experience with the intransigence of Rhodesian whites and with resolute white power in Southern Africa. Moreover Zambia confronted an explosive situation at home which made every confrontation with Rhodesia a matter of highest risk to Zambia's vital interests. In the face of these dangers and frustrations, perhaps unprecedented for a new government and arising from a situation for which Zambia bore neither blame nor responsibility, the Zambian Government accused Britain of hypocrisy (now personified in Harold Wilson), argued with undeniable logic that the only way to achieve announced British ends in Rhodesia was to use British force, and concluded that effective pressure must be brought to bear against Wilson before it could be brought to bear against Smith. The most promising vehicle now was the Commonwealth.

VII

'NIBMAR'

No one knew better than Harold Wilson that the Commonwealth Prime Ministers' meeting which convened in London early in September 1966 was going to be the most critical in the history of that unique institution. Twenty-two of twenty-three Commonwealth members were represented (Nyerere's Tanzania was the exception). The contentious Rhodesian issue was first on the agenda and the debate would range across nine of the conference's ten days, precluding detailed consideration of any other issue.

The 'presence' of two absentees was almost palpable. President Kaunda stayed away in protest, but appeared in print in the *Sunday Times* of 4 September immediately before the conference opened. He advocated again both the use of force and the application of mandatory sanctions, and warned that Commonwealth failure to meet the Rhodesian challenge would threaten the organization's continued existence. 'We could not in all conscience,' he said, 'continue to belong to [such] an organization. . . .' President Nyerere's influence was equally felt. Late in July he and Kaunda had met in Dar es Salaam with Uganda's President Obote and Vice-President Murumbi of Kenya. The four agreed to press within the Commonwealth for a British commitment not to grant independence to Rhodesia before the achievement of majority rule. If only Wilson were to agree to this, an article in the Tanzanian *Nationalist* contended some weeks later (7 September), then at least Africa and the United Kingdom would be on the same side of the issue, and other problems could be worked out in due course. Almost certainly the article had been written by Nyerere himself. The day before the Commonwealth conference opened, African delegates assembled at the home of Sierra Leone's High Commissioner. They ratified the decision taken at Dar es Salaam. The doctrine was quickly reduced to the acronym NIBMAR ('no independence before majority rule'), now to take its place alongside U.D.I. as one of the distinguishing insignia of the Rhodesian affair.

In a way, what transpired served as a fitting (and, one is tempted to say, an appropriately daft) outcome for a policy which seemed incapable of matching effective means with announced ends, and which now clearly was controlled by short-term expediencies designed to minimize losses at the margin under circumstances where it could not achieve results at the centre. Wilson's antagonists threatened dissolution of the Commonwealth unless Britain agreed to 'no independence before majority rule' and mandatory sanctions at the United Nations. Under pain of accepting both of these conditions if a settlement with Smith were not forthcoming, Wilson now tried to extract a compromise solution from the rebels. Failing this, he then accepted NIBMAR as British policy and pledged himself to mandatory sanctions, thereby for the moment consolidating his position with militant Commonwealth members, but placing totally out of reach any conceivable resolution of the Rhodesian impasse and sacrificing at the same time even minimal consensus with the Tories in Parliament. To recoup these losses he would in time have to reverse himself, again endangering the Commonwealth and his policy at the United Nations, only to find once more that he could not extract a settlement from the rebels even minimally consistent with the guidelines laid down in the six principles. It had become a rudderless policy, caught repeatedly by contrary crosswinds.

Confrontation at Marlborough House

Delegates assembled at 10.00 a.m. on Tuesday, 6 September 1966, in the handsome Blenheim Salon of Marlborough House on Pall Mall, once the residence of Queen Mary, grandmother of Elizabeth II, and now the headquarters of the Commonwealth secretariat. Wilson opened the conference with a seventy-minute address heard in silence by his Commonwealth colleagues. He emphasized that from the beginning the United Kingdom had taken a clear and firm line of total opposition to U.D.I. While ruling out the use of force, Britain had employed sanctions to create a situation in which Rhodesia would be willing to end its rebellion and to reach a solution in accordance with the now familiar six principles. Wilson admitted that his prediction at Lagos concerning the speed with which sanctions would prove effective had been in error. More time was obviously needed, but sanctions were biting and would create increasing problems for the regime. Britain's seriousness of purpose was evidenced by the actions already taken and the resulting costs to the United Kingdom which he put at around £100 million ($280 million).* Britain would not be deterred by this financial drain even though it occurred at a time when the country could least afford it. Wilson then reviewed Britain's assistance to Zambia including both the airlift and the pending offer of some £14 million ($39 million). All Commonwealth countries, he suggested, might contribute to this important effort to enable Zambia to cut back further its trade with Rhodesia, thus helping to plug one of the major remaining gaps in the sanctions dike.

Referring to the 'talks about talks' of the previous four months, Wilson emphasized their informal and exploratory character and insisted that genuine negotiations must be preceded by the restoration of legality. With respect to the question of majority rule, the British Prime Minister pointed out that time was needed to train Africans and that an immediate transition was unrealistic. Heretofore the United Kingdom, when granting freedom to colonial areas, had insisted on majority rule before independence. (The two exceptions were South Africa in 1910 and Zanzibar in 1963.) The only circumstances under which it would now agree to independence prior to majority rule was if it could be demonstrated that such a solution was acceptable to all of the Rhodesian people.

The meeting was adjourned immediately after the Prime Minister's address. The Africans, now joined by the Caribbean Commonwealth countries together with the representative from India, gathered at Uganda House to puzzle over Wilson's speech. At Lagos they thought they had agreed that the object was to terminate Smith's regime. This would be followed by a period of direct rule, a constitutional conference and a settlement leading to majority rule. Wilson now seemed

---

* Everyone played the numbers game concerning the cost of sanctions. Estimates high or low became a function of the audience one addressed or the policy one favoured. Wilson wanted to impress the Commonwealth. His estimate was meant to be confidential, but it leaked and became the subject of a Parliamentary exchange on 21 February 1967. The Prime Minister told Tory critics that the earlier estimate given to the Commonwealth had been too high, and in any event represented the cost to Britain of the rebellion in general, not the cost of sanctions in particular nor the actual cost to the Exchequer or to Britain's balance of payments. The cost to the Exchequer he estimated at only £15 million ($42 million) from U.D.I. to 6 February 1967. Shortly thereafter the Rhodesian Finance Minister, for whom the calculations were meant to serve a very different purpose, conservatively estimated the cost of sanctions to the United Kingdom at not less than £150 million ($420 million)! Of course much depended also on what items one chose to include in the calculation.

to be saying that Britain might negotiate a settlement leaving intact a minority rule government, albeit surrounded by constitutional guarantees for the achievement of ultimate majority rule.*

The seriousness of the situation unfolded over the next three days as one delegate after another from the African, Caribbean and Asian countries made his reply. Zambia's Foreign Minister, Simon Kapwepwe, urged the conference to call on Britain to assure that a period of direct rule would precede independence, which would not be granted until majority rule was secured. The NIBMAR theme was repeatedly sounded. So were other concerns. Zambia's Finance Minister, Arthur Wina, commenting on Wilson's plea for Commonwealth assistance to Zambia, noted that there were many Commonwealth countries much poorer than Zambia. It was hardly justifiable that they should take bread out of their own people's mouths to help Zambia quell a rebellion which the United Kingdom had the power to crush if it wished to do so. He disparaged sanctions, predicting that Smith could hang on indefinitely so long as South Africa and Portugal assisted him. Singapore's brilliant Prime Minister, Lee Kuan Yew, predicted that the conference would have to decide upon more effective sanctions or run the risk of a massive African walkout. When on Friday afternoon, 9 September, the conference adjourned for the weekend, a tense stalemate had been reached.

On Saturday morning, Wilson held an extraordinary Cabinet meeting preparatory to his scheduled reply to the attacks made on British policy, which was due the following Monday. There had been the hint of a compromise position in a thirty-minute conference address made the previous day by Canada's Prime Minister, Lester Pearson. He appealed for more time to permit a stiffened version of existing sanctions to take effect suggesting that if they failed, a United Nations embargo on trade with Rhodesia could then be considered, starting perhaps with oil. The British Cabinet gave Pearson's idea careful consideration.

When the conference reconvened after the weekend, Wilson outlined a detailed *scenario* for achieving a negotiated settlement and a plan for stiffening the penalties against Rhodesia in the event of negotiations failing. The latter included mandatory sanctions against selected Rhodesian exports, perhaps ultimately to include oil. At the same time Wilson noted that the United Kingdom must exercise

---

* In fact the Lagos *communiqué* was ambiguous. The constitutional conference, representing all sections of the Rhodesian population, 'would be for the purpose of recommending a constitution leading to majority rule on a basis acceptable to the people of Rhodesia as a whole'. Nothing was said about NIBMAR.

caution to assure that mandatory sanctions would not expand into general economic warfare in Southern Africa, which Britain at all costs wished to avoid. Nothing was said about NIBMAR.

Once again the African, Asian and Caribbean group caucused. The technique was unique at Commonwealth meetings, normally run with clubroom decorum, and deeply disturbing to the older Commonwealth countries, particularly Australia and New Zealand. The caucus, which actually had assigned to it a large meeting room in the east wing of Marlborough House, included all the 'New' Commonwealth members (those states having become independent since the Second World War), except Malawi, Malta, Cyprus and Malaysia. The former two were a part of what might be called the 'Wilson group' which also included, in addition to the United Kingdom, Australia and New Zealand. Malaysia and Cyprus leaned strongly toward the New Commonwealth caucus without fully identifying themselves with it. Canada remained in the position of a true intermediary. The caucus now reaffirmed its demand for NIBMAR. Many also wanted to insist on the use of force. While the caucus met, the afternoon plenary session of the conference had to be postponed for a full hour. Though the older Commonwealth countries did not appreciate it at the time, the caucus also served to dampen the ardour of those, particularly Zambia's Foreign Minister, Simon Kapwepwe, who argued for a withdrawal from the conference or from the Commonwealth itself over the Rhodesian issue. And before the meetings had ended, the caucus would also have shunted aside proposals for separate *communiqués* or the attempt to railroad through a majority *communiqué* drafted by the Afro–Asian–Caribbean lobby.

The debate once it reopened raged on into Monday evening. Wilson, under constant attack, was becoming nettled and irritable. When the meeting finally broke up shortly before 11 p.m. an agreed Commonwealth position on Rhodesia appeared hopeless. 'It seemed', said the Ugandan President, Dr. Milton Obote, 'as if Britain had closed all the doors for us, and the conference would inevitably break up.' Late that same night another important meeting took place in Wilson's office in Marlborough House. It was agreed that if Smith refused to negotiate within the terms laid down by H.M. Government Britain would no longer be bound by any previous formula allowing for independence under minority rule. Envisaged was a package deal which would leave the initiative in British hands to have another attempt at a negotiated settlement with Smith, failing which Britain would move significantly toward NIBMAR as well as stronger sanctions under United Nations auspices.

Early the next morning, Tuesday, 13 September, Wilson met with Kenya's Joseph Murumbi and Tom Mboya, then with Uganda's

Milton Obote, Sierra Leone's Albert Margai and the Indian Foreign Minister Swaram Singh. Lester Pearson of Canada was also involved as was Secretary-General Arnold Smith. Though some progress towards an agreed formula was made in these individual meetings, the going continued to be rough. Wilson still declined to make an unconditional commitment to majority rule and many of the New Commonwealth states did not find his phased plan an adequate substitute. The Afro-Asian draft insisted either that the British use force or that the Security Council impose comprehensive mandatory sanctions. It also pressed for a time-table with a strict deadline for the U.N. sanctions policy to prove effective, a categorical declaration of no independence before majority rule, and a flat demand for a Rhodesian referendum based on one man, one vote on the terms of any final settlement. It was at this point that Wilson turned to Canada's Lester Pearson asking him if he would try his hand at marrying the British and Afro-Asian drafts. 'I wasn't sure whether I was being asked to commit polygamy or incest,' Pearson reflected later, 'but whatever it was, I did it.'

Zambia's Simon Kapwepwe decided not to wait for the result of Pearson's effort. He had been greatly upset by Wilson's position and the inability of the conference to face him down and now wanted to decamp. His colleague, Minister of Finance Arthur Wina, advised him that this would have the effect of a walkout: it was important to secure President Kaunda's permission. A telephone call went through to State House in Lusaka and Kaunda told Kapwepwe he wanted him back in any event. Wina was to stay on as the head of Zambia's delegation. Technically it would not be a walkout. Arnold Smith accompanied the Zambian Foreign Minister to his car past the waiting reporters without incident. When Kapwepwe arrived at the airport, however, newsmen pressed him for a statement. He declared that Africa had got absolutely nothing, then fired a parting short as he left. This conference, Kapwepwe said, 'makes us know Wilson is coming to be a racialist'.

The following morning, Wednesday, 14 September, Wilson was in a prickly mood. Kapwepwe's remark had deeply irritated him. The plenary session was due to convene at 10 a.m. On the Marlborough House bulletin board, predictably by this time, appeared a notice, '10.00 a.m. meeting of the Afro-Asian group.' For one and a half hours Wilson and the other non-caucus heads were kept waiting. The British Prime Minister let it be known he was seriously considering adjourning the conference. By the time the New Commonwealth delegations filed in he was in a temper. It was not simply the long delays, he complained. There had been regrettable leaks to the press. He responded in anger to Kapwepwe's charge, calling it 'actionable'.

It was a strong statement delivered, as he later recalled in his memoir, 'in a cold but controlled fury'.

Pearson had laboured late into the night on his compromise draft which was now available for the delegates. Remarkably and unexpectedly (it had been decided at their caucus, just concluded) the New Commonwealth group agreed to attempt a joint *communiqué* using the Pearson draft as a base. A committee was appointed to consider the draft in detail. By five that afternoon the task was finished. It took no more than thirty-five minutes for the delegates to approve its fourteen paragraphs one by one. There were no dissenting voices.

Broadly speaking the final *communiqué* recorded first, a majority position, and second, a series of British decisions 'noted' by the conference. The majority position, held by 'most Heads of Government', presented the New Commonwealth point of view. It advocated *inter alia* the use of force, no independence before majority rule, the termination of 'talks' with the illegal regime, and the imposition of comprehensive mandatory sanctions including under Article 42 military enforcement procedures. More important, since they fixed the guidelines of London's policy for the next several months, were the British decisions incorporated in the *communiqué* and 'noted' by the conference. These in turn fell into two categories: the basis of a negotiated settlement now to be presented to Rhodesia as an ultimatum, and the steps Britain would pursue if the proposed negotiated settlement were not accepted. The settlement *scenario* involved the following: termination of the rebellion; appointment by the Governor of a broadly-based representative administration; responsibility of the Governor for the security forces; release of political prisoners; and restoration of peaceful and democratic political activity. With this interim administration, the British Government would negotiate a new constitution, based on the six principles, which 'would be submitted for acceptance to the people of Rhodesia as a whole by appropriate democratic means' judged to be 'fair and free' by both the British Parliament and Government, and (a new concept) 'acceptable to the general world community'. This meant that 'there would be no independence before majority rule if the people of Rhodesia as a whole were shown to be opposed to it.'

Britain proposed immediately to communicate the foregoing through Governor Gibbs to all sections of opinion in Rhodesia. If the illegal regime refused 'to take the initial and indispensable steps' to bring the rebellion to an end and to vest authority in the Governor, then Britain would, first, withdraw all previous proposals and would not thereafter 'be prepared to submit to the British Parliament any settlement which involves independence before majority rule' and second, 'given the full support of Commonwealth representatives at the United Nations', would join in sponsoring in the Security Council before the end of the year a resolution providing for selective mandatory economic sanctions against Rhodesia.

At a concluding press conference, Wilson noted that 'the Commonwealth has been tested in the hottest of flames and it has survived.' For this accomplishment he owed much to Pearson whose drafting skills were exceeded if anything by the trust he inspired in many members of the New Commonwealth. 'We still don't trust Wilson an inch,' the representative of one of the new states told a reporter. 'But we trust Pearson to keep him from following his instincts.'

'Negotiations about Negotiations'

Ironically, the Commonwealth *communiqué*, resulting to a great extent from the efforts of African, Asian and Caribbean members to avert a negotiated deal between Britain and Rhodesia, now became the vehicle for renewing talks in Salisbury – and, beyond that, raising them to the ministerial level directly involving Smith himself. Strictly speaking, of course, Wilson's new Commonwealth Secretary, Herbert Bowden, was simply to present to all sectors of opinion in Rhodesia, including the illegal regime, Britain's final proposals as recorded in the *communiqué*. Genuine negotiations could take place only after the rebellion had ended and only with the newly formed, interim Government. If the previous exchanges at official level had involved only 'talks about talks', perhaps, as *The Times* suggested, the forthcoming ministerial contacts were not negotiations so much as 'negotiations about negotiations'. It was, however, as everyone now knew, a distinction without a difference. And lest anyone were still in doubt, Smith himself quickly put them straight. The British Government had shifted positions, he told the Rhodesian Front on 23 September. Despite 'subterfuge and camouflage, it cannot be denied that they are having discussions with our Government to see if they can find a way out of this predicament.'

Arrangements for the Bowden mission were made by a senior civil servant in the Commonwealth Office, Sir Morrice James, who was dispatched to Salisbury by Wilson before the Commonwealth Conference had ended to explain to Governor Gibbs why it was necessary, in order to save the Commonwealth from dissolution, to issue what amounted to an ultimatum to Smith. Gibbs was hardly enthusiastic about the prospective penalties which supported the ultimatum: recourse to U.N. mandatory sanctions and a refusal to grant independence before majority rule. But together with Beadle, he welcomed the ministerial mission (Bowden was to be accompanied by the Attorney General, Sir Elwyn Jones), and urged them to come without delay. Sir Morrice also won Smith's agreement for talks to be held at Government House under the Governor's aegis. On 19 September 1966, Bowden and the Attorney General became the first British Ministers to set foot on rebel territory since U.D.I. They were driven off in a police-escorted convoy to Government House where a detachment of Rhodesian police formed a tight security screen.

During the next ten days British Minister and rebel Prime Minister met no less than five times to discuss Rhodesia's future. (In accordance with his mandate set forth in the Commonwealth *communiqué*, Bowden also met numerous representatives of the Rhodesian community.) He hit it off well with Smith, leaving the impression, as Colin Legum writing for the *Observer* noted at the time, that there had been progress toward making a deal. The new Commonwealth Secretary had been hand-picked by Wilson for just this job in an unexpected Cabinet shuffle the previous August, at which time the genial and dedicated but quite unpredictable Arthur Bottomley had been eased out. (Bottomley had also made clear his aversion to 'talks about talks'.) Bowden was a realist. He was sure that Smith was the only credible leader in Rhodesia and the only person available to negotiate with, and he was equally certain that the basis for agreement would have to be the 1961 constitution, suitably amended. There was already speculation in *The Times* that if agreement could be gained on the broad outlines of a settlement, Smith himself might be included in an interim government, or, yet more astonishing, be invited to head it. It came as something of a surprise, then, that on his departure from Salisbury on 28 September, Bowden's prognosis was extremely cautious. The talks had been frank; the air had been cleared, but he was not optimistic. Both sides, he said, were going 'to retire to their corners to do a little thinking'.

Bowden carried back with him an *aide-mémoire* in which opposing views were recorded. It bears careful attention for it became the springboard from which the debate developed over the next two months. The paper encompassed first, the 'return to legality' (which the Rhodesians called 'restoration of normal relations') involving the renunciation of the rebellion, the establishment of an interim government, and the termination of sanctions; second, procedures for testing the acceptability to the whole of the Rhodesian people of whatever final constitutional settlement the two sides had agreed to; and third, the outlines of the new Rhodesian constitution itself.

The very first problem encountered was the sequence of the above steps – the old 'cart and horse' problem which had preoccupied the

Rhodesian and British officials in previous months. Britain insisted
that prior to everything else, the rebellion must end and a new interim
government be installed of broad compass, including Africans,
appointed by the Governor and approved by London. With this
interim government, Britain would then negotiate the final terms of a
new constitution and arrange for a test of its acceptability. Smith
insisted that a premature 'return to constitutionality would be an
invitation for Rhodesia to put its head into a noose.' The process
must be reversed. First, negotiate a new constitution with the existing
Rhodesian Government, test its acceptability and ratify it in London.
Then, new elections could be held bringing into being a government
which Britain could recognize as permanent and independent. Under
the Rhodesian formula there would be no 'interim' government
at all.

There were other differences. Britain stated that the security forces
must be responsible to the Governor during the interim period and
that installations at Kariba Dam be placed under special protection.
Rhodesia refused on both counts. (In subsequent exchanges Britain
also stipulated that it would reserve the right to provide military
assistance if requested by the Governor.) Finally, Britain wanted
political detainees to be released and normal political activity to be
permitted in order to assure a genuinely impartial referendum on the
terms of the final settlement; to which the Rhodesians added the not
unreasonable proviso that the detainees must give a 'genuine undertaking to abide by the law'. However Rhodesia later announced that
no detainees were being held on 'purely political grounds', and the
regime's requirements for releasing them stiffened significantly. In
short, there was virtually no agreement whatsoever on the procedures
to return the situation to legality.

The second broad area canvassed by the *aide-mémoire* concerned
the test of acceptability. This, Britain said, recalling Harold Wilson's
formula proposed in Salisbury just prior to U.D.I., would probably
be carried out by a Royal Commission authorized to determine how
best to ascertain the opinion of the various sections of the community
and then to implement these findings. Rhodesia accepted Britain's
requirement that it must be assured of the acceptability of a constitutional settlement to the people of Rhodesia, and would need only
to be satisfied as to the terms of reference, procedures and composition of such a Commission.

Finally there was the constitutional settlement itself which both
sides agreed should be based on an amended version of the 1961
constitution. However, as before, there were several points of serious
disagreement. Britain insisted on 'entrenching' in the constitution
(that is, making subject to the toughest amendment procedures)

those provisions which would prevent gerrymandering constituencies or otherwise upsetting the ratio of seats elected preponderantly by those possessing low qualifications for the franchise (the 'B' Roll seats, fifteen in number and largely occupied by Africans) and seats elected preponderantly by those possessing high qualifications for the franchise (the 'A' Roll seats, fifty in number and at the time all occupied by whites). Rhodesia objected that this proposal would deprive the Rhodesian Government of a 'braking mechanism', as Smith called it, against the premature advent of African rule. The matter was put as follows in the Rhodesian summary of the Bowden–Smith talks: 'Rhodesia felt strongly that she should be relatively free to alter the number of "A" Roll seats if, at any stage, this appeared necessary to prevent the premature assumption of majority rule, i.e. before Africans have acquired the necessary degree of responsibility, tolerance, fair play, etc. consistent with the maintenance of responsible government.' The prospect left the British Ministers aghast as manipulation of any kind to slow the pace toward African rule was hardly consonant with 'guarantees' respecting 'unimpeded progress to majority rule' called for in the first and second principles.

Britain further specified that a 'blocking mechanism' must be introduced respecting the amendment of the specially entrenched clauses. The idea was that Africans in the legislature, by combining their votes, could block constitutional amendments held not to be in the interests of the African community. That was to be the first safeguard against retrogressive actions. Britain also insisted on a second safeguard, that such amendments be made subject to the approval of some external authority such as a special committee of the Privy Council sitting in London. Rhodesia rejected any role for an external authority as incompatible with independence. While accepting the notion of a blocking percentage of African votes in Parliament (ultimately set at 25 per cent and known as 'the blocking quarter'), Salisbury proposed that the African seats be so distributed as to make necessary, in order to achieve the blocking percentage, the inclusion of some Government-appointed African chiefs.

The United Kingdom advocated relaxing further the 'B' Roll (low qualification) franchise requirements. This would not have increased African representation in Parliament but would draw more Africans into the political process; Rhodesia agreed, but as a *quid pro quo* insisted, as it had in earlier negotiations, that cross-voting be abolished. (The 1961 constitution, it will be recalled, had introduced this procedure to dilute the otherwise stark racial division between the 'B' Roll and the 'A' Roll. It allowed each roll to have a 25 per cent influence on the other.) Britain explicitly rejected this compromise; cross-voting as an expression of multi-racialism had to remain.

On 11 October, the 'Rhodesia Group' in the British Cabinet completed its review of the *aide-mémoire* and set forth its 'final terms' for a settlement (though there could still be discussion of details). The terms were somewhat more specific than those just reviewed, but no different in substance. Sir Morrice James carried the British paper to Rhodesia on 13 October. Smith's reaction when he read the document was no more encouraging than had been his interview with the Rhodesian *Sunday Mail* some days before. He had publicly rejected Britain's all-important proposal for a return to legality, declaring that the 'present Rhodesian Government was elected under the 1961 Constitution before 11 November, and Rhodesia expected the British Government to accept this as a fact of life.'

On 20 October, having received Smith's oral reply, Sir Morrice flew back to London. Smith had insisted once again that he would restore normal relations (return to legality) only after the final settlement was signed, sealed and delivered. He would be 'mad' to give up independence for an unknown constitution, he maintained. On 4 November, the regime's written reply to Britain's terms was received. Questions of clarification were then put by London on 11 November and answered by Salisbury six days later. By roughly mid November and despite all this paper-passing, the points of difference remained, if anything, deeper than ever.

By now time had all but run out. In the conclusion of its 4 November reply, the regime had averred that the differences remaining between the two sides were not so great that they could not be bridged by negotiations. The Rhodesians invited Bowden to return. There was no reply. Two days later, in an interview in the Rhodesian *Sunday Mail*, Smith said that he and Wilson were the only ones who could solve the problem, 'but Mr. Wilson won't talk to me'. Still no response came from London about renewed negotiations. On 22 November Smith told a New Zealand journalist that he was prepared to meet British leaders in London or Salisbury or perhaps at another venue. The following day the British Prime Minister spoke in the Commons of a 'very wide gap of principle' which still remained. There was little hope of any sudden breakthrough that would make it unnecessary for the United Kingdom to move the problem to the U.N. early in December. A question was put whether there might be a meeting between himself and Mr. Smith. Wilson answered, 'I shall be very happy to meet Mr. Smith or any other Prime Minister of Rhodesia . . .' – to which he added, with an ironic significance which soon would become apparent – 'when Rhodesia has returned to constitutional rule.'

Preparations for the Summit

By the fourth week in November 1966, the Rhodesian affair was moving steadily towards the denouement outlined in the Commonwealth *communiqué*. Wilson confessed that in all the exchanges that had taken place since the commencement of 'talks about talks' beginning in early May, there had been no progress whatsoever, 'not by one inch', towards an acceptable settlement. It came as something of a surprise, then, that after revealing to Parliament on 23 November his deep pessimism, Harold Wilson announced that Bowden would leave the following night for Rhodesia. Governor Gibbs had made an urgent appeal to the Commonwealth Secretary to pay one more visit to Salisbury.

When Bowden arrived, a staff of fourteen disembarked with him. There was seriousness of purpose about this final venture. The visit would be short, in keeping with the rapidly approaching deadline and the staccato schedule leading up to it. Bowden was to report to the British Cabinet on the morning of 28 November. The Prime Minister had scheduled a statement to the House of Commons for that same afternoon. A white paper, already drafted, would be issued on 29 November outlining Britain's effort to inform the people of Rhodesia of the requirements incorporated in the Commonwealth *communiqué* and the failure to gain an acceptable settlement within these terms of reference. Parliamentary debate would take place on 30 November and 1 December. The Commonwealth Sanctions Committee would convene on 2 December to assure Commonwealth support for Britain's approach to the U.N. Then during the week of 5 December a resolution requesting selective mandatory sanctions would be introduced in the Security Council. Already Mrs. Judith Hart, the Minister of State in the Commonwealth Office, and Malcolm MacDonald, the Special Representative for East and Central Africa, were conducting discussions in depth in Kenya, Uganda and Nigeria. The latter two countries were members of the Security Council.

In Salisbury, Bowden and Smith met with the Governor and Chief Justice Beadle, who had been more than ordinarily busy behind the scenes. The conversations ran on for two and a half hours. Bowden left for London at noon the following day. Chatting with reporters at his residence gate, Smith said he had been very satisfied with the talks, denying that the brevity of Mr. Bowden's visit indicated a failure. He added cryptically, 'Now it remains for Mr. Bowden to gain the concurrence of his Government.' Arriving in London early on Monday, 28 November, Bowden at the airport admitted that there were 'some minor concessions'. He hurried directly to a conference with the Prime Minister at 10 Downing Street.

Bowden had already cabled Smith's 'minor concessions' to Wilson from Salisbury. One point in particular caught Wilson's eye. Smith suggested that rather than introduce an interim broad-based government, he would consider once again accepting the 1961 constitution, in effect temporarily returning the Rhodesian situation to where it had been as of 10 November 1965 until the test of acceptability had been carried out and the new constitution approved. This would leave Smith in complete control of the situation whatever the outcome of the test of acceptability. But it had the appearance of a return to legality and suggested a degree of flexibility which might warrant further investigation. Smith had also suggested that some impartial mechanism might be set up to examine all detainees, releasing those who had not been guilty of criminal acts. Finally, he said he would consider the end of censorship.

It was hardly a leap forward. Nothing was said about the Governor assuming responsibility for the security forces nor about a United Kingdom military presence in Rhodesia during the transitional phase. And Smith's readiness to return to the 1961 constitution sounded more like a willingness on his part to reinstate the Governor than the other way round. Bowden left behind another set of questions to clarify the position further but clearly Smith's movement, however small, was titillating Wilson's imagination. According to Wilson's own account in his memoir, it was on Saturday evening, 26 November, with Bowden's cabled report in hand, that he conceived the Churchillian notion of a summit meeting on a cruiser. Perhaps it was not so much the content of Bowden's message as what it appeared to signify by way of a new mood in Salisbury. *The Times* had described it as a 'highly significant change of tone'. Wilson had a hunch that Smith might give more ground. Some in the British Government believed that South Africa's new Prime Minister, Balthazar Johannes Vorster, was urging the Rhodesians to settle. Vorster had succeeded the assassinated South African leader, Dr. Henrik Verwoerd, the previous September and had promptly declared his intention to follow Verwoerd's policy towards Rhodesia, regarding it as a domestic dispute in which South Africa would remain neutral. Undoubtedly he favoured a settlement and made his views known in London and Salisbury, though probably without bringing any pressure to bear on the latter.*

---

* According to Wilson (again as reported in his memoir), Prime Minister Salazar of Portugal also 'had intervened strongly with Mr. Smith' both immediately before and after the *Tiger* talks.

With Bowden in attendance, Wilson on Monday, 28 November, met twice with the 'Rhodesia Group' of Ministers unfolding his plan for a meeting with Smith on H.M.S. *Tiger*, a British cruiser currently on a goodwill visit to Casablanca and which could be made available at Gibraltar. It was, he argued, absurd to incur the cost of mandatory sanctions if Smith were ready to climb down on acceptable terms. And if he were not, the Labour Government would at least have scotched Tory accusations that negotiations had terminated prematurely. It was decided that though Bowden had just returned, Sir Morrice James would be sent out immediately to renew contact with the rebel Prime Minister. Late on 28 November, at one hour's notice, James secretly left London on an R.A.F. Comet for Salisbury.

The following day, Tuesday, 29 November, Wilson informed the Commons of Sir Morrice's return to Salisbury. Heath pledged full support so long as Wilson kept trying for an agreement. Keep talking and forget about time-tables and deadlines, the Tory Leader advised. Wilson's problem, however, was not the Opposition; it was his own back-benchers who were deeply apprehensive that a deal might be struck with Smith. During the protracted talks in Salisbury there had been considerable comment about voting against the Government if there were a sell-out, and even threats to resign the whip. Speculation about resignations extended even to Wilson's Cabinet. Rumour had it that the British representative to the U.N., Lord Caradon, threatened to step down over Rhodesian policy (as he had once before under a Conservative government in October 1962). Doubts were not exactly laid to rest when, on his arrival in London at the end of October, he explained to the press that the speculation was groundless 'at the moment'.

Motions had been tabled in the Commons demanding majority rule before independence, or the achievement of majority rule in less than ten years through enforceable and irrevocable procedures. These had attracted widespread back-bench support. One resolution gained 115 signatures. A pressure group was formed within the party to insist that there be no sell-out to Smith. The mood of many was epitomized by the story of a strongly pro-African Member of Parliament who, it was said, had seen President Kaunda and then, subsequently, Prime Minister Wilson. Wilson asked what the member had said to the Zambian President. 'I told him what I thought would happen.' 'What was that?' said Wilson. 'That there would be no sell-out,' came the answer. 'Good,' replied Wilson. 'I told him,' said the member, 'there would be no sell-out because Smith would not buy.'

Clearly, from Wilson's point of view the situation demanded careful cultivation. Chancellor of the Exchequer, James Callaghan, found an opportunity to talk to the Parliamentary Labour Party's economic group describing to them in vivid terms (as he had frequently to his Cabinet colleagues) the damage that continuing sanctions would do to an already limping economy. His estimate of the cost of sanctions to Britain during the first year of U.D.I. ran between £90 and £120 million ($252 and $336 million). The Prime Minister himself made time for a long and friendly chat with a number of young, left-wing Labour M.P.s in the Labour Party's smoking-room in Parliament. He talked about the nature of terms that would be acceptable from Smith and let it be known that consideration must be given to including oil in any mandatory sanctions programme – a subject of deep concern to the left wing of the party.

Sir Morrice James meanwhile arrived in Salisbury late on Tuesday afternoon, 29 November. That evening, he delivered to Smith Wilson's proposal to meet on the *Tiger*. Smith met with his Cabinet early the next morning. The answer was in the affirmative which James immediately reported to Bowden in London. Bowden in turn conveyed the message to an evening meeting of the 'Rhodesia Group' of Ministers. It was now Wednesday, 30 November. In Salisbury there was an exchange of 'safe conducts' – the one for Smith signed by Harold Wilson, and that for Governor Gibbs signed by Ian Smith. Wilson had asked Smith to give assurance to Sir Morrice that he would be possessed of full powers to negotiate and to settle and sign on behalf of the regime. According to Wilson's later testimony Smith did so; and indeed at the time Smith was heard to say to John Hennings, the head of Britain's residual mission in Salisbury, 'What's the use of my going if I don't have these powers?'

Even so, however, there was reason to question whether Smith would be, or could be, plenipotentiary. An article in the *Rhodesia Herald* asserted that many in the Rhodesian Front and even some members of the Cabinet were uneasy that Smith might go too far in meeting British demands. There had been almost no time to consult. Many members of the Cabinet were out of town and unavailable. Considerable opposition to the *Tiger* talks reportedly had been voiced by several Ministers including Rudland, Harper, Dunlop and Partridge. Lardner-Burke was out of the country at the time and probably would have joined the sceptics. So too almost certainly would that right-wing *éminence grise* Clifford Dupont, the Officer Administering the Government.

At 6.40 a.m. on Thursday, 1 December, news of the *Tiger* talks was released at 10 Downing Street. Wilson had planned his sensational announcement for later that morning. But a photographer had caught sight of Smith boarding the R.A.F. Comet at 4.00 a.m. and forced the untimely release. A riptide of anxiety now ran through the left wing of the Labour Party. That morning Wilson met with some half-dozen leaders of the pro-African group from among the Labour back-benchers. He assured them that if anyone were to give in it would be Smith and not himself. He referred as he had many times in the past to his hope that a split might occur in the Rhodesian Front. Wilson thought that Smith, if left to himself, would be numbered among the moderates, a theme which he had worked over many times since U.D.I.

The Parliamentarians expressed particular concern about Zambia. Wilson pondered whether President Kaunda might not have to make a spectacular departure from the Commonwealth, in which case he hoped Zambia would return later on. But he did not think the Commonwealth would break up. Kaunda in fact did not bolt the Commonwealth. Though hardly satisfied with the outcome of the September Commonwealth meeting, he had come to recognize that the organization was not subject to British control and indeed, to a limited degree, was responsive to Zambia's concerns. Moreover he wished to hold the threat of leaving the Commonwealth as an ultimate pressure on British policy, which he continued to censure in unbridled terms. On 1 December, during a B.B.C. broadcast, he expressed his disgust at the sea-borne summit about to get under way. 'It is now clear that the solemn deals of Wilson meant nothing at all,' he stated. Two weeks before, addressing the United Nations General Assembly, Kaunda had accused Britain of 'treachery' and 'duplicity' and preparing for a 'dishonourable and downright sell-out'.

The Parliamentarians had also questioned Wilson about a story then current in the lobbies that Washington had grown cold on the subject of sanctions. The point had also been made in an article appearing that day in the *Rhodesia Herald* speculating that South African pressure on Smith and pressure by President Johnson on Wilson may have produced the dramatic decision to meet at Gibraltar. 'President Johnson', the article alleged, 'is reported to be perturbed at the implications of sanctions and this point will have been made to Sir Saville Garner, British envoy now in Washington.' Wilson dismissed these accounts as rumours set in motion by Rhodesian interests.

Sir Saville Garner, the Permanent Under-Secretary of the Commonwealth Relations office, was in fact in Washington. His trip had been planned for some days and involved consultations both in the American capital and in Ottawa concerning selective mandatory sanctions. Sir Saville was present when Bowden reported to the 'Rhodesia Group' at a Cabinet meeting following his return from Salisbury. Now that imminent talks with the Rhodesians were in prospect, it was all the more important, Wilson said, that Sir Saville should go to Washington. He left the following day and upon arrival briefed the American Government on the talks with Smith which were now arranged, though not yet announced. The Department of State was understandably concerned that Sir Saville's visit might seem to implicate the United States in what everyone knew would be a very unpopular exercise. Press guidance was quickly prepared to clarify that the United States–United Kingdom consultations in Washington on 30 November were part of continuing discussions on Africa between the two countries and dealt only with a review of British plans, in the event of talks with Smith collapsing, to introduce a sanctions resolution in the Security Council in accordance with the September Commonwealth *communiqué*. In short, the American Government had had no notice of the *Tiger* talks prior to consultations with the British representative.

On the afternoon of Thursday, 1 December, Wilson made his official announcement in Parliament. He was appropriately cautious: 'Despite the signs of movement we have had in the past week there is still, so far as I can at this moment judge, a considerable gap to bridge.' The Prime Minister went on: 'The House will wish us to do everything in our power to get a settlement – and this we shall seek to do.' The Tories cheered. 'But the House equally will insist, as the Government are insisting, that there can be no question of a settlement which does not honour the principles which all of us in this House stand by.' Labour M.P.'s applauded. Wilson's statement ended at 4 p.m. He hurried upstairs for a final meeting with the Parliamentary Labour Party. Sceptical members of the pro-African group again questioned him carefully. Callaghan's warnings about the impact of continuing sanctions on the economy did not imply a lack of resolution, Wilson insisted. As to the forthcoming negotiations the Labour Government would take nothing less than 'copper-bottomed' guarantees on progress toward majority rule. It was an impressive performance and won a round of applause.

Wilson raced for the airport with his Commonwealth Secretary, Herbert Bowden, and the Attorney General, Sir Elwyn Jones. The R.A.F. Comet was airborne for Gibraltar before 6 p.m. As soon as they arrived, they boarded H.M.S. *Tiger*. Another R.A.F. Comet was en route from Salisbury to Ascension Island carrying Smith and his party which included his Minister of Information, J. H. Howman, and the Rhodesian Solicitor-General, G. B. Clarke. Also on board were Governor Gibbs, the Rhodesian Chief Justice, Sir Hugh Beadle, and Sir Morrice James. From Ascension Island to Gibraltar the party divided, Smith's group following Governor Gibbs and his colleagues in a separate plane in order that the Queen's personal representative in Rhodesia might be received first. Smith boarded the

Tiger at 2 a.m. on Friday, 2 December, half an hour after Gibbs and his party. There was rain. The clouds were lowering and the weather was filthy. H.M.S. *Tiger* proceeded to cruise the stormy Mediterranean between Gibraltar and the Moroccan coast. It would be a rough seventy-two hour voyage – to nowhere.

H.M.S. *Tiger*

On board the *Tiger* Wilson ran a tight ship. Quarters were cramped. The Admiral and the Captain had left their cabins to go forward to sleep in their battle stations. The Admiral's cabin had been turned over to Wilson. The Captain's quarters were shared by Gibbs and Beadle. Smith's party was assigned the Medical Officer's cabin and that of the Chaplain. The Rhodesians had available one small ward-room for all their collective activities – dining, conferences, secretarial and signal work. Rhodesia was in rebellion. Britain now provided a final opportunity to end the rebellion before applying further penalties. Wilson was not going to let the Rhodesians forget where they were and why.) Threat of further penalties)

The next morning, Friday, 2 December, Wilson and Smith, together with Bowden and Howman, met alone for an hour and a half. With cool politeness Smith addressed Wilson as 'Prime Minister', who in turn called the Rhodesian leader simply 'Mr. Smith'. They were then joined by their respective teams. The talks continued until midnight. By that time most of the proposals for a constitutional settlement had been pieced together leaving the thorny question of the return to legality. The constitutional proposals, designed to give at least minimal satisfaction to the six principles, followed the pattern laid down in previous talks. The first and second principles, unimpeded progress to majority rule and guarantees against retrogressive amendments to the constitution, were provided for by the 'blocking mechanism' to guard against racially inspired changes in the more important (entrenched) sections of the constitution. In order to amend such sections, twenty-five elected Africans in Parliament would have to concur, or one more than was needed for the 'blocking quarter'. In addition there would be the right of appeal against the amendment of a specially entrenched clause of the constitution, in the first instance to a Constitutional Commission in Rhodesia and from that Commission, as of right, to the Judicial Committee of the Privy Council.

The third principle, involving the immediate improvement in the political status of the African, would be provided for by extending the 'B' Roll franchise to cover all Africans over thirty, increasing the

'B' Roll seats in the lower house from fifteen to seventeen, retaining cross-voting and applying it to all seats, and granting to Africans fourteen seats out of a total of twenty-six in a newly created Senate. Eight of these would be elected popularly and six would be Chiefs elected by the Chiefs' Council on a provincial basis. The fourth principle, that which assured progress towards ending racial discrimination, would involve the establishment of a Royal Commission to study and make recommendations on the problems of racial discrimination and Land Apportionment. The sixth principle, protecting the rights of the racial minority, was to be satisfied by establishing seventeen reserve seats for whites in the lower house. Combined with the twelve white Senate seats, these would assure the white community a 'blocking quarter' following the eventual transition to majority rule.

The fifth principle, devising a means for testing the acceptability of the foregoing formula to the people of Rhodesia as a whole, remained linked to the problem of returning Rhodesia to lawful rule. It was here once again that the most serious problems were encountered. Gradually a working document was hammered out containing an outline of arrangements for the interim government and the test of acceptability. Governance would be under the 1961 constitution, modified by the following provisions. The existing legislature would be dissolved for a period not to exceed four months. The Governor would invite Mr. Smith to head a broad-based interim government to include independent members and Africans as well as representatives of existing political parties which the Governor would appoint in his discretion. Wilson indicated that he would be satisfied to see five non-Rhodesia Front ministers included, three whites and two Africans. During the interim period the Governor would be invested with legislative powers, but would act on the advice of ministers on all internal matters of administration. As regards his ultimate responsibility for the maintenance of law and order and the protection of human rights, he would be advised, in his capacity as Commander-in-Chief, by a Defence and Security Council, comprised of responsible ministers, the heads of the defence forces, the chief of police and a single representative of the British Government.

Also during this interim period, and before any test of opinion was carried out, censorship would be removed and normal political activities permitted if conducted peacefully, democratically and without intimidation. An impartial judicial tribunal, appointed by the Rhodesian Government but including one British representative nominated by the Lord Chancellor, would review the cases of those held in detention and restriction. Continuing confinement would not be authorized unless the tribunal were satisfied that acts of violence or intimidation were involved. Once legal government was restored and the interim administration established, the British Government would take all action in its power to bring about the immediate cessation of economic and other sanctions. As soon as possible after the return to legality, Britain would negotiate with the legal, interim government the details of the constitutional settlement for an independent Rhodesia in accordance with the agreed constitutional guidelines reviewed above.

The draft constitution would then be submitted to the test of acceptability involving the people of Rhodesia as a whole (in accordance with the fifth principle) by a Royal Commission, whose composition and terms of reference would be agreed by the British Government and the interim Rhodesian government. If the settlement were shown to be acceptable, the British Government would then introduce in the British Parliament the necessary legislation to grant independence to Rhodesia on that basis and elections in Rhodesia under the new constitution would be held as soon as possible. The two governments would also negotiate a treaty guaranteeing the independence constitution and hold discussions on a possible defence agreement. If the settlement were shown to be unacceptable to the people of Rhodesia as a whole, the two governments would together consider what steps should be taken to devise alternative proposals.

By tea-time on Saturday, 3 December, the draft was ready for final typing. Sipping brandy in the Admiral's quarters, Wilson was confident that a settlement was 'a hundred to one on'. Smith, however, had asked for time to study the final document. And it was clear that he was skittish. The evening before he had explained that some of the proposals involved new issues of principle which he must radio to Salisbury. Wilson concurred with great reluctance for Smith presumably had come with full powers to settle. Smith made it plain this was not his interpretation of the invitation; he could not possibly settle without consulting his colleagues.* He re-emphasized this

---

* A Rhodesian Government commentary on these affairs later observed: 'It seems peculiar that a Prime Minister, working under the Cabinet system of government, should be expected to reach a settlement of such vital importance without further consultation with his colleagues – especially when certain of the terms and conditions of settlement were new to the Rhodesians; unless this settlement was intended to be on the lines of an ultimatum already agreed upon fully by the British. This may well have been Mr. Wilson's intention. On the other hand, there may have been a genuine misunderstanding between Sir Morrice James and Mr. Smith; but this does not seem likely.' From *Comparison Between White Paper C.S.R. 49–1966 and British Blue Book Command 3171* (mimeographed), p. 8.

position at a private meeting with Wilson just before lunch on Saturday, indicating that he must return to Salisbury for consultations. The Rhodesian leader had serious doubts on a number of points, especially the return to constitutionality before completing the test of acceptability and the provision for a 'broad-based' interim government.

Smith's apprehensions may have been heightened by a message from Salisbury early on Saturday evening. At any rate, the Rhodesian leader demurred when, later that evening, Wilson asked for his concurrence to the final document. Smith said he would sign it – but only as a correct record of the proceedings. Wilson pressed him at least to agree to the proposals *ad referendum* his Cabinet, while warning that the document must either be accepted or rejected in its entirety. Smith said he could not commend the document to his colleagues without first convincing himself that the terms were adequate. Pressed further by Wilson, who was by now positively furious, the Rhodesian leader replied that if he were forced to decide 'yes' or 'no' then and there, the answer would have to be negative. The heated exchange ran on into the night. Wilson could see this last desperate chance slipping away. If he could not convince Smith, surely he could not convince Smith's Cabinet. There was also the mounting pressure of time. Beyond that, the exercise he was engaged in, not only the eleventh-hour talks but the terms of the constitutional settlement and the interim arrangements, would, once revealed, be highly questionable in the eyes of the left wing of his party and even among some members of his own Government. He was reluctant to see the matter opened for fresh debate.

Late on Saturday night, in a final meeting in the Admiral's day cabin, Wilson told Smith that the British Government was not going to be 'pushed around'. Did the Rhodesians really think Britain would permit the Commonwealth to break up over a country with only a fraction of 1 per cent of the population of the Commonwealth as a whole? If the present formula were rejected, the British Government would go on to the end. Mandatory sanctions and the commitment to 'no independence before majority rule' would be irrevocable, once adopted. 'There could be no going back and no more concessions of the kind the British Government had been ready to make....' Even the earlier decision not to use force might have to be withdrawn. Rhodesia should not be misled by Britain's economic problems. The United Kingdom was basically a strong country, never defeated in any task to which it had truly set its hand. Even if it took years to solve the problem Britain would not give up, however much it might be hurt in the process. In the midst of these stormy proceedings, Howman at one point whispered to Smith that he was a bit worried that they would be hustled off to the Tower of London. 'Don't worry about it,' Smith came back. 'If they should be foolish enough to do that we shall have won.'

It was close to 1.00 a.m. on Saturday, 4 December, when Wilson and Smith finally fixed their signatures to a simple statement that the H.M.S. *Tiger* document was worked out without commitment by either side and that both sides would decide by 10.00 a.m. G.M.T. on Monday, 5 December 1966, whether the document was accepted 'in its entirety' – a simple 'yes' or 'no' answer, Wilson said, was all that was required. Gibbs witnessed the signatures. The Rhodesian party disembarked and drove to the airport. As they boarded the Comet someone shouted, 'Head for Africa – anywhere in Africa!'

Almost before Smith had arrived in Salisbury, the British Cabinet announced its endorsement of the course of action recommended in the *Tiger* document.* Smith, greeted at the Salisbury airport by some 300 cheering whites, drove directly to his residence to confer briefly with his Ministers. The following morning, Monday, 5 December, the Rhodesian Cabinet convened at 8.00 a.m. As the deadline approached (10.00 a.m. G.M.T. or 12 noon Rhodesian time), the Cabinet Secretary telephoned to the British residual mission in Salisbury to advise that the Cabinet was continuing in session and did not expect to reach a decision until the end of the day.

Even assuming Smith had succeeded, as he had put it to Wilson, in commending the *Tiger* terms to himself, his position was awkward in the extreme. The proposals he laid before his thirteen-man Cabinet, had they been accepted, would have put six Ministers out of work during the interim period. If forced through, these terms would have split the Front. It was exactly this that Wilson was counting on. Smith might have been able to overrule the hardliners by carrying his case to the electorate where his appeal was by now beyond question. But such leadership was quite uncharacteristic, and in any event he probably remained uncertain in his own mind about the advisability of some of the terms. The right wing now moved to the attack warning against perfidious British motives and the risks involved in giving any ground at all. The more moderate members of the Cabinet had neither leadership nor a firm position. When during the afternoon Clifford Dupont arrived on the scene (he was not beyond warning the Rhodesian Prime Minister that he was ready to unseat him just as he

---

* The decision, as Wilson later described it, was 'virtually unanimous'. Had the *Tiger* terms actually been implemented granting Rhodesia independence before majority rule, it seems likely that both Arthur Bottomley and Barbara Castle would have resigned from the Cabinet.

had earlier led the cabal against Winston Field), consensus against the *Tiger* proposals no doubt concealed. Considerable attention was then given to the rationale behind the decision and what would be said to the press.

At approximately 8 p.m. Rhodesian time the meeting broke. Smith met the press. The Rhodesian Government, he said, was prepared to accept the constitutional proposals put forward by Wilson in fulfil-ment of his six principles as a basis for a constitution for an in-dependent Rhodesia. However, the Rhodesian Government found 'utterly irresponsible' Britain's expectation that Rhodesia should abandon its present (1965) constitution before the new constitution had been 'finally secured and put to the test of public opinion'. The interim government envisaged by Wilson, said Smith, was 'repugnant' in so far as it involved the control of security forces by the Governor, the right of the Governor to appoint Ministers, five of whom (includ-ing two Africans) were to be from outside the Government party, and the dissolution of Parliament with the Governor reserving the right in certain cases to exercise legislative powers at his discretion. The whole amounted to a 'surrender and submission of power'. The crowd of whites who had gathered to hear the statement cheered as Smith concluded, 'and so, ladies and gentlemen, as you might have guessed, the fight goes on.'

∘ ∘ ∘

Taking everything into account, one wonders whether to be more surprised that the *Tiger* terms were offered or that they were refused. For it was not their severity that might properly have raised a questioning eyebrow but their laxity when measured by the Lagos and London Commonwealth *communiqués* as well as Wilson's earlier repeated interventions in the Commons. Former Rhodesian Prime Minister Sir Edgar Whitehead, no flaming liberal, called it an astonishing document which would have postponed 'the possible date of African majority rule almost certainly beyond the end of the century'. It was Whitehead who had estimated that the 1961 con-stitution, which his Government had negotiated with London, would have brought majority rule by 1977.

Leave aside for the moment the enormity of negotiating the future of Rhodesia without a single voice directly representing the interests of 95 per cent of its population. And leave aside too the fact that the principal spokesman for the Rhodesians was the very captain of the rebellion with whom Wilson had time and again insisted he would never deal. There was to be 'direct rule' Wilson had agreed at Lagos. The phrase was omitted from the London *communiqué*, but nonethe-less the interim administration was to be 'broadly-based', 'representative' and 'appointed by the Governor'. According to the *Tiger* document it was, in point of fact, to be headed by none other than Mr. Smith himself. Smith could have been surrounded by as many as ten or eleven of his Rhodesian Front Ministers for Wilson was prepared to have him expand his thirteen-man Cabinet to sixteen in order to accommodate more easily the newcomers who were to 'broaden the base'. Rhodesian Front Ministers would have doubly outnumbered the three non-Front whites and the two Africans who would have been added. According to the British version of a restricted session of the talks, Smith surprisingly said he would prefer to reduce the total from thirteen to twelve which would have meant seven Front and five non-Front members; a total of six Front Ministers thus would have lost their appointments. The Rhodesian leader left the clear impression, according to the British document, that he would use this opportunity to get rid of some of his more extreme colleagues. The two men then reviewed both white and African candidates for the broadened Cabinet.* Hardly 'Governor's rule', the Cabinet clearly was to be pre-selected by Wilson and Smith themselves.

On the absolutely critical matter of force deployment, Wilson ceased his effort to place the security services directly under the Governor's control or to position British troops within the country during the interim period, substituting instead a council to advise the Governor on matters pertaining to 'law and order and the protection of human rights'. The council was to include the responsible Rhodesian Ministers, the heads of the Rhodesian defence forces, the Rhodesian chief of police – and one British representative. The Governor was to be vested with legislative powers pending a new election but these were to be used, consistent with the 1961 constitution, on the advice of Ministers (two-thirds of whom could have been members of the Front), except in cases where he was empowered to act on his own discretion, presumably limited again to the main-

---

* This exchange was not reproduced in the Rhodesian account of the *Tiger* talks. However at a press conference held in Salisbury on 6 December Smith revealed the names of some who had been considered for the new Cabinet. (Curiously the names mentioned in Wilson's memoir do not match those given earlier by Smith.) The British record also discloses Smith's agreement that during the interim period the Rhodesian legislature would be adjourned, pending new elections within four months as required by the 1961 Constitution. Wilson further contends that Smith said he welcomed this move as an opportunity for 'getting rid of thirty of my chaps'. Needless to say there has been no official confirmation of this version from Salisbury.

tenance of law and order and the protection of human rights where advice was to be rendered by a Rhodesian-dominated council and executed by exclusively Rhodesian forces.

Exactly how much the British Prime Minister had given away tended to be obscured because, having in mind his critics at the U.N., among importunate members of the New Commonwealth and within the Labour Party itself, Wilson wished to put as favourable a face as possible on the modalities of settlement. He was willing to countenance independence before majority rule and an administration led by the rebel leader. The only chance of making such a deal minimally palatable to any of his critics was to make as ironclad as possible the procedure by which it was formulated (officially in a negotiation with a legal, broadly-based, interim Government), the method by which it was ratified (a Royal Commission testing opinion in a truly open forum) and the form by which it was promulgated (an Act of Parliament at Westminster once it was satisfied that these procedures had faithfully been followed).

When, however, Wilson began parrying in the Commons specific criticisms by Tory leaders – a very different constituency – the contradictions in his policy came to the fore and the ironclad procedures faded quickly. The Opposition, for example, repeatedly made the point that the interim arrangements arrived at on H.M.S. *Tiger* were distrusted by the Rhodesians for they involved rule by the Governor in matters relating both to the armed forces and to the police. Wilson rejoined that the Governor 'would not have had any power to override the powers of the interim government in defence and law and order matters, and Mr. Smith understood this.' Heath advised that Wilson lay the matter to rest once and for all by confirming that it would not be possible for London to give any orders to the Governor, or instructions to the forces through the Defence Council. Wilson retorted that he had given such an undertaking, that Smith knew it and, what was more, had never raised any doubts about the matter on board the *Tiger*. Almost without realizing it, Wilson was admitting that the influence of the Governor and of London on the interim administration headed by Smith himself would be virtually inconsequential.* The implications for the revival of free political activity and debate leading to an authentic test of opinion of all Rhodesians were obvious.

If these arrangements were 'unconditional and abject surrender'

---

* In another round of negotiations almost two years later, Wilson moved substantially toward the Tory position (as he had repeatedly before), playing down further the notion of an 'interim' government (see Chapter X).

as the Rhodesians now claimed, then it must have been Washington who handed his sword to Cornwallis at Yorktown, Grant to Lee at Appomattox, while Roosevelt and his Rough Riders galloped to ignominious defeat at San Juan Hill! As Wilson later reported to the British people, 'Mr. Smith could have . . . left Gibraltar as Prime Minister-designate of Rhodesia. . . . By this time, had he signed, we would have started dismantling all the economic sanctions now in force.' That such interim arrangements were put forward (and even more, of course, the proposals for a permanent constitution which would have formalized independence long before the achievement of majority rule) indicated once more the essential weakness of Wilson's position which even the formidable surroundings of Gibraltar, a naval vessel cruising dark seas and Prime Ministerial bustle and bluster in the Admiral's day cabin, could ill conceal .

It also suggested that underlying the Rhodesian rejection of the *Tiger* proposals was more than just the fear, freely expressed then and since, that Britain would have used the interim period to invest Rhodesia with military forces or, assuming the test of acceptability had proved negative, would then gradually have increased its hold over the political life of the country, extracting ever greater concessions from the Rhodesians as the price for full independence. In the closed and apprehensive ambit of Salisbury in those days, such fears might have seemed more believable than any objective assessment would warrant. (Wilson himself, on the other hand, was deeply concerned that Rhodesia, during the interim phase when operating under the 1961 constitution, would declare a 'second U.D.I.' if the test of acceptability were unfavourable. To meet such a contingency he invoked the threat of mandatory sanctions and – with questionable credibility – even the possible use of force.)

Beyond these fears, Rhodesia's unwillingness to accept the *Tiger* settlement probably arose also from a rejection of many of the terms of the new constitution, despite the regime's announcement that it was willing to accept them. On 6 December the Rhodesian Information Service issued a summary of Rhodesia's position, drawn up before the *Tiger* meeting but nonetheless released in that sensitive period immediately after rejection of the working document. The Rhodesian summary rejected the expansion of the number of 'B' Roll seats from fifteen to seventeen; rejected the right of appeal on matters relating to constitutional amendments to the judicial committee of the Privy Council; and rejected cross-voting if the 'B' Roll franchise were extended to include all male Africans over the age of thirty. All of these items were essential elements of the constitutional settlement in the *Tiger* working document and ostensibly agreed to by the Cabinet. Though weak and essentially unpoliceable, the *Tiger* consti-

Commitment based on

tution was premised on ultimate majority rule. It was fear of majority rule that U.D.I. was all about in the first place.

At 8.55 p.m. Monday, 5 December, Wilson reported to a tense House of Commons Rhodesia's rejection of the working document. He concluded his exhaustive review of what had transpired by announcing the departure the next day of the Foreign Secretary to New York to take personal charge of Britain's request for selective mandatory sanctions. Already Britain's permanent representative at the United Nations, Lord Caradon, had been instructed to ask for an early meeting of the Security Council. The effect was electric. A substantial group of Labour back-benchers, fearing for more than half a year that a dishonourable deal with Smith might be in the making, cheered and threw order papers in the air to celebrate this turn towards a tough policy. 'I am not prepared to recommend to this House,' Wilson said, 'that we let the Commonwealth break up for the sake of a very small group of people in a country whose electorate is only one-tenth of 1 per cent of the population of the Commonwealth as a whole. . . .'

Opposition spokesmen were caustic. Noting the Prime Minister's 'remarkable' achievement of concluding a constitutional agreement based upon the six principles, Duncan Sandys, himself once an antagonist of Smith as Commonwealth Secretary in a Conservative government but now one of Wilson's most virulent critics, observed that 'the British people will need a great deal of convincing that he was right to throw [the constitutional agreement] away on account of disagreement over procedure in the interim.' There were shocked exclamations from Government benches while the Opposition cheered. Wilson's faltering consensus with the Conservatives was about to come to an end.

The Collapse of Consensus

The interparty alliance on Rhodesia had been a tentative affair from the first. Both sides were against U.D.I. and wished to end it. Sanctions played a part in the strategy of each, but the Tories had always been inclined to link a mild sanctions programme to the aim of encouraging negotiations with Smith. During the opening months of the crisis, consensus of a sort prevailed despite Conservative excoriation of Wilson for his tough 'no truck with the rebels' line and his apparent confidence that following the collapse of the rebellion an alternative government would emerge after a period of 'direct rule'. These tensions abated when Wilson, following the 31 March Election, moved decisively toward the Tory position and inaugurated 'talks about talks' with the Smith regime. The Commonwealth *communiqué* in September, however, placed interparty accord under stress once again. Heath insisted that the Commonwealth ultimatum with its accompanying threat of mandatory sanctions and no independence before majority rule constituted a new policy, requiring the recall of Parliament, a position which Wilson dismissed out of hand. During the autumn the strains relaxed once more as talks began again, culminating on board H.M.S. *Tiger*. Now suddenly, after the upsurge of optimism that accompanied the shipboard negotiations, the talks had collapsed altogether.

Wilson, under constant pressure from his own back-benchers and the African, Asian and Caribbean members of the Commonwealth (problems which the Opposition did not face), prepared for what appeared to be an irrevocable break with Salisbury and the unprecedented invocation of mandatory economic sanctions in the U.N. The fragile consensus between the Labour Party and the Tories suddenly blew apart in an explosion of vituperation. In the Commons, the debate on 7 and 8 December 1966, on a resolution deploring the illegal regime's rejection of the *Tiger* document and supporting the Government's decision to implement the undertakings of the Commonwealth *communiqué* was probably more emotional and bitter than any since the Suez disaster ten years before.

Much of the argument centred on the interim arrangements, including the return to legality. The Tories contended that the constitutional principles (concerning which there had appeared to be considerable agreement on the *Tiger*) and the modalities for ending the rebellion and returning to constitutional rule (on which there was no agreement) should be separated and negotiations continued. It was inconceivable, the Tories charged, that the Government could have achieved agreement on a constitutional settlement in accordance with the six principles only to abandon it because agreement had not yet been reached on the means for a return to legality. 'The Right Honourable gentleman must have gone right out of his mind,' sallied the redoubtable Duncan Sandys. The Prime Minister had secured everything he originally set out to achieve, and now, over a question of procedure and personal prestige, he hurled everything back.

Deputy Opposition Leader Reginald Maudling urged the immediate appointment of a Royal Commission which, following the end of censorship and the restoration of normal political activity, would itself judge whether or not a fair test of acceptability of the constitutional provisions could be carried out. If so, let it proceed, urged Maudling, neither ending the sanctions nor insisting upon a return to legality until the Commission had completed its work.

Maudling's recommendation evoked noises of disbelief and derision from the opposing benches. A not dissimilar idea had been put forward by Ian Smith in a press conference the night before.

Three M.P.'s immediately cabled Smith to elucidate. The Rhodesian leader replied that he would receive a Royal Commission, accept its findings, and implement the terms of the *Tiger* working document providing for the removal of censorship, the renewal of normal political activities and the release of detainees. These steps would be pursued, of course, without a return to legality and with the illegal regime still in full control. The release of detainees, who included the top echelon of African nationalist leaders, was held to be critically important by African, Asian and Caribbean members of the Commonwealth, for unless these leaders could participate in the political debate which preceded the testing of opinion, that test would be bound to be one-sided. Whether the Rhodesian regime would voluntarily release these political leaders and permit them free play in the political arena was of course always open to serious question. Doubt tended to be confirmed when in its release of 6 December the regime made clear that 'no persons are detained in Rhodesia on purely political grounds. They are detained because of political intimidation and disregard for law and order.'

Patrick Gordon Walker, a former Labour Minister, censured Maudling's ideas as worthy of a 'naive idiot' – to presume that a 'man who has all that power, who can put anyone in prison without a trial, who can reimpose censorship . . . , would make possible conditions in which a Royal Commission could work and produce any answer other than that which he wants. . . .' Wilson was even more explicit. The test of acceptability could not take place under the Government as it was presently constituted, for the people of Rhodesia 'must be free to say "yes" or "no" with no thought of the peril in which they place themselves by expressing their views,' seeing that 'plain clothes members of the African police' were 'reporting to the authorities on every sign of political deviation'. This was why the Labour Government insisted that the test of acceptability would be meaningless unless conducted under a new, legal, interim administration; and why therefore the modalities of settlement were just as important as, and indeed inseparable from, the settlement itself. (Of course, as we have noted, Wilson himself had made clear in a different context that the interim Government would remain largely under the control of Smith and the Rhodesian Front.) In any event, the Rhodesian leader had turned down the package 'either because he rejected the working document, or because he was overborne'. In either case, the Prime Minister concluded, 'the settlement we worked out with such care has been rejected. This is why there is no future in ingenious proposals for further talks with that regime as at present constituted.'

The Conservatives looked upon the *Tiger* impasse with incredulity and at an increased role for the United Nations with alarm. Maudling warned that Wilson was leading Britain toward 'one of the greatest disasters in our history'. The doctrine of refusing independence before majority rule was tantamount to unconditional surrender. United Nations' mandatory sanctions would not produce political change among a people now threatened with that alternative. Recourse to the United Nations in fact would do more harm than good. It could expand into a conflict involving all of Southern Africa. Sir Alec Douglas-Home added that mandatory sanctions would force Rhodesia towards South Africa both economically and politically, concluding that a vote for mandatory sanctions which necessarily must include South Africa and Portuguese Africa was a vote 'which might, which could, which I believe most certainly would, lead us into war at some future date'.

Recognizing these dangers and the risk of further imperilling Britain's wobbling economy, Wilson's approach to the U.N. was, in fact, to be extremely cautious, involving the submission of a selective list of sanctions while carefully avoiding any confrontation with South Africa. His policy was now caught in a crossfire. Rejected by the right as dangerous, it was attacked by the left as ineffective. 'I find it very difficult to believe,' said Liberal Party Leader Jo Grimond who also spoke for many Labour back-benchers, 'that Britain should be more frightened of provoking South Africa than South Africa is of provoking the rest of the world. What sort of people are we? We ape the Churchillian attitudes. The Prime Minister goes off in a cruiser as if it were a world-shaking event. But when South Africa says "shut up," we shut up. Is that really the British Government's position? If so, they had better take off their "Super Mac" clothes and get back into a much humbler station of life.'

Recriminatory bolts were hurled from either side. Former Tory Foreign Minister Selwyn Lloyd catalogued Wilson's bad estimates and repeated inconsistencies, then concluded: 'For a man of his intelligence it is surprising that he should be consistently wrong about so much.' Wilson in turn charged that the Tories encouraged Smith to reject the terms of the Commonwealth *communiqué*, recalling a speech Heath had made soon after the September conference in which he was reported to have asked his audience how they would have reacted to an ultimatum of the kind issued by the Commonwealth. Heath, according to Wilson, answered his own question: 'You would tell those who sent it to go to hell.'

It was a moral issue, Wilson said, drawing a parallel (as he often did) with the American Civil War and Abraham Lincoln. Then, too, Tories had condoned illegality and racialism. But the working men of Manchester, intoned Wilson, though suffering deep hardship and privation because their mills had closed down for want of cotton from the American South, nonetheless remained firm on the moral issue, inspiring the imperishable words of Lincoln in his Memorial to their steadfastness. A chorus of cheers swelled from the Labour benches. It was too much for Heath. What was the great moral principle today? he demanded to know. To invoke mandatory sanctions provided we do nothing about South Africa? How are sanctions to be effective when there could be no confrontation with South Africa? What were the people of Manchester to conclude about a moral principle like that? It was 'sheer hypocrisy of the basest kind'. A crescendo of noise and confusion overwhelmed the House of Commons.

The Tories were particularly incensed that Wilson should construe a vote against mandatory sanctions, bound to be both ineffectual and dangerous they thought, as a vote in favour of the Salisbury regime. But the Prime Minister persisted: 'Every one of the honourable gentlemen opposite is more interested in trying to get rid of the legal Government here than the illegal regime in Southern Rhodesia.' 'After tonight's vote,' he continued, 'we shall have a most extra-ordinary situation in that while no country in the world supports Salisbury, the British Conservative Party does.' Welded together by Wilson's unremitting attack on their leadership, the Conservatives filed into the lobby to vote against the resolution, only two of their members abstaining.* The consensus on Rhodesia was in ruins. Britain's policy was now to be programmed in accordance with the Commonwealth *communiqué*. The issue was to go to the Security Council. All previous offers to Rhodesia were to be withdrawn and independence accorded only following majority rule. That clearly was the *scenario*.

Or was it? The point about NIBMAR was pressed in Parliament time and again. But strangely, try as both back-benchers and Opposition might to extract the magic phrase from the Prime Minister, Wilson never let the acronym nor the words it signified pass his lips in those early months after the *Tiger* talks. He talked about 'Paragraph 10' of the *communiqué* (the one containing the NIBMAR formulation); he alluded to references in previous debates when he

---

* Labour also lost two votes. Two hours before the vote, Reginald Paget had resigned the Labour Whip and for the first time in twenty-one years voted against his Party. One other Labour member abstained. The resolution passed by 353 votes to 244.

presumably (though not actually) had endorsed 'no independence before majority rule'; he talked freely of withdrawing all previous offers; he even agreed in answer to a direct question that, 'yes', this was Britain's policy. In fact he went so far in an important exchange on 20 December 1966, that a correspondent for *The Times* could write of the 'acrid tang of burning boats in the Commons'. His Foreign Minister, Michael Stewart, avowed without adornment on 17 January 1967, that NIBMAR was Government policy. So did George Brown later after he had succeeded to that post. But not Wilson. In his curious circumlocutionary references, the phrase itself during those months was never used.

This was not considered particularly noteworthy at the time. In retrospect, it would be. A Conservative critic, Ian Lloyd, once dwelt on the dilemma of large ends and slender means. He ended by suggesting that NIBMAR was 'the most massive and monumental stumbling block since the Pharaohs tripped over the Pyramids'. Wilson of all men must have known this was true. He had not the means to extract a settlement based on minority rule. How could he now expect to gain one based on majority rule? The whole exercise had been a calculated risk. The Commonwealth ultimatum, carrying the penalty of mandatory sanctions and the threat of NIBMAR, might just have produced the compromise which would have allowed Britain to disengage from the problem. (Whether with or without honour was a different consideration altogether.) Failing the compromise settlement, the ultimatum at least had held the Commonwealth together. So too would Wilson's approach to the U.N., now about to get under way. If he were unable to react meaningfully to the Rhodesian problem, he could at least react to the reactions to Rhodesia and attenuate the damage to Britain. Still, NIBMAR was the ultimate stumbling block. It had become Government policy by default and he seemed somehow reluctant to utter it. Already one sensed that he was preparing a retreat.

VIII

Over to the United Nations

Harold Wilson had denied himself the means to solve the Rhodesian problem by direct intervention. Britain would not use force. He had (for the time being) foreclosed any possibility of a negotiated settlement. For Britain was pledged not to grant independence before majority rule, and there was no chance Smith would agree to that. Wilson now turned to the United Nations for compulsory sanctions, but again under conditions virtually assuring failure. For Britain clearly had no intention of paying the heavy price of a serious confrontation with South Africa over the implementation of U.N. sanctions, and it was out of the question that South Africa uncoerced would comply. Wilson was at a policy dead end. He had however committed himself to a course of action at the September Commonwealth meeting – and it was not impossible that, despite all the difficulties that could now be foreseen, recourse to the U.N. might offer the British Prime Minister certain tactical advantages. At what expense to the world organization was another matter.

Selective Mandatory Sanctions

At 5.00 p.m. on 8 December 1966, Dr. Pedro Berro of Uruguay gavelled to order the 1,331st meeting of the United Nations Security Council. The Chamber was packed, the aisles were filled and people were standing three deep in the visitors' section. The audience tensed as Britain's Foreign Minister, George Brown, moved a resolution which for the first time since November 1935 would obligate members of an international body to impose economic sanctions to penalize an errant regime. In the debates that followed there would be frequent allusions to the Italian invasion of Ethiopia, to imperfectly applied sanctions by the League of Nations and the consequent failure to stop a white take-over in Africa thirty years before, and to the rapid decline of the League thereafter. Brown's mood, however, was confident. 'It is unthinkable,' he told the Council, 'that this rebellion can succeed.'

The Foreign Minister described the object of the exercise in unadorned terms: 'to reduce Rhodesian economic activity and prospects to a point where even the most stubborn members of the Rhodesian Front party could see that there would be no tolerable economic future for their country if their present policy were pursued.' Already the impact of the voluntary sanctions programme had been great, he went on. Rhodesia's exports had been cut by nearly 40 per cent. Nevertheless the Salisbury regime persisted in rebellion, defying civilized opinion everywhere. The rebellion presented an ever greater challenge to the international community, producing a situation filled with the danger of interracial strife and bloodshed throughout the region and affecting 'not only the stability and progress of Rhodesia's immediate neighbours, but also the maintenance of international peace and security'. Accordingly, Brown said, 'We shall now ask the Council to place upon all nations the obligation to carry out with the same intensity the measures which we have ourselves taken. . . .' The sanctions he asked for were to be in accordance with Chapter VII of the Charter and thus legally binding on all members.

It was a forceful statement. But Brown immediately proceeded to qualify it with as much concern for what would not be included in the U.N.'s sanctions programme as for what would. The use of force could not be considered. Economic measures, he insisted, were 'both more certain of success and far more susceptible of proper control'. Sanctions must be selective, not all-inclusive, for the programme must be realistic and sustainable.* Moreover, he continued, it must be designed to safeguard the economic interests of neighbouring countries in the region which were for reasons of geography particularly vulnerable to the impact of the sanctions measures. Finally, Brown made clear that he was referring exclusively to selective sanctions against Rhodesia alone. If other countries failed to

---

* The selective list of Rhodesian exports at 1965 levels represented in earnings nearly 60 per cent of Rhodesia's foreign exchange receipts. The commodities were asbestos, iron-ore, chrome, pig-iron, sugar, tobacco, copper, meat and meat products, hides, skins, and leather. Imports on the sanctions list were limited to military equipment and materials for its maintenance and manufacture. At the last minute Britain had also included civilian aircraft and motor vehicles and the materials for their maintenance and manufacture.

implement the Council's measures a new situation would arise. It was best to proceed 'step by step'. But, he emphasized, not once but twice, there must be no 'confrontation', economic or military, involving South Africa.

Britain's programme won unqualified approval from the United States. Ambassador Arthur Goldberg, with that curious over-statement that affects so many pronouncements made at the U.N., said that selective mandatory sanctions would not only have a profound impact on Salisbury but would add lustre to the United Nations as a force for peace and justice throughout the world. Many officials in Washington, on the other hand, continued to have the most serious reservations about the efficacy of sanctions, not to mention the wisdom of using for the first time the mandatory provisions of Chapter VII under circumstances making their enforcement virtually impossible. It was an irresponsible use of the Council's august powers, and an open invitation to Afro-Asian states to revile the inconsistency of Britain and its associates. Yet, having come this far down the road, it was difficult to identify a preferred alternative. So Washington followed the British lead – with reluctance and scepticism. Afro-Asian delegates indeed reacted bitterly. Despite Britain's brave words about toppling the rebel regime, there had been high-level negotiations with the rebels themselves, resulting in a British offer to Smith on board H.M.S. *Tiger* which in the opinion of most non-white nations would permanently have assured white rule in Rhodesia had it been accepted. Now there was a new British sanctions programme – one studded with qualifications. It was, said the Senegalese delegate, a diversionary tactic calculated to calm Africans while consolidating the regime in Rhodesia.

The three African states on the Council, Nigeria, Uganda and Mali, with the assistance (as had been prescribed by the O.A.U.) of Zambia, Senegal, Sierra Leone and Algeria, now proceeded to draft amendments that would have wiped out all London's carefully designed reservations. The fate of these efforts was sealed from the outset since Britain could simply have vetoed them; it never came to that, however, for the amendments were emasculated in backstage negotiations or failed to achieve the required majorities in the Security Council, and the entire exercise served only to confirm the Afro-Asians in their suspicion and bitterness. One amendment scored 'the refusal of the United Kingdom to use every means, including force, to bring about the immediate downfall of the Ian Smith regime'. In the approved version of the resolution, the word 'force' did not appear at all. Another amendment would have deplored the action of states, notably Portugal and South Africa, in rendering support to Rhodesia. The final draft mentioned neither of these countries and simply reminded all members that failure to implement the sanctions programme constituted a breach of the Charter, without specifying any penalty for offenders.

As to the sanctions themselves, most Afro-Asian spokesmen found the British list inadequate. The most important omission was oil. London was opposed to mandatory oil sanctions, a curious position as Zambia's Foreign Minister, Simon Kapwepwe, angrily pointed out. He recalled that just one year ago Prime Minister Wilson had told him oil was the key to crippling Rhodesia. Zambia had supported Britain's voluntary oil embargo at enormous risk and sacrifice. Now, however, oil was not even mentioned in the British draft resolution. Ambassador Kironde from Uganda joined the issue squarely. 'I suggest,' he said, 'that the only effective measure that could be taken under the circumstances is a total banning of oil, no matter where the oil comes from, and no matter whether this involves, in the end, a confrontation with South Africa. South Africa is a member of this organization. South Africa has to abide by the rules of the Charter of the organization to which it belongs.'

It was of course precisely this confrontation, so desired by the Afro-Asians, that Britain above all else wished to avoid. British exports to the Republic were running at £260 million ($730 million) per annum (1965) with a favourable trade balance of approximately £78.5 million ($220 million). Hard-pressed British officials pointed out in private briefings that the Rhodesian situation already threatened to affect Britain's economic position adversely in South Africa as South African businessmen began to look elsewhere for items traditionally obtained in the United Kingdom. Though difficult to quantify, it was estimated that if selective sanctions were extended to South Africa in order to enforce an oil blockade, the initial impact might cost Britain some £55 to £70 million (roughly $150 to $200 million) the first year and probably rise sharply thereafter. It was a terrifying prospect given the parlous state of the British economy.

The view was nonetheless pressed within the British Cabinet that oil sanctions against Rhodesia could hardly be ignored given the strength of feeling on the subject and Britain's own dramatic involvement (together with that of the United Nations) in the Beira blockade the previous spring. An overwhelming majority of Commonwealth countries, acting within the Commonwealth Sanctions Committee, had just demanded that oil be included. The British Cabinet finally settled on a peculiar compromise. Britain would neither initiate the subject, nor would it oppose any move to add oil to the sanctions list, provided, as Judith Hart told the Commons on 8 December 1966, the amendment was worded 'in acceptable terms'. She added that this position was taken 'on the full understanding . . . of the importance of not allowing sanctions to escalate into economic confrontation with third countries', principally South Africa.

Indeed so strongly did the anti-confrontation current run that some Ministers thought H.M. Government should make a declaration in the Security Council that Britain would dissociate from enforcement measures on oil sanctions even to the point of casting a veto. It was agreed, however, that this was to give away more than was necessary and George Brown's ambivalences about proceeding 'step by step' and avoiding 'confrontation' were substituted instead. But when the African amendment came forward, it invited the British Government 'to prevent, by all means', the transport to Rhodesia of oil or oil products – hardly a formula for side-stepping conflict with offenders. Again the African formulation failed and the language in the approved resolution was less direct, simply obliging members not to participate in supplying oil to Rhodesia.

On 16 December the historic (and carefully hedged) resolution, which for the first time invoked United Nations mandatory sanctions, came into effect, eleven members of the Security Council approving and four abstaining: the Soviet Union, Bulgaria and Mali because, as Ambassador Keita of Mali put it, the resolution had been stripped 'of positive elements'; and France because (as previously contended) Rhodesia was a matter falling within Britain's domestic jurisdiction and thus beyond that of the U.N. Nigeria and Uganda, the two African Commonwealth countries on the Council, voted affirmatively but with little enthusiasm. 'What has been demonstrated by the result of the voting on the African amendments today,' remonstrated Nigeria's Chief Adebo, 'is the futility of relying upon the Security Council for adequate action to deal with the outstanding problems of Africa.' The most serious deficiency, as the Afro-Asians one after another had pointed out, was the calculated unwillingness of Britain to risk 'confrontation' in Southern Africa – understandable perhaps in view of Britain's faltering economy, but a position that seemed to consign the whole enterprise to futility.

Every indication from Pretoria and Lisbon suggested that this indeed would be the case. Prime Minister Vorster had issued an extraordinarily candid statement on 5 December 1966, three days before the Council convened, advising that in South Africa's view the problem was domestic in character and should not be taken to the U.N. He expressed the hope that even at this late date the issue might be resolved in accordance with the six principles (a remarkable statement for the world's leading impresario of apartheid, for the principles were premised on majority rule) and warned that South Africa would not participate in any sanctions programme whether voluntarily or under compulsion. The day following the passing of the resolution Minister of Transport Schoeman announced bluntly, 'We will carry on as before.'

For its part Lisbon continued to believe that where the question of sanctions was concerned, the best defence was a good offence. In response to the Secretary-General's request for a report on measures taken to implement the new resolution, Foreign Minister Franco Nogueira recalled his enquiry concerning the legality of the earlier Beira resolution.* This he explained had been followed by three subsequent letters, to none of which had substantive replies been received. Portugal's consideration of the Security Council's new resolution would have to await a clarification of the issues raised in these as yet unanswered Portuguese queries.

Meanwhile Portugal's stated position with respect to sanctions continued to be one of neutrality, doing nothing either to further or to frustrate British policy, while at the same time insisting that responsibility for implementing sanctions must fall to those countries whose nationals bought Rhodesian exports or sold Rhodesia its imports, rather than to Portugal which was simply the owner of the real estate through which these goods must pass.† When on one occasion the British Commonwealth Secretary found himself unable to give precise answers in Parliament to a question concerning the nationality of tankers carrying petrol to the Mozambique port of Lourenço Marques, the Portuguese Foreign Ministry quickly obliged: 'Given the shortage of information affecting Her Majesty's Government, the Portuguese Government is in a position to inform Mr. Whitaker [the questioner] that between April 1966 and May 1967, 169 tankers entered Lourenço Marques harbour of which 58 were of British nationality and working for British companies. . . . Of the 169 tankers mentioned, not one was Portuguese or in the service of any Portuguese company.' Britain subsequently denied the accuracy of the report.

But Portugal's offensive went well beyond such sparring. With complete aplomb, Lisbon turned to the U.N. to request compensation for economic damages done to its Province of Mozambique by the U.N. sanctions of 9 April and 16 December. Lisbon estimated that by the end of 1966 the reduction of traffic flowing through Beira and Lourenço Marques consequent on these actions amounted to a startling £9.8 million ($27.4 million). Citing Article 50 of the Charter,

---

* See above, pp. 142–3.

† Nogueira was backsliding from the position he took in a press conference on 3 May 1966. At that time he said that Portugal 'would not practise any action that would lead to the supply of oil to Rhodesia. . . .'

Portugal requested that consultations be initiated between the Portuguese Government and the Security Council to determine the modalities for recompensing these damages. It was a bravura performance! Another letter was submitted on 22 September 1967, in which Lisbon itemized an additional £5.3 million ($15 million) in damages. An editorial in the Philadelphia *Evening Bulletin* provided the only commentary necessary: 'No one can say the Portuguese don't have a sense of humor.'*

While the Security Council resolution was disdainfully turned aside in Pretoria and Lisbon, in Lusaka the Council's action prompted an agonized reappraisal. Zambia was in the grip of another economic crisis. Coal imports from the Rhodesian colliery had fallen so low that the copper companies had been forced to reduce production by one-third in November 1966. The primary cause was a decision by the Rhodesian Government that no wagon carrying coal into Zambia would be released at the border until an empty one had been returned. The object was to prevent Zambia from routing wagons of the jointly-owned railway system through Katanga and Angola to Lobito Bay on the Atlantic. Zambia had planned to do so and thus reduce its reliance on Rhodesia and Rhodesia's revenue from the railways. The one-for-one exchange added to the inefficiency of the already strained system and coal did not flow again in quantities adequate to permit full production until the following June.

Nor was this the only problem. Oil imports over the various land routes remained uncertain. Zambia moreover had become the target of Southern African espionage, psychological warfare and actual sabotage which further excited tensions arising from U.D.I. Nerves taut, the country was living on the edge of potential disaster. In late October an accidental fire in a petrol depot on the Copperbelt caused a spasm in a neighbouring African community where it was assumed that this was another instance of sabotage. In the ensuing riot a South African miner's wife was stoned to death.

The terrible pathos of Zambia was that a full year after the rebellion it was caught in a national crisis without any apparent purpose or easy solution. It had managed to pare its imports from Rhodesia by more than one-third, but this sacrifice was now quite unrelated to the earlier 'quick kill' or even 'protracted kill' schemes for ending the rebellion. The Rhodesian economy, aided by its white

---

* Even assuming the Portuguese claim was based on anticipated revenue, had Rhodesian traffic continued to grow at the same rate as in previous years, the figures submitted by Lisbon seemed excessively high. No action by the Security Council has ever been taken respecting these and subsequent claims.

neighbours, was too resilient for that. For Zambia, the object became despairingly simple – not to scuttle Rhodesia, but to keep itself afloat. The temptation quietly to disengage from sanctions by appealing to the Security Council for exceptional status, must have been almost overwhelming, the more so because the danger to Zambia if sanctions continued was as palpable as their effective impact on Rhodesia was problematic. 'Now he would be a foolish man,' Foreign Minister Kapwepwe had told the Security Council, 'who would accompany another man going to buy his own coffin.' Suspicion of British motives ran as deep as ever. Kapwepwe accused London of 'abominable dishonesty' and believed that Britain was perfectly willing to see Zambia in ruins rather than damage its trade with South Africa. But these views notwithstanding, Kaunda, on 6 February, announced that he would comply with the resolution 'despite our strong belief this method will not achieve the objective unless more effective measures are employed.' He said Zambia would tighten its belt further.*

Like everyone else Kaunda's choices were limited. He had no faith in the resolution of 16 December but for Zambia to have withdrawn might have started the process of unravelling not just the sanctions programme but the involvement, however presently inadequate, of the Western powers. The object was to keep them engaged and hopefully as time went on to stiffen the pressures on Rhodesia and its Southern African partners. Most dangerous of all, Kaunda reasoned, would have been for Zambia to have found itself left alone in Southern Africa, still dependent upon and still in profound opposition to the white regimes. So, however reluctantly, he agreed to the U.N. resolution.

In London, meanwhile, the resolution as the Opposition had promised provoked a round of protest. But it also had its uses. Earlier Wilson had been against U.N. mandatory sanctions. The preceding January an argument favouring such sanctions had been put forward in Parliament. Wilson insisted that Britain must keep the problem in its own hands. As time went on, however, he began to express the

---

* The sanctioned items had amounted to about £7 million (or something under $20 million) in Zambian imports in 1965. These had already been reduced to about £4 million ($11 million) and were now progressively cut back further. Kaunda also sent his Foreign Minister and Finance Minister to appeal to Secretary-General U Thant for U.N. assistance in handling the strain of sanctions. A mission headed by Sir Robert Jackson was immediately dispatched but little by way of tangible assistance materialized except a gradual increase in the number of technical assistants under various U.N. schemes.

view that he was also getting a bit tired of having to shelter the rebels from United Nations opinion. Now that the U.N. had acted, where did responsibility lie? Mainly with Britain, but not exclusively. The sanctions programme, no longer simply a recommendation but now a 'decision' of the Security Council, was the Council's responsibility too. 'It is a mistake to think that it is our responsibility,' a Government spokesman once said in Parliament responding to numerous questions about the sanctions performance of various countries, 'or that we have the means to enforce sanctions resolutions of the Security Council. It is a matter for the U.N. . . .'

It was a useful gambit, even though disingenuous. For Britain, together with many other countries including the United States, had not the slightest intention of permitting the Council to tighten compliance by threatening South Africa and Portugal, which in turn would have whiplashed the ailing British economy. So Britain launched the U.N. into an unprecedented venture without the final booster necessary to reach its target, and one wondered concerning this significant new commitment to effect change in Rhodesia whether the world organization wasn't destined to wander aimlessly and endlessly in some irrelevant orbit with insufficient power to complete its journey and no guidance system for turning back.

Measuring the Sanctions Bite

In Salisbury, the European community went about its Christmas shopping apparently unconcerned that it had just been made the object of an unprecedented economic siege by the Security Council in New York. Retail figures were down somewhat from pre-U.D.I. Christmas sales and some shortages were noted, none critical. There was, however, a hint of anxiety in the analogy drawn by Deputy Minister of Information, P. K. Van der Byl, between the period of voluntary sanctions and the 'phoney war' in Europe during late 1939 and early 1940. The 'phoney war' was over now, he warned, and Rhodesia, facing mandatory sanctions, must gird for action. There were many, however, who took a more relaxed view of Rhodesia's prospects. A few days before the Security Council convened, an editorial in *The Times* noted that the commercial arrangements already built up during the past year to cope with voluntary sanctions would serve well in blunting mandatory sanctions too. And Sir Roy Welensky, former Federal Prime Minister and no friend of the Smith regime, wrote two months after the Security Council's action that mandatory sanctions would be ineffective unless accompanied by force. There was in short no unanimity when it came to assessing sanctions. The available evidence could be made to yield wholly different conclusions.

The sanctioners called attention to an impressive 36 per cent drop in Rhodesia's exports in 1966, from £164.5 to £104.5 million ($461 million to $293 million). There was also a drop of 2.6 per cent in the value of the Gross National Product and a small net outflow of Europeans. The sanctions debunkers, on the other hand, pointed to a corresponding fall in Rhodesia's imports which at £101.5 million or $284 million (including invisibles) kept her balance of payments nicely in the black on current account – the result of scrupulous Government control. The contradictory evidence of 1966 persisted. Sanctions sceptics were quick to note that in 1967 virtually all sectors of the economy recorded some growth. G.N.P. was up by 8 per cent and there was a net increase in the European population. Moreover, Rhodesian exports in 1967 were down only 3.5 per cent from 1966 levels, despite the fact that U.N. sanctions in the meantime had become 'compulsory'. But sanctions supporters analysing the figures, had their doubts. The favourable G.N.P. figure may have included unsaleable stockpiled tobacco. In any event inflation in 1967 had almost certainly wiped out real growth. Meanwhile Rhodesia suffered in that year an unfavourable balance on current account when imports jumped by some £9 million ($25 million) as industry and distributors replenished depleted stocks.

The statistical veneer of trade balances and levels of economic activity concealed a most complex and controversial reality. One development, however, was incontestable. Tobacco had suffered enormously. Tobacco sanctions were effective because Britain was more directly in control of the Rhodesian market than was the case with other commodities, 40 per cent of the tobacco having tradition-ally gone to the United Kingdom. Moreover the Rhodesian leaf was easily identifiable to those interested in enforcing sanctions, and replaceable (though not always by tobacco of similar quality) in an already glutted world market. Only the United States used to export more flue-cured tobacco than the highly efficient Rhodesian industry. Sales before sanctions went as high as £46.5 million ($130 million) a year, earning close to 30 per cent of Rhodesia's foreign exchange. The annual tobacco sales in Salisbury had been festive social occa-sions, the auctioneers down in the sheds chanting out small fortunes which in turn touched off buying sprees that proliferated the earnings into widening circles of prosperity.

Sanctions had changed all that. The sales were now conducted in secret. A Government corporation bought the leaf from the grower at a fixed price and got what it could through surreptitious deals. Unsold tobacco was held in secret stores throughout the country, the largest located outside Salisbury on an abandoned airport. A building of corrugated iron 300 yards long and 80 yards wide housed a major portion of the unsold 1966 crop (an estimated 130 million lb. out of 250 million harvested); the building was extended by another 312 yards to help house the 1967 surplus (an estimated 95 million lb. out of a harvest of a little under 200 million). The price to the grower fell from an open market average of thirty-three pence per pound in the last sales before U.D.I. to Government-fixed prices ranging downwards from twenty-eight pence per pound. In 1965 growers earned a total of £34 million ($95 million). Two years later the sum total had been reduced to slightly more than £14 million ($40 million). Even at these depressed prices, however, the Government was probably paying out to growers two to three times as much as it was taking in on sales. In his July 1968 budget speech, the Rhodesian Finance Minister summarized the damages in figures probably calculated somewhat on the low side: the costs to the Government of the 1966 and 1967 tobacco crops, including all handling, storage and finance charges incurred to date, together with losses on sales already effected, amounted to more than £34 million (over $95 million)!*

In 1968, the Government fixed the new crop at 132 million lb., roughly half the 1965 bumper crop, and one-third of Rhodesia's tobacco growers agreed to surrender their marketing quotas – receiving six pence for every pound *not* grown. Already, at Government urging, production was increasing in corn, cotton, wheat, peanuts, soya beans and beef cattle. Diversification promised long term dividends and probably would have been undertaken gradually in any event. But in the short run, alternative crops couldn't begin to make up the lost income from tobacco. So profits sank and agricultural indebtedness soared. Cotton for example yielded less than one-third the income per acre than did tobacco. Nor were any of the tobacco-substitute crops labour intensive in the same degree. Fifty-four per cent of African wage earners in the agricultural sector were employed by tobacco farmers alone, a total of over 130,000 workers. They were laid off by the thousands.

Respecting no other commodity, however, were the results of sanctions so singularly dramatic. Sugar, which had earned some £3.5 million (about $10 million) per annum prior to U.D.I., was hard hit, but possibly this was as much due to an immense over-supply in world markets as it was to sanctions. There were other extraneous factors. The agricultural community as a whole was hurt

---

* For convenience dollar equivalents are calculated throughout this section at £1 = $2.80 even though some of the data post-dates Britain's 18 November 1967 devaluation.

in 1967–8, in some cases almost fatally, by the second severe drought in three years. According to old hands, nothing like it had been seen for thirty or forty years. 'Joshua's revenge', the Africans called it, referring to the nationalist leader, Joshua Nkomo, languishing in restriction at Gonakudzingwa near the Mozambique border.

Though the agricultural sector was the most important foreign exchange spinner prior to U.D.I., manufacturing made the single largest contribution to Rhodesia's overall income. The initial impact of voluntary sanctions had caused production in 1966 to fall by about 8 per cent. In 1967 there continued a steady decline of exports to Zambia, once a major market for the factories of Bulawayo, and under the pressure of sanctions both the Ford and British Motor Corporation assembly plants were closed.* Yet, surprisingly, the downward trend of 1966 was reversed. Rhodesian manufacturers, encouraged by the regime, were turning their attention to producing for the home market, now fully protected by strict import controls. The rush toward greater self-sufficiency touched off a minor industrial revolution. By early 1968 some 405 new industries had been approved of which 380 were already in production.

'Buy Rhodesian' signs were everywhere. It was even the theme for a nationwide essay competition for school children. Electric stoves, refrigerators and stereophonic record-players soon appeared, all 'made in Rhodesia'; so too men's suits (for which import licences now were no longer available) and women's dresses. Rhodesian garments were not about to set on fire the fashion capitals of the world, but textiles in the rebel colony nonetheless received an enormous boost. The Government announced major cuts in the imports of rayon and cotton fabrics and estimated that up to 1,000 new jobs would be created in the rapidly expanding spinning and weaving industry while several million pounds in foreign exchange would be saved. A cheap line of clothing goods was given access to the South African market, underselling local products and promptly arousing complaints from the South African clothing industry. (The same thing happened in tennis shoes and transistor radios.) Work began on a £16.8 million ($47 million) fertilizer plant (South African interests were involved) which would result in foreign exchange savings of up to £3.5 million ($10 million) annually.

---

* While Rhodesian manufactured goods were not proscribed by the Security Council Resolution of 16 December 1966, that resolution did however prohibit the sale or delivery of materials for the manufacture of motor vehicles. Moreover, Britain under 'voluntary' sanctions continued to try to curtail trade in Rhodesian manufactured goods, as indeed in all commodities.

Once again, however, as in agricultural diversification, there were some immediate costs involved. Even import substitution industries required imports – machinery and in many instances raw materials. Though the drain on scarce foreign exchange was less than would have been required to import the finished article, it was real enough nonetheless. More important, many of the new enterprises, judged by the usual standards of efficiency, were uneconomic. Catering primarily to the tiny Rhodesian market, they were the desperate attempt to extract a return from production resources that otherwise would have stood idle. In some cases heavy Government subsidies were needed to stifle price inflation. Instead of promoting sound economic growth in areas of natural economic advantage, badly needed to provide jobs for an exploding African population, a large proportion of Rhodesia's scarce resources went to subsidize agricultural and industrial diversification prompted largely (though not solely) by the need to beat sanctions. Government assistance to the agricultural sector alone was running, for example, at over £11 million ($30 million) a year, more than 10 per cent of Rhodesia's annual budget.

With agricultural and manufactured goods trailing as foreign exchange earners, the regime attached increasing importance to mineral exports, the third important sector of the economy. Here, at the same time, was the bull's-eye of the sanctions target. Leaving aside the all-important embargo on tobacco, five of the ten remaining items on the Security Council's sanctions list were minerals with a total value in foreign exchange of £18 million ($50 million). Despite sanctions, however, a major expansion within the mining industry took place in 1967. Indications of this were found in glowing but unverifiable reports to the Rhodesian Parliament. In one instance, however, the information was as hard as it must have been disconcerting to officials in London. Two producers announced plans to open three new nickel mining operations. One of the two, the Anglo-American Corporation of South Africa, scheduled a £10 million ($28 million) investment. It was estimated that the three mines at full production would produce nickel valued at over £7 million ($20 million) annually. In 1967, the mineral was in extremely short supply on the world market.

Movements of Rhodesia's regular mineral exports were clouded in official secrecy but indications were that copper was doing well, that asbestos sales were being maintained, while chrome and iron were selling at perhaps 50 per cent of pre-U.D.I. levels. In most instances, monetary returns to Rhodesia, after moving the minerals through the sanctions barrier, were well below those obtaining prior to U.D.I. Yet they were by no means insignificant.

If anything, getting goods into Rhodesia presented less of a problem to the regime than getting them out. Mandatory sanctions involved only 15 per cent of Rhodesia's normal imports. Voluntary sanctions of course were meant to cover the remainder. But the principal inhibition on imports were Rhodesia's own controls to limit the expenditure of foreign exchange and to protect its infant industries. Oil flowed freely (though expensively) from Mozambique and South Africa and by mid 1968 Rhodesia's liquid fuel consumption had almost returned to pre-U.D.I. levels with enough stocks on hand to last perhaps six months under rationing. American and British vehicles were no longer being produced, but the roads carried an increasing number of Mercedes, Fiats, Peugeots and Toyotas. Luxury items were often hard to come by – Portuguese brandy was sipped reluctantly in place of scotch and Rhodesian women contrived ingenious schemes to fetch cosmetics from South Africa – but despite a 10 to 15 per cent rise in the cost of living, Europeans were still faring well.

Meanwhile, for the financial years 1967 and 1968, the Rhodesian Government presented budgets tidily balanced and providing for increased expenditures with no significant rise in taxes. It was a hat trick made possible in part because the regime had repudiated its debts in the London market and its obligations due to the British Government, as well as those incurred to the World Bank under British Government guarantees. At the same time Salisbury had blocked all payments of dividends and interest to the United Kingdom.* To the money thus saved by these Rhodesian counter sanctions was added income from locally floated loans which rapidly soaked up liquid resources trapped within the country by stringent exchange controls. The absence of alternative investment opportunities and a decline in available consumer goods had assured a high rate of savings. Rhodesia was swimming in liquidity. Over the short term, at least, budgets could be balanced and the costs of economic sanctions (particularly financing the tobacco crops) could be defrayed without triggering a runaway inflation.

Such was the impact of the U.N.'s selective mandatory sanctions during 1967 and well into 1968 as seen from within Rhodesia –

---

* These actions were in answer to a freeze by Britain of some £9 million ($25 million) in foreign assets held abroad by Rhodesia's Reserve Bank. It was a serious blow to Rhodesia at the time. When however the regime did not collapse in accordance with Britain's 'quick kill' schedule, it became apparent that Rhodesia had gained much more by defaulting on loan and dividend payments than she had lost in the sequestrated funds of the Reserve Bank.

troublesome, in some cases serious, but in no sense crippling. When that impact was measured by the published statistics of Rhodesia's trading partners, on the other hand, one passed through the looking glass to another world where things looked the same, as Alice had noted, but all seemed to go the wrong way. According to these statistics, the sum of all Rhodesia's exports purchased in world markets in 1967 (plus a 'best guess' for South Africa which released no figures on its trade with Rhodesia) came to £28.5 million ($80 million) less than the figure Rhodesia herself claimed to have exported. In 1968, the gap between the world's announced imports from Rhodesia and Rhodesia's published exports to the rest of the world rose to £35.5 million ($100 million). Even larger discrepancies appeared in the analysis of Rhodesia's imports. In the roughest of terms these gaps measured the success of 'sanctions busting'.

It developed rapidly as a fine and variegated art, flourishing particularly in South Africa and Mozambique through which Rhodesian exports and imports now flowed in considerable quantity. What was taking place occasionally revealed itself with startling clarity, as when Japan in the first quarter of 1967 showed a decline in imports from Rhodesia by 95 per cent while her imports from South Africa rose by exactly the same figure. This phenomenon showed up in the trade statistics of several countries including Britain whose imports from Rhodesia plunged by 98 per cent while imports from South Africa during the same period rose by 20 per cent. The methods of evasion varied. Often Rhodesian goods were simply sold to a South African concern which, acting as a middleman and taking an appropriate percentage, resold them to a third party. In this case the goods turned up as South African exports (or re-exports, a distinction which was now omitted in South African statistics). In still other cases Rhodesian products were consumed in South Africa releasing equivalents for sale in former Rhodesian markets.

Probably the device used most frequently by forwarding agents for Rhodesian goods being conveyed through both Mozambique and South Africa was simply to falsify declarations of origin and bills of lading, the goods thus mysteriously changing their country of origin in mid passage. For example, a careful comparative analysis produced by the United Nations Secretariat found in 1967 that importing countries claimed to have received a total of 784,000 metric tons of chrome from South Africa, while South African statistics revealed that it had shipped to the same countries no more than 656,000 metric tons. The difference of 128,000 metric tons, in the U.N.'s diffident expression, 'raises the possibility that they are of Southern Rhodesian origin' – travelling presumably under false documentation.

Imports passed over the same routes, frequently manifested for

Zambia and dropped off en route in Rhodesia. It is not unlikely that
Zambia on occasion unwittingly paid for products subsequently
deflected into the Rhodesian market. For these services, middlemen
charged their fees allegedly running as high as 10 per cent. It was not
for nothing that grateful Rhodesians displayed car stickers reading
'Muito obrigado, Moçambique' or 'Dankie Suid Afrika'. Occasionally a cynical Rhodesian would add, 'Dankie Suid Afrika, plus
10 per cent.'

Despite the evasions, sanctions were not without effect. Rhodesia
was forced to sell cheap and buy dear. Inflationary pressures strained
at the controls thrown up by the astute managers of the economy.
Resources were being used, but often inefficiently. Employment levels
within the white community were being sustained, but frequently by
requiring that firms maintain their payrolls even when production had
fallen off, and by swelling the ranks of the public service. Local
investment capital, with nowhere else to go, drained into real estate
and financed a boom in the construction industry rather than
creating the instruments for fresh capital growth. Internal loans
maintained Government solvency but significant new foreign investment, desperately needed for rapid growth, was another matter. It
was questionable, some thought, how long Rhodesia could continue
to make ends meet by taking in its own wash.

These were problems, however, for the long haul. For the present,
as the *Financial Times* observed on 7 September 1967, the Rhodesian
economy was sufficiently resilient and broadly based to survive a
cutback in tobacco and still produce a modest increment in national
income. This was not a conclusion which the hard-pressed British
Government could come to easily, certainly not publicly. At the
United Nations in October 1967 a British delegate, Evan Luard,
dismissed in now familiar phrases the repeated assertions that
sanctions were failing. 'We have increasingly clear evidence,' he told
his sceptical colleagues, 'that the mandatory sanctions imposed last
December . . . are biting deeply into the Southern Rhodesian
economy.' But, as a discerning London editor pointed out, if
sanctions had bitten Rhodesia as frequently and severely as British
spokesmen alleged, that economy by now would have been masticated
beyond all recognition.

The fact was that selective mandatory sanctions were not about to
force Rhodesia to sue for terms. Wilson knew it. As time went on
so too did Smith with increasing certainty. In Rhodesia, at least in
the short term, events were to be determined less by the external
pressure of sanctions than by the internal play of politics. The trend
was decidedly to the right.

Rhodesia's Great Leap Backwards

While far from lethal, the new sanctions, together with the encounter on the *Tiger*, reverberated within Rhodesia and Ian Smith could now discern faint rumblings of discontent from both left and right. Church leaders expressed unease that legality had not been restored and multiracialism assured; advertisements appeared asking the Government to reflect on its decision to reject the *Tiger* proposals; businessmen, worried about the U.N. sanctions, urged the regime to think again; and Lord Malvern, a former Federal Prime Minister and the grand old man of Rhodesian politics, circulated a petition which secured nearly 4,000 signatures calling upon the Government to implement the *Tiger* constitution unilaterally and thereby re-establish Rhodesia's good faith and its right to recognition. The groups assembled to the left of the Front, however, represented a disorganized and essentially non-political minority. (Talk of forming an Opposition party among Europeans was recurrent but did not bear fruit until the emergence of the Centre Party in May 1968.)

The dissidence on the right was more serious for it was located within the Rhodesian Front itself. The Rhodesian political situation had a way of recurrently tilting to the right, capsizing its leaders and then submerging them, a fate that had overtaken Smith's three immediate predecessors. Once the handmaiden of the right, Smith now found himself the target of an anonymous attack from party extremists who criticized his Government for accepting Britain's six principles while deviating from those of the party, demanded an end to negotiations with London, and urged Smith to get on with declaring Rhodesia a Republic and implementing the policies of racial segregation and 'separate development'.

Smith walked his tight rope with scrupulous care. He repeatedly talked of a new constitution for Rhodesia, endorsed separate development ('a system which acknowledges our different communities and provides safeguards which will enable [them] to live according to their own wishes'), and on one occasion revealed that only the last of the six principles appealed to him ('no oppression of majority by minority or minority by majority'). He acquiesced in an amendment to the party principles deleting an affirmation of loyalty to the Queen and set up a committee to design a national flag and a national anthem. But he persistently put off the question of turning Rhodesia into a Republic. It was part of the larger question, he said, of constitutional reform, for the study of which a Commission was appointed and then permitted to pursue its work at a studied and leisurely pace. Smith was concerned that the right should not turn his flank, but equally he wanted to retain the possibility of renewed contacts with London.

Of course these requirements tended to be contradictory. In order to maintain a firm hold on the Front, Smith had to lead the Party progressively away from those legislative and negotiating positions that might have permitted a settlement. The whole process was deceptive, giving the Rhodesian Prime Minister now the image of a moderate or again that of a reactionary, depending on the angle of vision. At one point during a tense convention of the Front, a resolution was introduced which would have prohibited the display of the Union Jack and all professions of loyalty to the Queen as well as flatly rejecting the *Tiger* constitution. Smith flushed angrily, slowly rose from his chair and told the startled delegates, 'Anybody who votes for this resolution is either a monkey or a nut.' He won the vote handsomely. But in closed session, it was understood that he had assured the delegates that Rhodesia would in fact no longer accept a settlement along the lines of the *Tiger* proposals.

Wilson too was set upon by both right and left. He would have been content to keep Rhodesia off the front pages for a while, avoiding reminders of his failure to solve the problem. Pressed for his position, he would state simply that Rhodesia was perfectly free to end the rebellion by acknowledging the Governor and returning to legal self-government under the 1961 constitution, or even that constitution as amended on board H.M.S. *Tiger*. Sanctions would then end and one could turn again to a discussion of terms for full independence. Barring this, sanctions would grind on, H.M. Government content to wait for them finally to take effect. Not so the Conservatives, and particularly the Rhodesia lobby on the back benches. Prompted by occasional hints from Salisbury that Smith was willing to talk again and warnings from the same sources that impending decisions concerning Rhodesia's new constitution would soon foreclose a negotiated settlement altogether, the Conservatives pressed with rising insistence for renewed contacts between Britain and the rebels. NIBMAR of course was an insuperable barrier and the object of repeated expressions of dismay from the Parliamentary Opposition.

By June 1967 Wilson began to hedge. NIBMAR was still Government policy (even though the Prime Minister for the most part still eschewed the phrase), but a gloss now appeared on it: The Prime Minister suggested he would be prepared to discuss with the Commonwealth the abandonment of NIBMAR if 'there were a substantial change in circumstances' in Rhodesia. Like a recurrent natural phenomenon, a seasonal happening, British–Rhodesian talks seemed inexorably to take place in the fullness of time. The time had come again and the gloss on NIBMAR was a sign. (An earlier sign was that Ministers known to have had reservations about the *Tiger* settlement were shunted from jobs having to do with Rhodesia.) On 13 June, responding to another prod from his old adversary, Duncan Sandys, Wilson startled the Commons by announcing that Lord Alport was to be sent to Salisbury to determine whether a settlement might be possible. Equally startled were officials in the Commonwealth Office (Wilson was still acting as his own desk officer on Rhodesian affairs), not to mention Smith in Salisbury who had not been consulted and who responded by calling Alport an 'incredible' choice. It seemed that only Kenneth Kaunda had advance knowledge of the Alport mission; fortunately, Wilson had made a special point of informing him.

Cuthbert Alport, made a peer under the administration of Harold Macmillan, had gone to Salisbury in 1961 as British High Commissioner to the Federation of Rhodesia and Nyasaland and ended up presiding over its liquidation. In a book published later he denounced the Rhodesian Front for its 'emotion, prejudice, and narrow self-interest'. After U.D.I., Alport made frequent broadcasts over the B.B.C. beamed into Rhodesia from the Francistown transmitter urging settlement and a return to legality. He was however a Conservative and had served as a junior Minister under Sandys in the Commonwealth Office. Sandys expressed his 'relief' when Wilson announced Alport's mission to Rhodesia, while Smith described him as 'almost a listed enemy of Rhodesia'. From Wilson's point of view, it was an astute choice.

The Prime Minister's motives were not difficult to determine. There had been a flurry of reports from a variety of sources indicating that Smith was ready to talk. (The regime's Agriculture Minister, George Rudland, had just announced that tobacco plantings for the coming season would have to be cut by half.) Wilson was not adverse to testing the situation particularly if in the process he could spike the guns of the Opposition, at least for a while. Governor Gibbs too had been pressing for a new initiative. Alport's visit would boost his morale. At the same time Wilson was not optimistic. He would confine himself to reacting to Smith's proposals rather than permitting Smith to shoot down his.

After a breakneck three-week effort, during which Alport saw an estimated 1,000 Rhodesians and had three talks with Smith, Wilson's emissary brought back an inconclusive report. There was a widespread desire for a resumption of talks. Alport was sure, as he wrote later, that a majority of Rhodesians of all races wanted a negotiated settlement and were prepared to accept something along the lines of the *Tiger* proposals. But he was even more impressed with the tough obstinacy of Front leaders and with Smith's lack of manœuvrability. In a meeting with all six of the Party's area chairmen, Alport noted both their fidelity to party principles and loyalty to Mr Smith. Pointing to a picture of former Prime Minister Winston Field on the wall behind them, he asked whether their loyalty to Smith were greater than that felt for Field, who had been dumped by the Party for failing to implement its 'principles'. There was no answer.

"I'm considering giving you another chance to pull me out."

On another occasion Alport received a plain-spoken reply from a group representing the Party's rank-and-file. If Smith betrayed the principles of the Party, they told Alport, they would know 'what to do with bastards like that'. Alport was not optimistic that Rhodesians favouring settlement would (or even could) assert their position in a politically meaningful way, or that Smith himself would attempt to cast off the Party's right wing and mobilize the moderate centre. However, Smith said he was willing to resume talks. He told Alport he would accept a constitution based on the *Tiger* terms, though 'some details' would have to be looked at again. There was also the larger problem of ending the rebellion and returning to legality. Still, believing that the passage of time diminished further the prospects for settlement, Alport recommended that the matter be pursued further.

Wilson pondered his next move. Ninety-five Labour M.P.s had signed a motion calling upon the Government to give no ground on its NIBMAR pledge. Conservatives were equally insistent that Alport's initiative should not be lost. And indeed the Prime Minister himself wished to lose no opportunity, no matter how slight, to settle the Rhodesian situation and brighten his waning political fortunes.

It was indeed a bleak season. The Arab–Israeli Six-Day War had closed the Suez Canal, further compounding Britain's economic problems. (The decision to devalue the pound would be made a few months hence.) In the Middle East the United Kingdom was facing a possible Arab oil boycott, and the situation in Aden where Britain was trying to disengage from another colonial responsibility, was volatile. Entry to the European Common Market, on which Wilson had set his sights, involved apparently insuperable obstacles. The Labour Party had sunk to a new low in the opinion polls.

The prudent move, Wilson concluded, was to encourage Smith to elucidate those 'details' that required a second look. If Smith's proposals seemed minimally acceptable, the Prime Minister could agree to them as an act of statesmanship; if they were not, he could reject them as a defender of the Commonwealth position. It would at least be a further delaying action, holding off Parliamentary Opposition and, just as important, reducing the risk of a precipitate move to republican status in Rhodesia at the Front's annual Party congress scheduled for early autumn.

On 25 July 1967, Wilson told Parliament that, on Alport's recommendation, he was authorizing Governor Gibbs to clarify with Smith those aspects of the *Tiger* constitution he and his colleagues would wish changed. Meanwhile Britain fully reserved its position on NIBMAR and would consult further with African Commonwealth states. The whole debate lasted only thirty minutes. The Prime Minister, by keeping the Alport initiative alive while himself giving away nothing, had once again achieved his tactical objective, stifling protests from both sides of the House. A momentarily subdued Duncan Sandys, warmly welcoming the Prime Minister's statement, expressed the hope his sentiment would not be 'the kiss of death'. Wilson responded that he would never regard a statement by Sandys as a kiss of death – 'to me, anyway'. But he added severely that if Sandys continued to cast doubt on Britain's intentions to stand firm on majority rule, 'I would regard any approach from him, if not as the kiss of death, as the kiss of dishonour.' A few days before, however, when Labour M.P. Frank Judd attempted to get Wilson to agree that NIBMAR constituted 'a fundamental point of political morality at stake in the situation', Wilson deftly side-stepped any commitment, replying that the only fundamentals involved were the six principles. The Prime Minister knew better than anyone that there was no point in talking to the Rhodesians if one were serious about NIBMAR.

Despite Wilson's renewed flexibility, the notes that now passed between London and Salisbury opened to grave question whether there was any point at all in attempting to renew negotiations. Each side seemed to remain studiously unresponsive to the questions of the other, a kind of dialogue of the deaf, which continued, as so often was the case, principally because each wished to place on the other the onus for breaking it off. 'The exchanges so far have not been encouraging,' Wilson reported tersely to the Commons on 24 October.

There was emerging, however, another reason to continue these exchanges. South Africa clearly wished to see the Rhodesian affair settled. And South Africa, Rhodesia's principal prop against the weight of sanctions, continued to hold the key to Rhodesia's future. On one occasion Pretoria's Foreign Minister was heard to refer to the 'catastrophic results' if the impasse were not ended. Prime Minister Vorster had earlier expressed considerable concern at the failure of the *Tiger* negotiations. Prior to these talks he had encouraged Smith to arrange a settlement and even after the effort had aborted, he urged both sides through private as well as public channels to try again before Britain consigned the matter to the U.N. All this of course had been to no avail. In a mood of some exasperation, the influential Afrikaans-language newspaper, *Die Burger*, suggested (22 December 1966) that Rhodesia abandon U.D.I. and return to colonial status. Its editor wondered out loud whether independence had not become 'an empty shell', 'a greater obstacle than a help to Rhodesia's own case', and 'an embarrassment to her best friends'. The South African Government quickly denied that these views represented official thinking, but Pretoria was apprehensive about the trend of events and probably was not unhappy to have *Die Burger* (which with its companion paper *Die Beeld* subsequently published other editorials critical of the direction of the Rhodesian regime) dampen somewhat the ardour of Salisbury's supporters throughout the Republic.

After Alport's mission, the attention of both London and Pretoria came to focus on a trip to Africa scheduled for late October 1967 by the newly appointed Commonwealth Secretary, George Thomson. (He had replaced Herbert Bowden who had retired and received a peerage in September.) The occasion was the conference of the Commonwealth Parliamentary Association in Uganda. En route Thomson was to visit a number of Commonwealth African countries. When Governor Gibbs heard of the trip he urged that Thomson should stop in Salisbury as he was anxious to meet the new man in charge of Rhodesian policy – as well as to give a new impetus to the lagging contacts between the Salisbury regime and London.

The South Africans were deeply interested in this new opening. Wilson was too – and wanted a free hand to expoit it. He went to considerable lengths to keep the Rhodesian issue off the agenda of the Labour Party annual conference which opened at Scarborough on 2 October, for he wished to give the left wing of the Party no opportunity to curtail his manœuvrability. At the U.N. General Assembly meetings a few days before the Party conference, Foreign Ministers Hilgard Muller of South Africa and George Brown of Britain had had conversations which by Brown's account had gone very well. Now, with embarrassing haste, Muller turned up in London immediately after the Scarborough Labour Party conference. Brown and Muller again conferred, then continued their conversation in an unscheduled visit to the Prime Minister across Downing Street from Brown's ornate office.

Wilson was anxious to dissipate fears, inspired by the NIBMAR pledge, that Britain demanded a rapid transition to majority rule. That this was not the case he no doubt now made clear to Muller. Ideally Britain hoped to end the rebellion, to return Rhodesia to legal status, and only thereafter to arrange a gradual transition to genuine independence. The South Africans were certain, however, that Smith would face insuperable difficulties if he were to contemplate ending the rebellion prior to the full legitimization of Rhodesia's independence, so great were suspicions of British motives in Salisbury, and Muller for his part doubtless reviewed these considerations for Wilson. Both sides, however, wanted a settlement and there is reason to believe that the South Africans concurred with the British that in general the *Tiger* constitution presented a reasonable basis for agreement.

The matter did not end there, however. As a part of his African tour Thomson was to cross South Africa en route to meetings in Botswana with that country's President and the Prime Minister of Lesotho. Two days before Thomson's scheduled change of planes in South Africa, Whitehall announced that he would meet with Foreign Minister Muller in Pretoria. The stop, which seemed to have been carefully prepared, featured a protocol luncheon given by the British Ambassador for the two Ministers. Indeed Thomson's mission to Pretoria and Salisbury increasingly took on the air of an extremely important venture. Sir Saville Garner, top civil servant in the Commonwealth Office and Head of Britain's Diplomatic Service, had joined Thomson's entourage immediately following Sir Saville's return from a trip to Ottawa. There, he had not only opened British Week in the Canadian capital where he had once served as High Commissioner, but had had an unannounced luncheon with Prime Minister Lester Pearson. Pearson, it will be remembered, had been largely responsible for hammering out the compromise Commonwealth formula the year before which now committed Britain to NIBMAR – and NIBMAR was the single most serious impediment to a settlement.

When Thomson and Muller met in Pretoria, then, it was obvious that both sides looked with the deepest interest upon the imminent negotiations in Salisbury. South Africa's concern had been further validated a fortnight before when Vorster had received Ian Smith at the Prime Minister's Pretoria mansion, 'Libertas'. Vorster impressed upon Smith the importance of an early settlement and so informed Wilson by letter. The South African Prime Minister, in fact, had been lacing his public comments with repeated references to the significance for all concerned of bringing the Rhodesian constitutional crisis to an end. Upon that outcome, he maintained, depended the prosperity and stability of Southern Africa.

With preliminaries like these one might be excused for assuming that once Thomson and Smith at last met in Salisbury on 8 November tangible progress towards a negotiated settlement would pour forth like water from Moses' smitten rock. In fact, the exact opposite occurred, indicating once more just how intractable the impasse had become. Smith's and Wilson's requirements were pulling in opposite directions. As Alport had observed, Smith's problems with his party gave him very little room to manœuvre. Not long before Thomson arrived Smith told the annual congress of the Rhodesian Front that Rhodesians would be 'stark, staring mad' to permit a settlement with Britain to deflect them from the political course they had set for themselves. Thomson in the meantime had been subjected to blistering attacks from Afro-Asian Commonwealth delegates at the Parliamentarians Conference which he had just attended in Uganda and was obliged to state publicly and flatly before leaving East Africa that Britain would stand by its NIBMAR pledge. Not even the urgent appeals of South Africa could harmonize these divergent views. It was impossible in any event for South Africa in its relations with Rhodesia to pass beyond the point where counsel became command. Given the views of the South African electorate the political liabilities were too great.

Nonetheless, it must have come as a shock to Thomson when Smith made perfectly clear that he had taken a giant step away from the *Tiger* formula. Under the proposed Rhodesian changes, the safeguards against retrogressive amendments to the independence constitution were systematically disassembled. All African members of the Senate were to be chiefs, thus making protection against discriminatory amendments dependent upon the support of chiefs who in turn, as Thomson told the British Parliament, were dependent 'on the Rhodesian authorities for their pay and allowances, and in the last analysis for their appointment or dismissal'. The internal safeguard gravely weakened, the external safeguard, appeal to the Privy Council, was to be dropped altogether. Those 'details' which Smith had told Alport would have to be looked at again turned out to be, in London's view, changes 'fundamentally incompatible' with the six principles. *The Times* examined these revelations and wondered whether any Rhodesian constitution presuming to assure progress towards majority rule would be worth the paper it was written on.

Following Thomson's abortive effort, there appeared to be a corresponding decline in South Africa's interest in promoting an accommodation. Vorster continued to declare that the Rhodesian question could and must be solved, calling it the 'fly in the ointment as far as development in Southern Africa is concerned'. But there was a marked change in his apparent willingness to work with Britain to achieve a solution. The devaluation of the British pound which took place on 20 November dramatized Britain's incapacity. British sanctions against Rhodesia, Vorster warned, were a luxury Britain could now ill afford. The South African leader may have reasoned that Britain would soon be forced to abandon sanctions altogether. Even more important, the British Cabinet after prolonged consideration had decided in December to maintain its boycott on arms to South Africa in accordance with a Security Council resolution passed in 1963. Rumours had circulated for months that a deal was afoot to lift the embargo in return for South African pressures on Smith to settle. Whether or not there was substance to these stories, London was now farther from an agreement with Salisbury than ever, and South Africa no closer to restoration of its traditional arms supply from the United Kingdom.* Anglo-South African exchanges dropped off sharply for the time being, and Rhodesia's determination to hang on stiffened further.

The Friendly Face Across the Great Limpopo

A corresponding hardening in Rhodesian domestic policy was also taking place, quite at variance with the direction pointed by Britain's

---

* Allusions to a deal between London and Pretoria appeared frequently in the British press. *The Economist* on 8 July 1967, traced the rumours to 'the lobbies of the South African Parliament' and, on 11 November, to official South African support for the vigorous lobbying on the arms issue undertaken by British industrialists in London. Whether or not linked to a deal respecting Rhodesia, there was no doubt that the South African arms embargo issue seriously divided the Cabinet and created a delicate crisis for Wilson both within his own Government and with pro-African Labour backbenchers.

six principles which among other things called for progress in ending racial discrimination. The tendency was detected in a perceptive editorial published on 31 December 1966, once more in the prestigious South African paper, *Die Burger*. If Mr. Smith truly subscribes to the six principles for progress towards majority rule, ran the argument, let him by all means settle with Wilson. But because Rhodesia rejected the *Tiger* formula, 'we have the right to ask . . . how sincere the Rhodesian belief in integration and eventual majority government really is. We get the impression that we have to do with people who sometimes talk like Mrs. Suzman [a stellar liberal in South African political life] and sometimes like . . . barefaced *baaskap* people [white supremacists].' There was no question but that Rhodesia was increasingly showing its *baaskap* face.

Among the official principles of the Rhodesian Front was one recognizing the 'right of government at all levels to provide separate facilities and amenities for the various groups'. A new bill, the Municipal Amendment Act of 1967, would empower municipalities to segregate recreational and athletic facilities (parks, sports grounds, swimming pools, public conveniences and the like). There was a 'separate but equal' proviso, but equitable facilities were to be defined 'according to the needs of each race' – a formula of marvellous elasticity. The bill was rejected by Rhodesia's Constitutional Council as discriminatory, an action which could be overridden by a two-thirds vote in the Legislative Assembly. The Front brooked no delay and forced the measure through the Assembly on the very eve of Thomson's arrival for his talks with Smith.

Some months before, and again responsive to pressures from within the Party, the Minister of Local Government, Mark Partridge, announced in Parliament that he would soon introduce legislation designed to assure the racial segregation of residential communities. A draft of the measure, the Property Owners (Residential Protection) Bill, was circulated not long before Thomson's visit. Similar to South Africa's Group Areas Act, it provided a mechanism for excluding Asians and Coloureds from owning property in European areas, Africans having already been excluded under the Land Apportionment Act. It incorporated a novel 'do-it-yourself' feature. A petition to restrict an area to persons of one race would be granted when signed by fifteen property owners. A tribunal would be established to classify individuals into racial groups, taking into account a person's appearance and any other factors thought relevant. The measure reflected the mood of many of the Front's most ardent supporters.

In the educational field, private schools were now effectively prohibited from admitting more African students. Barriers to interracial sporting events at Rhodesian public schools were thrown up by

the Ministry of Education which required that such events 1
be approved by local parent–teacher associations and that
facilities for the different races must be provided. At the
Congress of the Rhodesian Front held at the end of September
delegates voted overwhelmingly to end multiracialism in hos,
after hearing complaints that the same surgical instruments were
being used for both whites and non-whites, while white nurses were
having to eat at the same tables as non-whites (though not at the same
times). An alarmed delegate also warned of the infiltration of blacks
onto Rhodesia's television screens. His evidence was a black
youngster in kilts on a children's programme called *Cabby*. When
another delegate remonstrated that after all 'it was only a child,'
he was shouted down.

Developments in the field of civil liberties were just as ominous.
Restrictive legislation of course had long predated U.D.I. and the
advent of the Rhodesian Front Government – the same was true in
the area of civil rights – but these early restrictions were constantly
being added to. A pamphlet entitled 'Rhodesia and Ourselves',
published in 1967 by the Joint International Representatives of the
British Council of Churches and the Conference of British Missionary
Societies gave a poignant summary of the impact over the years of the
basic legislation affecting civil liberties, the Law and Order Maintenance Act, passed originally in 1960. (It was so notorious an instrument of arbitrary government that it occasioned the resignation in
protest of the Federal Chief Justice, Sir Robert Tredgold.)

'One of the tragedies of Rhodesia is that most Europeans do
not know how fellow African citizens have been muzzled and
controlled as a result of [The Law and Order Maintenance Act].
This is why they react so passionately to any suggestion that
Rhodesia is a police state. Yet the facts speak for themselves.
In the last six years thousands of Africans have been kept for
longer or shorter periods of detention or restriction without
trial, some for periods of five years. Some of these were guilty
of physical intimidation of their fellows; but the great majority
have been treated this way because of their political views,
because they were known to speak against minority white
government and racial segregation, or had previously sought to
organize political parties to express their opposition. (The
African political parties were banned under the "Unlawful
Organizations Act" of 1962.) Cases are known of re-arrest and
detention as many as three times. . . . It is difficult not to
conclude that this is being used as a method of intimidation
of the African elite!'

An amendment to the Law and Order Maintenance Act, which came into force in November 1967, provided a mandatory death penalty for anyone guilty of possessing arms of war with intent to endanger the maintenance of law and order in Rhodesia or in any neighbouring territory, and capital punishment or thirty years' imprisonment for anyone guilty of 'any act of terrorism or sabotage' done with similar intent. So sweeping was the definition of terrorism and sabotage that even the organization of a strike or boycott might fall within its ambit, or the advocacy of forceful intervention in Rhodesia by the United Kingdom. Just as alarming, the accused, according to the amendment, was presumed to have had criminal intent unless he could disprove it 'beyond a reasonable doubt'.

Such draconian measures, though deplorable anywhere, were hardly unique to Rhodesia. But in the Rhodesian case they were of particular consequence for two reasons. First, Smith went out of his way to defend Rhodesia as a bastion of Western democratic and Christian values. Second, they demonstrated the increasing incompatability between announced British requirements for a settlement and Rhodesian realities. Nor was the United Nations, which had now assumed a direct interest in these developments, any more able to affect them, at least in the short run, than was the United Kingdom. It too had assumed responsibility without corresponding capability. Sanctions might have some relevance in that undefined future the British called 'the long haul', but their only effect now was to prompt Salisbury to bolster its defences against outside interference and to consolidate its position within.

Since the logic of multiracialism was integration, and the logic of integration was majority rule, it was hardly surprising that a regime which had declared illegal independence to avoid majority rule would now move towards the logical alternative, which was of course separate development, the Anglo-Saxon euphemism for apartheid. A couple of guitar-playing folk-singers in Salisbury provided the theme for this drift towards South Africa as the moorings to Britain were cut one by one. Everyone was humming it. 'If you look across the river,' it began, 'you'll find a friendly face; the great Limpopo River, full of power, full of grace.' There were many whites in Rhodesia unhappy about this drift toward the Republic but not enough to reverse the process; and many in Pretoria who were equally disturbed at the thought of assuming increasing responsibility for Rhodesia and still hoped that a constitutional settlement between Britain and Rhodesia would allow the problem to disappear.

But the Rhodesian question, though few really wanted it that way, was slowly sinking into the general problem of Southern Africa, subject less and less to British and U.N. interventions and more and more to the flow of forces within that region. No one understood this better or feared it more than Kenneth Kaunda whose country to the north, across another great river, had been appointed by geography and politics and by the vocation of its unusual leader to play a role filled with risk and potential importance.

IX

The Crisis Deepens

For some 400 miles the Zambezi River defines Rhodesia's northern boundary – broad and pacid in the west above Victoria Falls, untamed and violent in the time-hewn gorges below the cataract where after a period the turbulence dissipates in the vast reservoir backed up behind the mighty dam at Kariba. Below the wall, the thwarted river is again set free thundering in due course under the arching road bridge at Chirundu and thence to Feira in the east where at the confluence of the Luangwa it enters Mozambique and finally empties into the Indian Ocean. The primeval countryside along its hot humid banks remains for the most part forbidding and sparsely populated except for wild game. On the northern shore lies the new African state which had taken its very identity from this remarkable waterway. To enter Rhodesia from black-controlled Africa to the north, one must cross the Zambezi from Zambia.

Not only was this the likely invasion route had London decided to use force to quell the rebellion. It was virtually the only avenue available to Rhodesian Africans intent on guerrilla warfare. If neither Britain nor the U.N. could achieve political change in Rhodesia, perhaps there was no alternative to a protracted guerrilla campaign. One remembered the words of Ambassador Arsene Usher spoken at the Security Council shortly after U.D.I. 'Do you believe in your soul and conscience,' he said, addressing himself primarily to Britain and America, 'that the Africans have not the right to free their brothers taken as hostages by white rebels under a regime condemned by you and considered by world public opinion as illegal . . . ?' It was of course primarily this contingency, and the danger of racial war which followed from it, that was cited to justify the Beira resolution and mandatory sanctions. These were held to be necessary responses to a situation endangering international peace as defined under Chapter VII of the Charter. U.N. efforts, however, had thus far been ineffective. Perhaps guerrilla warfare would be less so.

The risks were obvious. A guerrilla campaign launched over the Zambezi from Zambia would encourage further co-operation between Rhodesia and South Africa; it would also expose Zambia to counter-attack, and raise a host of intricate diplomatic problems for the absentee 'administering authority' of Rhodesia, Great Britain. Not as easily foreseen was another problem. Guerrilla attacks would prompt the rebel Government to take sterner measures at home against those who had committed acts of violence. This would set in motion a final test in Rhodesia's courts concerning the legal status of the rebel Government, a test which under the circumstances Britain had little hope of winning. And these events in turn would catapult the Rhodesian issue back into the U.N. for another round of acrimonious debate leading to broadened sanctions, with by now predictable stormy repercussions within the British Parliament. A rudderless policy, caught by contrary cross-winds, sometimes ends up by going in circles.

The Guns of August

Close to one hundred armed African nationalists, infiltrating in four separate groups, made clandestine entry in August 1967 across the Zambezi now tamed by the absence of rain. At least two significant engagements took place in the valley of the Zambezi and in the area near Wankie some seventy miles south-east of Victoria Falls. Censored at first in Rhodesia, news of the action quickly appeared in the South African press. One magazine spoke of 'the crackling of rifles and the chatter of machine-gun fire' in fighting on a scale that hadn't been known for more than seventy years since the Ndebele and Shona rebellions against some of the earliest of Rhodes's settlers. Rhodesian forces at one stage were drawn into an ambush and found themselves pinned down for a substantial period. At another point they were forced into hand-to-hand combat. Air strikes against the insurgents, however, brought the situation quickly under control. Still, random skirmishes continued for over a month.

By the Government's own count seven members of its security forces had been killed, including two white officers, and fourteen wounded. The Rhodesians claimed thirty-one of the guerrillas killed, thirty captured and approximately another thirty apprehended in neighbouring Botswana – figures which, while unverifiable, were closer to reality than the exaggerated claims of the exiled nationalist organizations.* (One vivid report had it that more Rhodesians died than could be interred in the area and that trucks marked 'Fish for Bulawayo' moved corpses to graveyards farther south.) Reflecting later on the events of August, the Minister for Justice, Law and Order, Desmond Lardner-Burke, said to a sobered Rhodesian Parliament on 25 October 1967, 'This is a serious threat and probably a mounting one, and we must be prepared. The country has recently suffered and repulsed, not without loss of life, the worst invasion of armed terrorists from Zambia that it has been our misfortune to have to deal with.'

Since U.D.I., the Rhodesian nationalist organizations had inspired only marginal concern among white Rhodesians, while commanding little respect among black African leaders. It will be recalled that the Zimbabwe African Peoples' Union (ZAPU) had splintered in July 1963. The breakaway faction led by the Revd. Ndabaningi Sithole, a respected alumnus of Andover Newton Theological School of Massachusetts, called itself the Zimbabwe African National Union (ZANU). Both within and outside Rhodesia, ZAPU and ZANU adherents promptly began to squander precious energy in attacks on one another. The clashes were often bloody. Continuing efforts by eminent African leaders to bring the fighting factions together were totally without result. President Julius Nyerere called it a 'disgrace'.†

When U.D.I. came and Africans in Rhodesia did little to resist it, President Kenneth Kaunda exploded with indignation. He called the nationalist leaders 'traitors to the human race' insisting 'they are nothing, nothing.' Their activities seemed limited to issuing from outside Rhodesia incendiary (and highly irresponsible) statements rather than organizing a genuine resistance movement from within. '. . . all travelling vehicles must be stoned, must be hit with whatever you have in your hands,' ran a typical ZAPU radio commentary beamed from Zambia (a practice about which Kaunda must have had increasing reservations), 'and to the people who are inside do what you are able to do, as you squash a fly or a louse in your hand. . . .' Yet despite inflammable rhetoric, there was little evidence

---

* The number of captured guerrillas appearing in Rhodesian courts roughly substantiated Government claims at least concerning that category. Journalists on the spot also lent credence to Salisbury's figures. The number of Government casualties may have been deflated but not by much, at least for Europeans. The Rhodesian white community is so small that battle deaths could not have been kept secret for long.

† See above, pp. 36–41, 49.

of effective organization or mobilization. From early 1964 and probably for some time before, the nationalist organizations had been arranging for Rhodesian Africans to receive training in sabotage and guerrilla techniques in the Soviet Union, China, Cuba, North Korea, Ghana, Algeria and Tanzania. Arms were supplied largely from communist sources. When they returned, these men were smuggled across the Zambezi in small groups only to be picked up by Rhodesian security forces. An occasional scuffle would receive brief notice in the press and shortly thereafter the captured guerrillas would appear on trial in Salisbury.

President Kaunda, whose country was necessarily implicated, was at first less than enthusiastic about these attempts at violent assault on the white power structure of Rhodesia. Addressing himself to 'the freedom fighters' at a celebration of African Freedom Day in Lusaka on 25 May 1965, he recommended the path of non-violence emphasizing that a nationalist movement must have the support of the masses before a revolution could succeed. Repeatedly he tried to impress upon the Rhodesian African leaders the lessons learned from Zambia's own freedom struggle which had always emphasized (though often not practised) the non-violent techniques of dissent and confrontation and the disciplined organization of the masses. Kaunda laid down a tough policy concerning the transshipment of weapons. In a press conference on 9 September 1965, he warned against using Zambia as a transit route for arms. 'In the interests of Zambia and its people we cannot tolerate the presence of unsupervised arms in the country. . . . I have given fair warning to organizations who indulge in this activity. . . . They will contravene this at their own peril.'

Following U.D.I., however, Kaunda's view gradually shifted as his disillusionment with Britain intensified and as the rebellion persisted. A significant turning point occurred on 29 April 1966, when near the town of Sinoia only eighty-five miles from Salisbury a running fight occurred between Rhodesian security forces and a team of ZANU insurgents. Seven Africans were killed, considerable equipment recovered and many arrests made by the Rhodesians. Only two days before, Kaunda had learned of Wilson's intention to negotiate with Smith, the beginning of the famous 'talks about talks'. He now lost all confidence in the British leader and was all but convinced that Britain would never intervene to manage a gradual and peaceful change to majority rule and to a genuinely non-racial society in Rhodesia. More drastic techniques would have to be used.

Kaunda praised the martyrs of Sinoia. 'Blood, I am afraid, has got to be spilled,' he told a press conference on 12 May. 'It is the foundation of any freedom movement that leads to success.' This was a reluctant – and remarkable – concession for a disciple of Gandhi who believed deeply in the philosophy of non-violence. But Kaunda believed even more deeply in freedom. At the same press conference, he was asked whether Zambia would give increased aid to Rhodesian nationalists. 'It all depends on what assistance you mean,' he answered. 'Would you now allow gun-running through Zambia?' the questioner persisted. Kaunda's reply revealed no answer. This subject-matter became more delicate as time went on. Public pronouncements made clear that the Zambian Government could not possibly police the 2,800 miles of its frontier, much of which ran unmarked through remote bush areas. But neither would the Zambian Government assist the nationalist organizations in their military efforts. In a strictly literal sense, this assertion seems to have been accurate. Military training camps, as opposed to 'holding camps' or staging areas, probably were not permitted nor in all likelihood did the Government dispense from its own stocks materiel to the guerrillas. But concerning the transit of men and arms the policy, as it now evolved, was certainly one of sympathetic permissiveness.

Respecting this policy, President Kaunda understood well not only the stakes, but the risks. Indeed, his repeated insistence that the British use what he called 'legal force' to bring about ultimate majority rule in Rhodesia was based precisely upon his recognition that the final alternative would have to be 'illegal force' if Africans were to gain self-determination in their own homeland. In the racial tinder-box of Southern Africa, the dangers of such a development could not be overestimated. And yet, as he was to describe the situation in late August 1968 to a visiting American journalist, racial war and perhaps 'ideological' war seemed 'inevitable'.

'To expect Africans . . . to continue to remain docile under minority rule is not being realistic at all. History the world over shows that no matter how long it takes, the time does come when the people refuse to be subjected to that type of rule. . . .

'You had the Yugoslavs in 1948, the Hungarians in 1956 and now the Czechs in 1968. . . . I have no reasons to believe the people in Czechoslovakia are different from Rhodesians – they may have experienced this type of rule for a longer period, but still the feelings are the same. . . . Unlike Czechoslovakia, here we have a potentially explosive situation racially. And not only does it have this racial setting, but it also has the potential of being an ideological confrontation.

'Now, the people of the West have refused to help the freedom fighters. . . . This leaves these young men and women

with no choice at all but to go to the only area where they will
be supplied, namely, the East. So, as they go there to train in the
use of these various weapons, . . . you can rest assured that out
of a hundred, four, five or six will come out convinced
Communists, and so here is the beginning of an ideological
conflict. And yet the minority groups in Southern Africa
proclaim from the rooftops that they are defending Christian
values, Western values, Western civilization, that they are
combating Communism. And yet by their own behaviour they
are inviting Communism.'

There were a number of smaller incursions in the months that
followed the conflict at Sinoia. But the pitched battles of August
1967, inflicting on the Rhodesians for the first time a significant
number of casualties, came as a surprise to everyone. Meeting in the
Congolese capital of Kinshasa from 11 to 14 September, the
Assembly of Heads of State and Government of the Organization of
African Unity recommended that particular emphasis be given to
financial aid and other forms of assistance to the liberation movements of Zimbabwe. President Nyerere spoke for many of his
colleagues: 'Africa has no alternative but to rejoice and support this
fighting. For years we did all we could to avert the dangers of war
between Africans and Europeans because our aim, and that of
every human being, is not racial war. But it is now clear that in
Rhodesia a change of Government can be brought about only by
the struggle of Africans alone, by military means.'
    After a lull during the fall of 1967, a clandestine operation got
under way again, more sophisticated and potentially more dangerous.
Beginning in December 1967 insurgents began moving across the
Zambezi east of Lake Kariba into a wild and desolate area some
150 miles north-west of Salisbury. They established a series of camps,
the final one in particular carefully planned and dug in, with an
underground armoury. Over a period of many weeks the build-up
continued, reaching as many as 160 men, many trained in Cuba and
behind the Iron Curtain and all equipped with ample materiel from
Soviet, Czechoslovak and Chinese sources including the formidable
Chinese A.K. rifle. The objective was to move eastward through
Mtoka and Mrewa (known dissident areas) into the wooded and
mountainous regions of Inyanga and Umtali which were suitable for
guerrilla warfare. It was 16 March when they were discovered by an
observant Rhodesian ranger who noticed the print of a foreign boot
in the dust. The alarm sounded throughout the country. That night
notices were flashed on cinema screens in all the main towns ordering
troops to return to their units. Military police scoured pubs and

dance halls summoning soldiers to duty. The road north from Salisbury to the border was closed to all but military traffic.

In the actions that followed insurgent positions were hit from the air by jets and armed helicopters and from the ground by strong mobile forces. Their supply lines cut, their reserves virtually non-existent, and their numerical strength further dissipated by the tactical necessity of dividing into small (and thus more vulnerable) groups, the African guerrillas were quickly mauled by the Rhodesian forces which were overwhelming in both numbers and military skill. Nonetheless, sporadic fighting continued until the end of April by which time the Rhodesians had (by their count) killed fifty-six more guerrillas against five Rhodesian dead (four white and one African) and eight wounded. No guerrilla unit had broken through to target areas, though a handful of individuals may have done so. The Rhodesian forces, including Africans serving in the Rhodesian African Rifles, had fought dependably. Morale was high. Intelligence concerning the movement of suspect groups was still reliably transmitted through a well-cultivated net of tribal headmen living in the Zambezi valley.

The situation was hardly desperate – but it was disquieting. The African nationalists, though again quickly decimated, had established a temporary base within Rhodesia, lived off the land and gone about their business with a kind of tough and determined professionalism. 'We have come to the conclusion,' Smith said, 'that we may have to live with this sort of thing for quite a while.' In Moscow the Soviet newspaper *Pravda* pronounced authoritatively that the liberation struggle in Africa was entering a new phase, a phase of armed struggle.

Pravda's estimate and even Smith's concern, as it turned out, were decidedly premature – but no one could have been certain of that in the spring of 1968.* Meanwhile the guns which had shattered the silence of the Zambezi valley the previous August had created a complex set of new diplomatic problems. The incursions then and thereafter were mounted not only by Rhodesian Africans of the Zimbabwe African People's Union (ZAPU) but by South African blacks representing the historic African National Congress (A.N.C.). Frustration had turned the younger leaders of the South African freedom movement, as it had those from Rhodesia, to violent tactics in recent years and to a liaison with radical and communist states

---

* Another intrusion occurred in July and August 1968 involving around 100 guerrillas. They were rounded up with dispatch. The next major assault did not take place until January 1970. It too was quickly put down.

which were the only available sources of military training and materiel. On 19 August 1967, Oliver Tambo, Deputy President of the A.N.C. and James Chikerema, Vice-President of ZAPU, convened a joint press conference in Lusaka to announce a 'military alliance' between their two organizations. Their men were fighting as comrades-in-arms, they said, against Salisbury and Pretoria, each group bound for its own homeland.

The African 'alliance' found its counterpart in a similar liaison between the two white regimes. On 26 August 1967, journalists covering the fighting reported the presence of South African forces and helicopters helping Rhodesian units. (An unconfirmed report from ZAPU had earlier claimed that between 19 and 23 March more than 500 South African troops had arrived in Bulawayo to be deployed in the Zambezi valley.) On 8 September, Prime Minister Vorster publicly acknowledged the presence of units of the South African Police in Rhodesia. He explained that at the invitation of Rhodesian authorities, they were helping to fight guerrillas who were on their way to ravage South Africa. Earlier, debunking rumours of a defence agreement binding together South Africa, Portugal and Rhodesia, Vorster had said: 'We are good friends and good friends do not need an agreement to combat murderers.' The point was largely academic. Co-operation among the three, including periodic exchanges of military intelligence, was established practice and South Africa's open involvement in Rhodesia was now its most vivid expression. *Die Transvaler* announced matter-of-factly on 16 September that South Africa's security frontier was no longer the Limpopo but the Zambezi, while the Johannesburg *Star* of 28 August described Vorster's statement about 'good friends combating murderers' as a Monroe Doctrine for Southern Africa.

Moreover, the three white-controlled regimes made clear that they would not permit the incursions from black-controlled states to continue with impunity and the diplomatic temperature rose even higher than the fahrenheit readings along the humid Zambezi. Vorster warned Zambia of a blow so hard 'you will never forget it,' while leading politicians in both South Africa and Rhodesia publicly speculated about steps that might have to be taken to make Zambia understand the mounting danger if 'terrorists' were permitted to launch attacks from Zambian soil. In the South African media there was talk of Israeli-type punitive raids against terrorist camps north of the Zambezi. President Kaunda in turn charged that Rhodesian and South African planes had been violating Zambian air-space and noted that a military air strip had been completed in the Caprivi, a bare few miles from Zambia and hardly relevant in that advanced location to South African 'defence' operations. He called for an

East and Central African defence pact and announced a move to acquire defensive weapons, including missiles.

From both sides of the Zambezi, these animosities came to focus on Britain. On 14 September 1967, London had lodged a formal protest with the South African Government over the deployment of police units to Rhodesia. Vorster replied impatiently that South Africa would accept no dictation on this matter and that it would protect its interests as it saw fit; the police would remain as long as allowed and as long as was necessary. Smith meanwhile had instructed the head of his residual mission in London, S. F. Brice, to deliver a note to the Commonwealth Office calling attention to the fact that Zambia was allowing its territory to be used as a base for actions against Rhodesia and insisting that Britain had an obligation to press Zambia toward a policy of moderation. The letter, having come directly from the illegal regime rather than through Governor Gibbs, was handed back to Brice, an action which according to Smith (in a rather strange *non sequitur*), was a 'most blatant example of the British Government assisting and indeed encouraging the action of terrorists against a friendly [*sic*] country'.

Zambia, too, quickly laid the issue on London's doorstep. On 29 August 1967, Lusaka delivered a note to H.M. Government calling upon Britain to intervene in Rhodesia now that 'vestiges of law and order no longer exist'. Observing that South African forces had 'invaded Her Majesty's colony of Rhodesia', the Zambians contended that the crisis threatened rapidly to become 'a violent and destructive racial conflagration . . . which shall blaze from the Cape to the equator if not beyond,' a catastrophe which would be Britain's entire responsibility if it were to arise from Britain's mishandling of the Rhodesian situation.

More than three weeks passed before London's answer finally arrived. It drew particular attention to reports that Zambian authorities had permitted Zambian territory to be used as a base for armed attacks on Rhodesia. If true, London declared, the British Government would view such a dangerous and deplorable development as having 'damaging consequences for the situation as a whole and for the possibilities of a satisfactory settlement of the Rhodesian problem'. The British note asked for Zambia's assurance that it was not affording support to armed incursions into Rhodesia. The note, seen by the press as a regrettable gaffe, had been the result of the strongest representations from Governor Gibbs. Predictably, Zambia characterized it as 'ludicrous, nonsensical, and unhelpful', while a spokesman for the Ministry of Foreign Affairs in Lusaka suggested that the world was about to witness a new development in which Zambia and other well-intentioned countries would be accused by

Britain, through the Governor in Rhodesia, of helping to overthrow
the Smith regime.

The guerrilla attacks like pebbles thrown in a pool created expanding and intersecting repercussions. It was an anomaly compounded. Technically a British colony, Rhodesia was warring with
guerrillas staging from a Commonwealth base (Zambia) while
receiving, against Britain's wishes, 'police' aid from a third power
(South Africa), justified by the fact that among the insurgents were
South African blacks aiming ultimately at insurgency at home. South
Africa and Rhodesia thus had a complaint against Zambia for not
interdicting the insurgents; Britain a complaint against South Africa
for intervening in Rhodesia; and Zambia a complaint against Britain
for failing to bring under control a deteriorating situation in its
colony, which in turn threatened Zambian security. And each
complaint produced in turn reciprocal charges.

As always the controversy in Southern Africa produced its counterpart within Britain, and Wilson's administration picked its way carefully through the narrow path between opposing views. A pro-
Rhodesian Conservative back-bencher, insisting on Britain's
responsibility to protect Rhodesia from external aggression,
wondered when the Government would stop British aid to African
countries permitting terrorist attacks to be launched from their
territories. Commonwealth Secretary George Thomson allowed that
this was not a very helpful approach to a most difficult problem
arising from the fact that Rhodesia was in a state of rebellion.

Another back-bencher of similar persuasion reminded the Prime
Minister of the role being played in the affair by the Soviet Union,
Communist China and Cuba, and drew the retort that this was
precisely the danger foreseen by the Government when trying to
elicit from the Opposition more help in ending the rebellion. Wilson,
however, remained equally unresponsive when it was suggested that
the guerrillas deserved Britain's support. The Fabian socialist
journal, *Venture*, described them as 'freedom fighters',* while in
Parliament Sir Dingle Foot reminded his colleagues that in their
time Garibaldi, de Valera and Marshal Tito had all been stigmatized
as 'terrorists'. 'Africans who have come fighting into Rhodesia,'

---

* If the purpose of the guerrillas, the argument ran, is 'to damage
installations in Rhodesia, blowing up power lines and bridges, inter-
fering with Government services, stirring up African resistance to the
illegal regime, then it must surely be recognized that they are the allies
both of the sanctions policy and of the commitment to legality which
the British Government stands for.' (Vol. 19, No. 11, December 1965,
pp. 3–5.)

Sir Dingle said, 'are governed by precisely the same motives as were the people of Warsaw in 1944 or the people of Budapest in 1956.'

There was no such debate in Salisbury. Even members of the African Opposition in the Rhodesian Parliament censured the 'terrorists'. On 7 September 1967, the Minister of Justice, Law and Order introduced his bill making mandatory the death sentence for anyone found in possession of 'arms of war' (firearms, ammunition, explosives, grenades, bombs or similar missiles or devices); it was enacted 16 November. The guns of August in the Zambezi valley led not only to the mandatory death penalty of November, but to an international *cause célèbre* in Salisbury the following March – and to a further intensification of the Rhodesian problem.

The Salisbury Hangings

Shortly after 8.00 a.m. on Wednesday 6 March 1968, typewritten notices were posted on the heavy wooden doors of Salisbury Central Prison announcing that three African inmates, all convicted murderers, had been hanged that morning. They were Victor Mlambo, James Dhlamini and Duly Shadreck. The affair had astonishing repercussions around the world.

George Thomson in the Commons expressed 'shock and outrage'. Deputy Leader of the Opposition Reginald Maudling called it 'clearly a very grave situation'. In India, the Prime Minister said the executions were 'monstrous and barbarous', while the Lower House of Parliament observed a minute's silence in respect for the three Africans. Secretary-General U Thant at the United Nations said he was shocked. Pope Paul expressed deep pain over the hangings. In Ethiopia the British Ambassador was pelted with rocks outside his embassy. In Nairobi London's Deputy High Commissioner was showered with rotten tomatoes as 200 students rushed the police cordon surrounding the British High Commission. Jamaica's Prime Minister, Hugh Shearer, called for a Commonwealth Prime Minister's meeting to determine what course of action should now be taken to bring down the rebel regime. Thirty-six African countries requested an urgent session of the Security Council to consider the use of armed force against Rhodesia. And in a block-busting editorial, the prestigious *Guardian*, vanguard of the British liberal press, called on the British Government to invade Rhodesia. All in all it was an extraordinary response to capital punishment for premeditated murder meted out under long established laws, and even more extraordinary given the brutal nature of the crimes involved.

The response can be understood best in symbolic terms. The

executed men were viewed as prototypes of African resistance against racial oppression. The execution itself symbolized not only the arbitrary cruelty associated with racist rule, but the ultimate act of defiance of rebels against constituted authority. The whole episode provided a fixed target on which to focus cumulative feelings of anger, fear and frustration aroused by a problem which had touched the raw nerve of racial sensitivity. Symbolism however always foreshortens reality. The facts were somewhat more complex than the perception of them.

Some four years before, Mlambo and Dhlamini had become members of a guerrilla band calling itself the Crocodiles. They had been trained in Tanzania by ZANU and sent back to Rhodesia, pathetically ill-equipped, to help lay the groundwork for a nationalist revolution. On 5 July 1964, the two Crocodiles threw a crude barricade across an isolated mountain road near Umtali in eastern Rhodesia. It was dusk when a local white farmer, Petrus Johannes Oberholzer, drove up with his wife and young daughter. The unfortunate Oberholzer got out to remove the road block and was attacked. Though savagely beaten and bleeding terribly he managed to reach the car and drive it some one hundred yards down the road before collapsing. The vehicle overturned in a culvert. As the Crocodiles tried to set it afire, a second car approached. The Africans fled. Wife and daughter were saved but Oberholzer was dead. A local informant tipped off the authorities and Mlambo and Dhlamini were soon found hiding in a hillside cave. They were convicted and sentenced to death on 14 December 1964, almost a year before U.D.I.

Duly Shadreck's crime was described by the authorities as 'pure thuggery'. With another man he had killed an old Shangaan chief. A few days before, however, Shadreck and the chief had had a particularly violent argument. The chief had supported Smith's party to which Shadreck was bitterly opposed. Even in thuggery there was a trace of politics. Shadreck was sentenced to death on 27 September 1965, nearly seven weeks before U.D.I.

At the time of the rebellion there were approximately thirty men in Salisbury Central Prison who had been condemned to die. By the end of August 1967 that number had climbed to eighty-two. No sentences had been carried out in the interim. Under Rhodesian law no death penalty could be executed without a warrant signed by the Governor on the advice of the Cabinet. The regime decided against submitting the cases to Clifford Dupont, the regime's surrogate for Governor Gibbs. To have done so would have prompted counsel for the defence to apply for interdicts to stay the executions. This immediately would have raised with the judiciary the issue of the regime's constitutional legality. From the outset Smith had been unsure of the loyalty of the High Court judges. The Chief Justice, Sir Hugh Beadle, had after all actually moved into Government House and was serving as Governor Gibbs's chief confidant.

At the end of August 1967, however, the regime decided that despite the risks involved, the time had come to move ahead. The recent serious altercations with African guerrillas argued strongly for tough Government measures as a deterrent. These in fact were being insisted upon by an increasing number of Rhodesian Front militants. Moreover Smith felt that by now the judges might end up supporting his regime in the legal contest bound to follow. Accordingly on 31 August the Minister for Justice, Law and Order, Desmond Lardner-Burke, advised Parliament that death sentences were to be carried out against Mlambo, Dhlamini and Shadreck. (Three other death sentences were commuted and the balance were to be reviewed.) Dupont signed the warrants and the three men were advised of their fate.

The ensuing confrontation involved, however, not only the Court but Britain itself. Since U.D.I., two insubstantial threads had continued to bind Rhodesia to the United Kingdom – the judicial system and the Crown. The regime had scrupulously challenged neither, while Rhodesian courts had avoided passing judgement one way or the other on the legality of the regime. But before this crisis was to run its course, both threads would be frayed to the breaking point. The same day that Lardner-Burke made his announcement to the Rhodesian Parliament, the Commonwealth Office in London expressed 'great concern', warning that executions not warranted by Governor Gibbs would be tantamount to murder, imposing the heaviest responsibility on everyone involved. Britain's representative in Salisbury, John Hennings, made the point bluntly to Beadle himself and talked about collective responsibility for 'judicial murder' if the courts upheld the regime. As the legal battle got under way, officials in London watched as intently as the condemned men in Salisbury.

Predictably on 2 September the decision to hang the three Africans was challenged in court. The defence attorneys argued that the execution order could only be valid if signed by the Governor and that substitution of the 'Officer Administering the Government' (Dupont) was 'prima facie invalid, unconstitutional and *ultra vires*'. An interim interdict granting a stay of execution, which had been scheduled for 4 September, was handed down. When however, on 22 September, the lawyers for the condemned men asked that the interim interdict be made 'perpetual', the judge refused, arguing that the Smith regime was the *de facto* authority and that Dupont was indeed empowered to grant clemency or to order the executions. The court did however extend the temporary stay pending appeal to the Appellate Division of the High Court, the highest tribunal within Rhodesia.

The grounds of the appeal to the Appellate Division were of course that the Smith regime was not legally competent to carry out the death sentences. Meandering through the courts for some two years had been another case, that of Daniel Madzimbamuto, designed precisely to challenge the legality of the Smith regime. The two cases now converged in time. Madzimbamuto, together with a white lawyer named Leo Baron, had originally been detained under the Emergency Powers Act shortly before U.D.I. The detention was valid for only three months. Counsel for Madzimbamuto and Baron (the latter was subsequently released and dropped out of the case) appealed against its renewal, arguing that Dupont in signing it was *ultra vires* as a member of an illegal regime. An application for a writ of habeas corpus was dismissed, however, and the case was then appealed to the Appellate Division of the High Court.

For a full year the proceedings dragged on. Finally on 29 January 1968, a peculiar judgement, but one of singular importance, was handed down. Four out of five judges agreed that the present Rhodesian regime could lawfully do anything its predecessors could lawfully have done. According to the legal doctrine thus set forth, the 1961 constitution was still in force, not the post-U.D.I. (thus illegal) 1965 constitution. Nonetheless the regime, though not a government *de jure* was a government *de facto* and must be endowed with all the powers held by the officers of its predecessor Governments. The Rhodesian courts had handed Smith a signal legal victory.

A month later, on 29 February, the case of the three condemned men came before the Appellate Division of the High Court. Based on the Madzimbamuto case, it was decided that a *de facto* government had the duty to govern and that duty included, as one of the judges had put it, 'the unpleasant task' of carrying out death sentences. For this purpose the Officer Administering the Government must be able to perform all the acts which the Governor had been able to perform. This established the legal competence of the regime to proceed with the executions and the petition of the condemned men was thus denied. Only one more step now remained in the long process of legal appeal.

Under the 1961 constitution, the authority of which had not yet been questioned by the judges, the right of final appeal lay with the Judicial Committee of the Privy Council sitting in London. Counsel for the three condemned men thus immediately made application to the Appellate Division for such an appeal. Lardner-Burke in the meantime however, had filed an affidavit on behalf of the Rhodesian

Government making clear that it would not respect appeals made beyond Rhodesia's own High Court. Accordingly Beadle, in turning down the application for an appeal to the Privy Council, found that 'no judgement would be of any value inside this territory. . . . it would be wholly ineffective and would not prevent the execution of the appellants if the Government decided to exercise its prerogative to carry out the sentences.' He added that to grant the application to appeal 'would only raise their hopes where there is no hope, and would be an act of gratuitous cruelty by increasing the delay.' It was now Friday, 1 March. A spokesman for the Rhodesian Government announced laconically that 'the normal processes of law' would be followed.

Officials in the Commonwealth Office, observing with acute interest these tortuous but legally significant proceedings, now issued a warning that the views of Rhodesia's courts could not be regarded as conclusive, that the final appellate court for Rhodesia remained the Judicial Committee of the Privy Council, and that 'any person who takes part in the carrying out of a death sentence without the confirmation required by law as eventually declared by the Judicial Committee will bear the gravest personal responsibility.' The warning was unlikely to have much effect for Smith now had all but won legitimacy from Rhodesia's courts. In finding Dupont competent to warrant the executions, the High Court had granted *de facto* status to the regime, though recognizing the legality of only the 1961 constitution. In denying appeal to the Privy Council, a right guaranteed under the 1961 constitution but deleted from the illegal 1965 constitution, the High Court seemed to be granting *de jure* status to the regime as well.* Underlying all of this was a clear legal challenge to Britain. It could hardly have been ignored, for to have done so would have meant to acquiesce in a High Court decision imputing legality to the rebel regime.

On Friday night, 1 March, the Commonwealth Secretary and the Attorney General met with the British Prime Minister. There was only one move left to be taken – to issue a reprieve. This was the Queen's prerogative but one which was exercised only on 'advice' from her ministers. During the night by diplomatic wireless, George

---

* Mr. Justice Fieldsend resigned from the Court in protest on 4 March, stating that denial of appeal to the Privy Council 'renders nugatory the protection which the Court can afford to rights enshrined in the 1961 constitution'. He was the only one of five members of the Court to dissent from the ruling in the Madzimbamuto case that Smith's regime was the *de facto* Government of Rhodesia, with power of life and death over its citizens.

Thomson informed Governor Gibbs of his prospective action. The Governor raised no objection. The Queen was contacted on Saturday, 2 March. She signified her assent. On Monday morning, 4 March, counsel for the condemned men urgently applied to the Appellate Division of the High Court for a stay of execution in response to the Royal reprieve, which had commuted the sentences to life in prison. Beadle stated again that the present Rhodesian Government was fully *de facto* and determined that under the 1961 constitution, which had granted internal sovereignty to Rhodesia, only the Rhodesian Government was empowered to exercise the prerogative of mercy. (London argued to the contrary, that though the Royal Prerogative of Mercy had been delegated to the Governor-in-Council, the Queen was not thereby 'emptied' of her right; moreover, the Governor himself clearly could not act on the advice of his Council since the Rhodesian Cabinet was illegal.) Beadle then deplored the fact that the Queen had been brought into the case by her Government in London. 'Her Majesty is quite powerless in this matter,' he went on. The second thread linking Rhodesia and Britain, loyalty to the Crown, had now been badly frayed. So too the relationship between Governor Gibbs and the Chief Justice. It could hardly have survived Beadle's rejection of the Queen's reprieve. Upon Gibbs's order, he packed his bags and moved out of Government House that day.

Rhodesian Cabinet members sat for seven hours on Tuesday, 5 March. Before them were petitions for clemency which had just been submitted to Dupont by the three men waiting in the death cell. In the balance, however, were not only three lives but a range of other weighty considerations. If the sentences were commuted by the regime (as Governor Gibbs now privately urged) the crisis would abort before reaching its climax and relations with Britain would then perhaps not be beyond ultimate repair. Only a few days before the hanging crisis, Sir Alec Douglas-Home, former Prime Minister and respected elder statesman of the Conservative Party, had made a private visit to Salisbury at the urging of Governor Gibbs (an old school friend) and Sir Roy Welensky. Sir Alec and Smith had agreed on a formula which nudged Smith part way back to the *Tiger* constitution. The Rhodesian leader said he would accept the internal safeguard – the blocking quarter of elected Africans – as the basis for renewed negotiations.* If the sentences were carried out Sir Alec's

---

* Smith had placed himself at a propaganda disadvantage the previous November when in talks with George Thomson he retreated so conspicuously from the *Tiger* terms. His limited concessions to Douglas-Home were, in part at least, an attempt to diminish Wilson's tactical advantage. The Rhodesian leader, however, evidently stopped

initiative would be lost, and further penalties would be likely to be heaped upon Rhodesia. On the other hand, the viability of the regime and the security of Rhodesia, it was argued, demanded full retribution for acts of terrorism, as indeed many in the Front were insisting. In due course the decision to hang was arrived at. The men died on the scaffold the following morning.

Rhodesia was now in a no nonsense mood. Reuters on the day of the hangings reported from 'reliable sources' that the regime was considering the possible execution of more prisoners held under sentence of death and would be dealing 'chronologically' with the condemned men held in the prisons which by this time had climbed to a figure of 116. On the day following the hangings, eight more Africans were sentenced to death by the Salisbury High Court under the mandatory death penalty clause of the Law and Order Maintenance Act (passed the previous November) for entering Rhodesia with lethal weapons. A ninth person, fifteen years old, was given twenty years in prison. By the following week-end it was clear that six more convicted men were scheduled for execution on 11 March. Detailed consideration again was given by the Cabinet to petitions and appeals for clemency. By now, however, the uproar abroad and growing concern within the Rhodesian civil service were getting through to Ministers in Salisbury, and when 11 March arrived only two of the six were hanged. (They had been found guilty of killing a sub-chief.) Over the next two days some forty-four reprieves were announced. The hangings had ceased. But a bitter legacy and some basic issues remained.

'Who is the Government?'

It was said that early in the morning of 11 March outside Salisbury Central Prison, an old African awaiting notice of the executions about to take place confronted a prison guard. 'By whose right is this being done?' the old man asked. 'The Government's', came the reply. 'Who is the Government?' the old man persisted. 'We don't know who the Government is.' Though layered over by complex legal doctrine, at bottom was the basic issue: who governs?

H.M. Government in London expressed concern that the sentences were executed after such a long delay; indignation that the cases were consummated before the final appeal was exhausted, that to the

---

short of endorsing any external safeguard such as the right of appeal to the Privy Council, as both Harold Wilson and Sir Alec Douglas-Home acknowledged in the Commons debate of 27 March 1968.

Privy Council; and shock that the Royal Prerogative of Mercy had been defiantly ignored. For some there must have been a sense of despair that politically inspired crimes and the inevitable punishment had resulted from Britain's failure (or inability, depending on one's point of view) to establish authority commensurate with its responsibility, thus giving rise to the dreadful complaint, 'We don't know who the Government is.'

There was nothing new in all this. As Edward Heath took pains to point out to Wilson in a subsequent Parliamentary debate, 'the writ of the Queen as advised by the Secretary of State for Commonwealth Affairs does not run in Rhodesia, and neither does any decision of Her Majesty's Government in the Parliament of Westminster.' But the unpleasant truth was the more bitter because the Rhodesian High Court, once impartial, had now invested the regime with new legitimacy and because the Queen's reprieve had been turned aside. The last vestige of British authority had been stripped off.

The regime accused Britain of cruelly using the condemned men as 'pawns in a political game, to be manipulated in an attempt to undermine the authority of the Rhodesian Government. . . .' Smith, like Beadle, deplored the fact that British Government policy hid 'behind the skirts of their Queen'. The reprieve was nothing more than a mechanism devised by the British Government in its contest with Salisbury. There was substance to these accusations for all along London had hoped to create a damaging confrontation between the judiciary and the regime and, by invoking loyalty to the Crown, to reduce Smith's support within the white electorate. But of course Smith and his regime had been equally manipulative, using the condemned Africans as political weapons in an effort to gain from the courts formal recognition of their power, and avowing unqualified loyalty to the Queen while tearing up the constitution which acknowledged her as Head of State and repudiating the Governor who was her personal representative.* The object on both sides was to see who ultimately would govern in Rhodesia.

Wilson himself had been in part responsible for the ironic situation that had now developed. The British Prime Minister shortly after U.D.I. had told Rhodesia's public servants, singling out the judiciary

---

* Derek Ingram, the head of Gemini News Service, made this point forcefully in a release carried by the *Times of Zambia*, 13 March 1968. The pattern of Smith's behaviour was not new, he asserted. 'It has been followed by Rhodesians ever since Cecil Rhodes used Queen Victoria's name to his advantage in dealing with African chiefs over mineral rights, often against the wishes of the Government in Britain.'

in particular, to carry on with their jobs and to help maintain law and order. Each must be the judge of any action he might be asked to take which would be illegal in the sense of furthering the rebellion. There was here an implicit contradiction which in the course of time could not help but overtake Britain's policy. For there can be no law and order without executive authority which is the essence of government. Britain's writ, as Heath had said, clearly did not run in Rhodesia. That of the rebel regime clearly did. And a government 'in fact' becomes in time a government 'in law'. For there is an inevitable accretion of legitimacy as commands are issued and obeyed, monies are raised and dispensed, order is maintained and the normal processes of society carried forward without serious internal challenge. Under these circumstances the acquiescence of the judiciary adds to legitimacy. For it to be otherwise, the judiciary must finally abdicate its vocation of maintaining the law.

It should have come as no surprise, therefore, that the implicit recognition of the Smith regime contained in the Madzimbamuto case and the cases of three condemned men would shortly become explicit. Indeed, the High Court gave the Rhodesian Government full legal (*de jure*) recognition under the 1965 constitution in a judgement handed down on 13 September 1968. The Chief Justice found the Smith Government in effective control with no prospect that sanctions would alter that condition. He found 'no other factors which might succeed in doing so, force having repeatedly been rejected'. Who is the Government? Mr. Justice MacDonald in the same decision noted that Rhodesians faced a choice between two Governments, one created in Britain by the enactments of 16 November 1965, but which had made no attempt to govern; and a second elected Government which had illegally declared independence, been dismissed but nonetheless continued to govern. MacDonald concluded that in these circumstances Britain had forfeited its authority. Beadle framed the choice as follows: 'Is it better to remain and carry on with the peaceful task of protecting the fabric of society and maintaining law and order as a court, other than a 1961-constitution Court, or is it better to go, even though going may (to quote Lord Pearce) cause "chaos and work great hardship on the citizens of all races and incidentally damage that part of the realm to the detriment of whoever may be ultimately successful"? In the circumstances it is better for the judges to carry on as a court in the new situation.'

Within Rhodesia the hangings had helped to resolve the question, who governs? But not so outside Rhodesia. At the United Nations, the hangings reconfirmed the illegitimacy of the regime.

Comprehensive Mandatory Sanctions

The whole affair had dramatized Britain's dilemma and deepened its sense of frustration. In general, however, few Britons viewed the prisoners as anything other than convicted murderers. The perspective among Afro-Asians was otherwise which helps to explain the vehemence of their reaction. Wilson himself once acknowledged that the executed men in the eyes of their fellow Africans would be seen as 'freedom fighters' and the way they were put to death would transform them from murderers to martyrs. He was quite right. The day following the first executions the U.N. Special Committee on Colonialism expressed shock, not at the executions but at the 'assassinations'. When the Security Council convened on 19 March 1968, the Algerians recommended that the 'murderers' in the rebel regime be treated as 'international criminals'. India talked of 'cold-blooded assassination' and Pakistan of the 'collapse of the rule of law'.

A tough resolution was in prospect, but not simply because the Afro-Asian states demanded it. It was in prospect equally because the United Kingdom Government once more found itself in the position of having to 'do something' in order to maintain the credibility of its policy. Wilson told the Commons (as he had often before) that he would neither use force nor surrender. Nor indeed would he negotiate 'in the shadow of the gallows' with a repressive and racist regime. That left only a new move at the United Nations, which in any event might serve to appease the wrath of that organization and of the Commonwealth. For Wilson, the U.N. had by now become a rather useful device, offering a kind of diversionary tactic when it was impossible to meet a problem head on. It was a place where one could co-opt others to share responsibility for effecting a solution or – who knows? – could distribute blame in the event of failure. The implications for the U.N. were something else again, for the world organization was about to deepen its involvement in an impasse which remained as intractable as ever and to expand its commitment to a sanctions strategy which gave little promise of success. For their own reasons, the Afro-Asians wished to force Britain beyond its limited tactical objectives, obliging either the use of force or a direct confrontation with South Africa. So once again Britain's Permanent Representative to the U.N., Lord Caradon, found himself in private and arduous negotiations with the Afro-Asians hammering out a new resolution. The talks ran on for an interminable ten weeks.

The result was one of the most detailed and complex resolutions ever passed by the Security Council, running to twenty-three operational paragraphs. Like the resolution of 16 December 1966, it found the situation a threat to the peace and invoked the mandatory provisions of Chapter VII. The Council 'decided' that member-states should prevent imports from or exports to Rhodesia of all products and commodities regardless of prior contracts or licences. Thus the selective sanctions of December 1966 were now made comprehensive. Excepted only were exports to Rhodesia for medical, educational and informational purposes. It forbade the transfer of all funds except for the purposes just cited, or for pensions or strictly humanitarian reasons. It enjoined members from permitting shipment by whatever conveyance of Rhodesian exports or imports or from allowing air traffic to or from Rhodesia or flights that would connect with Rhodesian aircraft. It required members to deny entry to anyone carrying a Rhodesian passport or anyone ordinarily resident in Rhodesia who had furthered or was likely to further the unlawful actions of the illegal regime.

In addition to these legally binding provisions, the resolution, using more permissive language, recommended a number of other measures. Of particular interest, it 'emphasized the need' to cut consular and trade representation in Rhodesia, in fact to terminate all communications with the rebel colony. The Afro-Asians wished to make these provisions mandatory. Britain and the United States demurred, the former because as administering authority it wished to keep open a channel of communication with Rhodesia and the latter because the requirement to interdict communications would have raised serious constitutional problems.

As before, the special situation of Zambia became an issue. The original British draft would have required the land-locked Southern African states to implement sanctions 'only in so far as their position permits'. In Lusaka it was assumed that this was an oblique warning from London that Zambia must look to her own interests and expect no further aid from the United Kingdom in return for strengthening its sanctions effort – once considered by Britain to be a matter of the greatest importance. The final draft called for priority assistance from all states to help Zambia overcome the economic problems arising from the application of sanctions. Not only did this deny Zambia any loophole, but, as it turned out, no help of any consequence was ever forthcoming; nor did Zambia, which of course was unable fully to comply with the resolution given its continuing reliance on Rhodesia, ever apply for relief under Article 50 of the Charter. In short everyone including Zambia failed to honour this part of the resolution.*

---

* Article 50 allows a state confronted with special economic problems arising from fulfilment of enforcement measures under

Perhaps the most controversial paragraph of the entire document was one urging all members 'to render moral and material assistance to the peoples of Southern Rhodesia in their struggle to achieve their freedom and independence'. The Conservatives in the British Parliament (not to mention Smith in Salisbury) found here an open invitation to commit 'terrorism' in Rhodesia. Their anxiety was not abated when Guinea's Ambassador to the United Nations noted with satisfaction that this was the first time the Council had 'approved a guerrilla struggle in Rhodesia . . . as well as assistance by individual states to freedom fighters.' The British Government flatly rejected this interpretation insisting that the help envisaged would continue to be peaceful. As the Commonwealth Secretary, George Thomson, pointed out, the Afro-Asian states had begun by insisting on a resolution demanding the use of force and ended with one containing no mention of force whatsoever.

Caradon in fact had managed once more to avoid all the pitfalls – or from the Afro-Asian point of view to thwart every effort to make the resolution effective. Thus, a provision that the United Kingdom should take 'all requisite measures' to stop the executions in Rhodesia came through in the final draft as a call for 'all possible measures'. While the Afro-Asians proposed to 'censure' South Africa and Portugal for assisting Rhodesia and to require the Council to levy sanctions against them if they continued to defy the decisions of the Council, the final draft generally deplored non-compliance and censured non-compliers without naming names or invoking threats. Britain repeatedly made clear that both force and a confrontation with South Africa were out of the question. 'It is best,' said Caradon to the Council, 'that these things should be openly stated and honestly faced.'

As to the requirement not to grant independence before majority rule, Caradon, through five major speeches during the prolonged Council debates, nimbly avoided any commitment to NIBMAR. He talked instead, with such calculated ambiguity as to inspire admiration for his dexterity, about 'democratic advance' and 'free govern-

---

Chapter VII to consult the Security Council regarding a solution to those problems. The other 'land-locked states of Southern Africa', Botswana, Malawi, Lesotho and Swaziland have also been unable to comply with mandatory sanctions, though their trade with Rhodesia has been of marginal importance as compared with that of Zambia. Only Botswana has taken the formal step of asking to 'consult' with the Security Council under Article 50. Even though the language submitted by Britain was never formalized in a resolution, it is generally conceded that these land-locked states fall in a special category.

ment' and, for Rhodesian Africans, 'the prospect of full participation in the government of their country'. The resolution itself was equally artful, requiring only that the United Kingdom 'should ensure that no settlement is reached without taking into account the views of the people of Southern Rhodesia, and in particular the political parties favouring majority rule, and that is acceptable to the people of Southern Rhodesia as a whole'. It was all well within the six principles, Thomson told Parliament – which was to say simply that the additional NIBMAR requirement had been successfully circumvented.

To assist in policing this elaborate schedule of requirements there was to be established a special committee of the Council, the so-called Sanctions Committee. It was to examine the reports to be submitted to the Secretary-General by member-states while seeking from members further information regarding trade or the activities of their nationals that might constitute evasion of sanctions measures. All members were called upon to supply such information and Britain, as the administering power, was asked to provide maximum assistance.

On 29 May 1968, the resolution was passed unanimously winning the concurring votes of all fifteen members of the Council. France for the first time voted affirmatively. This about-face placed the French in a curious position. France continued to assert that the U.N. lacked competence, as the Rhodesian affair fell within the domestic jurisdiction of Britain. At the same time, noting the vast depth of feeling created by the Rhodesian crisis, the legitimate impatience of the Africans, and the fact that 'the Rhodesian affair has increasingly assumed the aspect of a general crisis affecting the whole world,' the French Ambassador voted for the resolution in order to express French feelings 'in the clearest possible terms'. France thus ringingly endorsed a resolution which, by its own assessment, was entirely lacking in competence.

Lord Caradon summed things up after the vote. There would be no speedy or spectacular victories. The bywords were determination and perseverance to convince the Rhodesians of the hopelessness of their course, which led only to stagnation and isolation and which could be reversed only by 'a return to the high road of legality and democratic advance'. This was, he said, 'a job not for the cavalry but for the sappers'.

When, however, the affair returned to Parliament for consideration of the Order extending sanctions to cover the requirements of the new resolution, it was apparent that many of Caradon's sappers were in the Conservative Party, intent on undermining his delicate accomplishment. The Conservatives would have nothing to do with the expanded sanctions policy and vied with one another in hurling epithets, finding it vindictive, punitive, dangerous and futile. But the most eloquent critic was once again the curmudgeon of the Labour backbenchers, Reginald Paget, who accused the Government of 'a petulant attempt to punish where we cannot correct. . . . We simply divert ourselves and the United Nations,' he went on, 'to upset an economy when we cannot upset a regime: we make its government more difficult when we have no alternative government, no means of government, no change that we can establish. It is shocking policy and a shocking mess in which to find the United Nations.'

Quite on the contrary, George Thomson replied. The position was no force, no surrender and steadily increasing pressures, not to impose hardship for its own sake but to induce change. Britain's policy was not vindictive but a reflection of the condemnation of the illegal regime by the entire world community. One took no joy in applying sanctions over the long haul, a wasteful and painful prospect. But more damaging still to British interests and to Britain's moral standing in the international community, he claimed, would be to connive at a settlement which would sell Rhodesia's Africans down the river. When the division took place on 17 June, the Order was approved by seventy-three votes.*

The core of Wilson's dispute with the Opposition continued to turn on prospects for a negotiated settlement. For over a year the Conservatives had insisted that negotiations with Smith provided the only sure way through the Rhodesian morass. Particularly after the hangings, Wilson would have none of it. He revealed that his Government had been giving thorough consideration to the proposal for a settlement which Sir Alec Douglas-Home had just brought back when Salisbury decided to proceed with the executions, thus 'slamming the door' on further contacts. He called the Rhodesian regime on one occasion 'essentially evil' and confessed that he had indeed taken a serious risk in offering 'to men of that character' the rights of independence before the achievement of majority rule. In a free-swinging attack he accused the Salisbury rebels of subverting and perverting everything underlying the rule of law.

But Wilson was not a man to minimize his options. Immediately

---

* In an unprecedented move, the House of Lords defeated it the following day. The Labour Party accused the Conservatives of abusing their majority in the Upper House to frustrate the foreign policy of the elected Government, while a vengeful Wilson threatened legislation to abolish the House of Lords altogether. A second Order came into operation on 3 July, was approved in Commons on 15 July and this time, three days later, gained the consent of Lords.

after one of his bitterest denunciations, occasioned by the hangings, he had quietly dispatched a high official from the Commonwealth Office to Salisbury privately to assure the distraught Governor that negotiations on a settlement were not ruled out; and in the course of his indignant accusations he paused long enough to suggest that it might again be possible to talk when Rhodesian leaders had 'broken with racialism' and when responsible men had appeared (an oblique reference to changes in Smith's cabinet) who could be trusted to make an honourable agreement.

The perspicacious Commonwealth correspondent for the *Guardian*, Patrick Keatley, on the day after the first hangings when emotions were at white heat, estimated that contact between London and Salisbury might well be resumed within four or five months. He was a shade optimistic. Contact was re-established in five months and twelve days. And within seven months the two Prime Ministers were talking again on board a British warship. It was this erratic quality that so annoyed Heath. 'What can be more humiliating for this country,' he once complained after one of Wilson's tumultuous attacks, 'than for the Prime Minister to keep on heaping insults on them and saying it is impossible to talk to them and then two months go by and he tries to negotiate a settlement.'

X

The *Fearless* Interlude

On 8 October 1968, just twenty-two months after the abortive talks on board H.M.S. *Tiger* and following protracted, secret negotiations which were virtual carbon copies of those preceding the earlier talks, the Prime Ministers of Britain and rebel Rhodesia boarded R.A.F. planes in their respective capitals and headed once more for Gibraltar. There, as before, they clambered aboard a British assault ship, this time H.M.S. *Fearless*, to conduct negotiations about a settlement which, given their separate terms of reference, were almost certainly destined to fail – as they had failed earlier. The whole episode had about it the sense of *déjà vu*.

The residuum of British power was as deceptive now as before, the great rock fortress, the sleek fighting ships, naval efficiency, the visible trappings of empire and the instruments for projecting power and holding sway over distant populations. But these nostalgic symbols were irrelevant. There was no British power in Rhodesia, and there was no will and only slender capability to impose it. Symbolically more to the point perhaps was the last major operation of the *Fearless* before sailing to Gibraltar: she had assisted in the evacuation of British forces from Aden. Reflecting upon this disjunction between responsibility and power, Charles Fletcher-Cooke, M.P., reminded the Commons that Lord Salisbury, the British Prime Minister at the end of the nineteenth century (whose name Cecil Rhodes cunningly gave to the capital of the newly acquired area between the Limpopo and the Zambezi Rivers), had resisted going into Central Africa at all. Salisbury maintained that it was wrong to accept the allegiance of a population of whatever colour in areas beyond the reach 'of either the Royal Navy or the Indian Army'. 'We have reaped that lesson,' Fletcher-Cooke concluded, 'because we cannot protect them.'

Though subject to the continuing harassment of sanctions, Smith indeed had thus far remained effectively uncoerced and could afford to await the further attenuation of British demands, or if this were not forthcoming, continue to go his own way. In an extraordinarily frank interview with Ian Waller in the *Sunday Telegraph* of 28 April 1968, Smith had all but slammed the door on anything approaching settlement on British terms. The Rhodesian leader was asked if agreement on the principle of eventual majority rule would be acceptable, and replied that he didn't think any white person in Rhodesia accepted it, except possibly former Prime Minister Garfield Todd and perhaps a dozen others. 'If they thought it was coming in the next twenty years or so I think 99 per cent of Rhodesians would turn it down.' The only way one could sell majority rule, he went on, was to convince people it really meant nothing for the next hundred years. How thus the two Prime Ministers had come together once again at Gibraltar to attempt to reconcile their divergent positions – Wilson's premised on the ultimate achievement of majority rule and Smith's on its avoidance – is worth careful examination.

Preparing for *Fearless*

In Pretoria

The South African Government, as we have seen, had reservations about U.D.I. from the start. Needlessly, the rebellion had introduced new uncertainties within and unleashed new forces affecting the southern tip of the continent. The comprehensive mandatory sanctions passed by the U.N. Security Council at the end of May 1968 called fresh attention to South Africa's complicity in the nettlesome Rhodesian affair. The Reserve Bank in Pretoria continued to serve as a clearing house for Rhodesia's foreign transactions, accepting Rhodesian currency at par. Deficits in Rhodesia's trade balance were carried either by the Reserve Bank which presumably accumulated Rhodesian currency not acceptable elsewhere, or were offset by investment in and credit to Rhodesia made available by South Africa's private economic sector. Meanwhile South African middlemen, as well as Portuguese, were busy helping to facilitate Rhodesia's import and export deals.

The unsolved Rhodesian dispute further complicated Pretoria's relations with both London and Washington. It also threw up a formidable barrier to South Africa's so-called 'outward' policy, the effort to establish better relations with selected black-controlled states. A prime object was to develop within Southern and Central Africa a buffer between South Africa and the more militant black African states farther north. Some officials in Pretoria (however unrealistically) considered Zambia the vital link in this *cordon sanitaire* and there could be no meaningful approach to Zambia as long as Rhodesia remained in rebellion and was sustained in that role by South African connivance in sanctions-busting.

The problem was further aggravated by continuing, though sporadic and low-level, guerrilla activity within Rhodesia emanating from Zambia. Since August 1967 South African security forces in relatively small numbers had been positioned in the Zambezi valley.* Almost a year later, in a clash between a South African unit and a guerrilla force on 19 July 1968, three South African policemen were injured and one young constable, Danie du Toit, was killed. In South Africa, there were resounding Ministerial statements and a flow of commentary in the press which served to heighten public apprehension further. It was said that a new generation of 'terrorists' had emerged, many trained in communist countries, better armed and disciplined than their rag-tag predecessors. One paper described du Toit's death as the first shot in communism's war of conquest on South Africa. Wildly exaggerated reports circulated that some 2,500 well-armed and well-trained men were waiting in Zambian camps to enter Rhodesia.

In point of fact, the guerrilla bands, tiny and isolated with few reserves, were no match for white units well-trained in counter-insurgency tactics. Officials in Pretoria, however, were not adverse to using the situation in order to arouse popular emotions, to emphasize the importance of solidarity within the White Redoubt and to demonstrate South Africa's determination to remain master in its own backyard. The day following du Toit's death, Defence Minister P. W. Botha declared that 'South Africa has an interest in what happens in Angola, Rhodesia and Mozambique. . . . The onslaughts there are aimed at the Republic of South Africa in the final instance.' And in a significant article published on the same day in the German publication, *Die Welt*, Prime Minister Vorster announced South

---

* Estimates have varied between 300 and 800 men, excluding of course South African forces in the nearby Caprivi Strip. Assignments have been in part for training purposes in counter-insurgency techniques, involving a rotation of personnel roughly every three months. The South Africans have made a point of emphasizing that these were police units but in fact there has been an admixture of military personnel. South African Air Force helicopters and observation planes have also played an important supporting role. It will be recalled that the South Africans originally justified sending units into Rhodesia on the grounds that the guerrillas included elements of the African National Congress whose destination was South Africa, not Rhodesia.

Africa's willingness, if called upon to do so, to lend to other neighbouring countries assistance similar to that rendered to Rhodesia.
Shortly after Vorster's open offer to provide aid, the Republic's
army conducted in the northern Transvaal a nine-day, highly publi-
cized exercise ('Operation Sibasa') in counter-guerrilla warfare.
Some 5,000 South African soldiers were involved.

For Pretoria the Rhodesian situation was if anything more vexed
than ever. Rhodesia was an indispensable element in South Africa's
security system. Clearly the Republic could have no part in sanctions,
and certainly could not permit them to succeed. But if it was unthinkable that South Africa should force Rhodesia's capitulation, it was
also true that unresolved, the Rhodesian problem might well become
a growing source of internal and international irritation and an
increasing liability to South African policies. Only a negotiated
settlement between Salisbury and London could avoid the horns of
this dilemma. In South Africa, interest in a negotiated settlement,
which had dissipated after Thomson's abortive mission to Salisbury
the previous November, now revived.

The timing seemed hardly coincidental when Ian Smith turned up
in Pretoria on 26 July 1968, having come to South Africa ostensibly
to see the final Rugby test between the British Lions and the South
African Springboks. The week-end provided an opportunity for long
talks between Vorster and Smith. These no doubt touched on the
problem of 'terrorism' and the pressure of sanctions. It seems likely
that Vorster also stressed the importance of winning a tolerable
settlement from Britain which would exorcise sanctions, reduce the
risk of black–white confrontation and open the way for South
Africa's larger design – to break out of its isolation by achieving a
rapprochement with selected black states to the north.

In Salisbury

Smith had in fact repeatedly and characteristically asserted his
willingness to reopen talks. It was good public relations to appear
'reasonable'. It refurbished his support within certain sectors of the
Conservative Party in Britain, gave the Tories ammunition to fire at
the Labour Government's Rhodesia policy, and by appealing over
Wilson's head to the British public helped keep the Prime Minister
somewhat off-balance. In an interview with London's *Evening
Standard* on 19 June 1968, Smith went so far as to call for urgent
negotiations. Time after time he called a settlement with Britain his
'first prize'. One could never be entirely sure, of course, whether this
was only good public relations or possibly a serious overture. For it
was difficult to measure with precision the pressures that might be
restraining him from, or moving him toward, meeting British con-

ditions. A gathering crisis within the Rhodesian Front during the summer of 1968 might yield some answers, it was thought, and the phenomenon was observed from London with intense interest.

The issue was a new constitution for Rhodesia. On 5 April 1968, a Government-appointed Commission headed by W. R. 'Sam' Whaley had published its constitutional recommendations which were so coolly received by the Rhodesian Front that almost immediately the party proceeded to draft alternative proposals.* Hardly a prescription for liberalism, however, the Whaley Commission envisaged no majority rule – ever. It prescribed the gradual growth of African representation in the Legislative Assembly to the point where it might one distant day equal, but never exceed, white representation. It was, however, a multi-racial document in the limited sense that Africans and whites were to sit in the same legislature; there was to be a common voters roll for electing one-fourth of the members of the Lower House; and, while segregation was to remain the rule, multiracial facilities were to be extended 'for those who wish or find themselves suited to this way of life'.

Taken as a whole, however, the Whaley constitution was pathetically retrogressive from the 1961 constitution and the *Tiger* terms. Nevertheless many in the Front found Whaley's proposals dangerously extreme. For them the object was not only to annul forever the possibility of majority rule but to substitute the strictest segregation for even the vaguest evidences of multi-racialism and advancement by merit. The extremists also wanted to complete the break with Britain, declaring Rhodesia a Republic and ending forthwith the search for a settlement, fearing a sell-out if negotiations were renewed. On the very day the Whaley Commission published its findings, a founding member of the Rhodesian Front, Len Idensohn, established the break-away Rhodesian National Party, advocating precisely Republican status, racial segregation and separate development. Idensohn, a sewage engineer by trade, had earlier resigned as chairman of the Front's Salisbury East division in protest (of all things) 'against the clandestine racial integration which is taking place under Mr. Smith's leadership.' The Candour League was another ultra-right-wing group which contended that the Whaley constitution was the 'betrayal of the white man in Rhodesia'.

---

* The Rhodesia Constitutional Commission had been appointed in March 1967 to 'advise the Government of Rhodesia on the constitutional framework which is best suited to the sovereign independent status of Rhodesia'. Its members besides Whaley included two whites, S. W. Morris and R. H. Cole, and two Africans, L. C. Mzingeli and Chief S. M. Sigola.

In less strident terms, these views were voiced too within Smith's
Cabinet by men like William Harper, Minister of Internal Affairs;
Lord Graham, Minister of External Affairs and Defence; Philip
van Heerden, Minister of Lands; and A. P. Smith, Minister of
Education. As to Ian Smith's own predilections, he had made it clear
time and again that as far as he was concerned multi-racialism would
never be transformed into majority rule until some point in the future
so remote as to have no bearing on present realities or expectations.
Smith did however hope that a settlement with Britain on terms
acceptable to Rhodesia might still be possible, if not with the
present Labour Government then with a future Conservative one,
remembering that new elections in Britain would have to take place
no later than April 1971. Any new constitutional formula, Smith
believed, must therefore buy time and assure a margin of flexibility.
The trick was to produce such a formula without demolishing the
Front or jeopardizing his own position.

Accordingly with Smith's backing, a joint committee composed of
the Party caucus and local Party chairmen developed new constitutional guidelines which became known as the 'Yellow Paper'. It
proposed a two-stage affair. Stage one called for a Lower House in a
bicameral legislature which would be half white (as in the Whaley
Constitution), roughly one-quarter African (mainly chiefs) and the
balance elected by a common voters roll. As was true of the 'A' Roll
of the 1961 constitution, the common roll would be dominated for
years by white voters by virtue of its high qualifications for the
franchise.

Under stage two, not to come into effect for five years, Rhodesia
would change to a provincial system of government. Three provincial
councils would have jurisdiction over a limited range of regional and
local affairs. One council would be for whites and the other two
would represent the two major tribal groupings in Rhodesia, the
Matabele and the Mashona. A national Parliament would control
external affairs, defence, finance, internal security, justice, law and
order as well as important economic projects. Provincial representation in the national Parliament would be based on the contributions
made by each of the three provinces from personal income taxes to
the national exchequer. Since the African community was presently
contributing less than 1 per cent in income taxes, and since tax
increases could be achieved in a variety of ways other than levies on
income, the prospect almost certainly was for an all-white national
Parliament for a very long time to come, if not indefinitely.

The Yellow Paper had the tactical advantage of promising the
extremists a move in due course towards separate development – even
the ultimate possibility of partition was mentioned – and an all-white

national Parliament, while at the same time retaining for a five-year period a multi-racial legislature which might be useful in renewed negotiations with London. Some suggested that a bargaining counter on Rhodesia's side in such negotiations might be the non-application of stage two. It was of course this very prospect which the ultra-rightists in the Front found disturbing, for it conjured up again the prospect raised in the Whaley report of ultimate racial parity – hardly consonant with notions of complete segregation and separate development. The extreme right wanted African representatives 'faded out' of Parliament, not ensconced. On 2 July 1968, the Yellow Paper was presented to the Front's forty-nine member parliamentary caucus and accepted by a paper-thin margin of only two votes. According to press reports, four cabinet ministers were among Smith's opponents; William Harper had led the opposition. Two days later, under circumstances which never received an adequate public explanation, the Cabinet Office announced that at Smith's request Harper had tendered his resignation as Minister of Internal Affairs.*

The Rhodesian Front's annual Party congress was scheduled for 5 to 7 September 1968. An advance agenda warned of more trouble. It contained some eighty amendments to the Yellow Paper proposed by party divisions all over the country. Almost all aimed at shrinking or eliminating African representation in the central Parliament. Many advocated skipping stage one of the proposed constitution altogether and moving directly to stage two. The day before the congress opened, Lord Graham (James Angus Graham, the quite extraordinary and thoroughly reactionary seventh Duke of Montrose) distributed to branches of the Front an alternative draft approved by Harper and written in the Ministry of Internal Affairs under the guidance of its hardlining Permanent Secretary, Hostes Nicolle. It called for a Parliament divided into entirely separate white and African chambers each elected exclusively by voters of the two respective races. Graham's proposals were circulated with Smith's permission, an indication of the Prime Minister's continuing regard for Graham's potential strength, backed by Harper – and typical too of his disposition to keep his options open.

When the congress convened, however, Smith surprisingly began

---

* Soon after, Harper also resigned both his seat in the Legislative Assembly and his membership in the Rhodesian Front. Smith later said Harper was sacked as a security risk, though the evidence was never revealed. More to the point was Harper's recognized ability and ambition. He was quite capable of threatening Smith's leadership. The Prime Minister had long sought an opportunity to remove him.

by pressing the multi-racial premise. 'Merit', he told the Front representatives, 'is going to be the criterion in Rhodesia. You can't call a black man a second-class citizen just because he is black. You have a special responsibility for black Rhodesians, because they are not represented at this congress tonight.' He insisted at the same time that there was to be no appeasement of Britain and then appealed for calm consideration of the party's constitutional proposals. As had always been the case with the Front, the ensuing debate pitted, not right against left, but right against ultra-right. Smith adroitly reversed his field, arguing at one point, according to a later report by Party secretary André Holland, that he indeed favoured 'separate development . . . as a just and safe future for Rhodesia', but wanted an interim five years for full preparation of the new policy. Even so he was heckled by angry delegates. Together with the loyal Party hierarchy Smith now began a desperate effort to round up the necessary votes and the Yellow Paper proposals passed by the slenderest 11-vote margin, 217 for and 206 against with some 60 abstentions.

The Bulawayo *Chronicle* surveyed the wreckage and concluded that the Front had 'emerged from the constitutional discussions in one piece, but battered, weary and chipped at the edges. Some delegates have already resigned,' the paper noted, 'and more are expected to do so after reporting back to branches.' Lord Graham himself resigned. There were rumours of efforts to recall the Party congress. At this point Party regulars stepped in. Newly-elected Front chairman, Ralph Nilson, on 13 September stated firmly: 'It now seems very clear to me that the Standing Committee of the Party is going to have to crack down hard on those members who are trying to destroy the Party from within. It would appear the time has come for a spring cleaning . . . [and] for those of our members who cannot support the majority view to seek another political home. . . .'

Five days later at the rural town of Gatooma, the Front marshalled its forces in a barometric by-election. The seat vacated by Harper was contested by Commander Chris Phillips, a former Deputy Chairman of the Front who was now running under Idensohn's extreme Rhodesian National Party banner and no-nonsense slogan, 'Vote Phillips for a white government.' (At one point Phillips referred to Smith as a 'white Kaffir' – a little like calling George Wallace a 'white Nigger'.) The Front candidate swept the field winning 870 ballots to Phillips's scant 65. Significantly Smith had closed the ideological gap shortly before the Election by once again stepping nimbly to the right. 'I see no deviation from separate development,' he said. 'It has always been and always will be Rhodesia's policy.' And on the sensitive subject of negotiations with Britain, he laid right-wing fears to rest with equal aplomb: 'I believe the only thing Britain is interested in is a sell-out of the Europeans in Rhodesia.' After a rocky passage Party affairs were back more or less under control. As for a possible settlement with Britain, Smith had done what he set out to do. He had bought more time and seemed to have retained a slender margin of flexibility.

In London

Wilson watched these remarkable affairs unfold in Rhodesia – and tended to draw the wrong conclusions. It was an understandable error. Smith had hived off two of the more extreme members of his entourage, Harper and Graham. Indeed he went further and removed the Minister of Agriculture, George Rudland, from the cabinet, making him a Minister without Portfolio. Rudland, who in any event was ill, had voted against Smith on the constitutional proposals, and was now replaced by David Smith, a relative moderate who favoured a settlement with Britain. Wilson expressed his satisfaction at 'the disappearance of intransigent racialists'. He had pressed the idea for years (partly no doubt for its divisive effect) that Smith was someone you could work with if only he could be disentangled from the extremists who surrounded him. The disentangling process seemed well-advanced.

The situation looked all the more promising when the regime in late September 1968 introduced a new bill in the Rhodesian Parliament to end the mandatory death sentence for certain terrorist offences. Press censorship had already been abandoned the previous April. Smith it seemed was now more the master in his own house, revealing in a press conference on 14 September his pleasure at the way things were turning out and inviting others who did not believe in the Party's principles to leave too. Repeatedly he returned to the desirability of renewed talks. All in all by the end of the summer of 1968, Wilson thought (or desperately wanted to think) that things looked rather more promising in Salisbury.

There was however a dimension of the Rhodesian reality which seemed to have been overlooked. Sanctions were to have brought political change in Rhodesia by strengthening the moderates, or, barring that, forcing concessions from Smith. But the political crisis within the Front in mid 1968 had less to do with sanctions than with the colour question, which for many apprehensive whites in Rhodesia ominously dominated everything else. Since U.D.I. more Africans had been added to Rhodesia's population by natural increase than the sum total of all whites living in that country. How was this floodtide to be channelled? That was the question the extremists asked. The split within the Front came from the right over race, and not from the left over sanctions as London had hoped. In no sense did it create the possibility of a new coalition of genuine moderates with real political power.

Smith had contained the revolt of the ultra-rightists but the result, as it had been often before, was deceptive. It made *him* look like a moderate. He was in fact anything but, as the constitution he himself championed made evident. Even stage one was based on no more than a remote racial parity. It made a mockery of Britain's very first principle: 'unimpeded progress to majority rule'. It is true that the Rhodesian Prime Minister had managed to remove three recalcitrant Ministers from his Cabinet. On the other hand, a number of hard-liners remained: P. van Heerden, M. H. H. Partridge, P. K. van der Byl, A. P. Smith and Lardner-Burke himself – not to mention the Officer Administering the Government, Clifford Dupont, in many ways the most influential right-winger of them all. The previous March, in fact, Wilson had singled out the latter two as men who could not be 'trusted'. In any event, the gap between the extremists and the less doctrinaire right represented by Smith tended to close as each side tried to convince the anxious Rhodesian white that it could best protect his interests. During the Gatooma by-election, Smith's Deputy Minister of Information pressed the cause of the Rhodesian Front candidate by assuring his audience that the Yellow Paper proposals would make majority rule impossible for centuries! He was warmly applauded.

It was not surprising then that though Smith talked about renewed negotiations, the evidence remained inconclusive that he was pre-pared to yield to British terms, as in fact Wilson's own inquiries now began to make clear. During August 1968 Sir Max Aitken, Chairman of the right-wing Beaverbrook group of newspapers which had generally supported Smith, arrived in Salisbury on a mission for Wilson so secret that not even Governor Gibbs was originally in-formed about it. (The whole affair however soon leaked to the press.) Aitken arranged for Smith to meet with Lord Goodman, Wilson's personal solicitor and close friend. Goodman and Aitken together had three meetings with Smith between 19 and 23 August, then returned to London with a long memorandum for the British Prime Minister. It substantiated Smith's willingness to talk, recorded his agreement to some though by no means all of Wilson's conditions, and thus helped to lay the foundation for a new summit meeting. A month after the Aitken–Goodman initiative, an Assistant Under-Secretary in the Commonwealth office, James Bottomley, paid a surprise visit to Salisbury. Smith again made it clear that he wanted talks but would not be drawn into negotiations with anyone less than the British Prime Minister himself.

Wilson was determined to proceed. Smith would not reveal his negotiating hand to intermediaries – that was understandable, Wilson said – but conceivably in a direct encounter and given his newly consolidated position within the Party, he might bend sufficiently to make a settlement possible. Besides, Wilson noted with unwarranted optimism, sanctions were leaving their mark. Business and commercial interests continued to report that Rhodesia was hurting financially more than the general public was aware and (as always) there was widespread and growing sentiment within the business community for settlement. For Wilson, renewed talks would also be politically expedient. The Conservatives were again raising the Rhodesian issue, calling for new negotiations. Another all-out attempt at settlement, even if unsuccessful, would help to silence Tory critics. If on the other hand agreement were reached on grounds for a settlement, Wilson could use this British accomplishment at the next Commonwealth meeting (now scheduled for January 1969) to argue that no further Commonwealth action should be undertaken pending the results of the 'test of acceptability', thus buying more time.

Added to these considerations was the fact that South Africa had once more taken a hand in the game. Contacts between London and Pretoria had been recurrent over nearly three years since U.D.I. They were now resumed. One of those principally concerned was Lord Walston who had figured importantly in the events leading up to the Beira Resolution more than two years before. Walston had been moved from his post as Parliamentary Under-Secretary in the Foreign Office at the end of 1966. He was one of several junior Ministers who had tried to get the cabinet to reconsider the decision not to use force.

In August of 1968, as a private citizen, he had come to the Republic to deliver the celebrated Richard Feetham Lecture on academic freedom at the University of Witswatersrand, a lonely citadel of liberalism in Johannesburg. Walston took the opportunity during this trip to renew the contact he had first had with Prime Minister Vorster several years earlier, before he had become a member of the Labour Government. This led to a series of conversations which were to continue until the autumn. Vorster expressed his growing concern about Rhodesia and made it clear that he would be glad to help. He made it equally apparent, however, that it was against his policy to interfere in the internal affairs of any other country.

Walston communicated these views to Wilson, following which arrangements were made for the Commonwealth Secretary, George Thomson, to meet with Vorster while crossing South Africa to attend the independence celebrations of Swaziland early in September. The

South African leader once again indicated his willingness to act as go-between in facilitating exchanges between London and Salisbury. In point of fact, however, all he accomplished was to confirm what had been made clear repeatedly, that Smith wanted talks but was unwilling to commit himself to Britain's central demands. Notwithstanding, Wilson resolutely pressed forward, perhaps believing (however unrealistically) that Pretoria could be prevailed upon to push Smith toward the British position.

The most formidable obstruction to renewed negotiations was now thrown up by Wilson's own party. The occasion was Labour's annual conference scheduled for the beginning of October 1968 at Blackpool. For the pro-African lobby among Labour back-benchers, who ever since the 'talks about talks' had begun in May of 1966 feared their Leader would finally capitulate to Smith, it was a matter of shocked concern when the agenda for the conference was published and Rhodesia was not even mentioned. The same thing, curiously enough, had happened the year before when, despite the backstage efforts of a number of able M.P.'s, the issue never came to debate at all. At that time, too, talks were in progress with the South Africans preparatory to renewed contacts with Smith.* Now, a year later, they noted that things were strikingly and disturbingly similar. Immediately before the conference at Blackpool, South Africa's Foreign Minister, Hilgard Muller, turned up in London. George Thomson entertained him at an unannounced luncheon on the very day the conference opened. It was obvious that something was once more being planned and that Wilson wanted no complications from Labour conference members.

This time, however, under the leadership of Joan Lestor and Frank Judd, the Labour back-benchers persisted in their demands. A meeting with Wilson was arranged but left them as much ill at ease as ever. Thomson himself, when approached by a worried M.P., was reported to have said that there would be 'a few anxious weeks ahead'. Finally, reversing itself under pressure, the Party Executive allowed thirty minutes for a debate on Rhodesia – the final thirty minutes of the last afternoon's session, Thursday, 3 October. A resolution was introduced supporting the principle of no independence before majority rule (NIBMAR) and a continuing British role in Rhodesia until majority rule was established. Two additional paragraphs were critically important. One would have had the British Government withdraw the commitment not to use force. It was defeated at the urging of the National Executive Committee. The other paragraph called upon the Government to 'prepare a new Constitution for

* See above, pp. 224–5.

Rhodesia which would not be subject to negotiation with the rebels'. Despite backstage appeals from 'Harold' (as Labour members called him on such occasions) to defeat the resolution which contained this injunction, it passed by a comfortable margin. Thus, over the opposition of the National Executive Committee and Wilson himself, a majority of Labour Party delegates had unmistakably placed themselves on record as opposing further negotiations with Smith.

But even while the vote was being tallied a telegram was en route to Wilson from Smith accepting Wilson's invitation to meet at Gibraltar on 9 October. (The invitation had been delivered to Smith through Governor Gibbs on 28 September, the very eve of the Blackpool Labour Party Conference.) The following day, H.M.S. *Fearless* was secretly ordered to move to Gibraltar. At the same time Maurice Foley, then serving as Parliamentary Under-Secretary for the Navy in the Ministry of Defence, was summoned by Wilson and informed that arrangements had just been completed for another round of talks with Smith. Foley was briefed over the week-end and, carefully avoiding all publicity, rushed to Africa to advise key leaders that talks were to be renewed at the Prime Ministerial level. His most important stop was Lusaka where an apprehensive Kenneth Kaunda heard the news – this time some hours in advance of the public announcement.

Variations on a Theme from Gibraltar

At noon on Tuesday, 8 October 1968, a release from 10 Downing Street advised that talks 'aimed at discovering whether it would be possible to arrive at a settlement of the Rhodesian problem' would begin the following day at Gibraltar aboard the *Fearless*. Only two nights before the hapless Leader of the Opposition, with the talks already laid on but still unannounced, had expressed dismay at the refusal of Wilson 'to even talk to Mr. Smith'. Adroitly Wilson now left Heath clutching at air, pre-empting the headlines on the eve of the annual Conservative Party conference, and neatly forcing the deletion of the Rhodesian issue from the conference agenda for, as Sir Alec Douglas-Home was obliged to acknowledge, it would have been impolitic to comment while the summit talks were under way.

Interviewed just before leaving London, Wilson was guardedly optimistic. Smith, he said, was now more in charge than he had been during the *Tiger* talks. He had 'shown guts' to go 'all out' for a settlement, bearing in mind however that any arrangement must fulfil the six principles (nothing was said about NIBMAR), and be shown to be acceptable to Rhodesia's four million Africans. To accomplish this Smith would have to 'move a very very long way'.

In Salisbury the mood was one of hope edged with apprehension. While Smith and his party endured their twenty-hour flight from Salisbury to Gibraltar in a propeller-driven R.A.F. Britannia, hundreds of people crowded into Salisbury's Anglican Cathedral and spilled out through the entrance, answering an interdenominational call for prayers. It was noted that no such manifestation accompanied the *Tiger* talks. Economic indicators also mixed apprehension and hope. Though the regime had been surprisingly successful at containing inflation, sustaining a reasonable balance of payments, and maintaining a fair amount of economic activity including virtually full employment for non-Africans, the economy was nonetheless suffering from the comprehensive mandatory sanctions levied by the U.N. the previous May. It took longer and cost more to move goods through the new U.N. barriers as all concerned waited to see how faithfully Rhodesia's trading partners would abide by the new restrictions. Accordingly, there was a slump in retail trade, 'the worst few weeks in our history', one shopkeeper complained.

The seasonal heat was made worse by an unseasonal drought which again threatened agricultural catastrophe. The property market was in the doldrums. Orders for swimming pools – a big item in the Rhodesian capital which probably boasts more pools per (Caucasian) head than any community in the world except Beverly Hills – had virtually dried up. But the announcement of renewed talks sent a flutter through the Rhodesian Stock Exchange and many shares closed at their highest level in years. There was even renewed interest in sanctions-hit tobacco and sugar. In London buyers scrambled for Rhodesian securities as hopes for a settlement rose. Like Wilson, Smith hedged his hopes. He said again, as he had often before, that a settlement with Britain was 'the first prize'. Asked if he thought this was not the very last opportunity to snatch the prize, he replied, 'I believe there have been about a dozen so far.' But he warned that time was indeed rapidly running out. While welcoming the opportunity to negotiate a solution with Britain, he stressed he would contemplate nothing that would diminish Rhodesia's independence.

Wilson nonetheless was determined that nothing should diminish the chances for success (nor lend credence to Tory charges of mismanagement if a settlement failed to materialize) and he made every effort to create a congenial environment. In this single respect, the contrast to *Tiger* was so marked as to be almost comical. Before, the Rhodesian Governor and the rebel leader were treated each according to his station, Gibbs as the Queen's personal representative and 'Mr. Smith' as a cashiered Prime Minister. Now Gibbs and Smith travelled in the same plane. There was occasional friendly banter and at one point – as Smith later took pains to inform the waiting reporters – he offered the Governor advice on how to play his cards at bridge. (He also said wryly that he had 'offered Sir Humphrey a lift.') Before, the quarters were cramped, a subject of concern somewhat more perhaps to Smith's sympathizers in the Conservative Party in London than to Smith himself. Wilson now guaranteed that there would be no conceivable cause for complaint. Smith and his party had a ship of their own berthed alongside the *Fearless*, the newer and more expensive guided missile destroyer, H.M.S. *Kent*. The rebel Prime Minister occupied the Admiral's cabin. Before, there was the pressure of time and the threat of an ultimatum. On H.M.S. *Fearless*, Wilson stressed that time was no object. Discussions could proceed as long as necessary and 'Ian' (with whom Wilson was now on first-name terms) could thereafter consult at his pleasure with his colleagues in Salisbury. Before, there was concern to drop the hardliners in a reconstituted interim government. One of the chief among these was Desmond Lardner-Burke, Minister of Justice, Law and Order, who had presided over the hanging of three Africans after they had been granted the Queen's reprieve. Now Lardner-Burke was at Smith's elbow, his principal consultant.

It was small wonder that fears of a sell-out again swept through a number of African Commonwealth capitals. Coming from a meeting with Wilson's roving special representative, Malcolm MacDonald, President Nyerere was asked to comment on the Gibraltar talks. His simple, one word answer was, 'NIBMAR.' The same refrain was sounded in Kenya, Uganda and Ghana. In Lusaka, shortly after Foley advised him of the imminent talks, Kaunda let it be known that he looked upon the negotiations with 'deep fear' and 'great apprehension'. The danger of a deal between the two Prime Ministers which would have sacrificed the interests of Rhodesia's Africans may have been overdrawn – as similarly were the hopes of those who looked for a compromise settlement and the end of the impasse. Both the fears and the hopes tended to overlook the limited manœuvrability of either side.

Admittedly Wilson was prepared to scuttle NIBMAR. That in itself was a sell-out from Nyerere's and Kaunda's view. But the British leader probably could have satisfied Smith only by jettisoning important constitutional formulae long associated with the six principles, such as the non-racial franchise, cross-voting and the appeal to the Privy Council.* He would thereby have enraged a

---

* These elements, among others, were in fact jettisoned in the accords worked out between Mr. Smith and Mr. Heath's Government in November 1971. See below, pp. 303–9.

substantial bloc within his party. In order then to have gained Parliamentary approval for a settlement he might well have found it necessary to depend upon Tory support – an unenviable and dangerous position. Smith in turn could have accepted Wilson's constitutional formulations only at the risk of a Cabinet split and a revolt by the right wing of his Party. This would have necessitated an attempt to form a new coalition of more moderate elements within and outside the Rhodesian Front – again a most dangerous business. The prospect of being unceremoniously removed from office by right-wing Party leaders, as had happened to his predecessor, Winston Field, must have preoccupied him. In short, each man found it extraordinarily difficult to meet the minimal demands of the other, perhaps for reasons of personal conviction and assuredly for reasons of political self-interest and perhaps even survival. (In communications exchanged just prior to the *Fearless* meeting, Smith had in fact flatly refused each one of Wilson's non-negotiable conditions.)

It was not surprising then that at the end of the first day's discussion, Wilson's press secretary, Trevor Lloyd-Hughes, told the journalists gathered at Gibraltar that 'it was tough going'. Smith himself called this description an understatement. Nor at the end of four days, including thirty hours of what Wilson later termed 'hard hitting' exchanges, had circumstances changed – not even when the two leaders, before the final day's session, joined at a naval church service in singing 'Lead Us, Heavenly Father, Lead Us.' A final *communiqué* referred to 'disagreement on fundamental issues' and 'a very wide gulf' still remaining. Smith left for Salisbury, as he had twenty-two months before, with a British document in his brief case setting forth the basis on which H.M. Government would be willing to ask Parliament's approval of an independence settlement and with the understanding that after adequate time for Cabinet consideration in Rhodesia, Smith would tender his reply. George Thomson was ready to fly to Salisbury for further deliberations if the Rhodesians desired. A headline in the conservative *Daily Mail* capsuled the situation: 'No success, no failure, no result.'

The British proposals were modelled after the *Tiger* terms. Specially entrenched provisions of the constitution were protected, as before, by an internal and external safeguard. Amendments to these clauses required the concurrence of at least three-quarters of the total membership of both Houses. Elected Africans were to constitute twenty-five out of a total of ninety-three members, or one-quarter plus one. The second, or external, safeguard against 'retrogressive' amendments of entrenched clauses involved an appeal procedure to the Judicial Committee of the Privy Council, which also remained essentially the same as that found in the *Tiger* formula. A proviso was added however exempting this system of appeal from any change for a period of fifteen years.

The 'test of acceptability', to make sure that the terms of settlement were agreeable to the population of Rhodesia taken as a whole, remained substantially unchanged except that the Royal Commission which was to design and execute the test was to be assigned the additional task of examining working arrangements for voter registration. It was to recommend improvements aimed at registering more qualified Africans, and Rhodesian authorities were to take urgent steps to give these recommendations effect. Also aimed at hastening African advance was an offer, derived from an idea first put forward by Sir Alec Douglas-Home when he was Prime Minister, of aid to African education up to £5 million ($12 million) per year for ten years to be matched by equal amounts from the Rhodesian Government and over and above scheduled expenditures.

During the test of acceptability normal political activities were to be resumed, with the media available to Opposition spokesmen. Concerning the African leaders in detention or under restriction, the *Fearless* formula differed slightly from that of the *Tiger*. The *Tiger* document forbade continued detention or restriction unless the review tribunal were satisfied that the person concerned had 'committed, or incited the commission of, acts of violence or intimidation'. Under the *Fearless* terms, the tribunal had to be satisfied only that the individual was 'likely to commit, or incite or inspire the commission of, acts of violence or intimidation'.*

All of these were minor modifications of or amendments to the *Tiger* proposals. The major change involved a reversal of Britain's stand on the 'return to legality' provisions. These had been central to Britain's position and the avowed reason for Rhodesia's refusal to accede to the earlier document. A test of opinion without a return to legality would have been an absolute mockery, the Commonwealth Secretary told the Commons after returning from the *Tiger* talks. Wilson in that same debate excoriated Opposition sceptics who questioned the advisability of insisting on a return to legality prior to testing opinion. He conjured up the spectre of 'a coerced, submissive

---

* Whether the latter formula would have worked in favour of the detained Africans is arguable and in fact was debated in the Commons. In practice, however, the procedures in either case were pathetically inadequate. The 'impartial tribunal' under both *Tiger* and *Fearless* terms would have consisted of two Rhodesian nominees, certainly acceptable to Smith, and only one Briton. It is hard to see how a Rhodesian-dominated tribunal would have released many of the African leaders under either formula.

African population only too well aware that the penalty of political deviation could well be imprisonment without trial,' then suggested that the Royal Commission would have great problems under these circumstances in obtaining an 'uninhibited view'.

Now, in the *Fearless* proposals, the question of returning to legality was not even mentioned. Responding some months before to Conservative criticism, George Thomson had insisted that any settlement with Rhodesia must be '*Tiger*-plus'. But the *Fearless* proposals were clearly '*Tiger*-minus'. The testing of Rhodesian opinion on the terms for independence was to take place with the rebel regime still in unquestioned control, not only in fact (which was in large part the case under the *Tiger* proposals too) but in law as well. Smith indeed was to 'form a broad-based administration as soon as possible,' but it was generally agreed that the formula meant nothing more than adding two Africans to the Rhodesian Government. Their rank was not specified.

The question of the Governor, whose prestige and whose role in the interim period were considered so important in the *Tiger* terms, was bypassed entirely. Since there was to be no change in the *status quo* during the test of acceptability, sanctions were to remain in force. In this one respect, the *Fearless* formula strengthened the *Tiger* terms. If the Commission's findings were negative, everything evidently would have gone on as before, unless it were decided to renew negotiations. If the Commission's findings were affirmative, Britain agreed to submit for Parliament's approval the Rhodesian Independence Constitution. (Nowhere in this process, by the way, was reference made to consultations with the Commonwealth to seek a release from the NIBMAR pledge, which Wilson had said he would be willing to do only if there had occurred a substantial change of circumstances in the Rhodesian situation.) Once the constitution was accepted, Britain would take all possible action to end sanctions immediately. Elections would then take place under the new constitution and a new government would be formed.

With almost clinical precision *Fearless* repeated the essentials of the *Tiger* proposals while introducing two significant variables: there was to be no 'return to legality' and the time-pressed and threatening environment of the earlier encounter gave way to the relaxed congeniality of the later meeting. Since these two factors had repeatedly been blamed for the failure of *Tiger*, it was of more than passing interest to see what effect these changes would now have on the outcome.

'H.M.S. Cheerless'

While the talks were in progress, the editors of *The Economist*
produced a bleak prognosis under the above title. Early indications
from Salisbury after Smith's flight home did nothing to brighten the
outlook. The Rhodesian Front chairman, Ralph Nilson, delivered a
swift reaction: 'To have accepted the British proposals would have
been total, abject surrender.' The Cabinet nonetheless began long
deliberations and Smith on 15 October said he was not about to rush
into a decision on 'this tremendously important and complicated
question', nor indeed would he hasten 'to close doors'. The following
day in the Rhodesian Parliament, however, there was an audible
clicking of locks behind doors no longer ajar as Smith declared that
the demand for a broadly based government was 'obnoxious', that
the 'blocking quarter' must include African chiefs, and that the right
of appeal to the Privy Council involved in the external safeguard
would derogate from Rhodesia's sovereignty and result in 'second-
class independence'.* Evidently, nothing had changed. In a broadcast
that evening, Smith gave special attention to the external safeguard,
appealing to Wilson to remove 'this impossible and indeed ridiculous
obstacle from our path'. If this could be accomplished, he continued,
'then I believe there is a distinct possibility that we will be able to
reconcile our differences'.†

---

* Much confusion has surrounded this point. The Judicial Committee of the Privy Council has served as a final court of appeal for
certain independent countries of the Commonwealth which have
chosen to retain limited rights of appeal to it. What was being
suggested for Rhodesia, therefore, had ample precedent. Entirely
independent of both the British executive and the Crown, the
committee includes not only representatives of high judicial office in
Britain, but also eminent legal personalities appointed by those
countries which have retained in their law the right of appeal to the
Judicial Committee. As of the autumn of 1968, those countries
included Australia, New Zealand, Ceylon, Kenya, Jamaica, Uganda,
Trinidad and Tobago, and Sierra Leone.

† Not everyone in Rhodesia was prepared to scuttle the *Fearless*
terms. The Rhodesia Constitutional Association, members of the
non-political Forum, business leaders, the *Rhodesia Herald* and the
new Centre Party which had been formed in May 1968 all mounted a
campaign to accept the settlement, or at least to put the *Fearless*
formula to a popular referendum. These several groups, however,
continued to speak for a relatively small minority of white
Rhodesians.

It was not until 22 October, nine days after the talks had ended, that the Cabinet in Salisbury set out the precise terms of its reply. The Rhodesian *aide-mémoire* arrived in London that evening and was handed to Wilson in the House of Commons shortly before the conclusion of a heated debate on the *Fearless* proposals. As forewarned in Smith's public statements, the message flatly rejected the second safeguard, and again implied that if the Privy Council appeal could be got out of the way, the remaining problems would not be insoluble. However, the Commons debate which was in full swing demonstrated a deep distrust on the part of many Labour members of even the unadulterated *Fearless* terms. (A few days before, a delegation of twelve Labour M.P.s had called on the Government Chief Whip to inform him of the strong opposition within the Parliamentary Labour Party to any settlement short of NIBMAR. They said they spoke for at least sixty-five Labour M.P.s.) The debate was now about to climax in a vote bound to be embarrassing to Wilson. In an effort to head it off the Prime Minister interrupted his remarks to announce that Salisbury's reply had just been received, adding that he could hardly be expected under these circumstances to examine it carefully or to render a snap judgement on it. 'Why mention it?' an irate Labour M.P. shouted. The matter had gone too far. Those demanding a vote were not to be turned back.

The controversy had proceeded almost entirely within Labour's own ranks, to the immense pleasure of the Conservatives who themselves found little to quarrel with in Wilson's position. Sir Alec Douglas-Home noted (quite correctly) that when George Thomson gave his lengthy defence of the *Fearless* terms he was talking more to his own side of the House than across the floor. It was a topsy-turvy scene with Wilson, Heath and Douglas-Home exchanging elaborate compliments, while Labour critics offered spirited and unyielding dissent. Frank Judd, who had often crossed swords with Wilson on Rhodesia policy, found only a hair's breadth of safety in the *Fearless* proposals. He asked what would be the position if the Privy Council were to uphold an appeal and the Rhodesian Government then were to ignore it? Thomson had argued that once the Rhodesian economy was booming again Rhodesian whites would 'think twice, and more than twice' before taking any action that would risk a return to the penalties of sanctions. To which Judd rejoined that Rhodesia's major trading partners would 'think twice and more than twice' before reassembling a dismantled sanctions machine. What had happened, Judd wanted to know, to the NIBMAR pledge and its implied period of direct rule? Was it only a gimmick momentarily to reassure the Commonwealth?

Sir Dingle Foot, a former Labour Solicitor General, in a sweeping denunciation found the *Fearless* premise wholly in error. 'There is no formula', he declared, 'which would satisfy the racialists of Salisbury and which could honourably be accepted by a British Government.' Sir Dingle scoffed at guarantees against retrogressive amendments to the constitution, noting that after independence one would not have to alter the constitution at all, but simply proclaim a state of emergency and govern under emergency regulations. Others insisted that the only real assurance of unimpeded progress to majority rule was to establish a British military presence in Rhodesia, though almost no one any longer believed this to be a feasible alternative.

Discontent was matched by acute frustration. Alexander Lyon, speaking for the Labour pro-African lobby, expressed the prevailing mood to a T when he quoted Cromwell's reply to a question about a substitute for the Episcopalian Church. 'I can tell you, Sirs, what I would not have, though I cannot what I would.' Lyon, too, was unsure 'what he would'. But he knew with certainty what he did not want. He could not accept the compromise represented by the *Fearless* proposals. He readily confessed that he did not know what would happen if sanctions were continued. Britain might ultimately lose – in which case, he said, he would prefer honourable defeat to dishonourable compromise. He insisted the matter be brought to a vote. While acknowledging that it was only a gesture, he wished to record his opposition, for 'I do not want it said, when Mr. Smith says "Yes" to some proposal signed in a rowing boat on the Serpentine, that I did not make a protest earlier. . . .' Andrew Faulds, a bearded and explosive Scot, his eyes burning into the back of George Thomson's head, declared, 'There are Ministers on the front bench who should be ashamed at their connivance in such a settlement.'

Wilson seemed imperturbable in the face of this ruckus. He gave a self-assured and polished performance, insisting again that the *Fearless* formula was consistent with the six principles. After nearly seven hours of argument, the House divided. Fifty-eight members, fifty-one of them Labour, voted against the Government to signify their conviction that Wilson had in fact gone too far. An undetermined number of Labour M.P.s joined the Opposition in abstaining, while 177 members voted for the Government. The significance of this situation – still manageable but nonetheless volatile under the continuing pressure of a vocal and disaffected minority within the Party – was not missed by Wilson who acknowledged that the 'lesson of today's debate [is] . . . that there is a limit to what Parliament will accept, and that it has been reached.'*

---

* The *Sunday Times* on 27 October 1968, published an opinion poll which found that five out of eight respondents felt Wilson should

The outlook for Wilson was equally cheerless at the United Nations and in Africa. On 25 October, ninety-two votes were cast in the U.N. General Assembly favouring a resolution calling again for no independence in Rhodesia before majority rule. South Africa and Portugal submitted the only negative votes while the United Kingdom and the United States were among the seventeen states abstaining. Canada, of pivotal importance within the Commonwealth, voted for it, her Foreign Minister, Mitchell Sharp, having already maintained that 'the only basis for solving the Rhodesia question is for independence to be withheld until majority rule is established.' Two weeks later, on 7 November, a second resolution reached the floor of the General Assembly calling this time for Britain to use force against Rhodesia and asking for sanctions against South Africa and Portugal on the grounds that they had 'blatantly refused to carry out the mandatory decisions of the Security Council'. It was passed by eighty-six to nine with nineteen abstentions. Britain and the United States joined South Africa and Portugal in voting against the resolution, together with Australia, Belgium, the Netherlands and Luxembourg. Meanwhile, Tanzania's President Julius Nyerere, who only the previous June had at last decided to restore diplomatic relations with Britain, let it be known that his country would leave the Commonwealth if a settlement short of NIBMAR were concluded. Nor would Tanzania be alone. Observers concluded that Uganda, Kenya and India might follow suit – and, almost certainly, Zambia.

On 17 October the *Times of Zambia* carried a king-size banner headline quoting President Kaunda's reaction to the *Fearless* proposals: 'A Despicable Surrender', it read. The Zambian leader claimed to have irrefutable evidence that a deal had been arranged and that a sell-out had already been accomplished. Smith's intractability and Wilson's firmness regarding the sticking points in the *Fearless* formula were just shadow play. No explanation was ever offered for Kaunda's accusation. Conspiracy theories in fact ran like a contagion throughout the entire episode, inspired partly by the secretive mission of Lord Goodman and Sir Max Aitken to Salisbury in August. Ironically the extreme right in Rhodesia took the Goodman–Aitken mission as a signal that Smith was about to fold before

---

not have made any further concessions to Smith, while four out of five thought Smith should have made more concessions to Britain. Five out of eight advocated maintaining sanctions until Smith agreed to most of Britain's demands while only one in three thought Britain should make the best available deal even if that meant agreeing to most of Smith's demands.

Wilson's unconscionable demands, while in Lusaka Kaunda was equally certain Wilson was about to capitulate to Smith.

For the Zambian President in particular the Goodman–Aitken visit had been a painful affair, bound to inspire the deepest mistrust. The previous month Kaunda had visited London, his first personal contact with Wilson since the two had met briefly in Lusaka following the Lagos Commonwealth conference in January 1966 and had set 15 February as the 'quick kill' target date. So strained had the relationship become in the intervening two and a half years that the London visit was months in gestation before it was finally realized. Now, within weeks of his return, Kaunda learned that Wilson's good friend and personal solicitor, in the company of a right-wing publisher known for his support for Smith, was engaged in intensive and highly confidential talks with the rebel leader. The Zambian President was convinced that, far from remaining faithful to the NIBMAR pledge which Wilson had given to his Commonwealth colleagues in September 1966, he now meant to present the Commonwealth with a *fait accompli* when the Heads of Government convened next in January 1969. Needless to say, Wilson had given Kaunda no notice of or background concerning the Goodman–Aitken affair. 'We are back to square one here,' the Zambian leader concluded bitterly.

Only in Pretoria had the *Fearless* interlude not yet produced grave doubt or despondence. When the Gibraltar talks failed to achieve agreement, Vorster sent as a special envoy to Salisbury the Permanent Secretary of his Foreign Ministry, Brand Fourie. At about the same time, Rhodesia's External Affairs Minister, J. H. Howman, made a secret trip to South Africa for a meeting with Vorster. The South African leader seemed convinced that he could get Smith to accept the balance of the *Fearless* formula if the external safeguard (the appeal to the Privy Council) were dropped – which in any event he thought was an unreasonable demand. He so informed Wilson. Vorster appeared confident that the crisis at long last would be settled. It was a question of 'when', not 'if'. And once settled, his 'outward' policy could be made to encompass Zambia. 'Kaunda will come around,' he was heard to say confidently, predicting that there would be a South African trade commissioner in Zambia within two years of a Rhodesian settlement. Vorster's ostensible optimism dimmed however when word was received in Pretoria that Wilson was holding firm to some form of external safeguard. Clearly, as had been true from the start, there would be limits as to how far South Africa could move and shake the angular Rhodesian problem into place.

The external safeguard was the principal impediment and Wilson must have cast his eye longingly beyond it to an agenda at last free of this vexing issue. Equally discernible, however, were deep discontent within his own Party, renewed unrest in the Commonwealth and strident voices raised once more at the U.N. To compromise the *Fearless* terms would call forth a diplomatic holocaust. But conceivably he might ride out the storm if somehow he could get the terms accepted *in toto*. He decided to have one more try. Smith had asked George Thomson to come to Salisbury. After a dignified delay, Wilson agreed.

Labour's Last Try

The British Cabinet sat on the morning of 31 October 1968, and set its seal on George Thomson's trip. At 8.45 a.m. the following day Thomson with Maurice Foley and a team of officials left London and, after breaking their trip at Ascension Island, arrived in Salisbury late on 2 November. In Parliament the Conservative response again was embarrassingly warm. Tory M.P. John Biggs-Davison wished the Labour Minister well on his mission to Salisbury, whereupon Labour M.P. Frank Judd replied that it was impossible for many in the House to express hope for the success of this particular journey. Michael Foot spoke of the growing numbers of members on the Government's side of the House who would oppose to the limit of their ability any Rhodesia independence bill based on the *Fearless* terms since these provided no guarantee of majority rule.

Equally predictable was the reaction in Africa. Kaunda expressed shock that his long-time friend, George Thomson, should have associated himself with this mission, headlined in the Lusaka press as 'Operation Sell-Out'. In Pretoria, amidst renewed speculation that Vorster was busy behind the scenes, the South African Prime Minister said he was glad the matter had moved another step forward with the dispatch of Mr. Thomson and emphasized the great importance of settling the dispute through good statesmanship and good will. Salisbury, still awash in rumours of a secret deal, now sustained a totally unreal optimism that a settlement was imminent. Thomson's arrival after all was proof of it. Governor Gibbs was ebullient, predicting privately that it would all be over in six weeks. Thomson for his part said simply on arrival that the differences had narrowed, but remained deep. He had felt the pressure of the backbenchers since disembarking from H.M.S. *Fearless* and was determined to yield nothing more.

At long and difficult sessions held intermittently over the ensuing week, the areas so frequently tracked before were covered once again, but the high ground of agreement remained unclaimed. On the morning of 7 November Thomson and Foley broke away to meet the two nationalist leaders, Joshua Nkomo of ZAPU and Ndabaningi Sithole of ZANU. Pressed hard by the British Government, the Rhodesian regime reluctantly agreed to bring them from their places of detention to the New Sarum military airport near Salisbury, each accompanied by two supporters. The British Ministers met the nationalist delegations at separate two-hour sittings. Thomson explained the British settlement proposals, leaving each leader a copy. Reportedly, each took a hard line demanding that Britain use force to end the rebellion and, barring that, continue sanctions in the hope that direct British rule might eventually become a possibility. The *Rhodesia Herald* carried reports of this encounter between the British Ministers and the detained leaders and street sales shot up by 50 per cent as Africans flocked to read of the nationalist leaders who had last been permitted a British visitor when Harold Wilson saw them on the very eve of U.D.I.

Papas in The Guardian, London

"Well, Smith—let's reach an agreement."

The third anniversary of the rebellion occurred on 11 November and Thomson's party withdrew discreetly two days before, not to return until the conclusion of the celebrations. The British Ministers made a hastily arranged circuit of neighbouring Commonwealth states to brief these Leaders on developments in Salisbury. In Tanzania, Thomson detailed for President Nyerere Britain's effort to place a double lock (the blocking quarter and the appeal to the Privy Council) on the mechanism which was meant to insure that Rhodesia moved forward to majority rule. Nyerere responded that the

Rhodesians would wrench open any lock devised by Britain once independence was granted. Thomson pointed out that the present impasse meant indefinite stagnation for the African, a drift toward South Africa and the ascendancy of apartheid in Rhodesia. Speaking with great depth of feeling, Nyerere replied that the principle of NIBMAR must remain unalterable, that it was preferable to do nothing than to conclude a dishonourable settlement, and that in his view Africans in Rhodesia would prefer a long and difficult passage rather than to secure immediate independence 'for Smith', knowing that meanwhile more hands would be raised against minority rule as time went on.*

The talks in Salisbury resumed on 13 November and by mutual agreement, adjourned four days later completely deadlocked. As predicted the principal (but by no means only) obstacle was the external safeguard. Before the talks began Smith had accepted both the broader based government, which involved appointing two Africans to his administration for the duration of the test of acceptability, and the internal safeguard, a bare blocking quarter of elected Africans. (He later raised it to a blocking quarter plus one to meet the British figure.) Thomson argued again that this internal lock was 'too fragile a safeguard on its own', though as time passed and more Africans won seats in the legislature, it would of course become stronger. In the meantime an external safeguard was indispensable to assure against retrogressive amendments. The Rhodesians had made transparently clear that they would not consider any of the alternative formulations Britain put forward, including a simple treaty obligation not to alter the entrenched clauses for fifteen years. Both the Conservative Party in Britain and Prime Minister Vorster in South Africa had expressed interest in such a treaty to serve as the external guarantee, but it was a proposal in which Mr. Smith 'seemed to find no interest', as Thomson later explained to Sir Alec Douglas-Home in the Commons. Nor did the Rhodesians themselves suggest any alternative. 'I have never believed any safeguard to be

---

* Nyerere's assertion certainly applied to Nkomo and Sithole of ZAPU and ZANU. However, even Percy M'Kudu, Leader of the African Opposition in Rhodesia's Parliament, contended (as reported in the Bulawayo *Chronicle* of 17 June 1968) that it was not true that Africans wanted sanctions stopped because they suffered more than the whites. 'The African masses', he insisted, 'would rather suffer sanctions than give up their right and heritage.' This view was demonstrated conclusively during the 'test of acceptability' in early 1972 following the British–Rhodesian accords of November 1971. See below pp. 317–20.

necessary,' Smith remarked during his report to the Rhodesian people after the negotiations had concluded.

Thomson countered that the whole object after all was to assure that a white-dominated government could not legally take steps prejudicial to African political advancement. 'So long as the great majority of the people of Rhodesia remain unenfranchised,' Thomson had put it a few days before in a speech in the House of Commons, 'it would be contrary to our legal and moral obligations to them to concede unfettered sovereignty to the Parliament of Rhodesia.' While the safeguards insisted upon by Britain were unusual, so too was the situation. The Rhodesian minority might complain of restraints on their independence, but what about the majority who are dependent on them?

Smith had several times suggested that all remaining differences could have been resolved once agreement was reached on the external safeguard.* Perhaps. But it was one thing to gain agreement on general formulations and something else again to make them operationally precise. For example, when considering the criteria by which those in detention or under restriction should be released to take part in the test of acceptability, Smith introduced a gloss on the *Fearless* formula. That formula would have disqualified those likely to commit or incite or conspire with others to commit acts of violence or intimidation. Smith's emendation would have disqualified anyone whose release, quite irrespective of his intent or his own activity, might have caused others to respond with violence. Britain refused. There was also considerable debate over what would constitute 'normal political activity' during the test, the procedures whereby radio and television facilities would be made available to the Opposition, and whether ZAPU and ZANU would be permitted to resume political activity under their old names.

Smith said he was taken aback by the proposal that banned terrorist organizations, which with communist training and arms had attempted to infiltrate the country and kill Rhodesians of all races, should now be permitted to resuscitate themselves – a situation comparable, he continued, to advocating the resurrection of the

---

* Outstanding issues included *inter alia* the exact composition of the legislature; cross-voting procedures between the two rolls of electors, the one predominantly European and the other principally African; the delimitation of constituencies; the question of reinstating civil servants who had resigned following U.D.I.; the length of the period of a state of emergency permitted under the new constitution; and the use of the Privy Council as a final court of appeal for ordinary judicial cases.

Nazi Party in Germany after the war. It was a cruel analogy even taking into account the often ill-advised and reckless tactics of the African nationalist movement over the years. The fact remained that many African nationalists had accepted guerrilla warfare only when it had become apparent that all peaceful avenues for moving toward majority rule had been blocked and the top echelon of their leaders had been locked up. 'We want a government of all people and people must elect the government they want,' a captured African nationalist testified in a Rhodesian court a few days after Thomson's departure. He had come armed into the country, he said, to 'free the people of Zimbabwe'. Asked if he were eager to shoot Rhodesian soldiers, he replied, 'This was war. What did you expect me to do?'

From the point of view of a minority white community seeking to maintain its position Smith's concern was understandable. The British team in fact succeeded in getting the Cabinet in London to modify its earlier insistence that the old names, ZAPU and ZANU, remain in use, but agreement on procedural details governing the activities of nationalist leaders and organizations remained elusive. In point of fact the contradictions were simply overwhelming. It was quite unimaginable that a government dominated by the Rhodesian Front would have allowed Joshua Nkomo or Ndabaningi Sithole access to television in order to argue not only that the *Fearless* terms were a sell-out but that Africans must enjoy majority rule in their own country. It is not just that the sentiment would have been repugnant to the rank and file of the Rhodesian Front and indeed to most white Rhodesians, but that, given the circumstances, such a performance might well have been incendiary. A truly free debate involving the principal African leaders required totally new circumstances. These could have been provided only by direct British rule and the capacity to enforce impartial procedures on all parties. But direct rule was neither acceptable to Smith nor achievable by Wilson at acceptable political cost.*

This is only to say once again that the objectives of the two antagonists were radically at cross-purposes. And each lacked either the capacity (in the case of Smith) or the will (in the case of Wilson) to

---

* During the test of acceptability following the November 1971 agreements, spokesmen for the political parties represented in Parliament were in fact permitted access to radio and television. This however excluded the mainstream African movements. Nor were there any provisions to release detainees prior to the test of acceptability (though the regime of its own volition released a substantial number). Even so the test, as we shall see, evoked stormy demonstrations and considerable violence, validating the general point made here.

bring the other to terms. All the intricate constitutional formulations and complex legal efforts to reconcile the opposing positions were bound to be unavailing. Despite ingenious attempts on both sides to camouflage the real impact of their proposals, these nonetheless poked through with undisguised clarity whenever the conversation turned to concrete cases. A recognized African nationalist leader on television demanding majority rule during the test of acceptability? Symbolically it was as essential to the British Labour position as it would have been anathema to white Rhodesia.

So the talks ended without result, though the sparring continued into the following spring with the exchange of several complex, tendentious and repetitive memoranda. Kaunda, Nyerere and the 'New' Commonwealth had needlessly feared a sell-out, but so too had the ultra-rightists in Rhodesia – politics making strange bedfellows. Parliamentarians of liberal persuasion in London had fought against Wilson to defeat this settlement, while liberal whites (by Rhodesian standards) in Salisbury had fought against Smith to achieve it – bedfellows (of sorts) making strange politics. South Africa, and no doubt Portugal, had hoped for an end to the dispute. Vorster privately admitted defeat when it became apparent, despite his advice to the contrary, that Britain meant to make the external safeguard the sticking point. It neither jibed with his own convictions, nor was it ever politically possible for him to have imposed it on Rhodesia, given his domestic political constraints. Challenged in Parliament by both the Opposition United Party and the dissident right within his own National Party, Vorster found it necessary at one point to express surprise that anyone should accuse him of putting pressure on Rhodesia. After all, he contended, his own son was defending the Fatherland serving with a South African police unit in the Zambezi valley. As to Wilson, he failed in his last try for a settlement, leaving the Rhodesian problem farther from solution than ever. It was clear that the odious 'return to legality' formula in the *Tiger* terms and the unpleasantness of those earlier proceedings had not been the reason for failure then. And one wondered whether the withdrawal of the external safeguard would by itself have gained a settlement now. Rhodesia's own principal daily, the *Herald*, concluded on 26 November 1968, that the Rhodesian Government 'never intended to settle with Britain except on terms guaranteeing continuation at will of unqualified white parliamentary rule'.

But the final judgement was given by Smith himself in a broadcast to Rhodesians on 19 November 1965. 'It was clear to us throughout the talks that the British were obsessed with the question of African majority rule,' Smith remarked, as if suddenly struck by some blinding revelation. And when Thomson tried to get the Rhodesian leader to insert in the final terms of settlement a bland statement that 'the new constitution makes the same provision as the 1961 constitution for steady advancement to majority rule, and ensures that no impediment shall be placed in its way,' Smith would have none of it. 'Such a statement has no appeal for Rhodesians,' Salisbury's white paper commented later. Smith himself fell back to his now familiar assertion: 'There will be no majority rule in my lifetime' – adding at one point, 'or in my children's.'

'Into Cold Storage'

Negotiations with the Labour Government at an end, attention in Rhodesia turned once more to the formulation of a new constitution and preparations for declaring Rhodesia a republic. A referendum on both issues was scheduled for 20 June 1969. One month before, Ian Smith released a draft of the Government's proposed constitution which combined Sam Whaley's 'parity' approach and the first stage proposal of the so-called Yellow Paper.* A separate roll for whites (which included also Asians and Coloureds) was to elect fifty members to the House of Assembly (formerly the Legislative Assembly). Sixteen African members were to be elected also on separate rolls, eight directly by popular ballot and eight indirectly to represent chiefs and tribal interests.

The number of white seats would remain constant while the number of African seats would be increased in proportion as the personal income tax assessed on the African community taken as a whole rose in relation to the income tax assessed on the white community. At the end of the process, when the total income tax paid by Africans equalled the total paid by whites, each community would have fifty representatives seated in the House of Assembly. But there the process would stop. Once parity was reached, there would be no further increase in African representation.

Parity itself, by every calculation, was light years away. The African community currently was contributing approximately one-half of 1 per cent of the nation's personal income tax revenue. There could be no further increase in African representation in the House until that figure had advanced to over 24 per cent of total income tax revenue.† The six year span from 1963 to 1969 showed an average

---

* See above, pp. 261–63.

† That is, advanced to more than sixteen-sixty-sixths of the total. There were to be sixty-six seats in the House, sixteen of which were allocated to Africans at the outset.

annual improvement of approximately 0.05 per cent of the contribution to income tax revenue as compared with tha white community. Extrapolating from this trend, it would tak 460 years before any increase in representation would occur b the original sixteen seats allocated by the constitution and 980 for parity to be reached! Even assuming this rate increaseu by ten times to 0.5 per cent annually, parity would not be reached for almost a century. The ingenious community income tax formula effectively ruled out any meaningful African parliamentary advance whatsoever.

Even as an indication of African income or African contributions to governmental revenue, the proposed constitution was grossly unfair. In 1969 some 697,000 African workers in the cash economy earned 41 per cent of the cash income, while 99,200 non-Africans earned the balance. That Africans paid so little in personal income tax was accounted for by a relatively progressive income tax structure and by the depressed level of African earnings, an average of ten times lower than non-African earnings. The fact was that the African contributed to the high income of his individual or corporate employer by reason of his own low wages. Moreover, the real assessment of the African community by the national exchequer based on the full range of direct and indirect taxes (sales taxes, for example) was estimated to run anywhere between 8.5 per cent to 15 per cent of total collections. Further to compound these inequities, nothing in the constitution forebade a future legislative decision to decrease personal income taxes further in favour of indirect taxes which could wipe out any marginal gains Africans might have made in improving their ratio of income tax contributions and thus their ultimate representation in Parliament.

The draft constitution also incorporated amending procedures which placed control squarely in the hands of the white members of the legislature and, in the case of specially entrenched clauses, required the concurrence of only three African chiefs seated in an otherwise largely powerless upper house, or Senate. A new Declaration of Rights was written into the constitution – and explicitly removed from enforcement in the courts. While acknowledging the right of the individual to be protected from unjust discrimination, the Declaration opened wide the door to such practices if they could be justified as allowing for 'economic, social or cultural differences' among various peoples. Ironically the Declaration also authorized preventive detention and arrest, and the regulation of the press and other media.

Not without reason Smith contended that his new constitution would 'entrench government in the hands of civilized Rhodesians for all time' and, opening the referendum campaign, boasted that it would 'sound the death knell' for the principle of majority rule. Even pro-Rhodesian observers seemed nonplussed. For example the conservative American journal, *National Review*, on 17 June 1969, found the proposed constitution a 'racist' and 'despotic' document, 'immoral, unnecessary and imprudent'. Notwithstanding, 72.5 per cent of those voting in the referendum on 20 June 1969 approved the constitutional draft, while 84.5 per cent agreed that Rhodesia should sever its link with the British crown and become a republic.*

Now committed to republican status under a constitution which forever foreclosed majority rule, Rhodesia's break with Britain seemed at last complete. On 24 June, the British Foreign Minister announced in the Commons the withdrawal of Britain's residual mission in Salisbury and the imminent closure of Rhodesia House on London's Strand, while the Queen indicated her acceptance of Sir Humphrey Gibbs's resignation as Governor. Meeting with newsmen in the dining-room of Government House in Salisbury, the sixty-six-year-old Gibbs, his voice and hands trembling, said that no further purpose would be served by his remaining in office. He insisted however that his going did not mean that the Queen was abandoning her subjects in Rhodesia including the interests of the unenfranchised masses. Meanwhile, the usual 'informed sources' in London confirmed once more that legal sovereignty for Rhodesia would indeed continue to reside with Britain – as it had all along. A more accurate summary of the situation was provided by the title of a *Times* editorial on 25 June 1969 which announced tersely: 'Into Cold Storage'.

It had been almost forty-four months since Sir Humphrey, the symbol of British sovereignty in Rhodesia, voluntarily assumed his position of quasi-house arrest, not daring to leave his residence for more than a few hours lest he be barred from re-entry by the Smith regime. Now as they drove through the gates of Government House for the last time, Sir Humphrey and Lady Gibbs were bidden farewell by some 500 Rhodesian loyalists many waving small Union Jacks. It was a scene as humanly touching as it was politically irrelevant.

In November the new constitution was passed by the Rhodesian

---

* With less than 10,000 non whites on the voters rolls, however, the constitutional issue was in fact approved by only 1.1 per cent of the total Rhodesian population. Respecting the new constitution, 76,705 votes were cast; 54,724 were affirmative and 20,776 were negative, while 1,206 were spoiled ballots. On the republican issue, 76,709 votes were cast; 61,130 voted yes and 14,372 voted no while 1,207 were spoiled ballots.

Parliament. Rhodesia was declared a republic at midnight, 1–2 March 1970, some eighty years after it had first been tied to Britain by Royal Charter. Clifford Dupont was made interim President pending elections under the new constitution which were announced for 10 April. 'Five million tears will be shed over these laws,' said African Opposition Member of Parliament Philip Chigogo on the occasion of the new constitution's final passage in the Rhodesian legislature. Smith held a rather different view. To a group of visiting American journalists mostly from the Deep South, he spoke with evident candour shortly after Rhodesia had assumed republican status. 'Sixty years ago,' he said referring to Rhodesia's African citizens, 'these people were uncivilized – I do not want to be unkind – savages walking around in skins. They have made great strides but they still have a long way to go.'

The 'cold storage' Britain had in mind was to include Rhodesia's complete diplomatic isolation. Ever since the referendum and its own break with Salisbury, London had urged the United States to follow suit recognizing that if America were to close its consulate most of the dozen consulates still remaining would close too. The United States had refused, in part because the White House was concerned about the more than 1,000 Americans then residing in Rhodesia, in part because the small residual mission provided a valuable listening post, and in part because the American administration generally favoured wherever possible the principle of maintaining communications links rather than rupturing them.

Shortly after Rhodesia announced it had assumed republican status, however, Foreign Minister Michael Stewart called in Ambassador Walter Annenberg and handed him an aide-mémoire on the consulate affair, an unusual procedure for two close allies. Annenberg was reminded that the American consul's exequatur had been signed by her Britannic Majesty. At issue was not recognition of the Smith regime, for consuls may be accredited without being accorded diplomatic recognition. An example was Britain's own consular mission to Hanoi, as Stewart had just acknowledged on the floor of the Commons. Rather the issue was whether the United States was willing to cast doubt on Britain's technical jurisdiction over Rhodesian affairs. Once the matter was joined in an aide-mémoire at the Stewart–Annenberg level, the White House, having no graceful alternative, acquiesced. All other consulates closed too excepting only those of South Africa and Portugal.

London meanwhile faced yet another a difficult passage at the United Nations. Lord Caradon, as so often before, was first off the mark hoping to outflank Britain's critics. He called for an immediate meeting of the Security Council to condemn Rhodesia's 'purported assumption of republican status', and to decide (under Article 41) 'that all member states of the United Nations shall refrain from recognizing this illegal regime or from rendering any assistance to it.' Once again, the Afro-Asian states fashioned a tough resolution with which to challenge Caradon's vacuous formulation. It condemned Britain's refusal to use force, called for sanctions against Portugal and South Africa and the severance of all transportation and communications links with Rhodesia. The resolution was unacceptable not only to Britain but to the United States.

Unacceptable resolutions had been put forward before: for example the previous June when a similar Afro-Asian effort had failed because it lacked by one the nine affirmative votes needed for acceptance. Now, however, the Afro-Asian states had struck a deal with Spain which previously had dissented, not wishing to agree to sanctions against its Iberian partner, Portugal. The Afro-Asians offered Spain the chance to vote 'No' on the offending Portuguese paragraph. Spain then concurred in the edited resolution, delighted at the opportunity to condemn Britain while gaining favour with Afro-Asians which would be useful when soliciting future support for the Spanish position (*vis-à-vis* Britain) on Gibraltar. With Spain's concurrence the requisite nine votes were in hand. Under these circumstances America's negative vote, along with Britain's, constituted a 'veto', Washington's first and London's fourth since the Council first sat in January of 1946. The following day, 18 March, a compromise resolution put forward by Finland recast the controversial passages of the vetoed resolution while calling for more 'stringent measures' in support of existing sanctions. It won approval by fourteen to nil with one abstention.

These developments were scarcely noticed in Rhodesia where an electoral campaign, the first under the new constitution, was in progress. On 10 April 1970 the Rhodesian Front again swept the field. All fifty white seats went to the ruling party. The multi-racial Centre Party which had put forward sixteen white candidates and eight Africans succeeded in electing seven of its African candidates and no whites at all. (The eighth directly elected African seat was taken by the veteran African politician, Josiah Gondo, representing the National Peoples Union, an all-African party.) Only 8,300 Africans had in fact registered to vote and their disillusionment was hardly allayed when, in the course of the campaign, Smith let it be known that he envisaged further steps towards legalized separation of the races as 'the only way to preserve our civilization'.

Shortly thereafter another electoral campaign got under way. Harold Wilson on 18 May 1970 announced that Elections in Britain would be held one month later. Both Edward Heath, Leader of the

Opposition, and Sir Alec Douglas-Home, Shadow Foreign Minister, had made clear that should the Conservatives win at the polls there would be one final attempt to reach a settlement with Salisbury. They would shortly have an opportunity to try for, when the returns were in, Harold Wilson had been removed from office.

XI

The End – and the Beginning

Looking back, the Rhodesian imbroglio seems a tale told by an idiot, full of foolish estimates and silly superlatives, dramatic encounters on naval vessels cruising dark seas, the giving of ultimata followed by one 'final' offer after another until the last curtain falls – behind which continues the persistent rustling of deals proffered and refused and then offered again. It has been a madcap adventure, yet with frightening overtones.

Fearing their 'civilization' would be overwhelmed by an African population twenty times their number, a tiny enclave of whites in Central Africa, no more populous than the English town of Portsmouth, promulgated a rebellion in defiance of a power which a mere twenty-five years before had ruled the largest empire ever known. Britain imposed economic sanctions and vowed it would unseat the 'rebels' (as they were then pointedly called), return the situation to legality and assure unimpeded progress to majority rule. In the first year alone this policy cost London by its own calculations upwards of £100 million ($280 million). It placed Rhodesia's neighbour, Zambia, in mortal danger, came within an ace of destroying the multiracial Commonwealth, and promoted an unprecedented involvement of the United Nations in programmes of dubious effectiveness and therefore of questionable wisdom.

As we shall see, the final outcome of all this extraordinary activity was at long last a signed agreement between the new Tory Government in London and the Salisbury regime. Had it been implemented, it would have conferred upon Rhodesia legal independence in return for hard won concessions from the rebels – resulting in an amended Rhodesian constitution more reactionary by far than that of 1961 which both the Conservative and Labour Parties at the time flatly refused to acknowledge as the basis for Rhodesian sovereignty. It is difficult to imagine a greater disproportion between frenetic effort and meagre result. Before turning to these concluding events, however, a summary evaluation of Labour's policy is in order.

Wilson's Policy Assessed

Harold Wilson decided from the outset not to use force to reverse the rebellion. Formidable logistical problems, the kith and kin factor and negative advice from military commanders helped shape the decision. But underlying all else were the economic and the parliamentary crisis which gripped Britain at the time. For a brief moment Wilson seemed to believe that indirect measures could achieve his objectives. Sanctions would galvanize an effective opposition to the rebel regime in Rhodesia and he would be able to work with a reconstituted moderate Government. It was to be a middle-of-the-road revolution led by businessmen, a double contradiction and a shockingly bad estimate.*

Thereafter Wilson hoped that massive participation in sanctions by neighbouring Zambia would produce, in his celebrated phrase, a 'quick kill'. After intensive contingency preparations, Zambia, according to the British scheme, was to break completely its extensive economic ties with Rhodesia and be placed in a kind of 'care and maintenance' coma for some two months while the added weight of Zambian sanctions hammered Smith to his knees. It was a fanciful and irresponsible *scenario* for it assumed that Zambia should accept a level of risk which Britain itself had refused. Wilson also appeared to have placed a margin of hope on South Africa's willingness not to frustrate the oil embargo. It was another bad estimate. No one had more to lose than South Africa if sanctions had succeeded against Rhodesia.

By the time of the British elections at the end of March 1966, when Labour was returned with a handsome ninety-seven-vote majority, Wilson had concluded that these several ploys were not going to unseat Smith and produce the swift settlement he had hoped for. He had no stomach to re-examine a military solution, the more so because by now white Rhodesians had rallied behind Smith and so too the South Africans. It was out of this unenviable situation that his real policy began to emerge.

---

* Rhodesian businessmen themselves had contributed to the confusion. Both prior to and following U.D.I., they consistently exaggerated the economic impact of sanctions in order first to dissuade those contemplating the illegal seizure of independence and later to convince them that a settlement was indispensable.

Reversing himself, Wilson now set out to extract a compromise settlement from the rebels whom at first he had vowed to remove. Here too his efforts repeatedly failed. Unable therefore to react meaningfully to the Rhodesian problem, he found himself instead reacting more and more to the reactions to Rhodesia in order to minimize damage to British interests in collateral areas. Of principal concern to him in assessing those interests were four 'constituencies' as he once called them – the Tory Opposition in Britain, the Commonwealth, the U.N. and South Africa – and it was the mixture of his responses to the cross-cutting requirements of these 'constituents' that gave his policy that special madcap flair. Commenting on this exasperating situation, Wilson once noted in Parliament that every action he took, no matter how appropriate it might be in one constituency, seemed disastrous in another. Carried away, he mixed a metaphor that delighted his colleagues. 'What we are trying to do is to go straight down the middle of the road in a four-dimensional situation.'

Wilson was anxious that the Tories should not turn his flank thus undermining his position with the electorate. It was a requirement of the highest importance when he commanded a paper-thin majority in Commons. For this reason among others, his approach to sanctions was at first cautious and gradual. From the outset Heath had appealed for negotiations with the Smith regime, and Wilson, beginning with 'talks about talks' in April 1966, found that recurrent contacts with Salisbury were also useful in spiking Opposition guns at home.

Negotiations with the rebels were of course anathema to most of the Caribbean-Afro-Asian members of the Commonwealth and to none more than sensitive and strategic Zambia. The Commonwealth was Wilson's second constituency. For most of the new non-white members the objectives were straightforward enough: to press Britain to forceful intervention in Rhodesia; barring that, to broaden the sanctions war to include South Africa and Portugal; and barring that, to gain from Britain a commitment that there would be 'no independence before majority rule'. So heated did the confrontation become that, during the course of the September 1966 meeting in London, the Labour Cabinet agreed to pledge NIBMAR rather than see that unique assembly of former British colonies break up.

Wilson's third constituency was the United Nations where he sought to maintain the initiative in each move within the Security Council in order to head off resolutions demanding methods that Britain wished to avoid, and to strengthen so far as possible economic pressures on Salisbury. The escalating measures in the Security Council were also useful in containing recurrently enflamed Afro-

Asian reactions. Of equal importance was Wilson's constant attempt to balance two incompatible objectives at the U.N. He insisted upon maintaining British responsibility for the ultimate outcome of the Rhodesian affair, while at the same time moving to multilateralize through the U.N. both the problem and its solution. The first requirement was important for it would facilitate Britain's disengagement from U.N. commitments should a settlement be achieved; the second requirement was important as a means of placing greater pressure on Rhodesia, while possibly providing a mechanism for dispersing blame should Britain's policy fail to bring about change in the rebel colony.

Wilson's final constituency was the Government in Pretoria. It was obvious that South Africa, serving as entrepôt for much of Rhodesia's trade and clearing-house for many of Rhodesia's international transactions, was the country best positioned to bring effective pressure to bear on the rebels. Thus, repeated (though futile) efforts were made to recruit Pretoria's assistance in negotiating a deal with Smith. These efforts were compromised from the start because Wilson was determined above all else to avoid an economic confrontation with South Africa. The size of Britain's investment there and the parlous state of the British economy argued the wisdom of such a policy, and during the entire Rhodesian affair Britain simultaneously and increasingly promoted its trade with South Africa.

The point of the foregoing is that Wilson's reactions to his several 'constituencies' produced a policy constantly working at cross-purposes, with initiatives repeatedly cancelling one another out. He imposed sanctions in stages which helped to maintain his delicate consensus with the Tories, but had the unfortunate effect of immunizing the rebel regime so that it developed a certain 'resistance' enabling it to cope more easily than otherwise would have been the case with each intensification of the sanctions campaign.* 'Talks' with the rebels excited apprehensions in the Commonwealth which were partially allayed only when Wilson accepted NIBMAR. That made further talks with Salisbury useless – until he reneged on his NIBMAR pledge, creating a new environment for negotiations and leaving the New Commonwealth nations outraged once more.

Recurrent negotiations with the rebels also worked at cross-purposes with the sanctions programme and compromised the

---

* Wilson said at the outset that he was going to throw the book at Smith. This he did, observed Theodore Bull in his *Rhodesia: Crisis of Colour*, 'by tearing out and flicking a few pages at a time, and finally, with "mandatory sanctions", tearing off one of the covers and lobbing it at him.'

seriousness of purpose Britain sought to convey in sponsoring resolutions involving unprecedented 'decisions' by the Security Council. Zambia surely had no interest in taking the slightest risk in pursuing sanctions against Rhodesia once it seemed likely, as negotiations with the rebels suggested, that at the end of the day a deal would be struck with Smith leaving intact a white minority, racist regime headed by the captain of the rebellion himself. For other nations too, recurrent negotiations called into question the seriousness of Britain's intentions to defeat the rebellion decisively. No one wished to be last in line to reopen profitable commercial links once a settlement with Smith appeared to be in prospect.

Meanwhile the U.N. initiatives, pursued in part to maintain Britain's credibility among Afro-Asian critics, made yet more difficult the task of gaining South Africa's co-operation in achieving a negotiated settlement, for Pretoria could hardly lend support to a programme which had now become in some measure the jurisdiction of the U.N. Security Council and which required the imposition of mandatory sanctions. It is true that economic sanctions never stood more than the remotest chance of achieving Britain's earliest announced aim, to put down the rebellion and to bring into being a responsible government with which Britain could work in managing a transition to majority rule. But whatever chance might have existed was surely diminished by Wilson's *ad hoc* responses to a recurring series of conflicting demands imposed by constituencies whose interests were in radical opposition.

The policy result was a set of negative guidelines bound to lead to a complete impasse: no force; no confrontation with South Africa; and no sell-out. Whether Wilson was in fact ready to sell out depended of course on one's point of view.* The *Fearless* terms were as far as he was willing to go in his quest for a settlement, and even those raised the most acute anxieties among Labour back-benchers who at times became perhaps the most important 'constituency' of all. In any event Wilson failed utterly in his attempt to win a settlement – and thereby avoided an ugly confrontation within his own party, in the Commonwealth and at the United Nations, while managing at the same time recurrently to deflate Tory charges that he had not done enough to come to an agreement with Smith. Perhaps this was the outcome he had intended all along knowing that Smith would not yield. At any rate with a failure like that, who needed success?

---

* It is argued below that, given conditions obtaining in Rhodesia, any settlement formula lacking enforcement mechanisms was likely to be a sell-out in the technical sense that ultimately its provisions probably would have been ignored or abrogated. See below pp. 311–12.

The only difficulty was that at the end of his administration Rhodesia remained as far from solution as ever. He had once called it 'the greatest moral issue which Britain has had to face in the post-war world'. But he accomplished nothing more than the shrewd manipulation of a string of recurring political problems deriving from it. A Prime Minister, he wrote in his memoirs, must be 'managing director' as well as the 'chairman' of his administration. 'He must be completely *au fait* . . . with every short-run occurrence of political importance.' It was a lucid self-assessment – and summed up his Rhodesia policy to a T.

The Tory Settlement

For Prime Minister Heath the inducements to settle with Smith were greater and the costs of settling were less than was the case for Harold Wilson. It is important to be clear about these considerations for they gave form to Tory policy. The Conservative Party, always ambivalent about the efficacy, purposes and even appropriateness of sanctions, found them increasingly anathema. Sanctions contravened finely honed commercial instincts not to mention specific commercial interests within Southern Africa, a factor Wilson never had to reckon with in the Labour Party. There was also from the outset an aversion among many Tories (again not present in the Labour Party) to any involvement on the part of the United Nations. Nor was there much sympathy among Conservative leaders, who prided themselves on their realism, for what they considered to be moral gestures or for that matter, reminders of British impotence. Finally a powerful lobby had emerged within the Tory Party arguing that Southern Africa represented an area of peculiar significance for Britain and the West, thus adding strategic considerations to economic reasons as to why confrontation with South Africa was to be avoided and the nettlesome Rhodesian question laid to rest once and for all. In short, while pressures from within the Labour Party repeatedly placed limits on how far Wilson felt he could go in gaining a settlement, the thrust within the Conservative Party was unmistakably in favour of settling or, barring that, perhaps disengaging entirely.

Meanwhile, the costs of settlement were declining, in turn providing greater latitude as to the terms of settlement. Prime Minister Heath confronted a much changed Africa. Among the Commonwealth nations, Kwame Nkrumah had gone. So too had Sir Albert Margai of Sierra Leone and Milton Obote of Uganda, each replaced by a less militant and, from Britain's point of view, more obliging Government. The reverse had taken place only in Nigeria where

General Gowon adopted a position considerably more critical of British policy towards Southern Africa than had Sir Abubakar Tafawa Balewa. African militancy was further mitigated by the notion which was gaining currency in some quarters that political change in white-controlled Southern Africa could not be imported, but must arise from dynamics internal to the region. Britain would have somewhat less difficulty now than heretofore in convincing many African states that a settlement with Rhodesia involving even limited concessions for Africans was better than maintaining apparently ineffective external pressures.

The fire had gone out of the Commonwealth too. President Julius Nyerere might quit that body once a British compromise settlement with Rhodesia had been implemented. President Kaunda would be sorely tempted to do so too, but increasing political problems at home and continuing vulnerability to attacks from surrounding white regimes might give him pause before isolating himself further. In any event, it was unlikely that the rot in the Commonwealth would spread beyond Tanzania and Zambia and certain that their withdrawal would not be much lamented by a Tory Government in London.

If the Conservatives were more disposed to settle than was Labour and if Heath enjoyed more manœuvrability in settlement negotiations than had Wilson, the same could not necessarily be said of Smith. The situation in Salisbury was as difficult to read as ever. On the surface nothing had changed. The iron law of Rhodesian politics remained a steady movement to the right. It had been further confirmed in the 1969 constitution. The Party organization, particularly at the grass roots, continued to be in the hands of hardlining militants. The 1970 elections further strengthened the Parliamentary lobby favouring a kind of creeping apartheid, Rhodesia-style.

The Government meanwhile was evolving its own plans for segregation. In 1969 the new Land Tenure Act further tightened the provisions of the old Land Apportionment Act, neatly dividing land holdings in Rhodesia between the Africans (44,944,500 acres for 4,900,000 people) and the whites (44,952,900 for 230,000 people). Respecting the ownership and occupation of land in white areas, the Act allowed for the enactment of laws making provision for 'different classes of Europeans', a feature which presumably prepared for legislation to keep Asians and Coloureds out of white suburbs.* And since the Land Tenure Act defined attendance at or the use of schools, hospitals and hotels as 'occupancy', it gave the Government dis-

---

* This was the so-called Property Owners (Residential Protection) Bill. See above, p. 228.

cretionary power to prevent Africans from using these facilities in white areas in so far as Africans were forbidden to 'occupy' white land.

These trends were re-enforced by the rapidly changing character of the Caucasian population as whites left, among them liberals who had lost hope, to be replaced by infusions of immigrants from southern Europe, Zambia and South Africa whose attitudes generally added to the feeling of racial intransigence.* A private poll conducted among Rhodesian whites of all persuasions found that no respondent favoured majority rule and only 10 per cent thought that after a transition to black rule conditions for whites would remain tolerable. Even among supporters of the multiracial Centre Party, a majority admitted they would leave Rhodesia or expressed doubt about their willingness to remain following the establishment of an African Government. Two-thirds of the respondents expressed the view that white control would be necessary indefinitely primarily because they felt Africans were incapable of running a modern state. Dr. Morris Hirsch, a former member of the Rhodesian Parliament who conducted the poll, concluded: 'What is referred to as Ian Smith's obstinate right-wing is in fact the majority of his party and the majority of white Rhodesians.'

Meanwhile, *la dolce vita* continued to flourish as cheap labour and liquid assets trapped within the country contributed to a white economy which, despite the inconvenience of sanctions, was characterized by easy living and conspicuous consumption. It is doubtful that anywhere on earth could an annual income of, say, £3,000 ($7,200) go farther. For £5 to £6 ($12 to $15) a month (plus bed and meals) one could employ a full-time African servant. A good four-bedroom house on an acre of land could be bought for as little as £6,500 ($15,500). Add £5 ($12) per month to your home payments for the life of your mortgage and you could have a swimming pool as well. One firm alone in less than four months during 1971 announced it had built 700 pools in Salisbury suburbs.

Nor were pressures developing within the African community that might prompt the regime to take a new look at settlement terms.

---

* The Government's own figures showed a total white immigration from 1964 to 1970 of 69,184 and an emigration of 55,320 for the same period. This did not represent an absolute turnover, however, as many immigrants also turned up in the emigrant column, some having left the country within six months of their arrival. Government immigration figures for the nine years, 1955–63, showed (exclusive of Zambia and Malawi) a total influx of 95,058 whites and an emigration of 63,960.

Serious discontent among Africans, particularly the urbanized and educated, was evident enough to the discerning observer who had gained the confidence of his informant, but outward appearances conveyed more apathy than unrest. Outside Rhodesia, the exiled nationalist parties had fallen on hard times. During 1971 a bitter leadership struggle exacerbated by tribal differences had racked ZAPU requiring the forceful intervention of the Zambian Government and resulting in the deportation of several leaders. Squabbling within ZANU had further debilitated that movement as well. The last anti-Rhodesian guerrilla sortie of any consequence had taken place at the beginning of 1970. It included an attack on Victoria Falls airport and ended with a dozen nationalists and two members of the Rhodesian security forces being killed.

There were in addition some positive disincentives to settlement. The financial implications could be ominous (though perhaps susceptible of negotiation with Britain) as Rhodesia following legal independence, assumed responsibility for defaulted debt repayments. Those to the World Bank alone were running at about £3 million ($7 million) annually and had been assumed by Britain as guarantor of the loan. The Council of the Corporation of Foreign Bondholders reported that as of July 1971, sterling loans issued in London on behalf of the Government of Rhodesia were in default to the amount of £40 million ($96 million), including frustrated interest and dividend repayments and matured securities which had been frozen by the Rhodesian Government.* Unscrambling the financial results of sanctions and countersanctions would be difficult, and clearly the Salisbury regime would come out on the short end.

All things considered, then, it was not surprising that in the midst of exploratory talks undertaken by the new Conservative Government, Ian Smith blandly told a British television audience on 13 July 1971 that 'the five principles have never really been of much consequence. . . . They are of even less consequence in the circumstances of today.' Of these, it will be recalled, the first and salient principle was 'unimpeded progress to majority rule'. Yet despite the apparent impasse, talks continued during the spring, summer and autumn of 1971. The not inconsiderable figure of Lord Goodman, who had been designated by Heath to continue the probes first begun under Wilson in the summer of 1968, dominated these exchanges, which were otherwise meant to remain clandestine.

---

* *The Economist* on 22 April 1972 estimated Rhodesia's arrears on bond issues and debts to the British Government amounted to close to £100 million ($240 million) with possibly as much again owed to private parties.

The exercise finally culminated in a visit to Salisbury by the British Foreign Minister himself and, astonishingly enough, the Proposals for a Settlement which had eluded so many negotiators for so long were signed on 24 November 1971. That Smith and the Rhodesian Front at long last could have agreed to amend their constitution to make room again for the distant implementation of the principle of majority rule signified not only a further relaxation of British demands (which we shall examine in a moment) but the ascendancy among Rhodesians of economic anxiety over hardening political and racial prejudices. For despite surface appearances, some difficult problems had been accumulating.

This was the more surprising because 1969 had seen the first marked upswing of the Rhodesian economy since U.D.I. The gross national product had increased in real terms by almost 10 per cent. Agriculture had made a dramatic recovery from the previous drought-stricken years. Virtually all spare manufacturing and construction capacity was being utilized. Exports rose by 20 per cent creating a surplus in current transactions after two successive years of large deficits. Employment was up while the rise in prices remained tolerably low. There seemed to be substance after all to the boast of the Rhodesia Promotion Council that 'sanctions spur on Rhodesia'.

But in 1970 and 1971, the more sobering trend of the earlier post-U.D.I. years re-emerged. Real economic growth fell by more than half to 4.6 per cent in 1970. The causes were many and the potential results deeply disturbing to the Salisbury regime. Agricultural output was thwarted once more by poor climatic conditions. Output in other sectors advanced but world terms of trade were turning against Rhodesia as commodity prices fell while freight costs and import prices (a reflection of inflationary trends in supplier countries) continued to rise. Between 1965 and 1970, Rhodesia's terms of trade deteriorated by more than 14 per cent. Mineral output, which despite sanctions had grown more than 45 per cent between 1966 and 1970 and which earlier had benefited from a rise in the world price of base metals, fell 8 per cent in value during the first five months of 1971. Copper which had been selling at £600 ($1,440) a ton eighteen months before was down to £411 ($986) by November 1971, and nickel seemed hard to move at any price. The sanctions programme too continued to take its toll for, as Ian Smith put it, Rhodesia was obliged 'to sell at a discount and buy at a premium' in order to move goods in and out through the sanctions barrier. Even more important, sanctions denied to Rhodesia major sources of development capital.

Meanwhile commitments for imported goods and services were steadily increasing, rising more rapidly than export earnings. The basic reason was that Rhodesia as a part of the national effort to weather sanctions had been postponing the replacement needs of both private industry and the public sector. The most vital requirements were in the field of transportation. Antiquated equipment on the railways no longer could cope with the agricultural and mining traffic which in terms of volume (though not in value) was at record levels. So heavy were the demands on foreign exchange in order to service and replace infra-structure that foreign currency allocations to the private sector fell far short of requirements which, as the Finance Minister acknowledged in his annual budget statement on 15 July 1971, would inevitably have the effect of slowing down the national growth rate.

The end result of these several trends and requirements was a cumulative balance of payments deficit leading to a foreign exchange crisis of major proportions, a situation described by some as more difficult than any faced by Rhodesia since U.D.I. In October 1971 the regime published revised balance of payments figures for the first five years of U.D.I. In only one year, 1969, had Rhodesia managed a surplus on current account. The cumulative current account deficit for the other four years came to over £42 million ($100 million).* Substantial capital inflows from abroad had closed the gap but these of course involved later drains on the balance of payments when loans would have to be serviced and repaid. The situation was aggravated further by economic difficulties in neighbouring South Africa whose assistance to Rhodesia since U.D.I. had been indispensable. After the boom years of the late sixties South Africa found itself in the grip of a serious inflation and a balance of payments deficit on current account running at an unparalleled £542 million ($1,300 million) per annum. *The Economist* on 13 November 1971 drew the sobering conclusion that, respecting Rhodesia, both Pretoria's cash and patience were running out.

The immediate problems created by Rhodesia's chronic balance of payments deficit and shortage of foreign exchange were rivalled by grim prospects in the longer term. Increasing numbers of educated young whites, sceptical about the future, were leaving the country, adding to Rhodesia's problem of recruiting much-needed skills. Between 1961 and 1969 the percentage of whites in the twenty-five to forty-four age group dropped from 30.6 per cent of the total to 26.3 per cent while those over forty-five increased as a percentage of total population from 23.3 to 27.2. Trends in the African population were even more disquieting. The per annum growth rate was 3.6 per

---

* The dollar equivalent is calculated at the devalued rate of £1 = $2.40.

cent, one of the world's highest. At that rate Rhodesia's five million Africans would double in eighteen years. Each year the African population was producing almost as many new babies as there were whites living in Rhodesia.

Calculations made in mid 1971 indicated that the net annual addition of potential African workers to the economy was 38,400. To absorb these numbers, the national income at constant prices would have to expand by no less than 9 to 10 per cent. The emigration of alien Africans resident in Rhodesia might reduce the pressure on existing jobs, and so too the tendency of many African males to fluctuate between the cash and the subsistence economies. Nonetheless, the high and rising birth rate prompted the Government's economic survey for 1970 to conclude that the imbalance of African children (2.3 million) in relation to the size of the economy (employing a total of only some 800,000) underlined 'the insuperable problem of creating sufficient employment opportunities in the money economy. . . .' Finance Minister John Wrathall called attention to the fact that while nearly 17 per cent of the African population was employed in the cash economy in 1961, the ratio had fallen to 14 per cent in 1970 despite economic growth. This meant that 3.1 million Africans of all ages who were *not* employed in the cash economy in 1961 had risen to 4.4 million in 1970 and, assuming the pattern remained unchanged, would rise to 6 million by 1980. These alarming problems would be difficult enough under the best of circumstances but certainly insoluble under continuing economic constraints.

Even so, taking the full measure of the intransigence of the Front leadership and given the attitudes of most whites to African political advancement, it seemed certain that the rebel regime would balk once more at settlement terms – unless they incorporated significant new concessions.

Settlement or Sell-Out?

The document signed by Sir Alec Douglas-Home and Ian Smith on 24 November 1971, incorporated a series of amendments aimed at liberalizing the sharply retrogressive constitution of 1969. It would have been hard not to have done so, so onerous were its terms. The concept of parity, beyond which Africans could never aspire, was amended to permit ultimate majority rule. The thoroughly unjust limitation on African advancement, which tied the level of parliamentary representation to the proportion of personal income taxes contributed by the African community taken as a whole, was replaced by a formula which once again linked representation to the number of individual Africans registered to vote. A justiciable Declaration of Rights replaced the non-justiciable version of the 1969 constitution and placed certain restraints on the Government's use of preventive detention. And a 'blocking mechanism' against retrogressive amendments gave the power of veto to popularly elected Africans in Parliament.

The result was deceptive. Any historical judgement of British policy must compare the 1971 settlement terms, not only with Rhodesia's retrogressive constitution of 1969 but with former British terms outlined on H.M.S. *Tiger* and *Fearless* and with the 1961 constitution on which those terms were based. Viewed in this light it was not the Rhodesian Front, but the Conservative Party that had made the concessions, and on virtually every one of the five principles.

The most critical passages dealt with African advance to majority rule required by the first principle. Political progress for the African community would start from the base provided by the 1969 constitution. This included, it will be recalled, fifty white members of the House of Assembly elected by a separate white roll, eight popularly elected Africans and eight elected indirectly to represent chiefs and tribal interests. These seats would remain intact. A new African higher roll would then be created involving the same income, property and educational qualifications as the white roll. African representation in the House of Assembly would increase as Africans were enfranchised under the higher roll qualifications. Seats would be added in increments of two. Each increment would be achieved as the number of Africans registered on the higher roll increased *in proportion to the total number of registered whites* by 6 per cent. The first two seats would be filled by direct election (that is, by the Africans voting on the higher roll), the next two indirectly by electoral colleges of chiefs who presumably would produce less militant legislators. The process would continue, alternating between directly elected and indirectly elected seats, until the total number of Africans in the House of Assembly equalled the total number of whites, fifty in each case. At this point there would be approximately the same number of voters on both the white and African higher rolls.*

---

* The fifty Africans in the House, however, would by now include an elaborate combination: the original eight elected popularly on what amounted to a lower roll franchise, eighteen new members popularly elected on the higher roll, and twenty-four elected indirectly representing the chiefs (the original eight plus sixteen new ones.) There would then take place a referendum among all African voters to decide whether the twenty-four indirectly elected members

Parity having been reached, the breakthrough to majority rule would be achieved by the creation of ten new seats to be filled by a Common Roll composed of higher-roll Africans and whites voting together. The presumption was that as African registrations continued to increase on the higher roll in relation to whites, the Africans would come to control the ten Common Roll seats and thus would be enabled to form the government. The question was, When? And this depended in turn on the qualifications for registration on the higher roll.

These were fixed to include all but a fraction of whites and to exclude all but a fraction of Africans – and at levels significantly higher than the qualifications for the 'A' Roll in the 1961 constitution, which subsequently were written into the *Tiger* and *Fearless* formulae though adjusted upwards to account for the inflationary factor in the economy. A voter could register on the higher roll under either one of two conditions. First, he could qualify if he owned immovable property with a net value of £2,100 ($5,040), exclusive of all encumbrances such as unpaid mortgage notes or instalments on the original purchase price, or had an annual income of £1,050 ($2,520). (Under the 1961 constitution the corresponding figures were £1,650 or $4,620 for the gross value of the property *including* mortgages and unpaid instalments, or an annual income of £792 or $2,218.) Second, he could qualify if he had four years of secondary education and owned immovable property valued at £1,400 ($3,360) net or an annual income of £700 ($1,680). (The 1961 equivalents were £550 or $1,540 gross for property and £330 or $924 annual income.)*

Moreover, cross-voting was dropped under the 1971 proposals since the voting rolls were to be racially segregated. The cross-voting procedure, a feature of the 1961 constitution retained in both the *Tiger* and *Fearless* proposals, permitted lower-roll voters (principally Africans) to have an impact on higher-roll elections (involving principally whites) up to 25 per cent of the votes cast. The reverse was also true, but the relevant point was that, at least theoretically, Africans could have an increasing impact on the higher-roll seats, not only by registering more African voters on the higher roll itself, but by the influence of the cross-vote.

---

should be replaced by twenty-four members directly elected by higher roll African voters. (Up to six of these seats could be transferred to the lower roll if Parliament had so decided prior to the referendum.)

* In comparing the terms of the 1971 proposals with the terms of the 1961 constitution, the dollar figures are more accurate as the pound sterling figures reflect the devaluation of November 1967.

Under any of these formulations of course, the Africans began their struggle for increased seats at a considerable disadvantage. For example, in 1971 the annual output of secondary school four-year graduates was 2,600 for the African community and 8,000 for the white community. African wages were one-tenth those of white wages.* Moreover since the Government and the economy were exclusively controlled by whites, African economic advance depended in substantial measure upon the goodwill of the white community. Already some 80,000 whites were enfranchised as against roughly 8,000 Africans. That would mean 4,800 new African registrations (6 per cent of 80,000) would be needed to win each additional two seats under the 1971 proposals. It was estimated that somewhere between 5,000 and 10,000 unregistered Africans might qualify for the Upper Roll, adding two to four more seats at the outset. But white registrations would not remain static either. Some observers thought there were as many as 50,000 eligible unregistered white voters. As these enrolled the proportionate number of Africans needed to win new seats would rise correspondingly. A total of 130,000 whites on the rolls, for example, would mean, not 4,800, but 7,800 new African registrations (6 per cent of 130,000) to win two additional seats. Add to this a factor for increased white immigration following the settlement with Britain and the obstacles became more formidable still.

Analysing these figures, Dr. Claire Palley, an eminent authority on Rhodesian constitutional law, estimated that majority rule under the most optimistic assumptions could not be claimed earlier than the year 2035. Advancement towards this goal would be achieved essentially by increasing the number of Africans receiving four years of education in relation to the number of whites. Dr. Palley estimated a 50 per cent expansion on current output (2,600 annually) for four-year African graduates during the first five years, and an expansion by 33.5 per cent for the next five. During this ten-year period, £50 million ($120 million) in British aid, which was a part of the settlement deal, would be available to assist educational development as well as other projects. Thereafter she assumed a 15 per cent expansion over each five-year period. Her calculations also posited that there would be no increase in the rate of white immigration (which was most unlikely), that Africans gaining four years of secondary education would also be able to meet the financial requirements for the franchise (which in many cases but surely not in all would seem reasonable), and that the Rhodesian administration would evidence

---

* In 1970, average white income from agriculture and forestry was £1,422 ($3,412) while Africans averaged £89 ($214). In manufacturing the differential was £2,103 ($5,048) to £279 ($669); and in construction, £1,909 ($4,582) to £250 ($599).

absolute good faith throughout the scores of years the process would take. Even so, she concluded that her target year of 2035 for the actual achievement of majority rule was indeed highly optimistic and admitted that 2055 would be a more reasonable estimate – eighty-four years from the signing of the proposals! And once majority rule was in hand there could never be less than fifty non-Africans nor more than sixty Africans in the House of Assembly, while voting requirements would leave the vast majority of blacks effectively disenfranchised as lower-roll seats would remain restricted to no more than 14 out of a total of 110. According to these guidelines, Government eighty-four years hence (if one accepted Palley's estimate) would be in the hands of a tiny African oligarchy presumably working hand-in-glove with a white supremacist élite.

"Would you settle for somewhat unimpeded progress towards majority rule?"
London Express Service.

So much for 'unimpeded progress to majority rule'. Guarantees against retrogressive amendments to the constitution, as called for in the second principle, were also enfeebled. Under the 1961 constitution changes in specially entrenched clauses required the approval of a majority of each community – African, Asian, Coloured and white – voting in a special referendum. Under both the *Tiger* and *Fearless* proposals, the so-called 'blocking mechanism' was introduced requiring the concurrence of three-quarters of the membership of both Houses voting together in order to amend specially entrenched clauses. Since popularly elected Africans would have constituted twenty-five out of the total of ninety-three members, they would have controlled one-quarter plus one of the votes needed to block prejudicial amendments. An additional safeguard was to be found in the right of appeal to the Judicial Committee of the Privy Council in the case of discriminatory amendments or amendments contravening the provisions of the Declaration of Rights. By the time the 1971 proposals were formulated this 'external guarantee' had long since been scrapped by the Tory Government. The 'blocking mechanism' however was preserved, but the paper-thin margin of one-quarter plus one was now shaved still further. White members could pass any amendment with the support of African chiefs plus a single popularly elected African.

As to the immediate improvement of the political status of the African community under the third principle, there was little to choose between the *Tiger*, *Fearless* or 1971 proposals. Each represented at the outset a marginal increase of African seats in Parliament. It might also be noted that while the 1961 constitution placed no limit on the number of seats Africans might one day hold in Parliament, *Tiger* and *Fearless* reserved to non-Africans in perpetuity seventeen seats out of sixty-seven in the lower house, and the 1971 proposals assigned indefinitely to non-Africans fifty out of 110 seats.

The requirement of the fourth principle, to make progress towards ending racial discrimination, involved basically the same mechanism in the several settlement formulae. While in each case the Declaration of Rights as it affected future legislation was to be enforceable in the courts, in no case were its provisions to be made retroactive, and by 1971 the amount of discriminatory legislation on the books had increased significantly. To handle existing discriminatory legislation and practice, a commission was to be established to study the situation, paying particular attention to the Land Apportionment Act and later the Land Tenure Act, and to make recommendations, though with no power of enforcement.

The fifth principle involved the test of acceptability. Here a steady deterioration had taken place in the formal requirements. The *Tiger* proposals had insisted that Rhodesia 'return to legality' under a 'broadly-based' interim government formed by the Governor, though headed by Ian Smith. Details of the constitutional settlement were to be negotiated with this entity, following which sanctions would be ended. Normal political activities were to be resumed and those in detention and restriction were to be released unless they had been found guilty by a special review tribunal of acts of violence or intimidation. A Royal Commission was then to ascertain by inquiry and interview whether or not the terms of the new constitution were acceptable to the Rhodesian people as a whole.

The *Fearless* proposals dropped entirely the formalities of a return to legality and the creation of an interim government. The rebel regime was to remain in unquestioned control in law as well as in fact throughout the test of acceptability. It was required only to form 'a broad-based administration' which was generally agreed to mean adding to the Government two Africans of unspecified rank. Once again a tribunal was to review the cases of those held in detention or restriction, this time continuing to hold only those who were 'likely to commit or incite or inspire the commission of acts of violence or intimidation'. Normal political activities would be resumed and the test of acceptability by a Royal Commission would proceed as under the *Tiger* proposals, though throughout the process (and unlike the *Tiger* proposals) sanctions would remain in force.

The 1971 formula dropped not only all reference to a 'return to legality' but to a 'broad-based' government as well. It permitted the resumption of normal political activities. However, access to radio and television was limited to those political parties represented in the House of Assembly which of course excluded ZAPU and ZANU. Finally, the 1971 proposals postponed the formal review of the cases of those Africans still remaining in detention or restriction (their numbers by now having dwindled to less than 100) until *after* the test of acceptability. Assuming the test were favourable, sanctions would remain in force until the agreed constitutional changes had been enacted.

To summarize, the 1971 proposals as compared with the earlier settlement terms established a racially segregated franchise, raised the qualifications for the critically important higher roll, eliminated cross-voting, made it impossible for Africans ever to attain more than a ten-seat majority in the lower house, did away entirely with the external guarantee against retrogressive amendments, weakened slightly the internal 'blocking mechanism' against such amendments, denied key nationalist leaders any possibility of freedom during the test of acceptability and excluded the voice of militant African nationalism from access to radio and television during the period of public debate associated with the test.

Even so, Smith and the Front once more approached the 1971 proposals with painful caution. Only after anguished and repeated second thoughts did they finally accept them. After all, despite further emasculation, the terms were premised on the rightness of majority rule and the wrongness of racial discrimination and, by implication, segregation as well. Yet even for many hardlining

Rhodesian Fronters these dreadful apparitions were now so hedged about or so distant as to lose their potency. The Land Tenure Act would remain on the books. Schools and hospitals would still be segregated. Control of all aspects of Rhodesia's life would remain in white hands for generations. And white Rhodesia would continue to be, as *The Economist* put it, 'a three-servant, two-car, one-swimming pool society'. Rhodesia's leading right-wing journal, the *Financial Gazette*, concluded buoyantly: 'Concessions, but it's a win for Smith and U.D.I.' Majority rule, it declared, '. . . is so far in the future that it cannot be considered a serious possibility at this stage'. Surely Smith and his colleagues were not about to chuck everything the Rhodesian Front had championed for over a decade in order to return to the multi-racial gradualism of a Whitehead or Welensky, nor was Britain about to oblige them to do so. Smith had promised repeatedly that there would be no majority rule in his lifetime. He was now fifty-two. If the 1971 proposals were any guide, he would not only fulfil his promise, but would give substance to that bit of hyperbole he so frequently added – 'nor in my children's either'.

All that remained now was to determine whether the Proposals were acceptable to the Rhodesian people as a whole. For Britain, the end of the road was in sight.

The End . . .

The Organization of African Unity promptly censured the Proposals as 'an outright sell-out'. No African in candour could possibly have said otherwise. Predictably the settlement was also condemned in the General Assembly and Security Council of the United Nations. Even London's prestigious *Sunday Times* said it was 'an ignoble end to empire.' It came with ill-grace, however, when the Labour Party made similar accusations in the House of Commons on 1 December 1971, as Sir Alec Douglas-Home reported on his meetings with Smith. True enough, the 1971 proposals were worse than those of *Fearless* as they in turn were in general worse than those of *Tiger* and as indeed both in some respects were worse than the 1961 constitution. But in point of fact the deterioration in each case had been technical and marginal more than substantive. Each of the constitutional formulations in turn had confronted Rhodesia's Africans (in a phrase a Labour spokesman had used to describe Sir Alec's settlement) with 'the greatest obstacle race of all time'.

Though preferable to the 1971 proposals, there was no assurance whatsoever of unimpeded progress to majority rule in the 'A' Roll franchise and the cross-voting provisions of the *Tiger* and *Fearless* proposals, as the progression could easily have been aborted by inserting administrative impedimenta or simply by declaring a state of emergency; nor was there any sure guarantee against retrogressive legislation in the appeal to the Privy Council, which after all had been available under the 1961 constitution and the decisions of which in any event could simply have been ignored by the Salisbury Government; nor was there any certainty that the test of acceptability under a 'legal', 'interim' and 'broadly-based government' (as prescribed in *Tiger*) would have been conducted impartially, without intimidation and after truly open debate, given the fact that that government would have been headed by Smith and controlled by a majority of Rhodesian Front Ministers.

Sir Alec, defending his settlement as the best that could be extracted from Salisbury at the time (about which he was undoubtedly right), said that it would have changed the course on which the Smith Government was headed (about which he was probably wrong). It is the ultimate irony of the whole Rhodesian affair that all of these extraordinary negotiations and the intricate formulations which flowed from them probably would not nor could not have changed the political realities one iota. And that is because these various constitutional provisions were unrelated to any capacity for enforcement save the implied and altogether tenuous threat to reimpose sanctions.

The Rhodesian problem, though constantly expressed in constitutional terms, has always been a problem of power, not law. We are dealing here with human forces too primordial to be sublimated by any legal turn of phrase – profound fear and distrust, entrenched privilege and intensifying demand, absolute dominance and subordinance defined absolutely by race and by sharply differing cultures. Writing of Rhodesia in 1959 six years before U.D.I., Colin Leys observed that 'a solution to the country's major problems is fundamentally impossible within the system. To solve them is to change it. . . .' This has been Britain's problem throughout, how to bring effective power to bear to change the system without applying that power directly. British policy in Rhodesia has been an exercise in the application of indirect measures, manipulation at a distance with the aim of decisively shifting the power balance within Rhodesian society by withholding or granting formal rights and by persuasion under pain of penalties for non-compliance imposed from outside. On the basis of the experience to date, some conclusions are called for.

To have fulfilled its stated objectives in Rhodesia, which were to assure a gradual but irreversible transition to majority rule, Britain would had to

have intervened by force and, in Dennis Austin's phrase, have assumed the role of 'imperial arbiter'.

It should be obvious that a controlling minority does not usually forswear its privileges except under some form of duress. When the privileged minority and the dispossessed majority are defined racially and where the history of repression has been long, bitter and at times violent, voluntary accommodations are doubly illusory. In short, how could one possibly take seriously the prospect that a ruling racial élite would voluntarily preside over the procedures which assured its own liquidation? This is only to say that the Rhodesian problem is not, and never has been, susceptible of solution through self-policed constitutional procedures. Because the problem is one of decolonization of a kind, an orderly solution cannot be achieved without a supervising authority, an 'imperial arbiter'. In the absence of such authority, there is no possibility, and probably never has been, of synthesizing Britain's insistence on an irreversible movement towards majority rule and Rhodesia's insistence on maintaining control over the pace of African advancement. Any formula which claims to do so would either be disingenuous or bound to be abrogated at some future date. No one perceived these realities with a clearer eye, incidentally, than Kenneth Kaunda of Zambia – nor with greater political astigmatism than the British Government.*

Moreover only direct intervention, immediate and definitive with appropriate warnings to Pretoria of Britain's determination, as well as assurances that Britain would indeed have remained to manage a responsible transition to African rule, had any chance of avoiding the risk of a critical confrontation with South Africa always inherent in economic sanctions. In fact a military solution in Rhodesia imposed directly after U.D.I. was probably the only available means for resolving the crippling contradiction between Britain's economic stake in South Africa (which precluded a confrontation with Pretoria over sanctions) and its political stake in Rhodesia (which demanded the assurance that majority rule would in time be realized under terms satisfactory to the new Commonwealth states).

If Britain had seized control of Rhodesia immediately after U.D.I. and then stayed to effect a gradual transition to majority rule, the impact

---

* It is noteworthy that in 1910 Britain granted South Africa its independence under a constitution entrenching the existing voting rights of both Coloureds and Africans in the Cape. The subsequent disappearance of such rights provides an often-cited and ominous parallel.

upon the region would have been profound, including the following possible consequences:

— Zambia's economic problems would have been substantially reduced as well as its vulnerability to military retaliation, while relations with Britain would have improved and opportunities for the involvement of major communist powers, with the attendant danger of a future great power confrontation, would correspondingly have been decreased.

— Botswana, bordering on a Rhodesia now assured of a favourable transition to majority rule, could have looked forward over a period of years to increasing economic viability not wholly, and ultimately perhaps not even largely, dependent on South Africa. Over the longer run, Zambia and Botswana as well as Rhodesia would have enjoyed improved opportunities to evidence substantial progress and stability under African-controlled governments. Had they succeeded, the demonstration effect one day might have had a favourable impact on white attitudes elsewhere in Southern Africa.

— For Portugal, the 'loss' of Rhodesia, once the transition to majority rule in that country had been accomplished, would have added to slowly intensifying pressures on Lisbon to arrange for some accommodation with black nationalism. (Once Rhodesia was under black rule, incidentally, Portugal's strategic Cabora Bassa hydroelectric development on the lower Zambezi would have been 'outflanked', surrounded on three sides by black-controlled states.)

— Faced with firm British action in Rhodesia, and the more so if it had won the clear support of the United States, South Africa might have been pressed towards some accommodation with the United Nations in South-West Africa. Admittedly this projection is open to serious question, but the environment created by the bold British move in Rhodesia here envisaged would have been so alien to the prevailing situation as to have opened up a range of opportunities now quite impossible to foresee.

— With a solution in train in Rhodesia which would have led in turn to new pressures on Mozambique and possibly on South-West Africa, prospects would have been improved for a fair number of black states, not excluding Zambia, one day to have sought diplomatic relations with South Africa as a means of penetrating the 'laager' of white South African misconceptions and fears. Concomitantly greater recognition might then have developed as to the several ways in which the South African problem is different from the other problems of Southern Africa, demanding in turn a different timescale and perhaps a different approach. For direct measures against an independent state and its internal racial system are legally in a different category (as are direct measures against South Africa's formidable power structure politically in a different category) from direct measures against a rebellious colony or direct action by colonial peoples seeking self-determination from Portugal. Be that as it may, a truly meaningful dialogue between South Africa and black Africa cannot take place as long as South Africa is seen to be extending its influence and lending its strength to shore up a Southern African bastion under white control.

It would be foolish to suggest that the foregoing developments would have followed automatically once the Rhodesian domino had been toppled, leading somehow to a tranquil solution of the Southern African dilemma. Each item in the above *scenario* is admittedly speculative. The gross estimate is simply this, that just as Rhodesia under white rule is geopolitically the keystone in South Africa's developing co-security system, so its removal, together with Britain's reinvolvement in the area, would have opened new opportunities for pressure, persuasion and manœuvre probably leading to eventual changes in Southern Africa less productive of racial violence and possible communist exploitation than otherwise would seem to be the case. The alternative – a trend now discernible in every detail – is the further coalescence of the White Redoubt under informal South African hegemony, a progressive diminution of options and hardening of racial attitudes, and the further erosion of African confidence in Western intentions, particularly on the part of Zambia and Tanzania and the exile guerrilla movements, creating further opportunities for access to the area by communist governments, notably the Chinese. The significance of the Rhodesian issue in the context of Southern Africa is that it represented, in almost a watershed sense, either the consolidation or the disruption of these trends. Viewed in this light, Britain's failure to have used force must be recorded as a missed opportunity of historically great significance.

On the other hand, to have forcibly intervened in Rhodesia would have meant a dramatic 'about face' for Britain – not impossible, but extraordinarily difficult and by any calculation most unlikely.

Britain has steadily been disengaging from Southern African responsibilities as it has elsewhere throughout the world. The 1961 Rhodesian constitution which forfeited the right of Britain to veto discriminatory legislation in that country, the dissolution of the Federation of Rhodesia and Nyasaland in 1963, the independence of Zambia and Malawi in 1964 and subsequently of the High Commission Territories (Botswana, Swaziland and Lesotho) all were manifestations of the persistent retrenchment of British responsibility and capability within the region, until finally only Rhodesia was left.

Repeatedly Britain has attempted to complete its formal dis-engagement from its self-governing colony (this is the most accurate way to describe the interminable negotiations following the ascend-ancy of the Rhodesian Front at the end of 1962) and repeatedly has been prevented from doing so by a combination of its own principles, reinforced by external and internal pressures, and the often irrational obstinacy of Rhodesian leaders themselves. To have reversed this process and to have elected a quite unprecedented involvement of unpredictable cost and duration at a time of acute economic and political uncertainty at home would have required an act of courage and leadership neither characteristic of Wilson's administration nor, one must add in fairness, common in the annals of statecraft.*

Finally, short of direct forceful intervention, the question must be raised as to whether Britain should have attempted to intervene at all.

The answer involves a paradox. Had Britain's policy succeeded (that is, had Britain won Rhodesia's consent for any of its settlement proposals), then one would be forced to conclude that Britain should indeed *not* have intervened at the level of 'indirect measures' or sanctions. Having failed of success (that is, having reached no settle-ment), the matter of indirect measures remains moot, and depends upon how they are viewed. This paradox arises from the following considerations. Britain's sanctions programme gave rise to a number of extraordinary misadventures and liabilities which have been documented at length in this book. Zambia (apart from Rhodesia's own African population) was the principal casualty. Serious liabilities attached also to U.N. involvement. The precedent would seem to have limited utility, that one should invoke a threat to the peace under the U.N. Charter and then impose mandatory sanctions under con-straints which virtually assured they could not achieve the prescribed end. The inevitable result has been further to debase the currency of international action under U.N. auspices. Moreover, sanctions and attendant pressures, while undoubtedly troublesome to the rebel regime, consolidated the white Rhodesian community, forced an increasing reliance of Rhodesia on South Africa and became an added incentive for increasing co-operation within the White Redoubt.

If the end result of such a remarkably costly policy had been – or is yet to be – a settlement which, lacking any enforcement measures, would necessarily have been a sell-out, the whole affair would

---

* The military problems entailed in direct intervention would have been difficult too, but not impossible. See the discussion above, pp. 55–65.

obviously have been irresponsibility compounded. Only white-ruled Southern Africa would then have been the beneficiary. Sanctions, and in a sense all forms of international pressures against white Southern African regimes, would have been discredited. Trade and investment with Rhodesia would have been resumed releasing South Africa from a salvage operation as costly in political terms as in economic. The impact on the multi-racial Commonwealth would have been adverse, though exactly how severe would be difficult to measure at this point. The U.N. would have been left in disarray, sharply divided as to the future of sanctions despite the 'settlement' and Britain's insistence that the rebellion was over. Some nations would have maintained that sanctions be continued (principally those without trading interests), and others that sanctions be terminated (principally those with trading interests). Inevitably the line drawn on commercial grounds would have coincided with an ideological division: militant Third World states strongly backed by Communist governments pitted against most Western and a few moderate Third World countries. This in turn would have strengthened the identification of Western powers with the white-controlled areas of Southern Africa and communist governments with black African aspirations, while adding to the tensions between the West and the more militant African states of Zambia and Tanzania.

In return for these substantial liabilities, Britain would at last have won formal disengagement from the Rhodesian mess – under circumstances assuring no significant changes whatsoever in Rhodesia's political life and under a constitution worse by far than that of 1961. Contemplating such a possibility, one can only recall Churchill's verdict on Abyssinia: 'We should not intervene in these matters unless we are earnest and prepared to carry out intervention to all necessary lengths.'

Having been brought to the very threshold of just such an outcome, Britain suddenly found the door to settlement slammed at the last conceivable moment, significantly by Rhodesia's Africans themselves. This concluding event invites us – in fact, obliges us – to assess Britain's (and the U.N.'s) indirect measures once more and in fresh perspective. For now, at long last, there is no alternative but to sweep aside the illusion that sanctions can do what Britain's intervention by force would have done – to effect an orderly transition to majority rule and a responsible end to Britain's stewardship in Rhodesia. Of course, Britain may yet arrange a settlement, or otherwise disengage from the problem. Even so, we must now acknowledge that we are not at the end at all, but only at the beginning of the Rhodesian drama.

. . . and the Beginning

Given the obvious desire of the Tory Government in London
itself of the Rhodesian issue and of the rebel regime in Salisb
make normal its relations with the international community
might have been excused for assuming that once the Proposals for a
Settlement were agreed to on 24 November 1971, the test of their
'acceptability' would have been a mere formality. In fact, the mission
assigned to Lord Pearce by the British Government was anything but
– resulting in a profoundly ironic turn of events.

As far back as 10 September 1964, it was agreed by Rhodesia and
Britain that independence terms must be 'acceptable to the people of
the country as a whole'. (In fact, the phrase was Smith's; it was
immediately seized upon by the Commonwealth Secretary, Duncan
Sandys, and the Prime Minister, Sir Alec Douglas-Home, and placed
in the joint *communiqué* of the above date. It later became the fifth
principle.) Salisbury was confident that the masses of rural Africans,
guided by white District Commissioners and Government-paid
chiefs, would be compliant. Many African leaders assumed the
same and dismissed the test as meaningless. Far from compliant,
however, huge numbers of rural Africans told Pearce's commissioners
that they rejected the Proposals, and it was now the Rhodesian
Government which argued that rural Africans, ignorant and intimidated, were incapable of a meaningful choice. Thus, feared by its
opponents as the capstone to a negotiated deal between two white
governments which would sell out Rhodesia's blacks, the Pearce
Commission (to Britain's very great credit) triggered what may have
been the most democratic exercise in Rhodesia's history. While in
London and Salisbury it was hoped that the test of acceptability
would settle the Rhodesian problem and stabilize the situation, in
the event it settled nothing and just possibly changed everything.

Almost 115,000 Africans or close to 6 per cent of the adult African
population were contacted by the teams Pearce sent all over the
country to explain the Proposals and to elicit responses. By Pearce's
reckoning, this large sample opposed the settlement terms by 36 to 1.
(Whites including Coloureds and Asians, on the other hand, favoured
the terms by 14 to 1.) The African protest was accompanied at the
outset of Pearce's mission by major demonstrations. In all, at least
fourteen Africans lost their lives, thirteen of them killed in police
actions. More than fifty were injured including several whites.
Hundreds of Africans were arrested. Politically inspired strikes
flared in several parts of the country. It was the first serious mass
protest since the abortive strikes organized within the first month

after U.D.I. and the most significant African uprising in almost a decade.

"Up the Garden Path"

Still more significant was the swift and effective organization of Africans to plead against the Proposals before the Pearce Commission. The vehicle was the newly formed African National Council (A.N.C.) chaired by Bishop Abel Muzorewa, the diminutive, quiet but determined leader of the United Methodist Church of Rhodesia. Much of the organizational skill was provided by recently released political detainees – a co-operative effort mounted by adherents of both wings of the African nationalist movement (ZAPU and ZANU) which, since the split in that movement almost nine years before, had been plagued with internecine conflict and largely immobilized within Rhodesia.

Most Rhodesian whites were taken off guard. Only in November, when the Proposals were agreed to, had Smith boasted, 'We have the happiest Africans in the world.' Embarrassed and perplexed, white leaders scurried for explanations. Desmond Frost, the Rhodesian Front Party Chairman, explained to the Pearce Commission that adverse African reactions were the work of 'agitators and self-seekers' who were intimidating the Africans and seriously endangering the good relations that had been built up between the races.* Minister of Internal Affairs, Lance Smith, claimed that those shouting 'No' were a 'small minority of rabid, militant, nationalist hooligans', not at all representative of the African people. Scores of international newsmen who converged on Rhodesia for Pearce's test of acceptability concluded the opposite. So too did Rhodesia's leading daily paper the *Rhodesia Herald,* which noted simply that 'the Government has been deluded about the extent of African support it enjoys'. Closer to the mark, one supposes, was Desmond Frost's second observation to Lord Pearce: 'The sooner your Commission completes its task and returns to England, the sooner we shall be able to return to the peace and tranquility that Rhodesia has enjoyed for the last decade.'

The Pearce Commission indeed had a disruptive impact for it provided the occasion for the mobilization of opinion and thereby the rudimentary politicization of vast numbers of people. Pearce made available a forum, provided worldwide publicity and lent to long-suppressed protest the aura of legitimacy. Even when it was clearly understood that a 'No' vote meant certain return to the *status quo ante* (for the proposals were set forth strictly on a 'take it or leave it' basis), there seemed generally not the slightest equivocation. Africans were being given an opportunity, as Bishop Muzorewa put it, 'to pass a verdict on white minority rule', to strike a blow against the Smith Government, to cast a veto against a plan devised without any consultation whatsoever with the representatives of 95 per cent of the population. Deputy Secretary-General of the A.N.C., Eddison J. Zvobgo, told Lord Pearce that had Africans en masse approved the proposals, they would have been 'the only species of human being who ever went down on record as saying, yes, it's nice to be ruled by a minority in your own land.'

Pearce's report could not have been other than negative and Britain could hardly have refused the verdict, which the Foreign Minister, Sir Alec Douglas-Home, announced to Parliament on 23 May 1972. It was the first time that Africans had been given the

---

* The Pearce Commission found instances of intimidation but on balance concluded that had there been none there would still have been a substantial majority against the Proposals. 'We found it improbable if not impossible that with such a tight security system as that which has existed in Rhodesia for several years, a minority could dominate a majority by intimidation in a few weeks. . . . We do not think that the African National Council would have obtained so great and so swift a response had they not met a potential desire among a majority of the people for leadership in a rejection of the terms and in a protest against the policies of the last few years.'

power of veto over the future of Rhodesia. But their power ended abruptly once the report was submitted by Pearce and accepted by Sir Alec. Smith dismissed the exercise as a 'farce' and said he would rule Rhodesia 'firmly'. The Chairman of the Front added that the Government would now concentrate on measures to 'remove racial friction' which clearly signalled further moves toward segregation.

By providing Africans with the occasion for mass protest, Pearce's test also accentuated white Rhodesia's apprehensions. For some, apprehension expressed itself in greater intransigence and a further tilt towards South Africa. A new far-right organization, the United Front Against Surrender, was formed under the chairmanship of tough, former Internal Affairs Minister, William Harper, favouring apartheid and charging that the Smith Government sought, of all things, black majority rule, total integration and appropriation of European lands. (It is a classic tactic in Rhodesian politics to invoke *swart gevaar*, or the 'black danger'. The Front used it to excellent effect in its successful campaign against Sir Edgar Whitehead in 1962.) Perhaps more immediately to the point, Smith's critics charged that in permitting the 'test of acceptability', he made the natives restless and abdicated the heretofore unquestioned authority of the white man in Rhodesia. 'The unsophisticated, indeed primitive, millions are confused and disturbed,' commented the Rhodesian right-wing monthly journal, *Property and Finance*, 'and it will take firmness and much hard work to repair the damage.' Expressing the significance of the African protest somewhat differently, a *Rhodesia Herald* editorial said, 'Let there be no illusion that we can resume from the point at which we were before. The effects of what has happened since are too far-reaching.'

When he announced H.M. Government's acceptance of Pearce's negative verdict and withdrew the Proposals for a Settlement, Sir Alec expressed to the Commons once more the hope that had animated British policy towards the stubborn Rhodesian issue for twenty years, that all Rhodesians might 'choose the way of compromise and . . . work together for orderly political change'. In realizing that hope, however, Britain, as always, could play only a negative role; it could deny but not dispose. It could permit Africans a veto, but nothing more. Joshua Nkomo, eight years in detention at remote Gonakudzingwa, dramatized Britain's chronic incapacity in a statement to Pearce remarkable for its pathos and statesmanlike moderation. Calling Britain's attention to the distressing fact that African leaders had been left to the mercy of the rebels who in turn were the principals with whom Britain negotiated Rhodesia's future, Nkomo added sadly that the African people were treated as if *they* had committed the rebellion and not the Rhodesian Front. He asked for a settlement which would bring about a reconciliation among all of Rhodesia's peoples and called upon Britain to convene a constitutional conference to that end.

In his statement to the Commons, Sir Alec went on to say that the Rhodesian problem could essentially only be solved by Rhodesians themselves, if not by compromise then in the end by racial polarization and conflict. Sanctions would remain as a part of that 'atmosphere' conducive to further discussion 'until we can judge whether or not an opportunity for a satisfactory settlement will occur'. But surely it was no longer credible that sanctions could be made effective within Britain's original terms of reference, resulting, that is, in a settlement guaranteeing irreversible progress to majority rule.

Was it conceivable, on the other hand, that there was now more to be gained than lost by terminating sanctions and international ostracism? Admittedly, as we have seen, a sell-out settlement, or in this case a simple capitulation, would be irresponsibility compounded when measured by the sacrifices and liabilities of a long and fruitless sanctions programme. Leaving aside the past, however, what about current options? These were limited to continuing sanctions without any prospect of bringing to power a genuinely reformist white administration in Rhodesia, or dropping sanctions entirely. Moreover, what if the sanctions programme had been wrongly conceived from the start? The renewed impasse in Rhodesia gave new force to a recurring argument. After all, everyone agreed that these external pressures seemed to push Rhodesia closer to South Africa and to add to the strength of reactionary forces at home. If this were the case, the reverse would also seem plausible. Open Rhodesia to normal contact with the world and moderate, liberalizing influences within Rhodesia, long smothered by fear and the instinct for survival, would reassert themselves. Once the pressure was removed, change could be facilitated by rational discourse and contributions to rapid economic development which in turn would give the Africans a greater stake in Rhodesia's future and more leverage to determine the shape of that future. But the argument missed a central historical fact. Rhodesia's shift to the right preceded both sanctions and universal ostracism, and was occasioned, as we have seen repeatedly, not by external pressures but by internal anxieties about African rule.

In any event, the coalescence of the white-controlled areas of Southern Africa could not now so easily be reversed. Assuming that sanctions were lifted and that Rhodesia were recognized by a number of Western states, these developments would not affect at all the basic antipathies and sympathies which play upon the alignment of forces throughout the region. Such an outcome of course would never be accepted by most black African states, nor by most politically aware Rhodesian Africans for that matter. Nationalist exiles from Southern Africa would continue to be trained in guerrilla conflict, many by communist tutors. Zambia would persist in its efforts to disengage from the southern sector, with massive help from the Chinese in constructing the railway to Dar es Salaam, and the Zambezi River would remain the hostile Mason–Dixon line of the continent.

Meanwhile, responsive to these developments, the hardening of the White Redoubt would continue. And Rhodesia, lacking any viable alternative under a white-dominated government, would find itself quite inevitably being absorbed into the larger problem of a racially stratified system under the informal hegemony of South Africa. To 'normalize' relations with Rhodesia at this point would have the effect, not of rescuing that country from the South African 'alternative', but in a sense validating it by withdrawing all pressure for any other.

At the same time, what was to be gained if sanctions and international ostracism continued? Another turn of the sanctions screw, or even sanctions maintained at the present level, might eventually wring a few more reluctant concessions from the Rhodesian Government in a new round of settlement negotiations, but probably not enough to matter in the long run. Sanctions might finally topple the present regime, but chances are it would fall to a more repressive one. The distressing point is that Britain's essential justification for sanctions was suspect from the start. They were supposed to induce meaningful white reform. Thus, it will be recalled, sanctions were to be carefully modulated, for if they became too threatening, pressures for reform would be transformed into a reactionary retreat. And periodically, the situation would have to be tested to see whether these reformative pressures had done their work, a reading which understandably became confused with Britain's desire to formalize its disengagement from the problem entirely. Sanctions probably should never have been viewed as a means for achieving fundamental white reform because in the Rhodesian context that could only mean black empowerment and the disappearance of white rule.

There is another way of looking at sanctions. It begins with the recognition that ultimately it must be the African people themselves who fuel the engines of change in Rhodesia, as elsewhere in Southern Africa. This was the symbolic significance of the outcome of Lord Pearce's test. It revealed beyond all doubt the depth and breadth of African animosity and provided a glimpse of a long-dormant capacity to politicize and to organize the African population. If sanctions are to have policy relevance at all, they must be seen not as inducements to white reform but as adjuncts to slowly developing black assertion. Involved here are no short-term pressures to gain renewed discussions with the white regime, but a long-term commitment to help achieve conditions favourable to those who seek to disrupt the system. Under this formula sanctions must remain intact, at whatever level they can be sustained, indefinitely.

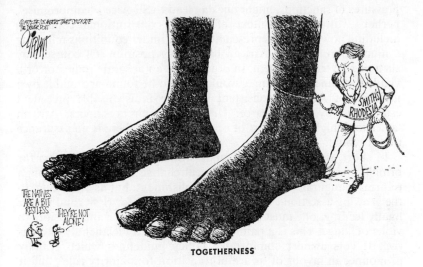

TOGETHERNESS

Even at its present level of relative ineffectiveness, the policy of making Rhodesia an international pariah curtails the flow of white immigrants into the country, encourages the drain of white young people from the country, and denies Rhodesia access to major money markets thus thwarting economic growth, hastening the rundown of infra-structure while increasing the cost to South Africa of sustaining its awkward and embarrassing northern neighbour. In time the situation will become more brittle and thus more capable of disruption. Even the emergence of a more repressive white regime might hasten the process of politicizing the African masses by adding further fuel to existing grievances. This is why all African nationalist organizations in Rhodesia, including now the A.N.C., have argued for the continuation of sanctions, even though Africans meanwhile will suffer disproportionately.

How long this process will take we cannot tell, though if we have learned anything from the tribulations of resistance movements in Southern Africa, we may expect that its course will be tortuous, marked by repeated reverses and extending over a number of years. Similarly, how the process will consummate we do not know, in part because the variables are too many and their possible interactions too complex, and in part because as the point of crisis is approached within Rhodesia – again, probably many years hence – the roles of other actors cannot accurately be forecast. It is not inconceivable, however, that African protests and a slowly expanding capacity for withholding co-operation and promoting disruption, combined with a gradual decline of the resilience of the white community under the pressures of sanctions, might one day lead to Sir Alec's 'compromise', perhaps within the context of a new constitutional conference including now African representation and under conditions reflecting a much more effective African bargaining position. Of course, any such negotiated settlement, in order to be an accurate indicator or a viable instrument of change, would have to be found acceptable by a majority of Africans consistent with the indispensable precedent established by Lord Pearce. Under these circumstances, African 'assertion' might stop short of open revolt. But there is no assurance that it would.

In short, sanctions must be understood, not as a mechanism for bringing orderly and peaceful political change to Rhodesia through reforms inaugurated by the white establishment, but as an adjunct to the growing assertion of the African population for rights and power finally leading, one must assume, to serious disorder and possibly to violent change. This is a painful diagnosis and a melancholy alternative. It cuts against comfortable policy guidelines which grandly pronounce in favour of 'peaceful transition to majority rule', and it strongly suggests that genuinely multiracial or non-racial options are simply not available. When all of this is fully understood by deeply unrevolutionary, commercially oriented, white Western governments, sanctions will probably wither faster than ever.* If so, this will be a

---

* The most dramatic defector recently has been the United States. In the autumn of 1971, Congress disallowed the prohibition or regulation of imports of strategic materials from non-communist sources so long as the import of such materials from communist countries was not also prohibited – legislative longhand for taking chrome (and a few other items of lesser importance) off the sanctions list. Though by no means as serious as the persistent and largely un-publicized violations of many other countries, the action placed the U.S. in the select company of South Africa and Portugal in open and voluntary breach of sanctions. Indeed, the U.S. became the only country in the world in explicit legislative defiance of its obligations under the Charter respecting sanctions. Until this congressional action – which was fought by the State Department but largely acquiesced in by the White House – the U.S. had an exemplary record for enforcing sanctions, and is still doing so in areas not exempted by Congress. Still, the impact of the American breach of chrome sanctions is likely to be far-reaching.

tragedy for, even though realism requires that the premise underlying sanctions and the expectations flowing from them must radically be changed, the justification for continuing international ostracism of Rhodesia has if anything increased.

First, sanctions signify that Rhodesia continues to be an international problem. Though it can be argued that it was both unjustified and unwise for the Security Council to have cited the Rhodesian situation as 'a threat to the peace',* it would be fatuous to suggest that the issue is not one of proper international concern, as are the anti-colonial conflicts in adjacent Mozambique and nearby Angola, and the U.N. trusteeship obligations of South Africa in neighbouring South-West Africa, and indeed, though in a more diffused sense, the question of human rights in South Africa itself. In any event, the Rhodesian question already has effectively been internationalized, not only by Britain's initiative in making it the object of repeated Security Council resolutions, but by the actions of South Africa and other states which, contrary to accepted international law, have assisted an unrecognized government in its rebellion. Moreover, it is inconceivable that black assertion for expanding rights and power throughout Southern Africa against strongly entrenched white minority communities (outnumbered by more than eight to one taking the region as a whole) could proceed without serious international implications. Already these involve the question of guerrilla incursions from neighbouring sanctuaries which in turn raises the equally delicate question of 'hot pursuit', the problem of foreign economic and military aid to the white regimes and to black exile movements, and the dangers of incipient great power confrontation. In the future, serious racial conflict in Southern Africa could ignite volatile racial situations far from that region.

Second, sanctions create an international milieu which will continue to be useful in prompting somewhat more caution than otherwise would obtain respecting the support of Pretoria and Lisbon for the rebel regime, or the reactions of the white regimes toward contiguous black-controlled states or possibly in some cases even the actions of the Rhodesian regime toward its own African population. Correspondingly, a continuing international involvement, hopefully including Britain as primus inter pares, could one day be helpful in providing an intermediary agency or conceivably even an intervening force should the confrontation within Rhodesia become truly critical.

Finally, sanctions oblige that members of the world community explicitly take sides on an issue of central importance to the future

---

* See above, pp. 139–41.

organization of Southern Africa. International pressure has increased Rhodesia's reliance on South Africa, but at the same time the
Rhodesian issue has complicated South Africa's task of organizing a
regional system subject to influence from Pretoria *and* free from
external interference. Sanctions indicate to Rhodesia's Africans (and
to exposed and vulnerable governments in Zambia and Botswana)
that they are not alone in their confrontation with the white power
structure of Southern Africa. Thus international involvement, while
offering no means of rescue, adds something to the legitimacy of the
struggle. Perhaps most significant of all, sanctions publicly commit
governments which otherwise would drift, under the pressure of
private financial and commercial interests, towards significant
de facto support of the rebel regime. In this way, sanctions help to
arrest a long term and ominous trend which has aligned the major
Western powers generally on the side of the white regimes and communist governments strongly on the side of African liberation. This
of course is exactly what the white regimes of Southern Africa *and* the
communists are promoting – the identification of the West with the
white power structure of the area. Nothing could be more dangerous
to Western interests throughout Africa and in other areas of the
world marked by racial tension than to permit the development of an
ideological overlay on racial polarization in Southern Africa.

None of the foregoing reasons for continuing sanctions depends
upon their more rigorous enforcement. That is fortunate because,
though desirable, it is not likely.* Indeed the problem will be to
maintain sanctions at all, together with the international involvement
they signify. We shall almost certainly fail to do so unless somehow
we can grasp the historical depth of the drama slowly unfolding
before us throughout that troubled region. It is perhaps worth

---

* Most schemes for strengthening sanctions call for improvements
in the work of the Security Council's Sanctions Committee. As of
June 1972, Britain had called to the attention of the Committee 170
cases of suspected breaches; in only four cases have prosecutions
been made. It is true that the U.N. Secretariat might have played a
more vigorous role under less flaccid leadership. However, schemes
for creating an international inspectorate to conduct on-the-spot
investigations of suspect cargoes (almost invariably identified by
British Intelligence) are probably non-starters. Such an inspectorate
could not do the job as effectively as national governments. And if
governments were willing to bring in international inspectors, they
would, one supposes, be willing to do the job themselves. The single
most important action to strengthen sanctions at the time of writing
would be to reverse the breach of chrome sanctions by the U.S.
Congress.

remembering in this connection that the most venerable political organization in Southern Africa, predating even the ruling Nationalist Party of the Afrikaner people, is the African National Congress of South Africa, after which Bishop Muzorewa's A.N.C. (like other movements before it) has styled itself. For more than a half a century the African National Congress has survived repeated repression and persecution – and in the process has given us Africa's only Nobel prizewinner, Chief Albert Luthuli.

Nor shall we respond with adequate sensitivity unless we can disentangle the central theme of the drama from the admitted complexities of the plot and the torment of the many antagonists. It has to do with the gradual and ponderous assertion of their rights and dignity by huge black populations against greatly privileged and desperately resistant white minorities. 'It is one thing to try, to fail, and to try again,' once commented Tanzania's President, Julius Nyerere, referring to the well-nigh universal struggle for racial and ethnic equality. 'It is an entirely different matter to base the whole structure of your society on the denial of human rights. With a society of that kind, we compromise at our peril. For ultimately humanity will not be denied.'

It is of course foolish to try to place a time-table on a drama of these enormous proportions. It is equally foolish to presume that because sentimental or stupid expectations have remained unfulfilled the drama is therefore not taking place, or that the *dramatis personae* have been wrongly identified, or that a dénouement will not have to be reached in the fullness of time. And the reckoning which will accompany it will affect regions far from Southern Africa – none perhaps more than Britain and America.

Bibliographical Notes

The interested reader should take note at the outset of a small collection of books directly related, in whole or in part, to the Rhodesian rebellion. (Other historical works are listed elsewhere in these notes.) For background to U.D.I., the two best studies are James Barber, *Rhodesia: The Road to Rebellion*, London and New York: Oxford University Press, 1967, and Frank Clements, *Rhodesia: The Course to Collision*, London: Pall Mall Press, 1969. In addition, the reader should consult the following: for a 'government establishment' view, Sir Roy Welensky, *Welensky's 4,000 Days*, London: Collins, 1964; for a view sympathetic to the Rhodesian rebel regime, Andrew Skeen, *Prelude to Independence*, Cape Town: Nasionale Boekhandel, 1966; for a vigorous dissent from the prevailing white view in Rhodesia, Judith Todd, *Rhodesia*, London: MacGibbon and Key, 1966; and for an account written from the point of view of Rhodesian African nationalism, Nathan Shamuyarira, *Crisis in Rhodesia*, London: André Deutsch, 1965.

There are no adequate studies of U.D.I. and its aftermath. A compilation of a few of the principal events is found in Donald Smith, *Rhodesia: The Problem*, London: Robert Maxwell, 1969. A ponderous review written from the perspective of the Rhodesian Government is Kenneth Young's *Rhodesia and Independence: A Study in British Colonial Policy*, London: J. M. Dent and Sons, 1969. For the British Labour Government's interpretation, see the relevant passages in Harold Wilson, *The Labour Government 1964–1970: A Personal Record*, London: Weidenfeld and Nicolson and Michael Joseph, 1971. And for many of these developments as they affected Zambia, see the excellent book by Richard Hall, *The High Price of Principles: Kaunda and the White South*, London: Hodder and Stoughton, 1969.

The present study relies on two kinds of sources. It makes use of insights deriving from a residence of almost four years in Zambia as

American Ambassador and, more importantly, some 300 interviews (many of them privileged) conducted since leaving government service. These unattributable materials have generally been supplemental to data available in the public domain, the second major source. The account given in this book has been built upon an exhaustive reading of British publications including the London *Times* and the *Sunday Times*; the *Observer*, particularly the columns of Colin Legum; the *Guardian* (formerly the *Manchester Guardian*), paying particular attention to the stories filed by John Worrall and Patrick Keatley; the *Financial Times*, with special reference to materials submitted by Anthony Hawkins and J. D. F. Jones; *The Economist;* and *Africa Confidential*.

Non-British publications, read more selectively, included the *New York Times*, the *Rhodesia Herald*, the *Times of Zambia*, *Die Burger*, the *Rand Daily Mail*, the *Johannesburg Star*, the Johannesburg *Financial Mail*, and on occasion other South African publications. An exhaustive review was also made of all British Parliamentary debates on Rhodesia, while more selective coverage was given to Parliamentary debates in Rhodesia and South Africa. Finally the verbatim reports of all United Nations Security Council debates on Rhodesia since U.D.I. were canvassed.

The notes which follow, arranged by chapter, do not even attempt to record the material deriving from the above sources which helped in constructing the narrative. That would have meant writing a companion volume to the present one. Rather they are highly selective, singling out only the most significant materials which the discerning reader may wish to consult, including here and there sources and materials supplemental to those actually used in the text.

◇   ◇   ◇

Chapter I. 11 November 1965

The best and most comprehensive source of reporting on 11 November 1965, and its immediate aftermath is *The Times*. Debates and exchanges in the Westminster Parliament on 11 and 12 November 1965 provide useful insights into the positions of the three British parties. See also Mollie Panter-Downes, 'Letter from London', *New Yorker*, 41:198–202 ff., 27 November 1965, as well as her subsequent article, *New Yorker*, 41:225 ff., 11 December 1965. A useful survey is found in Donald Rothchild, 'Rhodesian Rebellion and African Response', *African Quarterly*, 6:184–96, 1966. Two thoughtful essays dealing with the problems the United Kingdom faced in achieving its policy ends through sanctions are found in Grant Hugo,

Britain in Tomorrow's World: Principles of Foreign Policy, London: Chatto and Windus, 1969, pp. 112–21; and Brian Crozier, *The Masters of Power*, Boston: Little, Brown, 1969, pp. 285–303. The Harold Isaacs quote is from the essay, 'Color in World Affairs', *Foreign Affairs*, 47:235–50, January 1969.

Chapter II. Prelude to Rebellion

Of Pioneers and Imperialists. A number of books offer excellent historical background: T. O. Ranger, *Revolt in Southern Rhodesia*, London: Heinemann, 1967, and Evanston: Northwestern University Press, 1968; Clements, *op. cit.*; L. H. Gann, *A History of Southern Rhodesia: Early Days to 1934*, London: Chatto and Windus, 1965; Richard Gray, *Two Nations*, London: Oxford University Press, 1960; A. J. Hanna, *The Story of Rhodesia and Nyasaland*, London: Faber and Faber, 1965; Patrick Keatley, *The Politics of Partnership*, London: Penguin Books, 1963; Colin Leys, *European Politics in Southern Rhodesia*, London: Oxford University Press, 1959; Philip Mason, *The Birth of a Dilemma*, London: Oxford University Press, 1958; Claire Palley, *The Constitutional History and Law of Southern Rhodesia, 1888–1965*, London: Oxford University Press, 1966; and Lord C. Alport, *Sudden Assignment*, London: Hodder and Stoughton, 1965.

Collision Course. For the effect of Rhodesian–British consultations which often preceded legislation in Rhodesia affecting Africans, see Palley, *op. cit.*, pp. 68–9. See also Jack Halpern, 'Britain's Complicity in Rhodesia's Race Laws', *Race Today*, 4:2, Feb. 1972, p. 37. Huggins's account of his conversations with Creech Jones is found *inter alia* in 'Where We Went Awry', Parts One and Two, *Rhodesia Herald*, 21 and 22 January 1969. These long articles contain much fascinating material. A pithy account of why Rhodesia expected it would proceed to full Dominion status is found in the essay by Charles Burton Marshall, 'Crisis Over Rhodesia: A Skeptical View', Studies in International Affairs, Number 3, Baltimore: The Johns Hopkins Press, 1967.

For the Malvern–Welensky period, including the Federation, see Philip Mason, *Year of Decision: Rhodesia and Nyasaland in 1960*, London: Oxford University Press, 1960; E. M. Clegg, *Race and Politics: Partnership in the Federation of Rhodesia and Nyasaland*, London: Oxford University Press, 1960; Welensky, *op. cit.*; and Alport, *op. cit.* The two best accounts of this period by African nationalists are Ndabaningi Sithole, *African Nationalism*, London:

Oxford University Press, 1954; and Shamuyarira, *op. cit.* The Monckton Report on the future of Federation is available from H.M. Stationery Office, London, under the title, *The Report of the Advisory Commission on the Review of the Constitution of Rhodesia and Nyasaland*, 11 October 1960.

An excellent account of the Whitehead years, the 1961 constitution and the emergence of the Rhodesian Front is found in Barber, *op. cit.*, pp. 20–195. Sociological insights and attitudinal factors as they affected Rhodesian politics are found in Cyril A. Rogers and C. Frantz, *Racial Themes in Southern Rhodesia*, New Haven: Yale University Press, 1962.

Mr. Smith Goes to London. I am indebted to John Worrall for his reference to Smith's unrevolutionary demeanour in ' "Our Independence is Real", says Ian Smith,' *New York Times Magazine*, pp. 40–66, 27 October 1968. Charles Burton Marshall, *op. cit.*, among others, gives a trenchant account of Rhodesian anxieties over possible U.N. or Commonwealth initiatives against Rhodesia. Invaluable accounts of exchanges between Rhodesia and London, detailing the position of each side from March 1963 to U.D.I. in November 1965, are found in the British White Papers, Cmnd. 2073 and Cmnd. 2807 available from H.M. Stationery Office, London. Smith's London visit is detailed in the latter, pp. 21–39.

Mr. Wilson Goes to Salisbury. For a hard-hitting review of Labour Party policy and particularly that of Mr. Wilson on Rhodesia, see Paul Foot, *The Politics of Harold Wilson*, London: Penguin Books, 1968, pp. 249–70. Events in Rhodesia from the advent of the Wilson administration to U.D.I. are admirably handled in Barber, *op. cit.*, pp. 196–305. The same period seen from the white Rhodesian point of view is found in Kenneth Young, *op. cit.*, pp. 163–299. Harold Wilson's own account, *op. cit.*, is found in Chapters 2, 6, 10 and 11. Records of Smith's conversations with Wilson in London, 7–11 October 1965, are found on pp. 69–95, *Southern Rhodesia: Documents Relating to the Negotiations between the United Kingdom and the Southern Rhodesian Governments, November 1963–November 1965*, Cmnd. 2807, while Wilson's meetings in Salisbury, 26–29 October 1965, are recorded on pp. 102–32 of the same document.

For supplemental material, see Margery Perham, 'The Rhodesian Crisis: The Background', *International Affairs*, 42:1–13, 19 January 1966; J. Lelyveld, 'Mr. Smith Draws the Line in Africa', *New York Times Magazine*, p. 22, 22 August 1965; and M. Cable, 'We and They in Rhodesia', *New Yorker*, 41:36–41, 19 February 1966. For Smith's views, see, 'Other Side of the Rhodesian Story; Interview with I. D. Smith by A. J. Meyers', *U.S. News*, 59:68–72, 8 November 1965, and Ian Smith, 'Rhodesia: A Personal View', *Punch*, 250: 110–12, 26 January 1966.

Chapter III. Issues and Instruments

The Matter of Force. A few articles dealing with this subject are worth perusing: William Gutteridge, 'Rhodesia: The Use of Military Force', *World Today*, 21:499–503, Dec. 1965; Robert Sutcliffe, 'The Use of Force in Rhodesia', *Venture*, 19:5–7, April 1967; P. C. Rao, 'The Rhodesian Crisis and the Use of Force', *African Quarterly*, 6:285–96, Jan.–Mar. 1967; Neville Brown, 'Military Sanctions Against Rhodesia', *Venture*, 17:7–12, January 1966.

The matter was frequently alluded to in the British press. See particularly the exchanges between the Defence Correspondent of *The Times* and Government officials as reported in that newspaper 4–5 August 1965. See also the reports on Commonwealth Secretary Arthur Bottomley's discussion of force in the *Guardian*, 11 August 1965, and in *The Times*, 12 and 18 August 1965. Other selected articles or editorials for the balance of 1965 appeared in *The Times* on 7 August, 4, 9, 18 October, and 13, 15 November 1965; in the *Guardian* on 5, 8, 9, 11, 29 October, 1, 2, 13, 18, 26 November and 6, 10, 22 December 1965; in the *Observer*, 3, 10, 31 October and 14, 21 November 1965; and in the *Sunday Times*, 21, 28 November 1965. For a brief and to-the-point discussion of some of the repercussions and implications of the decision to return the Federation's Air Force to Southern Rhodesia, see Hall, *op. cit.*, p. 99.

A useful survey of British public opinion on Rhodesia during this period is Eric Silver's 'Mr. Wilson, the Public and Rhodesia', *Venture*, 18:4–5, February 1966. See also H. Brandon, 'Future of Rhodesia: Extremes of Political Opinion in Britain', *Saturday Review*, 48:9, 25 December 1965. Peter Calvocoressi for the Africa Publications Trust put out a summary of opinion polls on Rhodesia dated September 1968. For a fee, the Gallup organization in London will make available to the scholar the results of its polls. In addition the National Opinion Polls, Ltd. of the *Daily Mail* should be consulted.

The Sanctions Arsenal. The orders approved consequent on the passage of the Southern Rhodesia Bill are summarized in *Parliamentary Debates*, Commons, Vol. 721, cols. 522–714, 24 November 1965. Generally optimistic assessments of the impact of sanctions prevailed. See, for example, 'Tackling Rhodesia', *The Economist*,

13 November 1965 and estimates in *The Times*, 30 October, 24 November, and 2 December. Many of the more optimistic assumptions were reviewed by Russell Warren Howe, 'How Tight Is the Squeeze?', *Reporter*, 33:29–32, 2 December 1965. An early critical assessment is found in R. B. Sutcliffe, *Sanctions Against Rhodesia: The Economic Background*, London: The Africa Bureau, 21 January 1966. Dudley Seers's chapter is found on pp. 83–109 of Hugh Thomas, ed., *Crisis in the Civil Service*, London: Anthony Blond, 1968.

Problems at the U.N. A comprehensive review is found in J. Leo Cefkin, 'The Rhodesian Question at the United Nations', *International Organization*, 22:649–69, Summer 1968. An analysis of the changed circumstances which prompted Britain to bring the issue to the U.N. is found in Alex C. Castles, 'Law and Politics in the Rhodesian Dispute', *Australian Outlook*, 21:165–78, August 1967. See also 'Rhodesia Case at the U.N. Legal Basis Questioned', *Christian Science Monitor*, 16 December 1966 (Western Edition). The debates in the U.N. Security Council took place at the 1257–1265th meetings, 12–20 November 1965. The resolution was adopted at the 1265th meeting as S/RES/217 (1965). The reaction of the Tories to the Security Council resolution was fully reported by *The Times*, 23 November 1965. The debate in the Commons took place on the same day.

The Rebel Response. The confrontation between the regime and Gibbs was extensively reported in *The Times*. See, for example, stories filed on 13, 15–20, 24, 25, 27, 30 November, 3, 4, 9, 31 December 1965 and 1, 7 January 1966. Palley's expulsion from the Rhodesian Parliament is found in Rhodesia Legislative Assembly Debates, Vol. 62, 1965, cols. 1939–42. A review of church–state relations is found in *The Times*, 5 January 1966; see also Richard Brown, 'Prospects in Rhodesia', *Current History*, 52:162–7, March 1967. The stand of the Catholic Bishops has been particularly noteworthy. See *Shield*, a monthly magazine of the Catholic Church in Rhodesia and *Rhodesia – The Moral Issue*, Pastoral Letters of the Catholic Bishops, published by the Rhodesia Catholic Bishops' Conference, Gwelo: Mambo Press, 1968. Dissent at the University College of Rhodesia was recurrent. As just one example, see the booklet *We Protest!*, Proceedings of the 'Week of Protest', (18–21 May 1969) Teach-In on the Present Political Trends in Rhodesia, Editors: A. L. P. McAdam and T. I. Matthews, 1969.

As to general events in Rhodesia during this period, including sanctions, day-to-day reporting was extensive in many London papers, particularly *The Times*. Some interesting background for this period was provided in C. Trillon, 'Letter from Salisbury', *New Yorker*, 42:139–40, 12 November 1966, and J. Leo Cefkin, 'How Long Can Rhodesia Last?' *Reporter*, 34:42–5, 10 February 1966.

Chapter IV. Zambia and the 'Quick Kill'

Dealing with 'Hypothetical Situations'. General discussions of the economic implications for Zambia of U.D.I. in Rhodesia, as well as Zambia's efforts to meet these contingencies, include: Richard Hall, *op. cit.*, pp. 95–177; Richard L. Sklar, 'Zambia's Response to U.D.I.', *Mawazo*, 1:11–32, June 1968; F. Taylor Ostrander, 'Zambia in the Aftermath of Rhodesian U.D.I.: Logistical and Economic Problems', *African Forum*, 2:50–65, Winter 1967; R. B. Sutcliffe, 'Zambia and the Strains of U.D.I.', *The World Today*, 23:506–11, December 1967; and pp. 15–22 of Mike Faber's *Zambia – The Moulding of a Nation*, pamphlet privately printed in England, 1968. For a thorough analysis of the economic interrelationships between Rhodesia and Zambia, see Shirley Williams, *Central Africa: The Economics of Inequality*, London: The Africa Bureau, 1960. A review of the unified transport system is provided in Edwin T. Haefele and Eleanor B. Steinberg, *Government Controls on Transport: An African Case*, Washington, D.C.: The Brookings Institution, 1965.

For general studies of Zambia, see particularly Richard Hall, *Zambia*, London: Pall Mall, 1965; Kenneth D. Kaunda, *Zambia Shall Be Free*, London: Heinemann, 1962; Colin Legum (ed.), *Zambia, Independence and Beyond: The Speeches of Kenneth Kaunda*, London: Nelson, 1966. For an insight into the philosophy of Kaunda himself, see Kenneth D. Kaunda, *A Humanist in Africa*, London: Longmans, 1966.

The Crisis of Confidence. The debate concerning the dispatch of aircraft and troops to Zambia was extensively covered in *The Times*. See particularly reports in the issues of 18, 23, 24, 27, 29, 30 November and 1, 2, 4 December 1965. The principal debate in the Commons took place on 1 December 1965. See *Parliamentary Debates*, Commons, Vol. 721, cols. 1429–1441.

Pressure from the O.A.U. Again the most comprehensive reporting is found in *The Times*. See articles in issues for 3–6, 8, 9, 11, 13–18, 20 December 1965. A general review is found in Anirudha Gupta's 'The Rhodesian Crisis and the O.A.U.', *International Studies* (New Delhi), 9:55–64, July 1967.

Zambia at the Brink; 'The Quick Kill'; From Lagos to Lusaka; 'The Long Haul'. Once again, the best public sources for these events are *The Times* and the *Sunday Times* which should be consulted from 9 December 1965, to mid February 1966 for an account of the oil embargo, the airlift, U.K. contingency aid, the coal surcharge crisis, the Commonwealth meeting in Lagos, Wilson's visit to Lusaka and the abortive 15 February deadline. For Wilson's discussion of his views on reconstructing Rhodesia see the exchanges in Parliament 25 January 1966, *Parliamentary Debates*, Commons, Vol. 723, cols. 1–9.

Chapter V. Oil 'Spills' in Southern Africa

Beit Bridge on the Limpopo. Stories appeared virtually daily in the *Rand Daily Mail* from 1 February 1966. They were germane to the story for the next three weeks. Prime Minister Verwoerd's New Year's Day message was carried by, among other papers, *Die Transvaler*, 1 January 1966. The debates on Rhodesia are found in the South Africa House of Assembly Debates, Fifth Session, Second Parliament, Vol. 16, 25 January 1966, pp. 18–86. For additional evidence respecting the increasing flow of oil supplies, see *Die Burger*, 17 February 1966, and the *Cape Times*, 21 February 1966, as well as *The Times* for this period, particularly 14, 19, 21 and 22 February. Diplomatic exchanges are reported in *The Times* of 17, 18, 21 and 23 February and of course were widely reported in the South African press; see for example *Die Transvaler*, 18 February 1966, and the *Cape Argus*, 19 February 1966. Verwoerd's 28 February speech was extensively reported in both the *Johannesburg Star* and the *Rand Daily Mail* of 1 March 1966.

Tankers Away! For a comprehensive account of the *Joanna V* episode, see the report compiled by the 'Insight Team' in the *Sunday Times*, 10 April 1966. For Portugal's policy on Rhodesia the official statement issued in Lisbon on 25 November 1965, should be consulted; and for its policy on the *Joanna V*, the official statement of 6 April 1966. Both are found in the document entitled *Portuguese Foreign Policy*, Ministry of Foreign Affairs, 1965–7. Portugal's policy toward Zambia was outlined by the Portuguese Foreign Minister in a statement appearing in the *Daily Telegraph* of 30 December 1965. See also *The Times*, 27 January and 1 February 1966, and the official statements, 'Talks Between Zambia, Malawi and Portugal on Transport Problems', 28 February 1966, and 'Oil

Supplies to Zambia and Malawi', 29 April 1966, found in *Portuguese Foreign Policy, op. cit.*

Reports of the construction of special storage tanks in Beira were carried by *The Times*, 2–4 March 1966. British surveillance in the Mozambique Channel and accompanying protests, as well as the problem of the pipeline were recorded in reports published in *The Times*, particularly 5–7, 12, 17, 28 January, 23 February, 4, 8–12, 14–17, 19, 21–24, 28–31 March, 1, 2, 4–7 April. Lord Walston's Lisbon trip received attention in stories appearing in *The Times* of 7, 8 April 1966, and in an official Portuguese Government statement dated 8 April and titled 'Lord Walston's Visit to Lisbon – Demand of the British Government for a Meeting of the Security Council', published in *Portuguese Foreign Policy, op. cit.*

The Beira Resolution. The legal problems involved in stopping the *Joanna V* were discussed in a thoughtful *Times* editorial of 5 April. The Beira Resolution (S/RES/221 (1966) was passed after two meetings of the Security Council (the 1276th and 1277th) on 9 April 1966. Reactions to the resolution were reported in *The Times* of 12 April 1966. Portuguese positions were set forth in a series of documents: 'On the Resolution of the Security Council on the Question of Rhodesia', 28 April 1966; 'Comment on Portugal's Position on the Rhodesian Affair', 3 May 1966; 'Correspondence with the United Nations Secretary-General Analysed', 12 July 1966; 'Portugal and the Transit Problems of Landlocked Countries', 12 July 1966; and 'Portugal Doubts the Legitimacy of British Action in the Mozambique Channel', 29 July 1966 – all published in *Portuguese Foreign Policy, op. cit.*

A debate ensued over the legality of U.N. Security Council actions under Chapter VII of the Charter, gathering momentum as a result of subsequent Security Council meetings and actions in December 1966. Dean Acheson led a spirited and articulate campaign against U.N. intervention, claiming it both illegal and unwise. A number of his articles were collected in a pamphlet entitled 'Dean Acheson on the Rhodesian Question' and distributed by the Rhodesian Information Office, 2852 McGill Terrace, N.W., Washington, D.C. Equally energetic rebuttals came from many sources. See Arthur J. Goldberg, Letter to the Editor, *Washington Post*, 8 January 1967; Rosalind Higgins, 'International Law, Rhodesia, and the U.N.', *World Today*, 23:94–106, March 1967; Myres S. McDougal and W. Michael Reisman, 'Rhodesia and the U.N.: The Lawfulness of International Concern', *American Journal of International Law*, 62:1–19, January 1968; Thomas Franck, *Legality of Mandatory U.N. Sanctions Against Rhodesia*, Policy Paper, Center for International

Studies, New York University, 1968; and Ralph Zacklin, 'Challenge of Rhodesia', *International Conciliation*, No. 575, November 1969.

'One Miserable Tanker . . .' Activities relating to both the *Joanna V* and the *Manuela* following the Beira Resolution were summarized in reports in *The Times* of 9, 11–16, 18, 19 April and 9, 11, 19, 25 May 1966. Ian Smith's early morning broadcast of 16 April was reported in detail in *The Times* of 18 April 1966. The question of the continuing oil leak and its implications for Anglo-South African relations exercised both the British and South African press. See reports in *The Times* for 14–16, 18–21 April 1966. See *Die Vaterland*, 12, 20 April 1966; the *Rand Daily Mail*, 11, 15, 18, 19, 21 April 1966; the *Johannesburg Star*, 11, 18 April 1966; the *Cape Times*, 13, 18 April 1966; *Die Transvaler*, 15 April 1966; and *Die Burger*, 15, 16, 22 April 1966; the *Rand Daily Mail*, 11, 15, 18, 19, 21, April 1966; the South Africa, see Dennis Austin, *Britain and South Africa*, London: Oxford University Press, 1966. For Portugal's position, see 'Oil Supplies to Rhodesia from Mozambique', 11 May 1966, published in *Portuguese Foreign Policy, op. cit.*

Chapter VI. Talks About Talks

Talking about 'Talks' in Britain. A number of visits to Rhodesia, principally unofficial, were made prior to those directly leading to 'talks'. M.P.s who flew in included Sir Godfrey Nicholson, Reginald Paget, Peter Bessell, David Ennals, Christopher Rowland, Jeremy Bray, Patrick Wall and Jeremy Thorpe. These visits were covered by *The Times* in stories appearing between 30 December 1965 and 13 January 1966. The Rhodesian Chief Justice, Sir Hugh Beadle, visited London from 18 to 24 January 1966. See *The Times* particularly for 19, 20 January 1966. Assistant Under-Secretary at the Commonwealth Relations Office, Noel Duncan Watson, arrived in Salisbury in mid March for a two-week visit. Stories in *The Times* of 17, 18, 23 and 29 March 1966, summarized his visit. Selwyn Lloyd's nine-day trip during the first half of February was extensively covered by *The Times* in reports appearing on 4, 5, 7–12, 14–17, 19, 21 February 1966. For his report to the Conservative Shadow Cabinet see *The Times* for 22 February 1966. See also his later statement in Parliament, *Parliamentary Debates*, Commons, 1966–7, Vol. 727, 27 April 1966, cols. 743–4. A visit to Rhodesia by Lord Bolton in mid April was reported in *The Times* of 15, 16 April 1966.

J. Oliver Wright's mission to Salisbury was widely reported. See for example reports in *The Times* for 27–29 April 1966. Smith's statement in Rhodesia's Parliament on 26 April 1966 was fully covered in *The Times* of the following day. The principal debates in the Commons during this period took place on 31 January, 16 February and 27 April 1966. Conservative views were outlined in an article by Edward Heath, 'Rhodesia: The Conservative View', which appeared in *Punch*, 250:146–8, 2 February 1966. For selected reports on Rhodesia as an issue in the election campaign, see *The Times* for 12, 15, 19, 21, 22, 28–30 March 1966. For Wilson's earlier views repudiating any possibility of negotiating with Smith, see particularly, *Parliamentary Debates*, Commons, Vol. 722, 10 December 1965, col. 771, and 21 December 1965, col. 1928.

Listening to the News in Lusaka. Reports of President Kaunda's reaction to 'talks' were carried in *The Times* of 29, 30 April, and 2 May 1966. For an example of his earlier views expressed during the British election campaign see the *Times of Zambia*, 21 March 1966.

The Talks with Salisbury Begin. Scant attention is given in official British documents to the talks in London and Salisbury in May, June and August 1966. See *Rhodesia: Documents Relating to Proposals for a Settlement 1966*, Cmnd. 3171, pp. 4–5. The Rhodesian document, *Relations between the Rhodesian Government and the United Kingdom November 1965–December 1966*, C.S.R. 49–1966 gives somewhat more detail. See pp. 16–27, particularly pp. 21–2. For analytical articles about the talks see *The Times* for 1, 5, 8, 9 May, 1, 12, 19, 21 (editorial) June, 5, 6 (editorial) and 21 August 1966. A comprehensive wrap-up is provided by C. Johnson, 'Rhodesia – The Balance Sheet', *Financial Times*, 29 July 1966.

Another Look at Zambian Sanctions; The Commonwealth Affair. An overview of the continuing crisis in Zambian–British relations and negotiations respecting contingency aid can be gleaned from articles in *The Times* on the following dates: 10 (editorial), 23, 24 May, 2, 7, 16, 17, 30 June and 13, 21, 22 July 1966. See also the *Guardian*, 19 May and 8 June 1966; and the *Sunday Times*, 17, 24 July 1966. A thorough review of London–Lusaka aid relations is found in 'Some Aspects of British Aid to Zambia', *Central African Research Bulletin-6*, published by the Central Africa Research Office, 4 November 1968. For Britain's economic problems during this period see, for example, Harold Wilson's memoirs, *op. cit.*, pp. 183, 227–41. A review of the railway crisis of May and June 1966 may be had by scanning *The Times* for 16, 18–21, 24 (editorial), 27, 30, 31 May and 6, 9, 11, 14, 18, 22, 30 June 1966. See also *The Economist* of 28 May 1966, pp. 933–4. For the quotation from Dominic Mulaisho, I am indebted to Richard Hall, *The High Price of Principles*, *op. cit.*, pp. 163–4. His perceptive summary of these events is worth careful reading. The quote from President Kaunda is from an article by him published in the *Sunday Times* of 4 September 1966.

Chapter VII. 'NIBMAR'

Confrontation at Marlborough House. For a broad discussion of the post-war Commonwealth, see Nicholas Mansergh, *The Commonwealth Experience*, New York: Praeger, 1969; J. D. B. Miller, *The Commonwealth and the World*, London: Gerald Duckworth and Co., 3rd edition, 1965; and Derek Ingram, *Commonwealth for a Colour-Blind World*, London: George Allen and Unwin, 1965. In addition to the daily reports in the London press, two wrap-ups are of particular interest: 'The Night They Saved the Commonwealth', the *Observer*, 18 September 1966; and the feature by the 'Insight Team', 'How Everyone Won', the *Sunday Times*, 18 September 1966. The concluding assessment of Wilson and Pearson was quoted by Claire Sterling in 'Mr. Wilson Squeaks Through', *Reporter*, 35:32–3, 6 October 1966. The text of the final *communiqué* of the Commonwealth Prime Ministers' Meeting as it related to Rhodesia is found at Appendix A, pp. 13–15, Cmnd. 3171, *op. cit.*

'Negotiations about Negotiations'. A documentary review of the British–Rhodesian exchanges of September to November 1966 is found at Appendices B through I, pp. 16–37, Cmnd. 3171, *op. cit.* The same documents are presented, together with summaries of principal discussions prepared by the Rhodesians, on pp. 32–87 in C.S.R. 49–1966, *op. cit.*

Preparations for the Summit. These events were copiously covered in the press. Nora Beloff's well-informed account of Wilson's decision to meet Smith at Gibraltar published in the *Observer*, 4 December 1966, is instructive. So too is Mr. Wilson's own account in Chapter 17 of his *The Labour Government 1964–1970: A Personal Record*, *op. cit.* For the Rhodesian issue within the Labour Party, see the *Report of the Sixty-fifth Annual Conference of the Labour Party, Brighton, 1966*, published by the Labour Party, Transport House, Smith Square, London S.W.1, pp. 276–86. See also articles on Labour back-bench activity in both *The Times* and the *Guardian*, 8 November 1966. Concerning U.K.–U.S. talks prior to *Tiger*, see 'U.S. and U.K. Hold Talks on Southern Rhodesia – Joint Statement', *Department of State Bulletin*, 55:965, 26 December 1966.

H.M.S. 'Tiger'. Detailed records of the *Tiger* negotiations are found in the British version pp. 38–103, Cmnd. 3171, *op. cit.*, and in the Rhodesian version pp. 88–136, C.S.R. 49–1966, *op. cit.* See also the Rhodesian white paper, *Rhodesia Independence Constitution: Proposals for a Settlement Contained in the Working Document Produced at the Conference aboard H.M.S. Tiger*, C.S.R. 6-1967. Much supplemental information can be gleaned from articles by the 'Insight Team', 'Getting off the Hook', and 'Tiger Summit: The Inside Story', in the *Sunday Times*, 4 and 11 December 1966. Wilson's report to Parliament can be found in *Parliamentary Debates*, Commons, 1966–7, Vol. 737, 5 December 1966, cols. 1053–70. Numerous critiques have appeared. For a pro-Rhodesian view, see James Jackson Kilpatrick, René Albert Wormser, Walter Darnell Jacobs, 'Rhodesia: A Case History', *National Review*, 19:512–26, 16 May 1967; for an anti-Rhodesian (and anti-British) view see the lengthy analysis by Leo Baron published in the *Times of Zambia*, 1 September 1967.

The Collapse of Consensus. The high points of the debate on Rhodesia in the Commons on 7 and 8 December 1966 are found in *Parliamentary Debates*, Commons, 1966–7, Vol. 737, 7 December 1966, cols. 1389–1487; 8 December 1966, cols. 1587–1710. Examples of Wilson's later evasiveness concerning NIBMAR are found in *Parliamentary Debates*, Commons, 1966–7, Vol. 737, 5 December 1966, cols. 1076–7; Vol. 738, 20 December 1966, cols. 1176–80, 1182–3; Vol. 739, 19 January 1967, col. 653; Vol. 744, 13 April 1967, col. 1366.

Chapter VIII. Over to the United Nations

Selective Mandatory Sanctions. Concerning Rhodesia, the U.N. Security Council sat from 8 through 16 December 1966, encompassing meetings 1331–3 and 1335–40. Resolution S/RES/232/(1966) was adopted at the final meeting. A summary of South Africa's reaction to selective mandatory sanctions is found in *The Times*, 30 December 1966, and 2 January 1967. Portugal's position is presented in a letter from Foreign Minister Franco Nogueira to the Secretary-General of the U.N. dated 3 February 1967. A letter of the same date reports Portuguese losses consequent on sanctions, and a subsequent claim was contained in a letter from Franco Nogueira to the President of the Security Council dated 22 September 1967. Data concerning the nationality of tankers entering Lourenço Marques harbour between April 1966 and May 1967 was provided in a Portuguese official statement of 12 June 1967. All of these materials are collected in a document entitled *Portuguese Foreign Policy*, Ministry of Foreign Affairs, 1965–7, prepared by the Government of Portugal. For a comprehensive review of the Portuguese position, see Franco Nogueira's letter to the *Financial Times*, 13 February 1967, and a report by Roy Lewis in *The Times* on 8 June 1967, of an interview with the Portuguese Foreign Minister.

A brief review of the coal crisis in Zambia can be had by scanning reports in *The Times* for 5, 9, 17, 21 October and 5, 7, 14, 17 November 1966. A summary is provided in the *Wall Street Journal* of 13 June 1967. For an account of sabotage and espionage in Zambia, see Hall, *op. cit.*, Chapter 12, 'White Friends and White Spies', pp. 178–88. Richard Hall has also summarized Zambia's problems in 'Kaunda's Long Road to Dar', *Venture*, 20:5, May 1968, pp. 21–4. See too 'Zambia and Rhodesia: Effects of the Sanctions Policy', *Central Africa Research – 2*, published by the Central Africa Research Office, 12 March 1968. The Zambian position on selective mandatory sanctions was spelled out in a letter from the Zambian representative to the U.N. to the Secretary-General dated 23 February 1967 (S/7783).

Concerning the notion put forward by H.M. Government that the U.N., in enacting selective mandatory sanctions, had now assumed a measure of responsibility for Rhodesia, see for example exchanges in the Commons involving Frederick Mulley, Minister of State for Foreign Affairs, *Parliamentary Debates*, Commons, Vol. 757, cols. 14, 15, 22 January 1968, and Vol. 756, cols. 4, 5, 20 May 1968.

Measuring the Sanctions Bite. For general documentation, see *U.N. Economic Survey on Rhodesia 1966–67*, A/AC. 109/L. 445; *Economic Survey of Rhodesia* for 1967 and 1968, Central Statistical Office, Salisbury; *Public Sector Investment 1968–71*, C.S.R. 16-1968; and *Government of Rhodesia Budget Statements for 1967, 1968*, the Government Printer, Salisbury.

Two excellent theoretical discussions of sanctions are found in Johann Galtung, 'On the Effects of International Economic Sanctions with Examples from the Case of Rhodesia', *World Politics*, 19:378– 416, April 1967, and Fredrik Hoffmann, 'The Functions of Economic Sanctions: A Comparative Analysis', *Journal of Peace Research*, 4:140–60, 1967. The best reporting on the Rhodesian economy is found in the London *Financial Times* (note especially the pieces by Anthony Hawkins) and in the Johannesburg *Financial Mail* (particularly articles by Karl Keyter). See also the following analyses: R. B. Sutcliffe, *Sanctions Against Rhodesia: The Economic Background*, *op. cit.*; Sir Roy Welensky, 'Sanctions Will Not Break Rhodesia',

Indian and Foreign Review, 4:10–11, 15 February 1967; R. B. Sutcliffe and Brian Lapping, 'The Rhodesian Budget, 1966 . . . and Emigration Figures', *Venture*, 18:4–6, September 1966; Timothy Curtin and David Murray, 'Economic Sanctions and Rhodesia', Research Monograph 12, published by the Institute of Economic Affairs, September 1967; R. B. Sutcliffe, 'Rhodesia's Trade Since U.D.I.', *World Today*, 23:418–22, October 1967; 'Report from Rhodesia', *Fortune*, 74:73–4, November 1966.

The best popular reviews on sanctions busting have been compiled by the *Sunday Times* 'Insight Team': 'The Sanctions Busters', 27 August and 3 September 1967; and 'A New Rhodesian Coup as China Buys Chrome', 1 October 1967. See also Donald Trelford, 'How Rhodesia Dodges Sanctions', *Observer*, 17 March 1968, and 'How Backdoor Traffic Keeps Rhodesia Alive', *Business Abroad*, 12 December 1966. Systematic accounts of the impact of sanctions and the activities of sanctions violators have been published by the U.N. since the establishment of the Security Council Sanctions Committee in 1968. See *Report of the Committee Established in Pursuance of Resolution 253 (1968) of May 29, 1968*, 30 December 1968 (S/8954); Second Report, 12 June 1969 (S/9252/Add. 1); Third Report, 15 June 1970 (S/9844/Add. 1 and Add. 2); Fourth Report, 16 June 1971 (S/10229/Add. 1 and Add. 2).

Rhodesia's Great Leap Backwards. For selected accounts of political developments in Rhodesia at the beginning of 1967, see 'Has the Front Begun to Crack?', *Sunday Times*, 20 January 1967, and 'Rhodesia: Watch it, Smithy', *The Economist*, 21 January 1967. A sequence of reports about the Rhodesian Front Party Congress of 1967 are found in *The Times*, 28, 30 September 1967, the *New York Times*, 1 October 1967, *The Times*, 2 October 1967, the *Guardian*, 5 October 1967, and *The Economist*, 7 October 1967.

Respecting Lord Alport's mission, see his article, 'I know it's no use talking to Smith', *Sunday Times*, 23 June 1968. See also Patrick Keatley, 'Rhodesia is ready to settle – but on its own conditions', *Guardian*, 19 July 1967. Wilson's report to Parliament on Alport's mission is found in *Parliamentary Debates*, Commons, 1966–7, Vol. 751, cols. 325–30, 25 July 1967.

For details of changes in the *Tiger* formula proposed by Smith in his conversations with George Thomson in Salisbury in November 1967, see *Parliamentary Debates*, Commons, Vol. 756, cols. 219–22, 12 December 1967; for Thomson's report concerning these proceedings see *ibid.*, Vol. 754, cols. 231–4, 14 November 1967. Smith's reply was given to the Rhodesian Parliament, 20 December 1967, and 1 February 1968.

Respecting the rumours of a deal between London and Pretoria affecting the British arms embargo against South Africa and the debate within the British Cabinet concerning the maintenance of the embargo, see reports by Colin Legum (12 November 1967) and Nora Beloff (17 December 1967) in the *Observer* as well as reports in *The Times*, 15, 18, 19 December 1967. See also Harold Wilson, *op. cit.*, pp. 470–6.

The Friendly Face across the Great Limpopo. A comprehensive summary of developments affecting civil rights and civil liberties in Rhodesia is provided by Theodore Bull, ed., *Rhodesian Perspective*, London: Michael Joseph, 1967. See also Reg Austin, *The Character and Legislation of the Rhodesian Front since U.D.I.*, London: The Africa Bureau, March 1968. A review of many critical developments during this period is found in the reports of *The Times* for 2 June, 8, 14 September, 14, 27 October and 7, 17 November 1967.

Chapter IX. The Crisis Deepens

The Guns of August. On the Rhodesian nationalist movement see John Day, *International Nationalism: The Extra-Territorial Relations of Southern Rhodesian African Nationalists*, London: Routledge and Kegan Paul, 1967; and Nathan M. Shamuyarira, 'The Nationalist Movement in Zimbabwe', *African Forum*, 2:34–42, Winter 1967. For a review of the incursions of August 1967 and during the first half of 1968, see 'Black Man in Search of Power: 1. Drums Against White Africa', *The Times*, 11 March 1968; Alan Rake, 'Black Guerrillas in Rhodesia', *Africa Report*, 13:23–5, December 1968; and Nicholas Tomalin, 'The Dark Invaders', the *Sunday Times*, 15 December 1968. M. Bowyer Bell has provided a thorough review in his, 'The Frustration of Insurgency: The Rhodesian Example of the Sixties', *Military Affairs*, 35:1–5, February 1971. A number of instructive case histories of African nationalists have appeared. See for example Roy Terry, 'Africa: Guerrillas Against the White: Close-up of a Terrorist', *Atlas*, February 1968; and Musosa Kazembe, 'Why Should I Die? A Chinese-Trained Guerrilla of Africa – His Personal Story', *Atlas*, June 1968.

Comment in the South African press during this period is instructive, particularly articles and editorials on the guerrilla incursions, South Africa's involvement in Rhodesia and implications for Zambia. See for example *Die Burger*, 11, 25 September 1967, 23 March 1968; *Die Vaderland*, 5, 12 September 1967, 4 April 1968; *Die Beeld*, 27 August 1967; *Die Transvaler*, 26, 30 August, 4, 9, 16,

25 September 1967; *Dagbreek*, 21 April, 26 May 1968; the *Johannesburg Star*, 8 August, 1 September 1967, 24 May 1968; the *Cape Times*, 22 March 1968. For an interesting example of Rhodesia's concern about and precise information concerning guerrilla camps in Zambia, see 'Rhodesia gives details of how Zambia is helping armed gangs', Salisbury *Sunday Mail*, 28 April 1968. Examples of concern expressed in Parliament at Westminster are found in *Parliamentary Debates*, Commons, Vol. 752, 24 October 1967, cols. 1474–5; Vol. 753, 8 November 1967, cols. 1143–4; Vol. 764, 7 May 1968, cols. 212–13.

The Salisbury Hangings; 'Who is the Government?' Events leading to and flowing from the hangings were covered exhaustively in the press. A trenchant review is found in *The Times*, 'Rhodesia: the road that could only lead to the gallows', 10 March 1968. See also 'Sir Alec Douglas-Home and Developments in Rhodesia', *Central Africa Research Bulletin – 1*, published by the Central Africa Research Office, 23 February 1968. The House of Commons was briefed on these developments by George Thomson and Harold Wilson on 4, 6, 7, 11 and 14 March. See *Parliamentary Debates*, Commons, 1968, Vol. 760, cols. 37, 438–44, 653–6, 978–84, 1617–28. The parliamentary debate on the executions took place on 27 March 1968. See *Parliamentary Debates*, Commons, 1968, Vol. 761, cols. 1546–1672. See also Mollie Panter-Downes, 'Letter from London: Execution Crisis', *New Yorker*, 44:146 ff. 23 March 1968.

Comprehensive Mandatory Sanctions. Debates in the U.N. Security Council ran from 19 March to 29 May 1968, at meetings 1399, 1400, 1408, 1413, 1415 and 1428. At the final meeting on 29 May 1968 Resolution S/RES/253/(1968) was adopted. The parliamentary debate at Westminster on comprehensive mandatory sanctions took place on 17 June 1968. See *Parliamentary Debates*, Commons, Vol. 766, cols. 728–833.

Chapter X. The *Fearless* Interlude

Preparing for 'Fearless'. Rising South African concern was again reflected in the press. Respecting comprehensive mandatory sanctions, see for example *Die Burger*, 1 June 1968; and the *Sunday Tribune*, 2 June 1968. Concerning 'terrorism', see for example *Die Transvaler*, 26 June 1968; *Dagbreek*, 28 July 1968; *Die Burger*, 22 July 1968; *Die Vaderland* and the *Rand Daily Mail*, 23 July 1968. On Smith's visit to South Africa, see for example the *Johannesburg Star* and *Die Burger*, 29 July 1968. For South Africa's concern to see a settlement effected, see for example the *Sunday Tribune*, 4 August and 13 October 1968; and the *Johannesburg Star*, 12, 14 October 1968.

The Whaley Commission report is available from the Government Printer, Salisbury, under the title, *Report of the Constitutional Commission 1968*, 5 April 1968. The constitutional provisions of the so-called Yellow Paper were published in the *Rhodesia Herald*, 18 July 1968. For a sympathetic analysis of these proposals and a brief review of the turmoil within the Rhodesian Front, see Walter Darnell Jacobs, 'A Constitution for Rhodesia', African–American Affairs Association, November 1968. A careful review is provided in P. B. Harris, 'The Failure of a "Constitution"', *International Affairs*, 45: 234–5, April 1969. Excellent background articles are Larry W. Bowman's 'Rhodesia Since U.D.I.', *Africa Report*, 12:5–13, February 1967, and 'Strains in the Rhodesian Front', *Africa Report*, 13:16–20, December 1968. On Smith himself, two articles juxtaposed in the *Sunday Times* of 15 September 1968, are instructive: 'Ian Smith calls on extremists to quit party' (p. 7) and Malcolm Smith (former editor of the *Rhodesia Herald*), 'Illusions on Ian Smith' (p. 12).

Wilson's own account of these events is found in *The Labour Government 1964–1970: A Personal Record*, pp. 564–77. Respecting Labour Party consideration of Rhodesia, see *Report of the Sixty-Seventh Annual Conference of the Labour Party, Blackpool, 1968*, published by the Labour Party, Transport House, Smith Square, London S.W.1, pp. 287–92. Background on *Fearless* may be gleaned from Colin Legum's reports in the *Observer*, 13 October 1968, numerous reports in the *Sunday Times* of the same date and *Africa Confidential* of 11 October 1968.

Variations on a Theme from Gibraltar. For British Government documents respecting this period see *Rhodesia: Report on the Discussions Held on Board H.M.S. Fearless October, 1968*, Cmnd. 3793, and *Rhodesia: Report on Exchanges with the Regime since the Talks held in Salisbury in November, 1968*, Cmnd. 4065. The Rhodesian position is set forth in *Statement on Anglo-Rhodesian Relations, December, 1966 to May, 1969*, C.S.R. 36–1969. Speeches by both Wilson and Smith immediately following *Fearless* are found in *Africa Report*, 13:20–2, December 1968. For a detailed analysis of the *Fearless* proposals, see M. J. Christie, *Rhodesia: The 'Fearless' Proposals and the Six Principles*, London: The Africa Bureau, November 1968.

'H.M.S. Cheerless'. The controversial debate on Rhodesia on 22 October 1972, is found in *Parliamentary Debates*, Commons,

Vol. 770, cols. 1100–1225. See also Vol. 772, cols. 336, 693–4; and Colin Legum's analysis in the *Observer*, 27 October 1968.

Zambia's response to renewed negotiations with Rhodesia was summarized in the title, 'Grrrrrrr', of an article in the *Economist*, 30 September 1967. See also, for example, the *Zambian Mail*, 27 September and 18 October 1968; and the *Times of Zambia*, 9 and 17 October 1968. Zambia's increasing anxiety concerning defence is revealed in Kaunda's interview with Nicholas Carroll in the *Sunday Times*, 24 March 1968. See also 'Zambia: Rhodesia's Overspill' and 'Zambia's Air Defence', in *Africa Confidential* for 14 June and 9 August 1968. For a brief summary of developments during this period leading to Chinese construction of the rail link to Dar es Salaam, see the Chinese–Zambian *communiqué* in *The Peking Review*, 27:13, 30 June 1967; 'TanZam's Latest Link', *Africa Confidential*, 21 July 1967; Joseph R. L. Sterne, 'China's Rail Aid to Africa Fills the Gap the West Avoided', *Baltimore Sun*, 11 September 1967; Richard Hall, 'Kaunda's Long Road to Dar', *Venture*, 20:21–4, May 1968.

South Africa's reaction may be gleaned from articles in *Die Vaterland*, 18 October 1968, and the *Sunday Tribune* and *Dagbreek* for 20 October 1968. See also Stanley Uys in the *Observer* for 20 October 1968, and Colin Legum in the *Observer* for 3 November 1968; and the article titled 'Rhodesia: South African Pressure' in *Africa Confidential*, 25 October 1968.

Labour's Last Try. George Thomson's summary of his talks in Salisbury, followed by questions, is found in *Parliamentary Debates*, Commons, Vol. 773, cols. 896–912, 18 November 1968. Smith's summary is found in the series 'For the Record', No. 3 published by the Ministry of Information, Salisbury, 20 November 1968. For an analytical summary, see *The Times* editorials for 18, 19 November 1968. For Kaunda's reactions, see for example the *Zambian Mail*, 1 and 5 November 1968. For Vorster's reactions see the *Sunday Tribune*, 3 November 1968, and *Die Transvaler* and the *Johannesburg Star*, 4 November 1968. His comment in the South African House of Assembly about his son serving in Rhodesia is found in Debates, Fourth Session, Third Parliament, Vol. 26, p. 4580, 23 April 1969.

'Into Cold Storage'. Rhodesia's new constitution is available from the Government Printer, Salisbury, as C.S.R. 32-1969, *Proposals for a New Constitution for Rhodesia*. Debates concerning it are found in Rhodesia, *Parliamentary Debates*, Vol. 75, Nos. 15–19, 2, 7–10 October 1969. A summary of views with special emphasis on those of regime critic Dr. Ahrn Palley is found in a lengthy article in the

Rhodesia Herald, 9 October 1969, entitled, 'Palley on "True Reasons" for U.D.I.' See also Smith's Address to the Nation, 20 May 1969, published in 'For The Record', No. 10, by the Ministry of Information; and D. G. Clarke, 'The Political Economy of the Republican Constitution of Rhodesia', *The Rhodesian Journal of Economics,* 4:21–37, September 1970, to which I am indebted for projections concerning the African franchise. The United Nations Security Council considered the Rhodesian issue at meetings 1530–5. Draft resolution of S/9696 and Corr. 1, 2 was vetoed by the U.S. and Britain on 17 March 1970. The following day S/9709/Rev. 1 was passed to become Resolution S/RES/277/(1970).

Chapter XI. The End – and the Beginning

Wilson's Policy Assessed; The Tory Settlement. A recent and excellent assessment of discriminatory and repressive legislation and practice in Rhodesia is R. H. Randolph, S.J., *Church and State in Rhodesia 1969–1971: A Catholic View,* Gwelo: Mambo Press, 1971. See also James S. Read, 'Rhodesia: Equal Rights Indefinitely Postponed', *Race Today,* 4:52–54, February 1972, and 'Rhodesia: How the Other 95 Per Cent Lives', *The Economist,* 4 March 1972. For recent Rhodesian documents on the economic situation, see *Financial Statements 1971,* Cmd. R.R. 42-1971; *Economic Survey of Rhodesia 1971,* Cmd. R.R. 12-1971; and the *Monthly Digest of Statistics,* Central Statistical Office, Salisbury. For an assessment of sanctions during the period under review, see the Fourth Report of the U.N. Security Council Sanctions Committee, 16 June 1971 (S/10229/Add. 1 and Add. 2). See also J. D. F. Jones's analysis in the *Financial Times,* 23 June 1969; Ray Vicker, 'Rhodesia: Booming Despite Sanctions', *Wall Street Journal,* 11 September 1969; 'Rhodesia Under Sanctions', *The Economist,* 22 April 1972; and 'Rhodesia: The Impact of Economic Sanctions', *Africa Bureau Fact Sheet 17,* January 1972. Two other publications of the Africa Bureau should be consulted, both mimeographed: 'Sanctions Against Rhodesia 1965 to 1972', May 1972, and 'Rhodesia: Token Sanctions or Total Economic Warfare', September 1972. Colin Legum has provided a critical review of U.N. involvement in Rhodesian sanctions, together with recommendations for improving U.N. performance, in his 'The United Nations and Southern Africa', *ISIO Monographs,* first series, number three, 1970, published by the Institute for the Study of International Organizations, University of Sussex, pp. 26–34. See also *Sanctions as an Instrumentality of the United Nations,* Hearings before the Subcommittee on International Organizations and Movements of the Committee on Foreign Affairs, House of Representatives, 13, 15, 19 June 1972. For insight into Rhodesia's population problems, see the report of a speech by Sir Albert Robinson to the Bulawayo Chamber of Commerce, in the *Financial Mail*, 14 April 1972.

Settlement or Sell-out? The November 1971 proposals are found in *Rhodesia: Proposals for a Settlement*, Cmnd. 4835. Dr. Claire Palley's assessment is found under the title: 'Black's Best Hope – A Majority in 2035', *Sunday Times*, 28 November 1971. For problems of African education in Rhodesia see John Borrell, 'African Education in Rhodesia', *Rhodesia Herald*, 13 September 1971.

The End . . .; and the Beginning. Dennis Austin's reference to the need for an 'imperial arbiter' is found in a hard-headed and extremely perceptive article, 'Another Look at Rhodesia', *Venture*, 19:16–20, February 1967. The Pearce Report is available under the title: *Rhodesia: Report of the Commission on Rhodesian Opinion under the Chairmanship of the Rt. Hon. the Lord Pearce*, Cmnd. 4964. Some of the best reporting on the Pearce Commission hearings were articles by Jim Hoagland in the *Washington Post* (22, 23, 25, 29 January and 4 February 1972) and Charles Mohr in the *New York Times* (24, 25, 29 January and 14 February 1972). See also Martin Meredith, *Observer*, 30 January 1972; Nigel Lawson, *The Times*, 2 February 1972; Anthony Hawkins, *Financial Times*, 1 March 1972; Peter Niesewand, *Guardian*, 7, 9 March 1972; and Bridget Bloom, *Financial Times*, 2 June 1972.

Respecting the dynamics of Southern African politics, see Ernest A. Gross, 'The Coalescing Problem of Southern Africa', *Foreign Affairs*, 46:743–57, July 1968; Larry W. Bowman, 'The Subordinate State System of Southern Africa', *International Studies Quarterly*, 12:231–61, September 1968; Larry W. Bowman, 'South Africa's Outward Strategy: A Foreign Policy Dilemma for the United States', Papers in International Studies, Africa Series No. 13, Ohio University Center for International Studies, Africa Program, 1971; Douglas G. Anglin, 'Confrontation in Southern Africa: Zambia and Portugal', *International Journal*, 25:497–517, Summer 1970; J. E. Spence, *The Strategic Significance of Southern Africa*, London: Royal United Service Institution, 1970; Kenneth Grundy, *Confrontation and Accommodation in Southern Africa*, Berkeley: University of California Press, forthcoming; Robert Molteno, *Africa and South Africa: The Implications of South Africa's 'Outward Looking' Policy*, London: The Africa Bureau, February 1971.

For a brief selection of views from black Africa, see Julius K.

Nyerere, 'Rhodesia in the Context of Southern Africa', *Foreign Affairs*, 44:373–86, April 1966; 'We Have Lost Control of the Boat', an interview with President Kenneth D. Kaunda, *Newsweek*, 30 December 1968; and the Lusaka Manifesto in Charles C. Diggs, Jr. and Lester L. Wolff, *Report of Special Study Mission to Southern Africa*, Washington, D.C.: House of Representatives, Committee on Foreign Affairs, 1969, pp. 39–42. A review and critique of U.S. policy on chrome is available in *Rhodesia and United States Foreign Policy*, Hearings before the Subcommittee on Africa of the Committee on Foreign Affairs, House of Representatives, 17, 31 October, 7, 19 November 1969; and *Sanctions as an Instrumentality of the United Nations – Rhodesia as a Case Study, op. cit.*

For the reference to the longevity of the A.N.C., I am indebted to Alan Brooks, Letter to the Editor, *The Economist*, 6 July 1968.

Index

Index